Rebirth

Rebirth

THE REDEVELOPMENT OF
THE CHRISTIAN AND MISSIONARY ALLIANCE IN CANADA

by Lindsay Reynolds

More often than not, history teaches us our lessons obliquely. Not only what happened, but the meaning of what happened, concerns us.
—R. A. Knox

Copyright © 1992 by Lindsay Reynolds

All rights reserved. No part of this publication may be reproduced or transmitted in any form or by any means, electronic or mechanical, including photocopy, recording, or any information storage and retrieval system, without permission in writing from the publisher.

Published in 1992 by
The Christian and Missionary Alliance in Canada
Box 7900 Station B
Willowdale, Ontario M2K 2R6

Produced by
Evangelistic Enterprises
Box 600, Beaverlodge, Alberta T0H 0C0

Canadian Cataloguing in Publication Data

Reynolds, Lindsay, 1920-

Rebirth : the redevelopment of the Christian and Missionary Alliance in Canada

Includes bibliographical references.
ISBN 0-88965-099-3

1. Christian and Missionary Alliance in Canada—History.
I. Christian and Missionary Alliance in Canada.   II. Title.

BV2595.C47R49 1992   289.9   C92-098084-8

Printed in Canada

*Dedicated to the members and adherents
of The Christian and Missionary Alliance
in Canada*

Contents

Foreword		ix
Acknowledgements		xi
Preface		xiii
PART ONE	*Foundations*	
Chapter 1	American Roots	3
Chapter 2	Canadian Heritage	29
PART TWO	*A New Beginning*	
Chapter 3	The Aura of Uncertainty	45
Chapter 4	The Vision of Need	97
Chapter 5	Conflict of Interest	137
Chapter 6	Seedtime and Harvest	201
PART THREE	*From Sea to Sea*	
Chapter 7	Forging a Consensus	287
Chapter 8	The Education Struggle	329
Chapter 9	Canada's Other Sheep	365
Chapter 10	Canadian Identity Again	395
EPILOGUE	Until He Comes	445
Tables and Figures		449
Index		455

Foreword

Experience is the best teacher. In coming to know your history you come to know the experiences of past generations as you "read the minutes of the last meeting."

History does teach. When that fact is accepted we want to know the qualities of the person who records it. What is his vantage point? What are his credentials? Who is going to tell the story of The Christian and Missionary Alliance in Canada?

Dr. Lindsay Reynolds is a family member. He was born and raised in Montreal. He joined The Christian and Missionary Alliance in 1935, bringing with him many sterling qualities including a deep interest in history. The Alliance would benefit from his skills and knowledge in this field when he gave us *Footprints*, the first volume of this comprehensive historical record. *Footprints* took us to the year 1919. It begged an account of progress since that date. *Rebirth* provides that record.

Dr. Lindsay Reynolds is a person of integrity. He has always exhibited a clear commitment to our Lord and to His Church. I have never known anyone more committed to accuracy. His probing of the past has taken him past tradition and hearsay. He is stubbornly committed to establishing the facts.

In bringing together this chronological record of events, Dr. Reynolds exhibits both sensitivity and frankness. He describes those times and places when decisions were made that helped determine the subsequent destiny of our denomination.

Dr. Reynolds introduces the reader to some key people. Canadian historian John Barker reminds us "that history's primary subject is human beings." When you read *Rebirth* you feel you have met the

Foreword

people who have influenced our own beliefs and in different ways shaped our ecclesiastical environment. To understand how we have been affected by our history, we must know of their performance.

The writer is candid but fair as he sets forth his conclusions. He traces our metamorphosis from a spiritual agency with a priority on belief and experience in the truths of the Fourfold Gospel with a strong missionary emphasis, to a missionary denomination. This book tells how we reluctantly passed through those changes.

Rebirth tells the exciting story of church growth, the opening of new churches, and the establishing of new districts. It recounts the opening and closing of Bible schools and reminds us of the 12-year period when there was no Alliance school in Canada, and of the negative impact of that decision.

The book tells the story of the move to Canadian autonomy in 1981. It gives that account against the backdrop of 1897 when autonomy was relinquished by discontinuing what was known as the Canadian Auxiliary of The Christian and Missionary Alliance. All this and much more awaits the reader who would investigate the past.

History has lessons to teach. The truth may be satisfying, and it may also be painful. If we fail to learn from our history, then mistakes will be perpetuated and success cannot inspire.

This is the story of our family heritage. This is about you and me. It is our story. Read on.

        Melvin P. Sylvester, President
        The Christian and Missionary Alliance in Canada

Acknowledgements

I am indebted to many friends and organizations that have made this account possible.

My special thanks go to The Christian and Missionary Alliance, the A. B. Simpson Historical Library and the *Alliance Life*; to The Christian and Missionary Alliance in Canada and all five Canadian districts for making freely available to me their collections of historical materials.

My thanks go to former Alliance President Louis King, President Mel Sylvester, District Superintendents Jesse Jespersen, Robert Gould, Arnold Downey and Gordon Fowler, and to former District Superintendents Willis Brooks, Harvey Town, Alf Orthner and William Newell for their help and encouragement.

I wish to acknowledge the valuable assistance given by a large number of pastors, former pastors and pastors' widows, and for the use of valuable recollections and treasured letters. To the authors and publishers of many books, particularly those dealing with Canadian church history, I am deeply indebted.

To the owners of photographs and to the many who have helped in ways too many to mention individually, I offer my sincere thanks.

My personal thanks go to Mrs. Grace Bird for the many hours spent in computerizing the script, to Miss Esther Reimer for secretarial help, to my daughter, Elizabeth Reynolds, for indexing research materials, and to my wife, Jean, for her many suggestions for improvements.

Lastly, I wish to thank the Head of the Church for the privilege of writing about the progress of His Church.

Preface

Having identified progress with change, our western society finds it difficult to believe that yesterday has important lessons for today.

The great Anglican church historian of the last century, Bishop John B. Lightfoot, once told an audience in Saint Paul's Cathedral, "While it is necessary to face the problems of the present, it is not less important to review the experiences of the past. If we can only read them aright, the records of the difficulties, sufferings [and] the triumphs . . . are replete with lessons of immediate interest."

Writers of our own century echo similar opinions. In his book, *Heritage and Destiny*, Dr. John A. Mackay states, "A discovery of yesterday opens a new pathway to tomorrow, when, the awakening of a sense of heritage becomes a potent determinant of destiny." Dr. Mackay goes on to say, "We must cultivate once again the habit of retrospection. Men must learn to look back if they are to succeed in moving forward. The past is full of landmarks and danger signals which he must study who would advance into tomorrow. To look back, and even to retrace our steps for a time, need not be a flight from reality, nor yet an attempt to divinize the by-gone, nor to bind ourselves to a changeless yesterday."

The Christian and Missionary Alliance is a denomination of the Protestant tradition. As such, its history becomes a part of the history of the universal church of Jesus Christ. According to Archbishop R. C. Trench, "The history of the church is the history of the life of Christ in its members, not indeed without faults, infirmities and shortcomings; but despite all of these, a divine society. All that has been the true

Preface

expression of its divine life, all that has helped, and all too that has hindered, any true church history should tell us."

But how, we may ask, can a knowledge of past performance in different cultural settings be of any practical use in today's context? The answer is that as we study our past, we are impressed by the way in which basic human problems recur over and over again. The Alliance today faces situations not essentially different from those it experienced two, three or four generations ago. Of course we must distinguish between those features which were peculiar to the epoch of occurrence and those which have a permanent message. There is no need to repeat past errors and suffer again past consequences by ignoring past records.

Unfortunately, historical records usually exist as apparently disconnected cameos, rarely explained or set in the context of competing circumstances of thought and action. Moreover, history cannot be a simple recital of supposed facts, but must always involve a selection and interpretation in accord with the historian's insight into the meaning of the recorded information. History, therefore, does not speak for itself, but is dependent upon the idiosyncrasies of the human beings who interpret it. Dr. A. T. Pierson warned, "Undoubtedly, both the Word of God and the witness of history may be read through coloured glasses or distorted lenses." It therefore behooves the historian to do his research as thoroughly as he knows how before he commences to write. He must pick the data he considers significant from a mass that cannot all be used.

No developing movement or denomination exists by itself. To a large extent it is a product of its times, and is borne along by the theological, ecclesiastical, social and political currents swirling around it. The development of the Alliance in Canada has been the product of Canadian, European and American influences. The mix has been quite different from that which applied in the United States. The Canadian story therefore differs from the American. The author's former work, *Footprints*, provided an account of the Canadian early years. It was shown that the Alliance in Canada by 1919 was in such a state of disarray that rebirth rather than revival was required. It seemed appropriate, therefore, when providing an account of progress since 1919, to name this work *Rebirth*.

It was Pope Leo XIII's dictum that the first law of history is not to lie, and the second is not to be afraid to tell the whole truth. The author is aware that not all he has written falls into the popular mold.

Preface

He can only claim that the object of his work has been to present truth as far as it is ascertainable, not to perpetuate tradition on the one hand or to introduce novelty on the other.

Dr. Robert Speer has reminded us that "Christianity is a conviction and an experience, and Christ is the object of each. Conviction and experience are not to be separated. They were not separable at the beginning, and they are not today." This observation is of vital importance in the interpretation of church history. "Too often," says Dr. Timothy P. Webster, "historians of Christianity have studied theological aspects of the church's history to the neglect of how the beliefs were translated into daily life." The church's practice has often spoken louder than its professed faith. Too often, also, faith and practice have been assumed to be static, rather than dynamic. The element of time is most important, and the relative contributions of faith and practice and the relation that each bears to the other must be constantly updated with the passage of time if viable interpretations are to be achieved.

It has been the trait of the scribes of denominational progress to be quick to sound their victories, but slow to record their defeats. Therefore, a denominational historian should not restrict research to official records, but also consider the wider testimony of witnesses without.

To attempt to describe and interpret what happened during the last forty or fifty years is difficult and even dangerous. One is too near the events to assess objectively their importance or to see them in proper perspective. Nevertheless, an attempt has been made to chronicle certain developments and tendencies. No doubt, a very different account of this period will be written by another generation.

The great historian, Lord Macaulay, wrote in the introduction to his greatest work, "It will be my duty to faithfully record the disasters that have mingled with the triumphs of our past.... Unless I greatly deceive myself, the effect of this chequered narrative will be to excite thankfulness in all religious minds, and hope in the breasts of all patriots. No man who is correctly informed of the past will be disposed to take a morose or despondent view of the present." It is the hope and prayer of the author that the reading of this account will bring glory to the Head of the Church and a sense of thankfulness, hopefulness and purpose, particularly to the members of The Christian and Missionary Alliance in Canada.

PART ONE

Foundations

CHAPTER ONE

American Roots

History has no absolute beginnings. The key event which appears to initiate a new direction is itself tied in with earlier events, and is in some respect their result. Thus, the choice of an anniversary date to commemorate the beginning of a spiritual movement must always be open to question. The origin of The Christian and Missionary Alliance movement is particularly complicated, because its roots extend into at least five different earlier spiritual movements, namely, the evangelistic, the holiness, the divine healing, the pre-millennial, and the foreign missions movements. The progress of each of these root movements had its influence on how and when the Alliance started and how it evolved.

The founder of the Alliance, Rev. A. B. Simpson, in later years selected November 1881 as the point in time of the beginnings of his movement.[1] By that time his theological positions had reached considerable maturity, he had personally experienced the truth of his own beliefs, and, with his resignation as pastor of the Thirteenth Street Presbyterian Church in New York City, he had become free of the inhibitions of being a representative of Presbyterianism, with which he had reached serious disagreements in matters of both faith and practice.*

After first appealing for help in the form of "Christian workers," Simpson embarked on a ministry for the "evangelization of the neglected classes," advertising "free evangelistic services."[2] A news-

---

* By November 1881 Rev. A. B. Simpson's views on "free grace," sanctification (holiness) and baptism were untenable with Reformed positions, and his beliefs with respect to divine healing and premillennialism were at least embarrassments to the main body of his denomination.

/ 3

paper reported that Simpson proposed "to prosecute an anti-sectarian religious movement," in order to reach those "not within the active influence of the church," and that he intended to do this by "preaching and meetings of prayer and enquiry."[3]

Thus, Simpson's new work was viewed as just another of the many independent evangelistic works in New York, and as such, attracted little public or media attention. However, the converts soon began to multiply, and it became clear that they needed a church home and instruction beyond the level of evangelism. Obviously, the sheep first needed to be brought into the fold, but once there, they needed to be fed.[4]

In February of the following year an independent church was organized, a "Free Gospel Church," said Simpson, based on the "Scriptural and voluntary principles . . . [of] evangelistic and missionary work among the neglected and non-church-going population."[5] The sheep, therefore, were not only to be fed the doctrinal truths of Scripture beyond the conversion step, but were to be trained as missionaries to those around them.

Simpson was also greatly interested in foreign missions. He had published a non-sectarian missionary monthly, *The Gospel in All Lands*, during his ministry at Thirteenth Street Church, but had disassociated himself from it just before his resignation. Now, in January 1882 he founded a new monthly, *The Word, Work and World*. It was not just a new missionary monthly. It was a journal of all his great spiritual interests—evangelistic, doctrinal, experiential plus home and foreign missions, and a record of the principal events in the progress of his movement, as seen through the eyes of its founder.

From the very first issue of the new magazine, Simpson let his great concern for foreign missions be clearly understood. He sounded a call to his "paper parish," as he termed it, for a new non-sectarian missionary society, to send the gospel to the "unoccupied fields of the world." To make such a proposal possible, he advocated, first, the employment of lay people, "humble, devoted men and women who possess the requisite qualifications," and, second, the opening of a "missionary training school for the specific preparation of the labourers before they go out."

The next major development in the character of the movement occurred just four months later, in May 1882. Nearly a year had passed since Simpson's own stupendous healing, and now the president of the United States, James Garfield, lay dying from an assassin's bullet. Throughout the country much prayer had gone up that the attending physicians would be given the skill to bring him back to health. Simpson, still rejoicing in his experience of divine healing, had wished that someone would go to Garfield's bedside to anoint and pray for his healing. "I seemed to hear a voice," recalled Simpson, "asking me, 'will you go?'" He had not gone and the president had died shortly thereafter.[6]

Moreover, at the time of his own healing, he had solemnly covenanted with God "to use this blessing [healing] for the glory of God and the good of others, and to speak of it, or minister in connection with it, in any way in which God may call me or others may need me in the future."[7]

Simpson decided to take action. In May 1882, he commenced holding healing meetings every Friday afternoon. To emphasize his conviction that personal consecration and sanctification must precede healing, these meetings were termed "consecration meetings."[8] During the same month he dedicated a house as a "home for Faith and Physical Healing," where people could spend a few days or weeks in an atmosphere of prayer, affection and instruction, and where they could receive by "faith and consecration the promise of healing in the name of Jesus."[9]

Soon the Friday afternoon healing services grew to large proportions, and could no longer accommodate all the seekers for healing. Commencing in November of that year and continuing for twelve months, Simpson added a regular Sunday afternoon healing meeting. These too, became crowded.[10]*

Thus, the early phase of his ministry was strongly characterized by healings, and it was this characteristic that first attracted widespread public and media attention. It was reported during the fall of 1882 that "scores" had been converted and "scarce a less number have been cured of diseases, through prayer and the anointment of oil."[11]

---

* During his latter years, Dr. Simpson appears to have forgotten about these Sunday afternoon healing meetings. His biographer, Rev. A. E. Thompson, quotes from one of the founder's last addresses, in which he stated that "Sanctification and Divine healing, were not crowded upon the popular audiences,—but some of the week-day meetings were appointed for the purpose." However, frequent advertisements, together with occasional newspaper reports confirm that Sunday healing meetings were held. A *Hamilton Times* reporter was dispatched to report on the healing meeting of Sunday afternoon, December 31, 1882. In a long and detailed report, he said that 250 persons were in attendance. Thirty of these testified of being "cured through faith."

Simpson recognized the importance of this component of his ministry. "The subject of healing by faith in God," he said, "is receiving a great deal of earnest attention at this time."[12] A year later he commented, "Since the beginning [it] has been a somewhat prominent feature of the work."[13]

EARLY DISTINCTIVES

Despite his growing reputation in healing, Simpson had not forgotten his call for a new missionary society and training school. In March 1883 he and his church established the Missionary Union for the Evangelization of the World,[14]* and in October they opened the Missionary Training Institute.[15] It was immediately clear that Simpson envisioned both the missionary society and the training school to be agencies of his special doctrinal views. He wrote, "the blessed gospel of physical healing . . . is a sacred trust for a dying world. Those who accept it can no longer be satisfied with the present methods of missionary work. They must feel called to send these glad tidings to all the world."[16]

By the autumn of 1883, Simpson's distinctive doctrinal views on sanctification, divine healing and pre-millennialism were attracting wide media attention, but these, along with his foreign missions interest, were not his only concerns. He recognized that man was both spiritual and physical, and that these two aspects of his being came within the orb of the gospel. In 1886, he wrote, "He [God] wants us to have not only the mere preaching of the Gospel, but work for the poor and the lowly; work for the destitute and the sick; work for the rich and worldly."[17] Like Wesley, Simpson believed that true holiness would show itself as "social holiness." In addition to the home for healing, Simpson and his early followers established an orphanage, a home for fallen women, and no less than seven rescue missions. These institutions ministered to the temporal as well as the spiritual needs of the disturbed, the sick, the outcast, the abandoned, the debauched, and the hungry of society. Sanctification was made practical in loving service to man.

Notwithstanding these noble efforts, Simpson's "peculiar tenets" of sanctification, divine healing and pre-millennialism made his movement unpopular in the churches. Simpson was branded a

---

* The five and only missionaries of this agency were sent out by Simpson's church on an abortive mission to the Congo in November 1884.

"lunatic" and a "crank." Undaunted by these attacks, he admitted, "I am prosecuting a work which is regarded unfavourably by the great body of the clergy."[18]

In his salvation theology (soteriology), Simpson's views on "free grace" caused shock and disappointment among his former associates of the Reformed stamp. Presbyterians (along with other Calvinists) contended that God, in His sovereign grace, has elected to save some from among His fallen creatures. For the elect, alone, grace is free. Those chosen (elected) are enabled by the Holy Spirit to accept God's forgiveness. All others fall under the judgment of God, and are left without hope in their sins. In this administration of divine mercy and justice, God is unmoved by any response of man's choice, and is guided solely by the councils of His own will.[19]

However, Simpson now leaned toward Arminian* views. The sovereign grace of God, he said, "is free to all who will accept it— whosoever will may take it and live. . . . Two great truths run with unbroken clearness through the Word of God. One is the purpose of God, and the other is the freedom of man. . . . The Gospel is a personal message of love and mercy from God to every man. . . . Let us make sure of being inside God's purpose by choosing Christ ourselves."[20] These beliefs placed Simpson more behind Wesley than Knox, and Presbyterian leaders were unwilling to compromise on such a cardinal point. As Dr. A. A. Hodge of Princeton Theological Seminary saw it, "Every Christian must take one side or the other. If the means of grace is by the faith and repentance of man, he is an Arminian. If it is by the good pleasure of God, he is a Calvinist."[21]

Simpson's departure from Reformed belief on such a cardinal point made it impossible for many Presbyterians to think kindly about his independent ministry at all.

ISSUES OF CONTENTION

On the issue of sanctification, Simpson's chief opposition also came from the Reformed camp. Among his antagonists stood the renowned Dr. B. B. Warfield, also of Princeton, who lambasted

---

* Wesley's theology was termed "Arminian," because of certain modified similarities with views of Jacobus Arminius, who a century earlier claimed that the sovereignty of God was compatible with the will of man. However, Arminius was not the first to express such views. In 1532, Philip Melanchthon, the great Lutheran theologian, was the first Reformer to depart from Augustinian "particularity," and to advance the doctrine of the universality of God's offer of salvation, subject to the will of man.

Simpson for his "extravagant theories of mysticism."[22] For Presbyterians, sanctification was a life-long process of spiritual growth, through the work of the Holy Spirit, initiated at conversion. This process was conceived in terms of discipline, obedience and resolve.[23]

In contrast, Simpson held that sanctification was not a slow and painful growth, beginning at conversion, but a second work of grace, received by faith, in which Christ Himself was implanted instantaneously, enabling the believer to rise to a new and higher plane of living where Christ was in control. From this elevated plane, the sanctified Christian grew into spiritual maturity. "We do not grow into the sanctified life," Simpson said. "We go into it and then grow out from it into all the fullness of Christ, having the confidence that the grace that keeps for a moment can keep for a life-time."[24] In Simpson's view, the way of the sanctified life is the way of undeserved grace. God, not man, is the active agent in the state of holy living. God, Himself, becomes the new standard of the life hid in Christ. True Christian living is not the result of a struggle to do good works. Christ's righteousness is not only imputed to us for our salvation, but is also implanted in us for our sanctification.* It is God's gift to us, and the proper response should not be strain, but rather joyful acceptance.

This line of approach caused theologians with Reformed tendencies to claim that Simpson's dogma ignored the ethical dimensions of sanctification.

While there were similarities between Simpson and Wesley in their sanctification theology, there were also differences—at least in emphasis. John Wesley, always impelled by a sense of personal responsibility, was attracted chiefly to the objective or ethical aspects of sanctification. For him, the keeping of the two great commandments to love God and to love man, as enabled by the Spirit, was all important. He therefore thought of sanctification as "perfect love." On the other hand, A. B. Simpson, who had encountered spiritual

---

* Almost alone among the German Reformers, Andrew Osiander claimed that the gospel has two parts: the first, that Christ has satisfied the justice of God; the second, that He cleanses and justifies (makes acceptable). He insisted that justification did not hinge simply on the imputation of Christ's righteousness, but also on the implantation of Christ's righteousness, through the mystical union of the believer with the indwelling Spirit of Christ. Osiander's claim was rejected by the leading Lutheran Reformers, largely because of fear that it would weaken their great principle of justification by faith alone. However, the emphasis of the renovating work of the Spirit would emerge again and again. In the English-speaking world, mystics such as Jeremy Taylor in the seventeenth century and William Law in the early eighteenth century carried the torch of holiness teaching down through the years, until John Wesley founded Methodism. It is possible to claim that Osiander ignited the holiness fire in 1550 that 300 years later became the holiness blaze in which Simpson had a part.

desperation prior to his "deeper life" experience, responded primarily to the subjective or passive aspects of sanctification. He saw sanctification as the surrender of self to Christ, so that "the presence of Jesus comes between us and every temptation, and meets the adversary with vigilant discernment, rejection and victory."[25] He therefore thought of sanctification as "perfect trust." Taken together, these two concepts of sanctification emphasize the power of God and the obligation of man. For Simpson, the chief benefit of sanctifying grace lay not in the obtainment of gifts, but of the Giver Himself. As he expressed it in one of his best known hymns:

> Once it was the blessing, now it is the Lord;
> Once it was the feeling, now it is His Word.
> Once His gifts I wanted, now the Giver own;
> Once I sought for healing, now Himself alone.
>
> Once 'twas painful trying, now 'tis perfect trust;
> Once a half salvation, now the uttermost.
> Once 'twas ceaseless holding, now He holds me fast:
> Once 'twas constant drifting, now my anchor's cast.

But it was in the matter of divine healing that Simpson received the most virulent opposition from many quarters. He maintained that provision had been made for physical healing in the atonement of Christ. Quoting Isaiah, "He has borne our sorrows, and carried our sicknesses," Simpson added, "It makes the cross stand out clearly before us with Divine healing and Divine atonement on it. Our sicknesses are on one arm and our sins on the other. The blessed Christ has carried them both."[26]

Since the provisions of divine grace are received solely by faith, he reasoned, it follows that divine healing cannot be received through human agencies. The use of doctors and medicines is not wrong when faith cannot be exercised, but if we pray for healing in the name of Jesus, it must come by grace alone. "Healing faith" means confidence in the willingness of God to heal. "The very thought of resorting to old means is inadmissible," he said. Most persons are ready to admit that God can heal, but a vague hope in the possible acceptance of our prayer is not a faith definite enough to grapple with the forces of disease. No one would think of asking God to forgive his sins "if it be His will." No more should we doubt His promises to heal, by praying "if it be His will." A seeker with "healing faith" will abandon all remedies and medical treatments.[27]

Typical among the many who strongly opposed Simpson's beliefs and practices in divine healing was a Congregationalist clergyman who wrote, "We believe that this doctrine ... is a heresy which will contract the vision of everyone who is affected by it. By teaching men to rely on God for their healing," he said, "Dr. Simpson is blinding men to the stores of curative agencies with which God in His goodness has surrounded us."[28]

Equally critical, Presbyterian Dr. A. A. Hodge stated, "No sensible Christian will pray for the cure of his diseases without using all the means available. If he does, he mocks God, and God will mock him as sure as he lives."[29]

Simpson's belief in a pre-millennial return of Christ to establish His kingdom on earth was almost universally opposed by the mainline denominations of his day. The prevalent view of a post-millennial return of Christ claimed that the spread of the gospel would eventually triumph in the conversion of the world, producing universal peace, which would constitute the millennium. Christ would then return to a world prepared for His coming.

Among the churches, a pre-millennial view was generally associated with low education and low intelligence. Pre-millennialists were accused of being pessimistic and fatalistic, and of having no interest in improving the social order, or of providing relief for temporal sufferings. A Methodist periodical claimed that a pre-millennial belief "practically invalidates Christ's gospel, by asserting its incompetence to evangelize the world."[30] Dr. Albert H. Newman, a Baptist professor of church history, wrote, "Millennialism is likely to be the bane of any movement into which it may enter. ... Such thoughts are unspeakably revolting to the rightly instructed consciousness, and the fact that they are entertained by earnest and zealous men does not make them one iota less objectionable."[31]

Among the pre-millennialists, Simpson was an historicist, who believed that the prophetic Scriptures refer to events that have already occurred or are occurring.[32] This enabled Simpson to say that our Lord's return was imminent; it awaited no future event, and was dependent only on the completion of the task of world evangelism. Simpson's historicist views placed him in opposition to the futurist dispensationalists, such as C. I. Scofield and the followers of John N. Darby.

Simpson was also a pre-tribulationist, who believed that the church would be raptured some time before our Lord's return to earth. "There will be two appearings of Jesus Christ," he wrote, "the one to His own and the other, later, to the entire world.... The signs of one do not apply to the other."[33] In this view he was opposed by those of his fellow historicists, who held that the rapture of the church and the return to earth were both part of the one great event of the second coming.

Although Simpson's belief regarding baptism was not included in his doctrinal capsule of the "Fourfold Gospel," it was well known in ecclesiastical circles that he had been immersed in a Baptist church just prior to his resignation from the Presbyterian ministry, and had then publicly stated that he could no longer baptize infants. He was accused of being an Anabaptist (re-baptized), thus earning the disfavour of the otherwise benign Methodists. Even the Baptists were suspicious of Simpson for failing to identify with them. One of their spokesmen complained, "Practically, he is a Baptist: then why not say so?"[34]

PRACTICAL IMPLICATIONS

Simpsonian theology affected the area of practice. His philosophy of foreign missions clashed with that of the main denominations, especially those of the Reformed tradition. Because of their postmillennial belief that the preaching of the gospel would eventually result in the world-wide conversion of both Gentiles and Jews prior to the second coming of Christ, the denominations adopted long-range missionary plans. Permanent Christian centres were established in foreign countries, designed to teach and to train national leaders, that they in turn might spread the good news to their own people and establish national denominational churches. As Presbyterian missionary to India Alexander B. Campbell explained, "All history proclaims that this is the way in which God generally works. There are seasons of preparation; the truth is spread; obstacles are moved out of the way, and then God comes in power and turns the people to Himself."[35]

However, Simpson thought otherwise. In 1882 he wrote, "They [the denominations] are preaching the gospel in their respective fields; they are organizing churches and nurturing converts; they are establishing schools and teaching the young; they are circulating the Bible and infusing Christian influence into the social life of the nations. But are they ... evangelizing the regions beyond; itinerating through all tribes and provinces, sowing the seed 'beside all waters' and not staying for the present to reap the harvest, hastening to offer the message of mercy, once only, if need be, to all mankind before the Master comes, or the grave closes over these dying millions?" What was needed, according to Simpson, was "a class of foreign missionaries, fired with the love of Christ, called by the Holy Ghost, dedicated to the work . . . who, receiving a simple missionary training can go forth, inexpensively, not as settled missionaries, but as pioneers, evangelists, itinerant heralds of the great salvation, . . . who can tell the story of Jesus and pass on."[36]

Presbyterian Dr. A. A. Hodge retorted, "Millenarian missionaries have a style of their own. Their theory affects their work in the way of making them seek exclusively, or chiefly, the conversion of individual souls. The true and efficient missionary method is to aim directly, indeed, at soul winning, but at the same time to plant Christian institutions in heathen lands, which will, in turn, develop according to the genius of the nationalities."[37]

Simpson could hardly have expected his former ministerial colleagues to endorse his plan for foreign missions.

Some found fault with the conduct of Simpson's followers during public meetings. They charged that these "enthusiastic disciples" showed more passion than prudence. The evidence indicates that on occasions there probably was some truth in these charges. Nevertheless, there can be little doubt that the underlying reason for these attacks was prejudice and fear. The denominational theologians were provoked with Simpson because he violated their preserves and challenged their sacrosanct views.

It is therefore not difficult to see why Simpson's movement was unpopular, even among other evangelicals. However, Simpson was quite prepared to endure unpopularity for himself and his movement. He wrote, "We have risked the good opinion of thousands, by fearless testimony to the advanced truths of the Fourfold Gospel."[38]

Four Gospel Truths

Despite opposition, the movement grew, drawing increasing numbers of Christians from a wide variety of denominations into a supra-fellowship that transcended all ecclesiastical barriers.

Simpson believed the message of the gospel consisted of four parts: Christ has given 1) Himself as Saviour, 2) the indwelling Holy

American Roots / 13

1.1

1.2

1.1 An Alliance convention at Old Orchard, Maine, during the 1890s. The side-by-side display of "Old Glory" and the Union Jack denoted the bi-national character of the Alliance homeland.

1.2 Rev. A. B. Simpson, founder of the Christian Alliance and the Evangelical Missionary Alliance, as he appeared around the turn of the century.

Spirit to enable us to live in accordance with the will of God, 3) His resurrection body as the health of our mortal flesh, and 4) the glorious promise of His return to earth as millennial King, when the task of world evangelism is complete. Salvation is offered to any and all who will accept it, sanctification to all who possess salvation and are prepared to consecrate their lives to the will of the indwelling Holy Spirit, and divine health and healing is for all who are genuinely sanctified. These progressive blessings of grace are received by faith and authenticated by experience.[39]

However, far from believing that the blessings of the gospel are given for self-benefit, the founder held that they are given that the church might effectively engage in the work of God, which is to evangelize the world in preparation for Christ's return. Simpson stated that the experience of the Spirit-filled and Spirit-motivated life is the "first objective" of every serious Christian. It is the foundation on which the superstructure and "ultimate objective" of world evangelism is to be erected.[40]

This, then, was Simpson's great founding vision. First, a community of believing Christians experiencing the filling of the Spirit. Then, cleansed and made holy, directed and empowered by the Spirit, the community would reach out to evangelize the world, thus bringing back the King. As Dr. Henry Willson's epigram expressed it, "First saved, then sanctified, then sent." Terse but true!

The movement had no formal creed or rule of faith. However, Simpson embodied the above "four messages of the gospel" into a symbolic capsule of truth, which he termed "the Fourfold Gospel." Understood in its rich, Christ-centred fullness, involving restorative, invigorative, eschatological and evangelistic qualities, the Fourfold Gospel was clearly central in Simpson's thought. It held the conviction and fashioned the experience of his movement. Simpson held that the two central "folds" of the Fourfold Gospel were peculiarly important. Of sanctification, he said, it was not only the divine empowering for the work of world evangelism, it was also the divine empowering for missionary giving.

> The secret of liberality for missions is a deep spiritual life at home. Instead of missionary appeals, the best way to increase the missionary gifts ... would be to hold conventions throughout the country for the baptism of the Holy Ghost, and the consecration of selfish lives. When hearts

are broken and filled with the Spirit of Jesus, there is no lack of money and sacrifice for the spread of the gospel, and the evangelization of the world.[41]

As for the ministry of healing in his own church, he wrote, "It has proved the greatest spiritual force in connection with our work."[42] Again he wrote,

> The doctrine of Christ's healing power is so closely linked with the necessity of holiness and deeper truths and experiences of the spiritual life, that it tends, in a preeminent degree, to promote purity and earnestness.[43]

However, quite apart from the benefits enjoyed, "Divine healing is a command. It ceases to be a mere privilege. It is the Divine prescription for disease, and no obedient Christian can safely dispense with it. Any other method . . . is unauthorized."[44]

Finally, divine healing was an "invaluable handmaid to the cause of missions."[45] Having been told to preach the gospel, to lay hands on the sick, and they shall recover, "What right have we to go to the unbelieving world and demand their acceptance of our message," Simpson asked, "without these signs following?"[46]

EARLY ORGANIZATIONAL PATTERNS

In September 1884, Simpson held his first "Faith Convention." The stated objectives were:

> To gather Christians of common faith and spirit for fellowship; to study the Word of God; to promote a deeper spiritual life; to seek a better understanding of the teachings of the Scriptures respecting physical life in Christ; to wait upon the Lord for a special baptism of the Holy Spirit for life and service; to encourage each other's hearts in the prospect of the glorious appearing of the Lord; and to promote the work of evangelization at home and missions abroad.[47]

The order in which the objectives appear was not accidental. Simpson intended the main thrust of the convention would hinge on the topics of the "deeper spiritual life"—sanctification, divine healing and the second coming of Christ. These were to be the motivation for what was to follow—evangelism at home and abroad. Thus faith and experience in the founding doctrines of his movement were assigned a causative and initiative primacy in his whole scheme of Christian endeavour. So successful was this first convention that it became an annual event, not only in New York, but in four or five other selected locations. The name was altered to "Christian Convention" but the form remained unchanged.

The annual conventions were the principal public expressions of the soul and substance of the movement, in which healings played a prominent part. Indeed, in some of the locations, the conventions were termed "Faithcure" conventions. After one such occasion it was reported that "five hundred people of all ages rose at the close and held up their hands to show that they had been relieved of disease and suffering, by faith alone."[48]

Simpson was accused of being a "hypnotist" and a "charlatan" by some, but others were more charitable. One reporter wrote,

> Think what we may of these people, they do show the fruit of their faith.... They are not oppressed as most of us are with physical infirmities, and evidently their homes are not cluttered with medicine bottles or their desks encumbered with unpaid doctors' bills.[49]

Another reported that the convention meetings were remarkable for the absence of "outward demonstration or levity." He added that "all present seemed to be actuated by a spirit of reverence."[50] Thus, by foul or fair report, Simpson rose to a place of prominence in the religious world, known for his "peculiar tenets" of sanctification, divine healing and pre-millennialism.

During the summer of 1887, at an Old Orchard convention, two societies were organized: the Christian Alliance, "a fraternal union of all who hold in common the fullness of Jesus,"[51] and the Evangelical Missionary Alliance, "to carry the Gospel to all nations, with special reference to the unoccupied fields of the heathen world."[52] As a point of historical fact, the Christian Alliance was organized first, followed by the Evangelical Missionary Alliance, "an association within the Christian Alliance." The first concern of his movement was not the evangelization of the lost without, but the experience of the Spirit-filled life by its members within.

Simpson did not intend to start a new sect or denomination. He visualized a community of the Spirit, nurtured by the Christian Alliance, within the larger communities of the denominations. He wrote, "The Christian Alliance is not intended in any way to be an engine of division or antagonism in the churches, but on the contrary to embrace evangelical Christians of every name." He recognized that in certain circumstances, Christians would want to organize independent churches associated with the Alliance, but he anticipated that in the great majority of cases, members of the Alliance would be loyal to their denominational churches. He added, "At the same time there are special truths which need to be emphasized, and there are cords of spiritual unity more deep and clear than any denominational affinity."[53]

Membership in the Christian Alliance presupposed subscription to these "four great truths." However, an exception was made for those who "cannot yet fully accept the doctrine of Christ's premillennial coming," provided they "are willing to give this subject their candid and prayerful consideration."[54] This concession was indicative of Simpson's desire to avoid polemical divisions between Christians if at all possible.

The Christian Alliance was organized into three levels: a national administration in New York, a "state" (later district) organization, and local branches. The local branch executive consisted of a president, vice-president, treasurer, secretary and sometimes other officers. Not being a church, the local branch had no elders. The constitution enunciated its objectives, especially as they related to the local branches:

a) to promote and diffuse the truths of the Fourfold Gospel;
b) to lead Christians into the practical experience of the fullness of Jesus;
c) to afford a bond of union and fellowship for all who hold this common faith and life;
d) to pray for each other daily, for sanctification of believers, the progress of Christian truth, the evangelization of the world and the speedy coming of our Lord Jesus Christ.[55]

Herein lay the essence of Simpson's Christian Alliance. The local branch was a voluntary society, where the bond of union was not an external framework impressed from without, but a sense of fellowship springing from within.

The local branch was the Alliance equivalent of the Methodist class meeting. Simpson, like Wesley, believed in the necessity of mutual instruction, encouragement, prayer and love. Neither the Methodist class nor the Alliance branch were rivals of, nor substitutes for, the regular church ministries. Rather, both complemented the church by offering a more intense inter-personal relationship within the context of a small and intimate group, which usually met on Sunday afternoon or Friday night so as not to interfere with regular church activities.

The relationship of the local branch to the other agencies of both Alliances should not be overlooked. It was in the local branch meeting that the individual Alliance member was to learn that he or she was important to the whole cause, that fellow members really cared that every member had been filled with the Spirit and was living a life of victory over sin, that each was being kept physically well through the power of God, and was joyously anticipating the imminent return of the Lord. Perhaps the purpose of the local branch is best described by Simpson himself, who wrote, "His [Christ's] disciples need the mutual support which comes from acquaintance, communion, mutual prayer, the interchange of thought and experience, and the consciousness of sympathy and partnership."[56]

Experience filled a large place in the Christian Alliance economy, and in the Simpsonian sense, experience meant doctrine translated into human and living terms. The local branch, therefore, was not a church but a spiritual agency; not a ministry of evangelism for the unconverted, but a ministry of experiential theology for the saints, who were personally seeking the experience of the Spirit-filled life and enduement for Christian service.

The local branches were self-propagating. Someone who had sought and found the "blessings of entire sanctification" or who had been healed of some disease, would invite friends and neighbours to introductory home meetings, usually termed "circles." There would be prayer and perhaps a reading of one of Simpson's sermons, or a chapter from one of his books. The group would then "search the Scriptures to see if these things were so." Sometimes a special advocate of Alliance testimony would be invited to elaborate on some facet of truth. As the numbers grew, a room might be rented and the public invited to attend. A request would bring the district superintendent and a branch would be officially organized.[57]

There were exceptions to the general pattern of local branch activities as laid down by the Christian Alliance constitution. In order to meet local needs, a branch ministry might include the work of a rescue mission or even approach that of a church. Regardless of the variations, the central theme was the personal experience of the deeper spiritual life truths, and enduement for service.[58]

The Ascendancy of Missions

The Evangelical Missionary Alliance (later renamed the International Missionary Alliance) was the service arm of the Christian Alliance, or as Simpson expressed it, "an association within the Christian Alliance, designed to be purely missionary."[59]

It was a policy of the early Alliance to depend entirely on God's faithfulness to provide through the "voluntary gifts of His children . . . as He may dispose them to contribute," a policy which enabled Simpson to declare, "The Alliance has never asked for a cent."[60] The missionary appeal, therefore, was not portrayed as a financial need but as a "call to the people to send out their share of workers into the missionary field."

The first two missionaries of the Evangelical Missionary Alliance were dispatched in October 1887, just two months after the founding of the two Alliances. During the first four years, a total of 22 were sent out. However, death, sickness and re-identification with other sponsors reduced their number to 15 by the summer of 1891. Up to this time, voluntary offerings had been considered more or less sufficient for the unspectacular number of missionary candidates. But by the summer of 1891, Simpson became dissatisfied with the progress of Alliance missions. He proposed sending out 100 new missionaries in the next twelve months. Quickly, volunteers stepped forward. To meet the burgeoning financial requirements, Simpson changed his financial policy, and called for his first missionary offering and pledge. By the end of the summer, more than 100 volunteers were preparing to leave for the mission fields. During the next four years, an additional 200 missionaries were sent out.*

That the hand of the Lord was in this great expansion of the missionary witness would be difficult to deny. Yet, there was a negative side to this development which adversely altered the Alli-

---

* The total number of Alliance missionaries varied little from the 300 mark until after the death of Simpson in 1919.

ance character. Up to this point in its history the Alliance had been known chiefly for its faith and personal experience, as expressed in its great conventions and local branch work. Simpson's low-key approach to financial support for his fifteen or twenty missionaries had attracted little attention from the secular or religious media, who avidly reported his doctrinal positions and healing ministries, and not infrequently denounced them both. The local branch members had been happy to identify with their much maligned leader and the faith "once delivered to the saints." But now he was pleading for and receiving huge amounts of money for missions and saying comparatively little about the once paramount matters of a deeper life experience.

The press was quick to pick this up and stated that the "great faith healer" of former years had become the "champion money-raising clergyman of the country." Whereas doctrinal and experiential matters had previously claimed most of the time and attention at conventions, between 1891 and 1895 missionary topics came to predominate. From then on, the conventions were termed "missionary conventions" at which the crowning features were the counting of pledges, donations, and missionary volunteers.

Nor was the change restricted to the convention life of the Alliance. When the two Alliances had been founded in 1887, the special goals of the Christian Alliance had lent themselves to a flexible organization. On the other hand, the effective and efficient administration of the Missionary Alliance demanded a structured and disciplined organization. With the ascendancy of the missionary thrust during the early 1890s, the resulting rapid growth and complexity of administration demanded a streamlined, resource-conserving reorganization. In 1897 the two Alliances were amalgamated to form The Christian and Missionary Alliance. What resulted was not a proportional blending of the two founding natures, but a new Alliance whose paramount theme was foreign missions, having a network of home branches whose chief reason for existence was the support of the missionary program.[61] The Alliance character was reshaped perhaps not so much by deliberate choice as by a drift of circumstances set in motion through the interplay of competing forces, both within and without the Alliance system.

The Christian Alliance constitution of 1887 had recognized the inevitability of churches wanting to affiliate with it. When this had occurred, it had been customary for the local branch to hold separate meetings from its host church, as the functions were quite different. In the United States, after the turn of the century, because of the continual inroads of liberalism in the mainline churches, those who embraced the Fourfold Gospel became increasingly inclined to leave their denominations and to form independent churches, many of which affiliated with the Alliance. Progressively, the practice of holding separate branch meetings declined, and soon the churches themselves were termed branches. By 1919, the last of the old churchless branches had disappeared. The numerically larger church branch, motivated by evangelistic extroversion, proved to be a superior vehicle by which to campaign for missionary candidates and money, but the smaller fraternal branch, motivated by experiential introversion, had been a superior vehicle by which to maintain fervour of belief and experience in the founding doctrines.

Decline of Doctrinal Distinctives

By the turn of the century, the rise in missionary priority, together with a waning doctrinal priority, had resulted in variations of faith within the Alliance membership. In May 1906, a "Conference for prayer and counsel respecting uniformity in testimony and teaching of the Alliance" convened for four days in Nyack. The conference was called by the board of managers because "a common basis of testimony and teaching is becoming more and more urgent." Only the doctrines of the Fourfold Gospel were addressed.[62] The conference does not appear to have been very productive, and the need to clarify distinctive doctrines and to agree on their importance and place in the total Alliance economy became increasingly evident with the passage of time.

The doctrine of divine healing was the first distinctive Alliance doctrine to be questioned within the fellowship and de-emphasized. In 1885 the founder had said, "The gospel of healing is inseparably linked with the evangelizing of the world. God has given it to us as a testimony to the nations."[63] Again, in 1887 he had written, "The Cross stands out clearly before us with divine healing and divine atonement on it. Our sicknesses are on one arm and our sins on the other."[64] The "blessed gospel of physical healing" was "a sacred trust for a dying world." However, by 1904 he would say, "Healing of the body is not the primary blessing but a secondary blessing. The chief object of our testimony is Jesus Christ as Saviour and Sanctifier."[65]

There was probably a good reason why the Alliance distinctive of divine healing was de-emphasized during the later decades of the founder's life. In former days, healings had formed an important part of local branch and convention ministries, and numerous had been the testimonies to the efficacy of the teaching. Leaders had felt comfortable with the position that healing was assured to all who were truly sanctified, without the use of human agencies. A lack of healing pointed to a faulty sanctification or faith. In the face of markedly decreasing evidences of healing, this position became untenable in the eyes of many within the Alliance family. Still emphasizing that healing had been provided in the atonement of Christ, they now took the position that there was no Scriptural warrant to ignore the sovereignty of God by claiming that healing was universal and immutable, limited only by the degree of sanctification and faith.

Salvationist Captain R. Kelso Carter, the hymn writer, and Episcopalian Dr. Kenneth MacKenzie, both long-time close friends and ardent supporters of Dr. Simpson, have emphatically stated that in his later years, the founder came around to adopting this modified view.[66] Another witness, Presbyterian Rev. W. T. Griffiths, a believer in divine healing, but not that it is an inherent provision of the atonement, claimed that he had personally challenged Simpson on this "fundamental issue," that the founder had admitted to him that his early teaching on healing had been "erroneous in the crucial point," and that "if ever he re-wrote his book he would alter it."[67]*

Be that as it may, apparently the founder has left us without any statement from his own pen or tongue that would confirm or deny a fundamental change from his early divine healing beliefs. Notwithstanding, the fact remains: the subject of divine healing was de-emphasized after the turn of the century.

By 1917, it was clear that all distinctive Alliance doctrines had lost their former position of foundational, primary importance. District Superintendent J. D. Williams says that Simpson, during his last deputational visit to St. Paul, "took occasion to emphasize in the strongest possible way the fact that the primary objective of the

---

* Writing in 1920, Rev. A. E. Thompson guardedly admits that "some have thought that Dr. Simpson changed his views and attitudes in his latter years." However, he claims that those who knew Simpson best would disagree. It would appear that Thompson decided to inquire no further, for he concludes his remarks on the subject with the statement, "We shall do well to be as wise as he [Simpson] was in leaving some things to be made manifest when we shall 'know as also we are known.'"

Alliance movement was not the teaching of special doctrines, but the salvation of souls. . . . He trusted that this should always be the primary ideal and aim of our work."[68]

This statement contrasts sharply with the founder's statement, made just before the turn of the century, in which he urged his followers,

> Let us never forget the special calling of our Alliance work. It is first to hold up Jesus in His fullness. Next, to lead God's hungry children to know their full inheritance of privilege and blessing for spirit, soul, and body. Next to witness to the imminent coming of the Lord Jesus Christ as our millennial king. And finally, to encourage and incite the people of God to do the neglected work of our age and time among the unchurched classes at home and the perishing heathen abroad. God will bless us as we are true to this trust.[69]

During the closing two decades of the founder's life, his great vision of a Spirit-filled, Spirit-empowered home constituency, reaching out to evangelize the masses at home and abroad, dimmed in several respects. Publicly, at least, the subject of foreign missions had become the dominant theme and consuming passion. Not only was it the "ultimate objective," it had also become the "first objective." No longer were belief and experience in the doctrines of the deeper spiritual life presented in their foundational and causative roles in the work of a successful evangelism. Instead they were presented as an optional benefit, the better way, rather than the "only way." Coincident with the swing away from the old style fraternal ministry towards a church ministry, and the de-emphasis of deeper life topics, was a decline in concern for social outreaches. In 1886, Simpson had written, "He [Christ] wants us to have not only mere preaching of the Gospel, but work for the poor and the lowly; work for the destitute and the sick; work for the rich and the worldly." However, by 1897 he would say, "They [social projects] have a place and value, but let the world take care of them." "Redeemed men and women," he said, "ought to be giving their strength and wealth to do the best things and not the second best."[70] It would appear that the founder had allowed his great passion for foreign missions (and perhaps a concern over the rising popularity of the "social gospel") to cast a deepening shadow across this once sparkling facet of the founding Alliance vision. Whatever the reason, by 1919, the early home missions projects for the orphaned, degraded and sick had virtually disappeared.

The Alliance had reached a point in its development where the value of homeland ministries would be seen by their direct contribution to foreign missions, rather than for their causative or foundational value of leading members first into an experience of the deeper spiritual life, and then into the work of evangelism.

Steps Toward Denominationalism

In 1907, the Alliance in the United States began to experience serious problems over the "tongues" issue, associated with the rise of Pentecostalism. Those with Pentecostal leanings claimed that speaking in tongues was a necessary evidence of the baptism of the Spirit. Simpson published an official Alliance stand on this matter, in which he opposed this view.[71] As a result, many withdrew from the Alliance fellowship, and took with them an alarming number of church properties.

By 1910, in an attempt to stem the tide of building losses, the Alliance took steps to gain control of properties belonging to affiliated churches. Pressure was brought to bear on district superintendents, who, in turn, exerted their powers of persuasion on local church boards or trustees. This process significantly advanced the trend towards denominationalism.

The General Council of 1912 adopted a new constitution. By that time most of the old style fraternal branches in the United States had been replaced by affiliated independent church branches. Among the provisions of major importance, the annual General Council henceforth would be the legislative body of the Alliance. Delegates to Council would include representatives from the branches. The board of managers would be the executive body. Local branches would come under the supervision of a district superintendent and a district executive committee, elected at an annual district conference.

Of particular significance, a "reversion clause" was included in the constitution of 1912. Briefly stated, deeds of property owned by local branches should contain a clause to the effect that in the event of the property ever ceasing to be used for Alliance purposes, title would convey to The Christian and Missionary Alliance.

The constitution of 1912 was of historic importance, for although several minor amendments would be made in the course of time, the basic concepts remained fixed for the next sixty years.*

THE END OF AN ERA

On October 29, 1919, Dr. A. B. Simpson, founder, chief architect and chief steward of the Alliance movement for its first 38 years, passed on. He left behind an Alliance appreciably changed from what he originally designed. It was no longer an interdenominational fraternity in the faith and experience of the "deeper spiritual life," committed to both home and foreign missions. It was now primarily a foreign missions society, working in sixteen countries with 259 missionaries, supported to a large extent by a fellowship of 239 home churches, connected by what was by then an ill-defined Fourfold Gospel. The Alliance had gained a measure of respectability and support among the Christian public as a result of its own uncertainties and de-emphasis of its most controversial doctrines. Its founding distinctives were becoming matters of historical interest rather than expressions of its living faith. The vision had undergone change. The primacy of foreign missions had become the new supremacy. "Historical drift," as it is sometimes termed, had already set in.

REFERENCES

1. George P. Pardington, *Twenty-five Wonderful Years* (New York: Christian Alliance Publishing Co., 1914), p. 6.
2. *New York Times*, 19 Dec 1881, p. 7; ibid., 31 Dec 1881, Religious; ibid., 4 February 1882, Religious.
3. New York newspaper clipping, unidentified.
4. *Word, Work and World* (New York), Mar 1883, p. 45.
5. Ibid., Jun 1882, p. 215.
6. *Hamilton Times*, 3 Jan 1883, p. 4; *Cornwall Freeholder*, 19 Jan 1883, p. 1; *Word, Work and World*, May & Jun 1883, editorial.
7. A. B. Simpson, *The Gospel of Healing* (Harrisburg: Christian Publications Inc., 1915), p. 161.

---

* Two very important advances in the field of women's ministries took place during the Council of 1914. Recognizing the importance of prayer in the success of missionary work, the women present were organized into "women's missionary prayer bands." Secondly, Council recommended that women workers be recognized as "deaconesses."

8. *Word, Work and World*, Aug 1882, p. 64; ibid., Nov 1882, p. 203; ibid., Mar 1883, pp. 37, 46.
9. Ibid., Mar 1883, p. 47; ibid., Jun 1883, p. 82.
10. *New York Times*, 4 Nov 1882-20 Oct 1883, every Saturday, Churches; *Hamilton Times*, 3 Jan 1883, p. 4;*Cornwall Freeholder*, 19 Jan 1883, p. 1.
11. *New York Tribune*, 19 Nov 1882, p. 10.
12. *Word, Work and World*, Feb 1883, editorial.
13. Ibid., Mar 1883, p. 46.
14. Ibid., Mar 1883, pp. 46, 47.
15. Ibid., Oct 1883, p. 154.
16. Ibid., Mar 1883, p. 47.
17. A. B. Simpson, *The Fullness of Jesus* (New York: The Christian Alliance Pub. Co., 1886), p. 25.
18. *New York Tribune*, 19 Nov 1882, p. 10.
19. Westminster Confession of Faith, Chapter X: Articles 1, 2, 3, 4; A. A. Hodge, *Outlines of Theology* (London: Thomas Nelson and Sons, 1886), pp. 447-449, 454, 455; B. B. Warfield, *Biblical and Theological Studies* (Philadelphia: Presbyterian and Reformed Publishing Co., 1968), pp. 325, 327.
20. A. B. Simpson, *The Fourfold Gospel* (Harrisburg: Christian Publications Inc., 1968), pp. 20, 22; ibid., *Christ in the Bible Vol. XIX Galatians/Ephesians* (New York: Alliance Press Co., 1904), pp. 75, 83-85, 90, 91, 110.
21. *Outlines of Theology*, p. 217.
22. B. B. Warfield, *Perfectionism* (Philadelphia: Presbyterian Board of Publishers, 1980), pp. 309, 357, 385-388.
23. A. A. Hodge, *Popular Lectures on Theological Themes* (Philadelphia: Presbyterian Board of Publishers, 1887), p. 341.
24. A. B. Simpson, *Wholly Sanctified* (Harrisburg: Christian Publications Inc., 1982), pp. 16, 19; ibid., *Christ our Sanctifier* (Harrisburg, Christian Publications Inc., 1947), pp. 6, 9, 10, 11; ibid., *Christ in the Bible* (New York: Alliance Press Co., 1904), Vol. XIX, *Christ in Galatians/Ephesians*, pp. 45, 46; *Word, Work and World*, Jul 1887, Distinctive Teachings, p. 2.
25. *Wholly Sanctified*, p. 87.
26. *Word, Work and World*, Aug & Sep 1887, p. 76.
27. A. B. Simpson, *The Gospel of Healing* (Harrisburg: Christian Publications Inc., 1915), pp. 31, 39, 67, 68, 76, 78, 88.
28. *The Canadian Independent* (Toronto), April 1889, pp. 115, 116.
29. A. A. Hodge, *Popular Lectures on Theological Themes* (Philadelphia: Presbyterian Board of Publication, 1887), p. 108.
30. *The Christian Advocate*, 7 Nov 1878, p. 712.
31. Albert H. Newman, *A Manual of Church History* (Philadelphia: American Baptist Publication Society, 1911), Vol. 2, p. 81.
32. A. B. Simpson, *The Fourfold Gospel* (Harrisburg: Christian Alliance Publishing Co., 1925), p. 84.
33. Ibid.

34. *The Canadian Baptist* (Toronto), 29 Nov 1881, p. 4.
35. Iain H. Murray, *The Puritan Hope* (London: The Banner of Truth Trust, 1971), p. 181.
36. *Word, Work and World*, Jan 1882, p. 33.
37. C. A. Salmond, *Princetonia* (Edinburgh: Oliphant, Anderson and Ferrier, 1888), pp. 238, 239.
38. *Christian Alliance*, Feb 1892.
39. *The Gospel of Healing*, p. 7.
40. *Word, Work and World*, Mar 1883, p. 46; ibid., Jul & Aug 1885, p. 197; A. B. Simpson, *Walking in the Spirit* (Harrisburg: Christian Publications Inc., no date), pp. 103-n107.
41. *Alliance Weekly*, 12 Jun 1920, p. 171.
42. *Word, Work and World*, May 1894, p. 472.
43. *The Gospel of Healing*, p. 70.
44. Ibid., p. 23.
45. *Word, Work and World*, Mar 1883, p. 47.
46. *The Gospel of Healing,*, p. 19.
47. *The Christian and Missionary Alliance* (New York), October 1884.
48. C. Donald McKaig, "Simpson's Scrapbook" (Nyack: by the author, 1971), unidentified newspaper clipping.
49. Ibid.; *The Alliance Weekly*, 5 Jul 1937, p. 358; 17 Jul 1937, pp. 452, 453.
50. *New York Times*, 13 Oct 1888, p. 8.
51. *Word, Work and World*, July & August, 1887, p. 110.
52. Ibid., p. 111.
53. Ibid., pp. 110, 111.
54. Ibid.
55. Ibid.
56. A. B. Simpson, "Why Should There Be a Christian Alliance?" (pamphlet, 1888).
57. *Alliance Weekly*, 20 Dec 1919, p. 215.
58. Ibid.
59. *Word, Work and World*, Nov 1887, p. 227.
60. *Toronto Empire*, 25 Sep 1891, p. 8.
61. C&MA Annual Report, 1892, p. 55.
62. *The Christian and Missionary Alliance*, 3 Mar 1906, p. 185; 19 May 1906, p. 297.
63. *Word, Work and World*, Jul & Aug 1885, p. 210.
64. Ibid., Aug & Sep 1887, p. 76.
65. Ibid., 7 Nov 1904, p. 2.
66. R. Kelso Carter, *Faith Healing Reviewed* (Boston: The ChristianWitness Co., 1897), pp. 112, 113, 114, 122, 124, 127; Kenneth MacKenzie, *Our Physical Heritage in Christ* (New York: Fleming H. Revell Co., 1924), pp. 27, 28; *Alliance Weekly*, 24 Jul 1937, p. 470; ibid., 7 Aug 1937, p. 500; ibid., 24 Aug 1937, p. 516; ibid., 4 Sep 1937, p. 566.

67. *The Life of Faith* (London), 13 Apr 1921, p. 415.
68. A. E. Thompson, *The Life of A. B. Simpson* (Harrisburg: Christian Publications Inc., 1920), p. 136.
69. *Alliance Weekly*, 11 Nov 1899.
70. *The Christian and Missionary Alliance*, 27 Oct 1897, p. 417.
71. Ibid., Apr 1910, p. 78.

CHAPTER TWO

Canadian Heritage

The cradle of The Christian and Missionary Alliance in Canada was southern Ontario. At the close of the American Revolutionary War in 1783, that territory, apart from a few French settlements scattered along the north shore of the St. Lawrence River, was a wilderness of timber and swamp, virtually uninhabited except for Indians and fur traders. The successful rebellion to the south had left many American families torn apart by competing loyalties. About 80,000 colonists who were not prepared to deny their allegiance to the British crown were disinherited, stripped of their goods and lands, and exiled. Some 40,000 of these took refuge in Britain, while the remainder made their way to what was left of British North America. During 1783 and 1784, 10,000 United Empire Loyalists settled along the Canadian shores of the St. Lawrence and Niagara Rivers, Lake Ontario and Lake Erie. A century later, Loyalist stock would become the backbone of the Fourfold Gospel movement in Canada.

VISION AND REVISION

In February 1790, William Losee, a one-armed Methodist from Long Island, New York, obtained permission to "range at large in Canada." He visited homesteads that year between Kingston and the Bay of Quinte, and learned first hand of the appalling spiritual needs of the settlers. The following year he returned as a duly appointed Methodist missionary to Canada. Losee's mission field was a difficult one. All but a few of its inhabitants lived in isolated farms, connected by roads little better than trails. In all of southern Ontario there were only six clergymen of all varieties.

Losee, and other saddle bag preachers who followed him, were nicknamed "the Methodist Cavalry." They carried the gospel from farm to farm, organizing little classes of believers, and subsequently churches. They preached not just a message of sins to be forgiven, but of lives to be changed by the indwelling presence of the Holy Spirit. Man was saved, they claimed, that he might be holy—a message startlingly similar to that of Dr. A. B. Simpson some ninety years later.

By 1830 the province had been rurally evangelized. Undoubtedly a major reason for this outstanding success had been that both the message and method of Methodism had been particularly suited to frontier conditions. They had identified with the people, had encouraged an "every member" ministry, and had found room for emotional expression, which other denominations had frowned upon. Thus, social as well as spiritual needs of the settlers were met.

The Methodists now turned their attention to the cities, and immediately found that they were not welcome. The sophisticated city dwellers refused to accept the rough Methodist preachers, and demanded an educated ministry as the price for their attention.

Up to this point the Church of England was the church of privilege. "Non-conformists" could not own land for churches or cemeteries, nor could they perform marriages or operate colleges. In 1830, the Methodists petitioned the governor, Sir John Colbourne, for permission to found an institution of higher learning, but he flatly refused.[1] Nothing daunted, the Methodists sent Egerton Ryerson to England with instructions not to return to Canada without a Royal Charter. He was successful, and to Upper Canada Academy at Cobourg (later Victoria College) was given the honour of being the first non-conformist college in the British Empire to receive a Royal Charter, and the first institution of university status, under any auspices, to become operational (1836) in Ontario.[2]

However, this success would cost the Methodists dearly. Their preoccupation with these matters during the 1830s caused them to forget that holiness was the "grand depositum" of Methodist heritage. The rising generation of educated clergy was not as committed in faith and holiness as were their predecessors. The principle of separation from the world was abandoned after 1840.[3]

By 1860 the Methodists had become well established in the towns and cities. But the build-up was not from the masses of the poor city dwellers as much as from the middle class of business people. By 1861 the provincial population had reached 1.4 million, and the largest denomination was the Methodists, embracing just under one-half of the total population. The rural sect had grown into the town and city church.[4] After 1870, the growth of wealth among the membership created a thirst for ever bigger and better church buildings. A program was put into effect to replace the "little wooden structures" with "handsome brick churches."[5] "We must have a fine church, by some means," lamented one Methodist writer. "Talk as we will about God meeting us in the humble cottage, let it be borne in mind that the difficulty in these days is to get people there to meet with Him."[6] The burgeoning building program brought about sweeping changes in arranging for pulpit placements. In effect, churches bid against each other for preachers with the greatest oratorical skills who could fill the churches in order to meet the debt payments. Churches came to depend upon people of wealth, and the criterion of membership was no longer those who could pray, but those who could pay. More and more, Canadian Methodism became a church of fashion, and less and less a church of the masses.[7]

By 1880, modernism had crept into the colleges and was affecting most of the young clergy. The old message of sin, repentance and faith gave way to a more gentle message of love and understanding. By 1880 it became difficult to find a clergyman, especially a young and talented clergyman, who shared his faith.[8] Moreover, by that time, positions of denominational influence were being filled by clergymen who, to use a phrase of A. M. Fairbairn, "had risen in the church by falling in the faith."

Caught in the web of an insatiable desire to spend and a critical need to economize, Canadian Methodism looked to the economies of reunion for a solution. In 1884 the Methodist Church of Canada united with the Primitive Methodist Church in Canada, the Bible Christian Church and the Methodist Episcopal Church in Canada. This was the price to be paid to secure the expansion of credit necessary to meet the heavy carrying charges on church buildings,[9] but the union of 1884 was the signal for the conservative laity to revolt against what they deemed to be the abandonment of Methodist orthodoxy by their liberal clergy. In their agony, many heart-broken Methodists looked around for alternatives to Methodism.

New Spiritual Movements

At this very point in time there occurred several separate events that cast their shadows across the path of distraught Methodists. In February of 1882, two recent immigrants from England held the first

Salvation Army meetings in Canada, on the streets of Toronto.[10] The Salvationist movement spread rapidly throughout the cities and towns of southern Ontario. Two years later, many unhappy Methodists who were prepared to leave their church, flocked to the ranks of the Salvation Army. For them, this was the answer to a crumbling Methodist church. The Army was clearly a holiness movement, and "a poor man's church," a direct descendant of true Methodism, oriented to the needs of the masses.[11]

The second significant event occurred in April 1882, when the Rev. John Salmon, a former Methodist, returned to Toronto from Britain where he had embraced the teachings of sanctification and divine healing, as taught by Dr. William E. Boardman. In December of that year he entered upon a ministry at the Hazelton Avenue Congregational Church, featuring Jesus Christ as Saviour, Sanctifier, Healer, and Coming King.

His teaching, especially regarding healing, although accepted by some, was opposed by others. Three years later, to minimize difficulties in his congregation, he commenced holding "meetings by invitation" in his home, emphasizing sanctification and divine healing. These meetings were attended particularly by Methodists, who spread word of his teachings to their spiritually hungry brethren still in the churches.[12]

The third important event occurred in October 1882, when a Presbyterian paralytic, Maggie Scott, was miraculously healed, apparently in answer to prayer on her behalf by Dr. Cullis in Boston. Within six months, the nineteen-year-old Maggie began holding evangelistic campaigns. The story of her healing became widely known throughout southern Ontario, and many believed in the "prayer of faith."[13]

On February 1, 1887, Salmon commenced an independent ministry in the Fourfold Gospel. He did not plan to form a sect, but conducted meetings in homes or wherever friends of any and all denominational backgrounds were willing to consider the truths of the Fourfold Gospel. Not all the disillusioned Methodists in Ontario had been prepared to leave their churches following the union of 1884. However, they longed for some kind of fellowship of evangelical faith and holiness experience. In Salmon's sapling movement they, along with others among the Congregationalists, Anglicans, Presbyterians, Quakers and Plymouth Brethren, found the answer to their needs. Very few of the first generation of Salmon's fraternity in the Fourfold

Gospel would ever see the need of leaving their denominations and forming separate churches.

News of Salmon's independent ministry spread rapidly, and soon he received invitations from across the province to make known his teachings. It was no accident that the majority of his followers were Methodists. They had little difficulty in adjusting to a slightly different version of sanctification,* and Maggie Scott had prepared the way for them to accept the teaching of divine healing.

The Dominion Auxiliary

In February 1889, the young Canadian movement invited Dr. Simpson to come to Canada to explain the function of the Christian Alliance, resulting in the union at that convention of the Canadian and American movements. There was to be a national body for all Canada, to be known as "The Dominion Auxiliary Branch of the Christian Alliance," headed by its own freely elected president and executive committee. The Alliance was stated to be a fraternity of faith in the Fourfold Gospel that transcended all denominational boundaries. This appealed to Canadians, especially the majority Methodists, who saw in the Alliance a means of providing Christian fellowship and spiritual fulfilment, while remaining loyal to all that was still good in Methodism. The term "Auxiliary" held special meaning for Canadians of Loyalist stock, with their characteristic aversion to being manipulated by Americans. They gladly accepted the connotation of a confederate or partner, acting under their own freely elected president and executive in support of an international cause.[14]

William Howland, previously Toronto's great reform mayor and ardent Anglican worker, was elected president (and chief administrator) of the Canadian Auxiliary. Among the vice-presidents was Congregationalist John Salmon, patriarch of the Canadian movement in the Fourfold Gospel and the prime causative influence in the auxiliary's development for the next 21 years. Presbyterian Maggie Scott also became a founding vice-president.[15]

---

* In Canada, until the emergence of the Salvation Army and Salmon's movement, there were no viable alternatives to decaying Methodism. This contrasts sharply with the situation in the United States, where, following an alarming decline in public morals associated with the Civil War, the national Association for the Promotion of Holiness was formed. The result was a profusion of assorted holiness teachings, of which Simpson's, in 1881, was a latecomer.

Howland, Salmon and their associates immediately put in motion a program of establishing local branches. It is remarkable that within six years, at least thirteen branches were organized in Ontario. In addition, there were formed an unknown number of "circles" (the embryo form of a branch). This is a measure of the acceptability of the fraternal branch concept in Ontario during the period 1887-1895.[16]

The Canadian Auxiliary never had more than five or six clergymen within its ranks. It was essentially a layman's society, characterized by a bubbling enthusiasm to expand the testimony of the Fourfold Gospel. Groups of as many as fourteen lay people accompanied Salmon as he travelled from town to town spreading the teaching.[17]

The Canadian Auxiliary members were at first somewhat slow to participate in the work of the Evangelical Missionary Alliance. This was due to existing commitments to their own denominational missionary programs and to a national distaste for the administration of their financial contributions by Americans. Dr. Simpson made an attempt to accommodate Canadian sensitivities by renaming his enterprise the International Missionary Alliance in recognition of the bi-national character of the Alliance.[18]

Salmon commenced holding independent church services in Toronto in November 1887 which resulted in the organization and incorporation of Bethany Church in 1891. It was the mother church of the Alliance in Canada. Like the mother church of the Alliance in the United States, the Gospel Tabernacle in New York, Bethany Church was also heavily engaged in evangelical social welfare. Its pastor and members founded Bethany Home for healing, Bethany Orphanage for destitute boys, Bethany Working Men's Home for homeless men, Bethany Mission for the debauched and destitute, and the Bethany Gospel Wagon, for the preaching and distribution of the printed word on the streets of Toronto. Both Pastor Salmon and Head Elder Howland were known city-wide for their work among the poor, the sick, and the degraded of Toronto's largest slum. Bethany Church was host to both the Toronto Branch of the Christian Alliance and the Toronto Missionary Training Institute, the first "Alliance" Bible school in Canada. Bethany Church, Toronto, gave its name to Alliance churches in Peterborough and Hopeville, and its Bethany "model" Constitution was the standard for any church wishing to affiliate with the Alliance in Canada.[19]

In September 1891, Simpson, acting on the recommendation of Salmon, conducted his first ordination in Canada. However, the

Canadian Heritage / 35

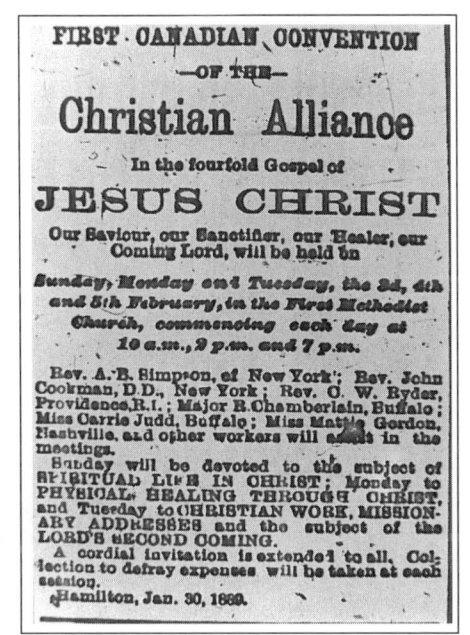

FIRST CANADIAN CONVENTION
—OF THE—
Christian Alliance
In the fourfold Gospel of
JESUS CHRIST
Our Saviour, our Sanctifier, our Healer, our Coming Lord, will be held on

Sunday, Monday and Tuesday, the 3d, 4th and 5th February, in the First Methodist Church, commencing each day at 10 a.m., 3 p.m. and 7 p.m.

Rev. A. B. Simpson, of New York; Rev. John Cookman, D.D., New York; Rev. C. W. Ryder, Providence, R.I.; Major R. Chamberlain, Buffalo; Miss Carrie Judd, Buffalo; Miss Mattie Gordon, Nashville, and other workers will assist in the meetings.

Sunday will be devoted to the subject of SPIRITUAL LIFE IN CHRIST; Monday to PHYSICAL HEALING THROUGH CHRIST, and Tuesday to CHRISTIAN WORK, MISSIONARY ADDRESSES and the subject of the LORD'S SECOND COMING.

A cordial invitation is extended to all. Collection to defray expenses will be taken at each session.

Hamilton, Jan. 30, 1889.

2.3

2.1 Evangelist Maggie Scott awakened southern Ontario to the teaching of divine healing and became a founding vice-president of the Dominion Auxiliary of the Christian Alliance.

2.2 Pastor John Salmon was patriarch of the Fourfold Gospel movement in Canada and its longest serving founding vice-president.

2.3 Announcement of the founding convention of the Christian Alliance in Canada, at which the Canadian movement linked up with the Christian Alliance in New York.

2.4 The Honourable William H. Howland, first president of the Dominion Auxiliary of the Christian Alliance.

2.5 "Blythe Cottage," Queens Park Crescent, Toronto, was the home of William Howland and was the first headquarters of the Alliance in Canada.

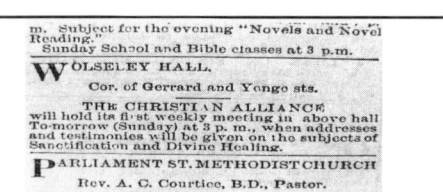

36 / *Canadian Heritage*

2.6 Newspaper notice of the first weekly meeting of the Alliance in Canada, February 24, 1889. Note the subjects addressed.

2.7 Bethany Chapel, on University Avenue, Toronto, was the first "permanent" home of the mother church of the Alliance in Canada.

2.8 John Salmon ministered to the Central China Conference of the Alliance in October 1917. Photographed with the delegates in the centre of the second row, Salmon is flanked by veteran Canadian Alliance missionaries Matthew Birrel (left) and Robert Jaffray (right).

2.9 The chapel of Toronto Bible College, on College Street. Here, on June 17, 1917, Dr. Simpson delivered his final address to a Canadian audience.

2.10 Parkdale Tabernacle, in a Toronto suburb, was the only Canadian church building to be dedicated by Dr. A. B. Simpson.

Canadian movement had linked up with Simpson on the assurance that the Alliance was not a denomination, but a fraternity of faith and experience among Christians of all denominations. The action of ordination was seen by many to be an infringement on the prerogatives of their denominations. The resulting division decimated Alliance ranks in Canada.

In Canada, as in the United States, annual conventions were a feature of all branches from the start. These great annual conventions sometimes featured as many as twenty guest speakers. Until 1893, the conventions were chiefly doctrinal and experiential in character, and were usually termed Christian Conventions. After 1895, they were termed Missionary Conventions, and featured predominantly (and in later years almost exclusively) missionary topics. The first missionary collection taken at an annual convention in Canada was delayed until the year 1900 because of a persistent adverse reaction to reports of Simpson's huge collections of money and jewels south of the border.[20]

Dr. Simpson's climactic missionary sermon of the Dominion Convention of 1917 on Sunday, June 17, was his final address to a Canadian audience, and was delivered before a capacity audience in the Toronto Bible College. It was, as the media reported, "a rousing closing" to the eight-day missionary convention. Simpson urged his Canadian audience not to look on the collection as money being sent to New York for the support of the Alliance missionary program, but rather as a Canadian project to send out new missionaries to as yet unevangelized fields, at an estimated cost of $850 each. What a thrill it must have been to his great missionary heart when it was announced that $20,800 had been received—enough "to send out twenty-four new missionaries." What a grand finale this was for his last appeal to the land of his birth![21] All told, Dr. Simpson had been the principal speaker at a total of 64 Alliance conventions in Canada.

As mentioned in the previous chapter, the amalgamation of the two Alliances in 1897 brought about profound changes in the structure and the nature of homeland work. For Canadians, it meant the dissolution of their cherished Auxiliary, with its freely elected president and executive committee. The Alliance in Canada suddenly lost its national character and became just one of many districts under an appointed district superintendent, answerable to a field superintendent residing in New York. It appeared to Canadians (with some justification) that they were no longer being treated as confederates, but rather as a territorial division to be administered. Canadians remembered that in 1889 they had voted for "alliance," not "absorption." It appeared that Dr. Simpson had forgotten their national distaste for being administered from beyond their borders. Nevertheless, the decision rested, and the Canadian Auxiliary passed into history. Simpson would later admit that the amalgamation "was accomplished with considerable strain." "It was a crisis," he said. "There were difficulties and misunderstandings."[22] It had not been a happy event for The Christian and Missionary Alliance within Canada, and the unfortunate turn of events would not pass without leaving persistent scars. The wonderful lay enthusiasm, which had characterized the early Canadian movement, gave way to apathy. A cloud of uncertainty which would not be lifted for several decades hung over the Canadian segment of the Alliance.

CANADIAN DISTINCTIVES

During the Dominion Convention of June 1907, in Toronto, the delegates frankly and coolly addressed the issue of Pentecostalism. The phenomenon of tongues was accepted as "genuine, modest and entirely scriptural," but a judicious balance was agreed upon "without serious strain." It was to the credit of the delegates of this convention that the work in Canada was thus "preserved from extravagance and excess" and spared from division.[23]

As discussed in the last chapter, the same issue of Pentecostalism caused severe division within the constituency in the United States. In order to stem the tide of church building losses, steps were taken to gain control of properties belonging to affiliated churches. This was undoubtedly a wise move for the Alliance in the United States, but it was inappropriate for Canada. In the first place, affiliated churches in Canada had not experienced a problem with Pentecostalism. Moreover, the Canadian affiliated churches had been brought into the Alliance fellowship through Salmon, a Congregationalist, and they had adopted the Bethany Constitution which emphasized the importance of complete independence from outside ecclesiastical control.[24] Neither the churches nor Salmon were prepared to yield to pressure from New York. With Salmon it was a matter of Congregational conscience, and he concluded that he could no longer represent the Alliance to his constituent churches. In April 1910 he tendered his resignation from the district superintendency, "giving his reasons," but he carried on as pastor of Bethany Church.[25]

On their part, the churches and fraternal branches continued to regard Salmon as the patriarch of their movement until his retirement from the pastorate of Bethany Church a year later. It fell to "Travelling Superintendent" Harold Stephens, who was proclaimed district superintendent after the resignation of Salmon in 1910, to attempt to persuade the churches to commit their properties to the Alliance. He succeeded in persuading only the Parkdale Tabernacle Church, which he had founded, to go as far as agreeing to equal representation of New York Alliance officers and locals on its board of trustees. Stephens resigned from the Alliance one year later because of "excessive interference." This tension with its resulting human losses could have been avoided if the Canadian situation had been recognized prior to adoption of a new general policy.

Alliance successes in the maritime provinces had never been outstanding. From the beginning, the religious, political and economic vicissitudes of the area, combined to hinder the entry of new denominations. By the time a serious Alliance attempt was made, the ecclesiastical mix had stabilized, the area was fully churched and newcomers were not welcome. With the Methodists comprising just fourteen percent of the English speaking population (compared with fifty percent of the total Ontario population), the Alliance should not have expected, nor did it receive, widespread acceptance in the maritime provinces. The Alliance made its overture to the maritimes in 1896. Four years later, Rev. George Fisher (co-superintendent with Salmon), made an in-depth investigation of maritime conditions, during which he encountered widespread "prejudice and misunderstanding," but he was successful in organizing two branches.[26] Fisher's investigation led him to conclude "that a grand work could be done," provided the Alliance was prepared to appoint a resident maritime district superintendent.[27]

Fisher was supported in this conclusion by Salmon, who understood the difficulties of superintending from a 1,400-mile distance. However, the Home Department was not prepared to appoint a resident superintendent, on the basis of the existing missionary giving from the area. Salmon made a final appeal to the Council of 1909 for a resident maritime district superintendent to "hold on to what we have gained,"[28] but to no avail.

The situation in western Canada was no better. The first branch had been formed in 1895, and by 1911 there were four. However, the idea of an interdenominational fraternity of Fourfold Gospel faith and experience was never popular in the west. From 1885 onwards, with the opening of the trans-continental railway and the ever increasing flood of immigrant settlers, the urgent need in western Canada was seen as the evangelization of the vast number of settlers who knew absolutely nothing of Christ. For many years the western media was resentful of the Alliance collecting money for foreign missions, which they considered should be spent at home, alleviating the spiritual needs of the neglected immigrants.

A Waning Interest

The resignation of Stephens from the district superintendency in June 1911 triggered some action from New York. In September, the Rev. Louis J. Long of Corning, New York, was appointed district superintendent of eastern Canada only.[29] No superintendent was appointed for the west.

Rev. L. J. Long proceeded to advance the Alliance cause through city missionary conventions and new church affiliation, as practised in the United States. He showed little interest in the existing fraternal branches, generally located in small towns, which were dependent on the district superintendent to maintain vitality, and had been the backbone of the movement in Canada. However, Canadians generally, in the second decade of the century, were not prepared to abandon their denominational ties to form new churches. The arguments over the growing issue of church union in Canada had already reached fever pitch. Among the Methodists, Presbyterians and Congregationalists, those who were concerned about the preservation of their denominational distinctives were too busy working and praying for deliverance from the twin enemies of modernism and unionism to seriously consider the Alliance program for new churches. Compounding the problem during the four years of the war (1914-18) was the severe drain on human resources from the churches and fraternal branches, either by induction into the services or dislocation for wartime work.

In 1914 the Home Department decided "to take steps toward freeing Mr. Long from his pastoral responsibilities in Toronto, so as to give his whole time to the work throughout the Dominion."[30] But the decision was never carried through. Discouraged with the Canadian situation in 1918, Long made it known to the board of managers that he wished to return to a ministry in the United States. In the annual report delivered at Council in May 1918, a brief reference to Canadian affairs ended with, "We are praying that someone may be set free for aggressive work in opening new places."[31]

In July, the board of managers approved a recommendation of the Home Department to offer the superintendency of all Canada to Rev. P. W. Philpott of Hamilton.[32] Philpott turned down the opportunity and Long resigned in October. When he tallied the results of seven years of labour, Long found that he had gained two churches and lost the mother church of the Canadian movement. Of the twelve or more fraternal branches, all but two had been closed down. Once again, a general policy or practice, based on conditions in the United States, had proven to be unsuitable in Canada.

After the return of Long to the United States in October 1918, there was no district superintendent for any part of Canada. Thus, even before the founder of The Christian and Missionary Alliance, Dr. A. B. Simpson, departed this life on October 29, 1919, the affairs of his Canadian constituency were in disarray. Rejuvenation was virtually impossible. Rebirth was a necessity.

REFERENCES

1. J. Wesley Bready, *England before and after Wesley* (London: Hodder and Stoughton, 1938), p. 441.
2. "New Outlook," Toronto, 23 Sep 1936, pp. 874, 888.
3. S. D. Clark, *Church and Sect in Canada* (Toronto: University of Toronto Press, 1948), pp. 326, 327.
4. Ibid., p. 330.
5. Ibid., p. 201.
6. *Christian Journal*, 6 Aug 1875.
7. *Church and Sect in Canada*, p. 343.
8. Ibid., pp. 341, 342.
9. Ibid., p. 334.
10. R. G. Moyles, *The Blood and Fire in Canada* (Toronto: Peter Martin Associates Ltd., 1977), p. 6.
11. Ibid., pp. 12, 13.
12. Lindsay Reynolds, *Footprints* (Toronto: The Christian and Missionary Alliance in Canada, 1982), pp. 71, 73-82.
13. Ibid., pp. 71-73.
14. Ibid., pp. 106-111.
15. Ibid., p. 112.
16. Ibid., pp. 124-127; 528-531.

17. Ibid., pp. 124-128.
18. Ibid., pp. 128-132.
19. Ibid., pp. 188-204; 518-527.
20. Ibid., pp. 242-263.
21. *Toronto Globe*, 18 Jun 1917, p. 6; *Toronto Telegram*, 18 Jun 1917, p. 15.
22. *Christian and Missionary Alliance*, 11 May 1901, p. 258.
23. *Toronto Globe*, 24 Jun 1907, p. 2; *Christian and Missionary Alliance*, 6 Jul 1907, p. 1.
24. Ibid., p. 518.
25. Board of Managers, April 1910; ibid., 7 May 1910; C&MA Executive Committee, Minutes, 14 May 1910.
26. *Christian Alliance*, 19 Aug 1899, p. 184.
27. Annual Report, May 1900, p. 54.
28. Ibid., May 1909, p. 71.
29. Executive Committee, 23 Sep 1911.
30. C&MA Home Department, Minutes, 17 Jan 1914; 14 Jun 1914.
31. C&MA Report to Council, 13-17 May 1918, p. 62.
32. Board of Managers, 13 Jul 1918.

PART TWO

A New Beginning

CHAPTER 3

The Aura of Uncertainty

When World War I ended at the eleventh hour of the eleventh day of the eleventh month of 1918, it left a world not only shattered physically by fire and steel, but also shattered politically, financially, socially, and spiritually. The unbridled savagery of the conflict, which had killed 8.5 million men in uniform, apart from civilians, exploded the modernist dream of a world fast approaching utopia. It also destroyed man's faith in the institutions of law, government and religion.

As Canadian servicemen returned home from the European fields of blood, they had lost faith in both man and God. As historian Sir Arthur Bryant has said, before the war, men may not always have done right, but at least they thought they knew what was right and what was wrong. After the war, they did not know the difference.[1]

It is not surprising then that the 1920s were characterized by a general drifting away from spiritual values, as evidenced by a declining Bible influence, a falling off in church attendance and the secularization of the Lord's Day. This was the spirit of a society that had become detached from its former Christian moors.[2] These were the "fatuous and irresponsible 1920s."

Canadian churches had their own problems. Modernism, or moral idealism, had been creeping into many of them since before the turn of the century, not only denying evangelical doctrines but viewing traditional denominational differences as unacceptable. This required a surrender of distinctive denominational beliefs and practices and began a movement for cross-confessional church union.[3] However, as Stephen Neill has pointed out, churches cannot unite until and unless they are first willing to die.[4] This was the problem that faced the "unionists." Many conservatives, particularly among the laity, were not willing to die with their denominations. With Anglican H. M. Gwatkin, they believed that "the very divisions of churches are in some sense a sign of life."[5]

The suggestion of cross-confessional union in Canada was introduced in 1902. Controversies and increasing bitterness continued until 1917 when a truce was agreed upon, with the stipulation that no further action would be taken until "the second Assembly (Presbyterian) after the close of the war." The truce ended in June 1920, at which time invective and intrigue broke out within the churches. The issue of church union and its companion issue of modernism, was by far the greatest crisis faced by Canadian churches in the inter-war period. Canada's religious binge of bitterness, which was not finally settled until 1939, consumed an enormous amount of time and effort on the part of thousands of clergy and laity who should have been attending to more personal matters of religion.

Nor was the union/modernism controversy the sole concern of the churches. Cults were pushing their way into Canada, attracting a growing number of unstable denominationalists. What was even more alarming was a rapidly growing separatist movement, which threatened to syphon off the most orthodox Christians from the churches.

In 1919 the World's Christian Fundamental Association was formed out of the ruins of the former Niagara Conference.* Besides taking a strong stand for evangelical doctrines and a pre-millennial view, the "fundamentalists" as they became known, emphasized the "true church" of individual believers. Some of their leaders denounced the organized church as apostate, and sounded a call to believers to "come out from among them, and be ye separate." For this reason, the "fundamentalists" became most unpopular with the denominationalists and were branded as "schismatics" or "separatists."

---

* In 1868 a group of American pre-millennialists commenced holding annual "prophetic" conferences. The non-sectarian spirit of these meetings attracted a cross-section of evangelicals, including the followers of J. N. Darby (Brethren), who introduced dispensational teaching and a strong anti-ecclesiastical bent into the movement. But the conference leadership remained chiefly in Presbyterian hands, who kept separatist tendencies under control. From 1883 to 1897 the conference met at Niagara-on-the-Lake, Ontario. A Niagara Creed, patterned largely after the Keswick statement of faith, effectively maintained Reformist views and suppressed extremist tendencies. The conference disbanded in 1901 when its leadership could no longer agree on the timing of the rapture in relation to the tribulation of the last days.

ALLIANCE EFFORTS TO REBUILD

In this context of upheaval the Alliance made its first faltering post-war moves to become re-established in Canada. It could not identify with the main denominations without being accused of having modernist tendencies, yet the Alliance had always regarded itself as a friendly addition to church programs, an "interdenominational fraternity" in the truths of the "Deeper Spiritual Life." The bulk of money raised at Alliance missionary conventions in Canada had always come from denominationalists, and it was now more vital than ever to maintain a good relationship with them. Simpson himself said just nine years before that "we do long for the sympathy of all good men in this broad evangelical work which takes in all nations. We belong to all worthy evangelical churches."[6] Nor could the Alliance identify with the rising tide of "fundamentalism," without being accused of being extremist and separatist. This was also painful because the Alliance had always felt akin to teachers of premillennialism. The Alliance was caught in the middle, and therefore could not take sides in the national controversy. Yet it could not free itself from the powerful ecclesiastical and theological currents swirling around it, and would be borne along with them to a greater extent than is generally recognized.

The Rev. L. J. Long left the troubled District of Canada in October 1918, leaving the Parkdale Tabernacle Church without a pastor. Arrangements were made for the Rev. William T. (Daddy) MacArthur to fill the pulpit on an interim basis. A long-time friend of Dr. Simpson, he doubtless came to Toronto partly to assist in selecting a new superintendent in conjunction with a committee formed in Toronto for that purpose. His reputed acid frankness would be helpful, even if not always appreciated.[7] The Alliance lamp was barely flickering and might well have gone out during those days had it not been for an old friend, Rev. Dr. W. H. Griffith Thomas, Professor of Systematic Theology at Wycliffe College.* Dr. Thomas had been a "genuine admirer" of Dr. Simpson for many years. Now at this time

---

* Born in Shropshire, England, Dr. Griffith Thomas was for nine years vicar of St. Paul's, Portman Square, London, and later principal of Wycliffe Hall in Oxford. In 1910, he accepted a professorship at Wycliffe College, Toronto. In 1919, he began a continent-wide ministry of Bible lecturing and teaching in Bible schools, seminaries and at Keswick and "victorious life" conferences. In the preface of his book, *Principles of Theology*, he gives credit to Dr. George F. Pardington (late of Nyack College) and his *Outline Studies in Christian Doctrine* for their contribution to his thoughts. He died in Duluth, Minnesota, in June 1924, at the age of 63.

of critical need, he gathered several friends and chaired a sponsoring committee for an "Alliance" convention in Toronto, during January and February of 1919. A choir of 400 was organized and the 3,400-seat Massey Hall was rented for nine days. Paul Rader, pastor of Moody Church, Chicago, was the featured speaker, assisted by Rev. A. E. Thompson, who later became Simpson's biographer. At that time, Paul Rader held no office in the Alliance, but was strongly sympathetic to the Alliance missionary cause.

The convention was an outstanding success. Huge crowds attended the 12 noon, 3 p.m. and 8 p.m. daily services and Toronto newspapers reported the proceedings daily with 20 to 35 column inches of print. Even the conservative Toronto *Globe* reported with such headlines as, "Rader Stirs Vast Audience," "Massey Hall Packed Again" and "Many Hundreds Converted." The *Globe* claimed that Rader had preached to 50,000 persons in nine days, and that the final service was "one of the most memorable religious meetings ever held in the city." On that occasion, not only was Massey Hall filled to capacity, but "many hundreds" were turned away, and an overflow of 600 were seated in the Bond Street Congregational Church. At the close of the convention, the venerable Dr. Griffith Thomas appealed for a missionary offering which was turned over to A. E. Thompson to take back to New York "for support in spreading the Gospel in other lands."[8]

So impressed were the leaders in New York and Rader himself that Home Secretary E. J. Richards immediately planned another missionary convention in Toronto, again featuring Rader, just four months later in June. Having been elected one month previously at the Council of May 1919, Rader was this time presented as the new vice-president and heir apparent to the presidency of the Alliance. At the convention, he was assisted by Rev. Gregory Mantle, a Wesleyan minister living in New York, veteran Canadian missionary Rev. Robert A. Jaffray, and others. This second conference, of six days duration, also concluded in a packed Massey Hall with a strong missionary appeal and an objective to raise $22,000. "How selfish we are that we do not give everything to God," cried Rader, "and how foolish we are if we do not pour out our money and our lives to evangelize the world." Then the missionary collection was taken up, and "when the grand total was announced," wrote a reporter, "Massey Hall shook with glad acclaim." Over $47,000 was received, the highest missionary collection ever taken in Canada! Canadians, despite their religious turmoil, were still able and willing to support

Alliance missions if aroused to do so, and Paul Rader was the man to do just that.[9]

In July, the members of the Toronto committee appointed to locate a new district superintendent agreed that he should be a Canadian, familiar with prevailing national tastes and conditions, and recommended Rev. A. W. Roffe, "provided he can devote his whole time to the work." The proviso was all important. The committee believed that the territory of Canada was far too great for one man to supervise unless he could be completely free of all other business obligations. The board of managers agreed that Roffe should be given "favourable consideration," and instructed the Home Department to "take action after consultation with Mr. Roffe."*[10]

Roffe agreed to give up the administration of his Missionary Rest Home but not his work as publisher and editor of *The Christian Worker*. However, he proposed that Lionel Watson, his general assistant, handle some of the district office work, especially when Roffe was on the road. Apparently, this compromise was acceptable to the Home Department and to the board of managers, which, on September 16, appointed Roffe as superintendent of all Canada. Lionel Watson** became part-time assistant in district affairs, and the district office at 33 Richmond Street West became one and the same as the publishing and editorial office of *The Christian Worker*.[11]

The Death of the Founder

Just when Canadian Alliance spirits were beginning to be encouraged by the appointment of a new national superintendent, they were saddened by the news of the passing of their beloved founder and president, Dr. Albert B. Simpson. The news was not

---

* Born in Mitchell (near Stratford), Ontario, in 1866, A.W. Roffe became an apprentice to his baker father. Converted in his youth, Roffe was one of those Methodists who forsook their denomination at the time of Methodist union in 1884, to find a new church home with the Salvationists. In 1891, together with Brigadier P.W. Philpott and Captain George E. Fisher, Adjutant Roffe was one of the leaders of the Salvation Army "seceders," who broke away and subsequently formed the Christian Workers Churches (later, the Associated Gospel Churches of Canada). That same year, the three leaders also became members of the Christian Alliance and were ordained by John Salmon. Recently, he had resigned his pastorate in the Christian Workers Bathurst Street Tabernacle and was giving his full time to the administration of his Missionary Rest Home in Mimico, and to editing and publishing a bi-monthly periodical, *The Christian Worker*.

** Born in Bradford, England, in 1879, Lionel Watson came to Canada at the age of four. A member of Dovercourt Road Baptist Church, he was secretary-treasurer for an electrical contractor in Toronto, before becoming assistant to Roffe. Throughout his life he had the reputation of being "a walking encyclopedia."

entirely unexpected. For about two years preceding his death, Dr. Simpson's activities had been tapering off. When, in June 1917, he had addressed the Annual Dominion Convention in Toronto for the last time, it had been noted that he was not at his best. In January 1918 he suffered a slight heart attack but made a rapid recovery. At the General Council of May 1918, he called upon Ulysses Lewis, vice-president of the Alliance, to preside, and "committed his business affairs to his brethren for settlement." Although he technically remained president, he effectively ceased to direct the affairs of the Alliance from that time on. Shortly after the conclusion of Council, Dr. Simpson went into a state of deep depression for several weeks, but emerged to spend the remaining year of his life in serenity. Early in May 1919 he suffered "a slight stroke of paralysis," but again made a good recovery. On October 28, at his home in South Nyack, he apparently suffered another stroke and passed peacefully to his reward the following day.[12]

Dr. Simpson's body lay in state in the chapel of the Missionary Training Institute from the following Sunday afternoon until the conclusion of a funeral service on Monday. After the service, some 300 students lined the roadways leading from the chapel to the South Nyack railway station, from where the casket was taken to New York for the final honours in the Gospel Tabernacle. So great was the crowd at this service that admission was restricted to ticket holders. Originally the family had planned for interment in Hamilton, Ontario, but conceded to a request from the board of managers that the founder's body be buried on the Nyack hillside on the institute property.[13]

Following the Gospel Tabernacle service, Dr. Simpson's casket was temporarily placed in a vault in Woodlawn Cemetery to await the selection and preparation of the Nyack hillside grave. Dr. Simpson's body was reinterred "by the loving hands of missionaries" on May 21, 1920, close to what is known as Pardington Hall.[14]

Many were the tributes and messages of sympathy received from all parts of the world. William G. Jaffray, publisher of the *Toronto Globe* and brother of Alliance missionary Robert A. Jaffray wrote, "The Christian and Missionary Alliance stands as a monument of his devotion to God's purpose for him in this life."[15] Recalling the early days of the Alliance movement, Jaffray lauded Simpson as a "benefactor of the poor, . . . a towering figure in the missionary work," concluding that, "Canada has given to the world few more useful or gifted men."[16]

Dr. D. McTavish, long time pastor of Central Presbyterian Church, Toronto, said, "Rev. A. B. Simpson was a man definitely laid

The Aura of Uncertainty / 51

3.1 Courtesy Wycliffe College

3.1 Rev. Dr. W. H. Griffith Thomas, vicar, principal, professor, lecturer, writer and friend of the Alliance. In 1919, he organized, underwrote, and conducted an "Alliance" missionary convention in Toronto.

3.2 Massey Hall, Toronto, erected in 1892, was the site of many important Alliance gatherings during the 1920s.

3.3 A seldom published photograph. The body of Dr. Simpson lies in state, in the chapel of Simpson Hall, at the Missionary Training Institute, Nyack.

3.2 Courtesy Metro Toronto Reference Library

3.3

3.4

3.4 Students line the path of Dr. Simpson's funeral cortege, as it made its way to South Nyack Station, on November 3, 1919.

52 / *The Aura of Uncertainty*

3.5

3.5 Dr. Simpson's gravestone can be seen at the extreme left. Stones of various colours, donated by and bearing the names of foreign fields and home districts were placed in the walls of the burial enclosure. The stone for the District of Canada is just to the right of the tree.

3.6 Rev. Paul Rader, second president of the Alliance, held office from October 1919 until January 1924.

3.7 Rev. A. W. Roffe, as he appeared during his superintendency of the District of Canada, from September 1919 until May 1925.

3.8 The board of managers in 1920. Several of its members played significant roles in the drama of the "reborn" Alliance in Canada. Mentioned in this narrative are, left to right, front row: Peter W. Philpott, H. M. Shuman, Paul Rader, G. Vernor Brown, E. J. Richards, ——, J. D. Williams. Second Row: ——, ——, A. E. Funk. Third Row: A. C. Snead, R. H. Glover, ——, Frederic H. Senft, Walter Turnbull, A. E. Thompson.

3.6

3.7

3.8

hold of by God to do a marvellous work. He was a great Gospel preacher, a great defender of 'the faith once for all delivered unto the saints,' a great missionary advocate, and a great-hearted Christian friend."[17] Dr. Rowland V. Bingham, once an Alliance worker in Toronto, and later the founder of the Sudan Interior Mission, commented, "As a speaker, Dr. Simpson swayed large audiences, not so much by oratory as by the forcefulness of convictions that dominated his own life and simply found expression through his lips. His missionary work will be his most lasting monument. He passes as one of the mightiest men of faith of this generation, and a man whose love embraced the whole church and the whole world."[18]

Much more was said in tribute to the man who was not only the founder but also the chief architect and builder of the Alliance movement during its first 38 years. If a movement is to be understood, it must be through an understanding of the key man who forged it during its formative years. The characteristics and influences that determine the mind of a founder become the essence of the movement he builds. Dr. Simpson combined the qualities of both a dreamer and a pragmatist. With a free mind he formed his thoughts and drew his conclusions. In intellect he was, perhaps, less rational than emotional and intuitive. His remarkable combination of conviction and determination enabled him not only to see visions but have the will to realize them too. However, Dr. Simpson was not a slave to vision for vision's sake. If change appeared desirable, the vision could and would be altered, and herein lies the key to a substantially altered Alliance vision by the time the founder departed. Just what the Alliance was all about in 1919 was not clear to many, both within and without the fellowship.

CANADIAN CHALLENGES

This was the first problem that faced the new national superintendent of Canada when he assumed his responsibilities in September 1919. What, precisely, were the beliefs, the purposes, the guiding principles and the priorities of the Alliance? What were his duties, particularly in the context of a Canadian inter-denominational upheaval? Clearly, the Alliance was no longer an inter-denominational fraternity, having long since abandoned the intimate fellowship of the fraternal branch with its passion for an every member experience in the "fullness of Christ" as its first objective. This was regrettable, as, with few exceptions, the fraternal branch had proven to be the only form of branch that was desirable and successful in over-churched eastern Canada, particularly in Ontario.

During the General Council of 1918, Home Secretary E. J. Richards noted that U.S. evangelicals were revolting against modernist teachings in their denominations and, seeking fellowship in new churches, were affiliating with the Alliance in increasing numbers. These new members were needed, he said, in order for the Alliance to pursue its missionary objectives.[19] Such a policy pressed upon Canada in 1919 would have alienated denominationalist sympathies and deprived the Alliance of its much needed missionary support.

Hampered from planting churches because of Canadian conditions, and discouraged from resuscitating fraternal branches by Alliance policy as determined by American conditions, there was little else that Roffe could do to further Alliance fortunes in Canada than hold missionary conventions in as many centres as possible. In his first report to Annual Council in May 1921, Roffe explained that "for a number of years the Alliance has not been honoured with many promising things as far as Canada is concerned. . . . Our larger communities are strongly held by the various denominations. We do not encourage organizing branches (churches) unless our heavenly Father clearly indicates such a step."[20] To the Council of the following year, he was more explicit about his predicament:

> The conditions and problems of the work in our Canadian District are so fundamentally unlike those met within other Home districts that our plans and methods have to be on a very different basis—so different that it is not possible to compare them with those of other districts. We have few, very few, distinctively Alliance churches. Two years ago the entire work could hardly have been in a more comatose condition, and retain any spark of life. For this reason our policy of necessity is to present the Alliance message by means of conventions, held in various denominational churches, where we can secure an entrance. Our larger communities are strongly held by the various denominations, and in the smaller ones the missionary offerings would look very small beside those resulting from the same time and effort on your side of the line. Our very long and narrow geographical layout causes excessive travelling expenses, and the temperament and enthusiasm of our people is different to yours.

Because we are not well known in Canada, we find it necessary to devote time and pains explaining what the Alliance is, what are its purposes and message, and answering what might appear to you to be odd and foolish questions. Is it a new denomination? Is it part of the Tongues movement? Has it anything to do with Christian Science? Is it an American organization? Having no local funds to fall back upon, it often means a venture in faith to undertake the conventions, even after the openings have been secured. These factors make Alliance work on our side of the line so different to that to which you are accustomed, that I fear few of you really understand it.[21]

Little wonder then that Roffe's first full year showed little progress, except in missionary collections. Thirteen conventions were held in the cities only. The smaller centres, where most of the fraternal branches had been located, and where there still must have existed sympathy for the Alliance, were entirely neglected because of a preoccupation with large collections for foreign missions. A three-day convention in Toronto's Massey Hall, featuring President Paul Rader, netted $51,000 for missions.

Describing the pulpit charisma of the new Alliance president/ evangelist, the *Toronto Globe* stated:

> Preaching not only with his voice, but with all the physical energy of his well-developed frame, using head and hands and body to point his moral, with the spiritual power of a Knox and the winsome pleading that only springs from the deepest spiritual conviction, Paul Rader of Chicago, ex prize fighter, cow puncher and world-famed evangelist opened his campaign.[22]

Reporting on one sermon, the *Globe* stated, "To make the Gospel plain, the evangelist said, was his aim, and plainer it could not have been made."[23]

An Uncertain Focus

During this campaign the new president made a startling statement about Alliance objectives: "God raised up The Christian and Missionary Alliance for one purpose," he said, "and that is to get the gospel to the ends of the earth."[24] There must have been many present who could remember Simpson's words of 21 years earlier:

> Let us never forget the special calling of our Alliance work. It is first to hold up Jesus in His fullness. Next, to lead God's hungry children to know their full inheritance of privilege and blessing for spirit, soul and body. Next, to witness to the imminent coming of the Lord Jesus Christ as our millennial king. And finally, to encourage and incite the people of God to do the neglected work of our age and time among the unchurched classes at home and the perishing heathen abroad.

A confused understanding or at least an inconsistent expression of the priorities for Alliance objectives was a feature of the early interwar period. This is not to say that the second generation of Alliance leaders, including Rader, were not aware of the seriousness of a religious movement failing to be clear on matters of its faith. Indeed, in his first report to the Council of May 1920, Rader warned that for the Alliance "neglected truths must be seen or we move without a message." He lamented the closing of Alliance homes for healing "which were so blessed in former years among us," and noted the demise of rescue and other home missions, reminding his audience that these ministries formed part of the founding Alliance vision. He also noted that in the early days of the movement hearts that hungered for holiness found Christ as their Sanctifier through the Alliance message of a personal crisis experience. The need of the hour, said Rader, was for a movement of "clear doctrine and clear method."[25]

Never were truer words spoken. The second generation leadership was paying lip service to the capsule of the Fourfold Gospel, but by its hesitancy to define the movement's distinctives or to present them publicly, it was exposing its own uncertainties.*

The following year, P. W. Philpott of Hamilton, serving on the board of managers, enquired regarding the "attitude of the Alliance

---

*The problem of variant views stemmed from the early days of the movement. Although Simpson's views were regarded as official, he was remarkably tolerant of other views, requiring only a declaration of belief in "Christ as Saviour, Sanctifier and Healer" for membership. Such an imprecise code of faith permitted a variation in views. Adding to the uncertainty was the fact that the founder was not primarily a theologian but rather a preacher. Many of his theological explanations were delivered orally to a variety of audiences, and he sometimes sacrificed consistency and precision, more concerned with presenting truth to be spiritually experienced than intellectually defended.

toward Divine Healing." There followed some discussion by the board, but no consensus was determined.[26]

Yet another year later, a report was directed to the board of managers concerning "Our Distinctive Testimony." It was a reiteration of early Simpsonian positions. Noteworthy were statements regarding Christ as Sanctifier and Healer, which in part read:

> *Christ our Sanctifier*: Assuming the following essential points: a definite second work of grace, distinct in nature from the experience of conversion, for personal holiness and victory over the world and sin.
>
> *Divine Healing*: It is understood that the Alliance holds and teaches provision for the body in the redemption of Christ; the will of God to heal the bodies of those who trust and obey Him, by His own direct power and without means.

The report was filed, but no action taken to clarify official, current positions.[27] Nor did the Official Manual of those years help to answer questions about Alliance belief. According to the manual, in order to become a member of the Alliance, in addition to acceptance of the usual evangelical doctrines and a "satisfactory evidence of regeneration," one needed only to affirm acceptances of "the doctrines of the Lord Jesus Christ as Saviour, Sanctifier, Healer and Coming King."[28] Apparently the Alliance of the 1920s was not prepared to risk internal controversy in order to define its distinctive faith and priorities.

In 1920, President Paul Rader was featured at a five-day convention in Ottawa held in the Westminster Presbyterian Church. So great was the attendance that meetings had to be moved to the larger Chalmers and then Knox Presbyterian Churches.[29] Among other noteworthy conventions that year were four days in Kingston, at the Bethel Congregational Church, a friend of the Alliance since Salmon's earliest days of independent ministry in 1887.[30]

In this initial spree of conventions, the maritime provinces were not overlooked. At Moncton, New Brunswick, in Central Methodist Church, Superintendent Roffe, "an evangelist of marked ability," kept the church well-attended for eight days. The Moncton *Daily Times* commented, "There is nothing sensational in Mr. Roffe's manner or method, but his preaching is a sane, spiritual and scriptural presentation of truth. He held the rapt attention of a large audience as he discoursed on Spiritual Vision. First, A vision of need, then A vision of self, and finally, A vision of God."[31] This presentation became a classic of Roffe's preaching. It would have particular significance in the reopening of an Alliance witness in western Canada.

In St. John, New Brunswick, a seven-day conference was held in Brussels Street Church (independent). The team made a tremendous impact on the city and particularly on the church. Indeed, the foundations were laid for the church coming under the Alliance banner seven years later.[32] The team also spent three days in Halifax, where a convention was held in St. Matthias' Anglican Church, "the rector (Rev. Craig Nicholls) manifesting a great interest, and asking for another convention next year."[33]

Although the district superintendent could not report the addition of any new branches that year, much had been done in the cause of Alliance missions. Headquarters was apparently satisfied with the more than $50,000 received from these conventions, as the *Alliance Weekly* reported, "Brother Roffe, Canadian Superintendent of The Christian and Missionary Alliance, is making strenuous efforts to open up that country to a vital missionary effort."[34]

THE MOVEMENT GAINS MOMENTUM

Two other events of great significance took place in 1920 in the District of Canada. On October 1, eight men met with Home Secretary Rev. E. J. Richards in the Old Colony Club of the King Edward Hotel in Toronto to form a district committee. The function of the committee would be solely "to consult with and advise the Superintendent in the work." However, as events would turn out, the committee would exert an influence much greater than the Home Secretary envisioned. Richards stated that the committee would be elected each year at an "annual conference of Alliance supporters." The founding district committee, appointed by the Home Secretary, consisted of:

> Rev. A. W. Roffe, Toronto, district superintendent
> W. H. Adamson, Toronto, insurance adjuster executive
> George R. Gregg, Toronto, Japanese goods importer
> Charles H. Grobb, Toronto, draughtsman
> Reuben Harvey, Toronto, biscuit salesman
> William G. Jaffray, Toronto, publisher and editor of the
>   *Toronto Globe*

Augustus G. Malcolm, Toronto, wholesale dry goods executive

John Patton, Ottawa, Dyer, C&MA local branch superintendent

Rev. P. W. Philpott, Hamilton, member of the board of managers, New York, and founder of Philpott Church

John J. Thompson, Toronto, brother of A. E. Thompson, Dr. Simpson's biographer

Dr. George Zimmerman, Toronto, dentist and son of Dr. R. J. Zimmerman, early Canadian Alliance leader [35]

The second important development took place late in December 1920 when Roffe received a telephone call from the Rev. Oswald J. Smith. He had been holding independent meetings close to Parkdale Tabernacle, which had proven to be a financial burden to him, or to use his own words, "a peculiar form of testing."[36] Smith wanted to discuss the possibility of an Alliance ministry for himself. Roffe's assistant, Lionel Watson, arranged to meet Smith on December 21, and at that historic meeting, the affairs of Parkdale Tabernacle Church were aired. The church was passing through perilous times. Without a pastor for seven months, attendance had dropped to about 35. Smith and Watson quickly agreed that Smith would close his work and have his people join with him as pastor of Parkdale Tabernacle Church. The following day, the tabernacle committee summarily agreed to the proposition, and without recourse to the tabernacle's constitutional requirement of a congregational call, Smith was appointed pastor.[37]

Some years later, Smith wrote that up to the time of his appointment, the Alliance had held little attraction for him. "It was," he said, "the last organization on the face of the earth with which I ever expected to be identified." He had embraced the doctrines of the Niagara Conference, which held closely to the Reformed view of sanctification. He had not yet established his position on divine healing,* nor had he been immersed as generally practised by the Alliance and specifically required by the constitution of Parkdale Tabernacle Church.[38] Moreover, Pastor Smith held strong dispensational and separatist beliefs which were quite foreign to the Alliance image of itself as a cooperative supplement to the denominations.[39]

---

* Three years would pass before Smith would announce his convictions about divine healing and then specifically align himself with those outside the Alliance.

That Smith should have been summarily appointed an Alliance pastor serves to underline the unimportant position assigned to Alliance distinctive doctrines at the time. One month later at a congregational meeting, a vote was taken and a retroactive call extended to Pastor Smith, which he retroactively accepted.[40] For the next six years Smith and the Alliance would do much for each other, but their inevitable separation would cause much hurt to both.

THE BOSWORTH CAMPAIGN

The year 1921 was a year of immense importance to the Alliance. Early in January, the district committee met to consider a request from Parkdale Tabernacle Church to bring to Toronto the Alliance evangelistic team of the Bosworth Brothers.* F. F. Bosworth had the reputation of being a "faith healer," but his chief emphasis was evangelistic. "As is known," commented the *Alliance Weekly*, "Brother Bosworth emphasizes salvation and sanctification in their proper order, and hundreds are saved, in addition to those who are healed as a result of the prayer of faith."[41] However, because of the numerous healings at Bosworth campaigns, the media usually featured this aspect of their ministry.

The district committee was aware of some unfavourable reports about the Bosworth meetings (as there always were when the subjects of sanctification and healing were preached). It was decided to send a team to Detroit where a Bosworth campaign was in progress to obtain "first hand information." In due course the team returned and reported. Two members of the team could not agree with a Bosworth claim that the "Baptism of the Spirit was a second work of Grace." Another noted that there had been definite cases of healing which he had seen, but there had been other cases where no healing occurred and he therefore questioned the Bosworth claim that "the removal of disease is an integral part of redeeming Grace, provided through the Atonement." These views (of the search team members) were in contradiction to those which had been held by the founder (see pages 9-10).

---

* F. F. Bosworth was the preacher and B. B. Bosworth the musician. An interesting minute of the Home Department dated January 24, 1921, reads, "Rev. F. F. Bosworth, convinced that God wants him to conduct revival work, can not continue as assistant to the South West District Superintendent. He is appointed Field Evangelist, thus keeping him in official touch with our society."

Programme of the **Christian *and* Missionary Alliance Convention**

TO BE HELD IN

BRUSSELS STREET CHURCH
81-85 BRUSSELS STREET
ST. JOHN, N. B.

February 27th to March 6th, 1921
(INCLUSIVE)

SPEAKERS:

REV. R. H. GLOVER, M. D., New York.
" OSWALD J. SMITH, Toronto, Can.
" A. W. ROFFE, " "
" FRANK IRWIN, French Indo-China.

3.9
3.9 Evangelist Rev. F. F. Bosworth featured the Fourfold Gospel doctrines.

3.10 Early in 1921, a convention was held in the independent Brussels Street Church in St. John, N.B. Seven years later, this church became the first Alliance church in the Atlantic provinces.

3.11 The Cedarvale Gospel Tabernacle, the first new church of the "reborn" Alliance in Canada and the consequence of the Toronto Bosworth campaign.

3.10

3.11

62 / *The Aura of Uncertainty*

3.12 Bella Tarlton was a founding member of the Onward Mission, Verdun.

3.13 Rev. (later Dr.) Oswald J. Smith. Through his vision of a great evangelistic centre for Toronto, the Alliance Tabernacle was known worldwide.

3.12

3.13

3.14 The Christie Street Tabernacle, originally seating 2,000, was enlarged to seat 2,700. During the ministry of Rev. O. J. Smith, it was filled regularly.

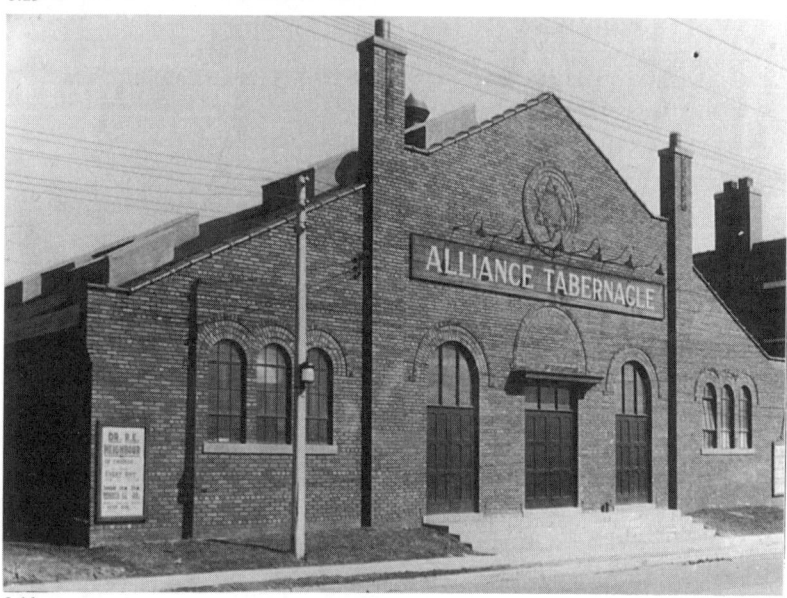

3.14

However, the team was agreed that the most remarkable thing about the meetings in Detroit had been the spontaneous way in which people came forward seeking salvation. All things considered, the district committee recommended that the Bosworths be invited to conduct a campaign in Toronto from mid-April until late May.[42]

The first week's meetings were held in Parkdale Tabernacle, and from the start the sanctuary was filled. By the fifth day, a newspaper reported:

> Last night the central section was filled up shortly after six o'clock and the doors had to be chained by a quarter after seven. This reporter witnessed scores of disappointed applicants at the door, refusing to go away. The hall is designed to accommodate 900 persons, yet there must have been 1,100 there last night.[43]

Commencing with the second week, all services were held in Massey Hall, seating 3,400. On several occasions hundreds had to be turned away. Day after day the newspapers printed long reports of the meetings, listing the names and addresses of those claiming to have been healed at the meetings. The reporters told their own stories:

> Interest in the revival and healing mission that the Bosworth Brothers are conducting in the City continues to grow apace, as was evidenced by the large gatherings that twice yesterday assembled in Massey Hall. Fully 6,000 people must have met there yesterday, while hundreds sought healing from various ailments, and many remarkable cures, besides conversions, were witnessed.[44]

> Evangelist Bosworth places the main emphasis on spiritual blessing, urging men to seek first the Kingdom of God and Christ as their Saviour, and then look to Him as the bearer of their infirmities and healer of their sicknesses.[45]

> In striking contrast with many evangelists who have visited Toronto, the preaching of evangelist Bosworth is characterized by an entire absence of sensationalism or any endeavour to excite emotional outburst on the part of the hearers. He is a plain man and preaches the plain old-fashioned Gospel.[46]

Unless they are consciously deceived, or unconsciously deceiving themselves, scores of people in Toronto, who a few weeks ago were suffering from diverse ills are today rejoicing in healed bodies.[47]

For four weeks the crowds daily poured into Massey Hall, and the newspapers continued printing lengthy reports. Everywhere people were talking about the conversions, sanctification, divine healing, the Bosworths and the Alliance. Not all the talk was favourable. Foremost among the critics was Rev. R. V. Bingham, editor of *The Evangelical Christian* and founder of the Sudan Interior Mission. In a sermon preached in High Park Baptist Church he said, "To teach that healing is a part of the atonement and that all Christians have therefore the right to expect and experience it, is to cause heartbreak and disappointment. Worse than that, it leads in some cases to spiritual darkness."[48] Bingham's remarks were understandably upsetting to former members of Bethany Chapel who remembered him as their former pastoral assistant.

Others, however, within and without the Alliance fellowship, were deeply impressed by what they heard, saw, or experienced at Massey Hall. One of those was District Superintendent Roffe and his family. His 30-year-old daughter, Ethel, had been confined to a sanatorium in Gravenhurst with advanced tuberculosis. Hearing of the Bosworth meetings in Toronto, she insisted on making the 100-mile journey against her doctor's advice. Her faith was rewarded as the Lord touched her in Massey Hall. Back at the sanatorium, the doctors, after several examinations and consultations, pronounced her healed! The incident greatly strengthened her father's preaching and writing on Alliance distinctive teachings. He wrote several books, two of which, *God's Way Up is Down* and *The Divine Touch*, were much used in spreading the teaching of the deeper life. Until Ethel Roffe graduated from Nyack and sailed for French West Africa three years later, she frequently accompanied her father on convention tours, giving "her testimony of miraculous deliverance from tuberculosis."[49]* At least one church would be brought into the Alliance fellowship because of this miracle.

---

* Ethel Roffe married George Bell and together they served as Alliance missionaries. Mrs. Bell served the Lord on the mission field for 34 years, passing on in 1983 at the age of 90. Who can deny the genuineness of her healing in 1921 through the ministry of the Bosworths?

CAMPAIGN AFTERMATH

Among many from without the Alliance who were deeply impressed by the Bosworth meetings was 29-year-old Rev. Oliver Crockford. He had been converted during his youth in the Parry Sound Methodist church, but because of growing convictions against infant baptism, had become a Baptist. By 1921, Crockford was pastor of the Woodbine Heights Baptist Church in the east end of Toronto. Concerned about the resistance in his church to his Methodistic preaching of separation and holiness, he attended the Massey Hall services to hear what would be said about sanctification. He came away captivated by the Bosworth presentation of divine healing. Directed to Dr. Simpson's books for further information,* Crockford became convinced that the Alliance positions on sanctification and divine healing were soundly scriptural, and he began to teach them in his own church. Unfortunately, the congregation became divided, whereupon Crockford resigned and began a new independent work.

On June 11, just two weeks after the conclusion of the Bosworth campaign, 34 charter members of Crockford's new following petitioned District Superintendent Roffe for affiliation with the Alliance.[50] An Alliance branch was organized and the work began immediately in the home of Mrs. W. H. Berry on Cedarvale Avenue. This was the first new branch of the reborn Alliance in Canada. The work developed rapidly and within a few weeks, services were relocated to a hall at Gerrard and Main Streets, then to a tent on Danforth Avenue, at the head of Glenhill Avenue.

With the passing of summer, it became clear that a building would have to be obtained. A lot on Cedarvale Avenue, just north of Danforth, owned by a lumber mill, was offered for sale at $1,700 cash. Crockford explained to the seller that his congregation had no money, but he was confident that God would provide for the need. The mill owner liked Crockford's faith. He agreed to sell the lot to the church for $1,200, with only $1 down payment, the balance to be paid "as God provides." Moreover, the lumber mill would supply all the lumber to build a 500-seat tabernacle, also to be paid for "as God provides."

The people had a mind to build. Working day and night, six days a week, the men and women of the congregation, led by their

---

* The habit of recommending the reading of Simpson's works, covering Fourfold Gospel topics, became popular following the founder's death. However, as most of the original materials of these books dates back to the early days of the movement, they do not reveal the subsequent development of Alliance thought, experience, interest or priority.

indefatigable pastor, erected and completed the tabernacle within a month! It was the cheapest possible frame building, typical of those popular in the United States for "sawdust trail" gospel meetings. The earthen floor was covered with wood chips, and the people sat on backless wooden benches. A single space heater supplied what heat it could. By any standards it must have been a fire trap, yet it served the congregation without mishap for fifteen years.[51]

Opening services of the Cedarvale Gospel Tabernacle were held on Sunday, September 25, "the faithful pastor and his co-workers having been busy up to a late hour the night previous, putting on the finishing touches," according to Roffe.[52] So pleased was President Rader with this "first fruit" of the new Alliance in Canada that he came to Toronto to dedicate the new tabernacle on New Year's Day, 1922.[53]

The effect of the Bosworth campaign on Parkdale Tabernacle in Toronto's west end, under Pastor Smith, was even more spectacular than that in the east under Pastor Crockford. Smith had never been content with being confined by the walls of the 900-seat Parkdale Tabernacle or restrained by its "Alliance" constitution, and now came the opportunity for something more. He had long dreamed of a Toronto work, where he would direct a "great centre of evangelism," a "soul-saving station."[54] Such a centre could not be an Alliance church, committed to a sanctification experience for each member. Now a full Bosworth tide was flowing and something had to be done immediately to maintain interest and attendance after their departure. Accommodation much greater than that of the tabernacle had to be provided in short order. As soon as the Bosworth meetings came to a close, very large newspaper advertisements announced that the Bosworth campaign was continuing with a steady stream of "spiritual men" who would be brought to the city night after night and every weekend.[55] A 90-foot square tent, seating 1,800 persons, was erected on College Street, one block west of Spadina. Tabernacle services were suspended and every effort made to attract a capacity audience for the first tent service. The public was invited to participate in a chair shower. On the day prior to the opening, chairs marked with their owner's name poured in from every part of the city until the tent was filled. This guaranteed a full house for the meetings. The tent was dedicated at the opening service on July 3, 1921, by the president, Rev. Paul Rader.[56]

Throughout the summer and fall, the tent was packed week after week until the late autumn weather necessitated reopening the overflowing Parkdale Tabernacle. Many had made their way up the sawdust covered aisles to make a public confession of their faith in Christ. Among them had been 25-year-old war veteran George Moffat, who would become a great missionary to Ecuador. In August, Smith announced that Parkdale Tabernacle was to be sold and that a much larger building would soon be erected. This announcement precipitated the first signs of fundamental tension between the pastor and his people. The Alliance and Parkdale Tabernacle Church were committed to democratic principles of government. On the other hand, Smith favoured a monocracy, where his views prevailed. He was not in favour of church membership, church constitution or elected representative church government. Rather, he preferred to make his own selection of helpers to assist in carrying out his plans. These views were contrary to the Alliance constitution for local churches, to which, under pressure from the Home Department and District Superintendent Rev. L. J. Long, Parkdale Tabernacle Church had been persuaded to commit itself just five years previously.

Pastor Smith's plans for a changed ministry did not envisage a relocation of the existing church, maintaining its commitment to an Alliance organization and program. Rather, Parkdale Tabernacle would be terminated. The building would be closed and sold. In its place, a new corporation would be formed with Pastor Smith as its president. Serving with the president, a committee of fourteen directors, selected by Smith for their "spirituality and godliness," would direct activities and establish rules. In a new and much larger building there would be a ministry to vast "adherent" crowds.

That the membership of Parkdale Tabernacle Church was persuaded to accept these plans is surprising, especially since the termination of the Parkdale Tabernacle Church would mean that the proceeds of sale of the property would be turned over to the Alliance for foreign missions. Nevertheless, only ineffective resistance was offered. It was hard to view in objective perspective a train of events which, within four months, had increased attendance some thirty times. At the district level, it is even more surprising that such actions were permitted. Yet, there is no evidence that any restraints emerged from the district office.

The search for a new location commenced immediately. Soon a suitable site was located on Christie Street, facing Willowvale Park. On October 12, 1921, Smith purchased property and signed a contract to build a tabernacle for $43,500, with only $3,000 on hand, committing himself to pay the balance with interest in two years' time. This represented a sum of money equal to thirteen years of Pastor Smith's salary! On April 12 of the following year, the promised new corporation came into legal existence as Alliance Tabernacle Willowvale Park Corporation. It immediately assumed all liabilities and assets in connection with the new enterprise. Less than a month later, on May 7, valedictory services were held in Parkdale Tabernacle and the church legally closed. This was probably the only case in Alliance experience where a church literally bursting its doors with regular attendances of 1,100 was corporately dissolved.

A New Work is Born

One week later, the opening and dedication of what would usually be termed "the Christie Street Tabernacle," took place. Rev. Paul Rader preached the dedicatory sermon. From the opening service, capacity audiences of 2,000 were commonplace. Occasionally, as many as 1,000 people were turned away. Early the following year, a sloping "amphitheatre" was built over the entrance end, seating an additional 500. A subsequent extension accommodated yet another 200. From then on, the total capacity of 2,700 was regularly utilized, and on several occasions hundreds were turned away.

The congregation sat on ill-suited pews recovered from the old Parkdale Tabernacle, augmented with plain wooden chairs. The barn-like structure, measuring 80 feet wide by 130 feet long, was constructed of hollow tile, bricked only in the front. Its uninsulated walls, corrugated steel roof, concrete floor, and inadequate heating system made it impossible to attain comfortable temperatures in either winter or summer. The sound of rain on the metal roof would obliterate the voices of the speakers.

But the rudimentary nature of the new facility suited the mission of the new enterprise, as Smith explained. "Our Lord did not tell us to build beautiful churches, but to evangelize the world," he said.[57]

> God is raising up a great nation-wide tabernacle movement. Necessarily, they are outside and apart from the churches. Most of them have no membership, because they are not churches. Their work is that of prolonged evangelistic campaigns. Their one objective is the salvation of souls at home and abroad. As long as a tabernacle

remains true to the original God-given vision, it prospers. As soon, however, as it seeks to become a church it fails.[58]

Smith's zeal made good sense to many but problems began to emerge. The Alliance Tabernacle became the church home of many new converts; it was not sufficient to preach only the gospel and raise support for missions. The believers needed spiritual meat as well as spiritual milk. Outside the tabernacle, Smith's strong dispensational bias alienated his denominational neighbours struggling to salvage the good in their denominations, and who were still the chief supporters of Alliance missions in Canada. "Organized Religion," he declared, "cannot survive. God speed the day! It cannot come too soon. . . . The mask is being torn off. A change is inevitable. The rising generation will probably live to see it judged."[59]

There was much of value in Smith's views on how best to reach the masses with the gospel, but his anti-ecclesiastical opinions could hardly have been more devastating in terms of the support and goodwill of denominationalists. Nor were his views on pastor/lay leader relationships apt to put at ease the members of the tabernacle committee who felt any responsibility to their fellow adherents or to the Alliance."All down through the centuries," wrote Smith, "it has been the same. When God wanted something done, He chose a man, equipped and fitted him for the task, placed him at the head of His people and told them to follow and obey. Never did He select a committee, never did He choose a board." Lay leaders should, according to Pastor Smith, "seek his [the pastor's] vision, get his viewpoint, accept his plans. Instead of dictating, assist, for if he is God's man he will have God's vision. To hold back and question, to oppose and criticize is to invite disaster."[60] It is not surprising that denominational opposition grew against the Alliance, and internal opposition grew against Pastor Smith from the tabernacle committee.

In the meantime, the Alliance in eastern Canada basked in the afterglow of Bosworth sunshine for some time. Many locations asked for Alliance conventions and Torontonians began to talk about another Bosworth campaign. However, enthusiasm for the Bosworths was dampened when in October 1921 President Rader emphasized to the District of Canada committee that the Alliance was a soul-saving organization and not a healing cult. He felt that the Bosworths were making a dangerous mistake in giving healing the prominence they did and that it would be a mistake to have them return to Toronto unless they were willing to radically change their methods of work.[61]

It was evident that the president was not alone in his views; two days later in New York, the board of managers addressed the same subject. Rader advised the board that he had recently investigated the Bosworth meetings and had suggestions for their improvement.[62] Home Secretary E. J. Richards expressed his concern during the following Council. "There are," he said, "possibly a few individuals in our ranks that seek the spectacular and magnify certain phases of truth out of just proportion to the other part of our testimony."[63]

These were strange words to emerge from the Alliance president and Home Secretary regarding the ministry of a credentialed evangelist. This less-than-whole-hearted support of the Bosworth ministry on the part of the top level Alliance leadership contrasted sharply with the position taken by several Toronto denominationalists, among whom was Dr. John Inkster of Knox Presbyterian Church who wrote, "I am thankful to say that I can endorse every word he [Bosworth] says. I know that God can heal all manner of disease. I have seen it and have experienced it.... It rejoices my heart to see men and women here who are interested in this great, vital truth, who want to be saved, their bodies healed and their lives filled with the Holy Spirit. It rejoices my heart to see work like that going on, and I am willing to lend my little influence to that end."[64]

As a comparatively new entrant to Alliance ranks, one can understand President Rader being concerned to avoid excesses and unnecessary adverse public opinion, but one may wonder if he was aware of the strong healing emphasis of Simpson and Salmon in the early days of the movement, or of the willingness of their first generation followers to suffer criticism and unpopularity for the founding faith of the Alliance.

CONVENTION EXCITEMENT

Meanwhile, Roffe pressed ahead with many missionary conventions. During his first year of superintendency he had conducted five. During his second, third, fourth and fifth, he conducted 13, 18, 23, and 28 respectively, and he simply wore himself out travelling and preaching. As the *Alliance Weekly* advised its readers, "District Superintendent Roffe, whose devotion to his work often seems to threaten his very life, is doing magnificent pioneer work in the Dominion, and has already far more open doors than he can enter."[65]

One week after the Christie Street Tabernacle was dedicated, an eight-day Annual Toronto Missionary Convention commenced.

Among the many speakers were Dr. John Inkster of Knox Presbyterian Church, Rev. T. T. Shields of Jarvis Street Baptist Church, Dr. Kenneth MacKenzie, Episcopalian, of Westport, Connecticut, and Rev. E. J. Richards, Alliance Home Secretary from New York. Among the array of missionaries present were veteran Robert A. Jaffray of South China, and Mrs. L. J. Cutler of India. From the first service, the 2,000-seat (later 2,700) tabernacle was filled to overflowing. Many were the pleas for missionary support as excitement rose towards the climax of the missionary offering. The *Alliance Weekly* reported that "faith rose steadily until there was an overflow of the joy of giving, which resulted in a splendid out-pouring for missions of over $38,000" ($600,000 at 1992 equivalent).[66]

Everyone was justly excited with the results. The pattern of conventions was yielding rich harvests for foreign missions. However, a subtle change had taken place in Alliance principles of missionary support. Formerly, the call to salvation had been directed to the masses, the call to sanctification had been directed to believers and the call to missionary support had been directed to the sanctified. Now, the call to missionary support was going directly to the conglomerate masses at large missionary conventions. Few seemed to remember the words of the founder in former days:

> The secret of liberality for missions is a deep spiritual life at home. Instead of missionary appeals, the best way to increase the missionary gifts of our churches would be to hold conventions throughout the country for the baptism of the Holy Ghost, and the consecration of selfish lives. When hearts are broken and filled with the Spirit of Jesus, there is no lack of money and sacrifice for the spread of the Gospel, and the evangelization of the world.[67]

Immediately following the dedication of the Cedarvale Tabernacle on New Year's Day, 1922, Rader, Roffe and Smith embarked on a ten-day convention tour of Kingston, Ottawa and Montreal. The Kingston meetings were held in the Old City Hall and the Ottawa services in Erskine Presbyterian Church. They attracted large crowds and $4,000 ($60,000 at 1992 equivalent) for Alliance missions. However, the three days in Montreal were of particular importance to the future of the Alliance in what was at that time Canada's metropolis. This was the first time that the city had been visited by Alliance leaders for twelve years, and by an Alliance president since 1895.

72 / *The Aura of Uncertainty*

Many former members of the disbanded fraternal branch came out to welcome the Alliance back. Among them was John Fraser, superintendent of Welcome Hall Mission,* a former friend of John Salmon. Others were Hannah Smith, matron of the Friendly Home, and Bella Tarlton, of the "little group of true hearts" that regularly attended the Old Orchard conventions. A founding member of Onward Mission, Verdun, she was destined to play a quiet but vital part over the years in the development of Alliance fortunes in Montreal.**

At the invitation of Rev. John Linton, the convention meetings were held in his Pointe St. Charles Baptist Church. So great were the crowds that it was found necessary to move to the large neighbouring Centenary Methodist Church. The missionary topics made a great impression on the capacity audiences. Seventeen people volunteered for missionary service and a large missionary offering was taken up. Roffe described the convention as "the greatest Protestant effort in a generation to stir Montreal."[68]

One of those who attended was Anglican Rev. Edgar T. Capel, superintendent of the Knowlton Conference Grounds, Quebec. He retired from church ministry that year, but served on the Alliance district committee for several years. Moreover, he offered his conference grounds for an annual Alliance conference.***

---

* Welcome Hall Mission and Onward Gospel Church still exist.

** Mary Isabella Tarlton was born in Ireland in 1867 and emigrated to Montreal as a child. Of Methodist persuasion, she was a member of the Montreal Alliance branch organized in 1891. Commencing studies at the Missionary Training Institute in New York, with the intention of becoming an Alliance missionary, her father's death and the subsequent physical degeneration of her mother led her to conclude that it was her first duty to provide a home for her younger brothers and invalid mother. As a result she never became a missionary. However, she did become a great prayer warrior for Alliance missionaries, a valued friend of local Alliance pastors, a loving worker among the Chinese, and a faithful member of the Alliance Community Church in the north end of Montreal. In later years, Miss Tarlton became very deaf, but she never doubted that the Lord would yet heal her. She passed away on August 12, 1959, at the age of 92, and was laid to rest in Mount Royal Cemetery.

*** Edgar Tracy Capel was born in Montreal in 1865. Graduating from the Diocesan Theological College with a Licentiate in Theology (L.Th.), he was ordained deacon in 1889 and priest in 1891. He became known as a great Sunday school worker and was unanimously chosen as general secretary of the Sunday School Union of Quebec. After serving for 33 years in various Quebec churches, including Christ Church Cathedral, Montreal, he retired from church ministry in 1922 to pursue a vision to establish a Christian family camp ground "where the children of God can meet for spiritual, mental and physical refreshing." He became chief founder and superintendent of the Knowlton Conference Association at Brome Lake. Capel fully retired ten years later and took up residence in Brantford, Ontario, where he died in 1946. The Knowlton Conference Ground is no more, but its site can still be traced by the street names of the area, such as Capel Avenue.

Situated on the shores of beautiful Brome Lake among the Eastern Township hills, some 60 miles southeast of Montreal, the accommodations were "second to none." For about ten years, the old institution of the Dominion Convention, originally held at Grimsby Park, Ontario, was revived as the Annual Knowlton Convention at Brome Lake, Quebec. Of the first Knowlton Convention held that summer of 1922, Roffe wrote, "One sensed the spiritual atmosphere of an old-fashioned Alliance convention."[69]

OPPORTUNITIES SEIZED AND MISSED

In July 1922, just two months after the opening of the Christie Street Tabernacle in Toronto, Dr. Charles S. Morris, a black evangelist and principal of the Boydton Institute (Virginia), an Alliance Bible School for blacks, held a four-week campaign in the tabernacle. He brought with him the Cleveland Coloured Quintette. This was their first appearance in Canada and they immediately became famous. During the engagement, the quintette sensed a divine call to leave their secular employment and give their time fully to a Christian ministry of song. For the first eighteen months they ministered in Canada, accompanying Roffe and Smith on their many convention tours across the country, and were frequently featured at the Christie Street Tabernacle between tours.[70] Their rich vociferous harmony was not only entertaining, it brought great blessing to hundreds of audiences. Their presence in any gathering guaranteed a large attendance. On August 31 of that year, the quintette was featured at the Canadian National Exhibition where they "delighted the great crowds who thronged about them."[71]

At the conclusion of an evangelistic campaign by Rev. C. B. Wallace of Detroit, Lionel Watson met with a group in Chatham, Ontario, on December 18, 1922, and organized a church of 50 charter members. Among the seven members of the original executive committee were Godfrey Rutledge, secretary-treasurer, and H. H. Dowling, superintendent of the Sunday school. Rev. William Browning was the first pastor. Although services were suspended for about one year in 1938, this church, in the town where Simpson grew up, has continued and today is known as Gregory Drive Alliance Church.[72]

During an eight-point convention tour in January and February 1923, Montreal was again visited by a large entourage which included Roffe, Rev. Gregory Mantle, an English Wesleyan, Mrs. L. J. Cutler of India, Miss Mary Butterfield of Palestine and Capel of the Knowlton

Conference Grounds. This time, meetings were held in the newly-dedicated Onward Mission, Verdun.[73]

The party then held important conventions in Truro, Halifax and Dartmouth. Capel was well-known in Quebec and the maritimes and was aptly described as "an Anglican clergyman who preaches and practices the victorious life in Christ Jesus, a man of beautiful spirit, who will prove a great accession to our ranks."[74] Public acceptance of the Alliance in the maritimes was unusually high that year. Particularly among the Methodists, a longing for fellowship in the deeper spiritual life was much in evidence. A Methodist minister wrote Roffe as follows:

> I have only known the Alliance through its literature, but the blessing both physical and spiritual that come to my life through this medium is beyond the power of words to express. I have never lost one iota of faith in the fourfold gospel that I embraced more than twenty years ago.... I sometimes have grown hungry for a bit of your fellowship.[75]

Another wrote, "I have followed the Alliance teaching for over twenty-five years, but have never had an opportunity of attending your meetings. I hope this will be the opening up of a mission in this place."[76]

If ever there was an opportunity for the Alliance to plant churches in eastern Canada, it was then, but a dearth of district funds and suitable pastors precluded many of these opportunities, unless a sizeable group or existing church requested the Alliance to make them an official branch. Roffe warned that:

> The Christian and Missionary Alliance in Canada is facing a crisis hour. Throughout our land, many individuals and groups are finding the subtle trend towards modernism a burden too heavy to bear.... God has raised up the Alliance to meet this need.... One reason why we have not been able to occupy new centres is a lack of men... who are seized with the Alliance message. It would appear that our task must be to develop our own leaders into a real understanding of Alliance fellowship and vision. Another problem is the question of finance. We have no district fund, and many times we are faced with open doors that we cannot enter because of a lack of money.

While we do not look to the opening of Alliance branches, we must answer the calls that are coming to us. To them we would gladly minister by means of an Alliance convention.[77]

And so, the work of many conventions and collections for Alliance missions continued to be the chief feature of the Alliance thrust, and Roffe continued to work himself into ill health.

New Recruits

Despite the lack of personnel and money, there were many developments to encourage the district superintendent. Several great churches and influential workers came into the Alliance fellowship during those difficult days. Edgar Lorimer, born in 1894 of Methodist stock, grew up in Haldimand–Norfolk County, Ontario. After serving in the army during the war, he became a Methodist lay preacher, his first charge being in Fisherville, near Toronto.* In May 1921, he attended some of the Toronto Bosworth meetings, becoming devoted to Fourfold Gospel teaching. Some eighteen months later, he concluded that his work was unchallenging, and he asked God to give him a "harder job." He also advised District Superintendent Roffe that he would like to become an Alliance pastor, provided he were offered a "hard job."

At that very time, Juanita Williams, a graduate of the Missionary Training Institute in Nyack, was working with a small independent church in Belleville, Ontario. She had explained the Alliance message and missionary program to both pastor and congregation. During the spring of 1923, Roffe's assistant, Lionel Watson, accompanied by Mrs. L. J. Cutler of India, visited the Belleville church and aroused further interest in the Alliance. During the summer, the church passed through a crisis during which its congregation became divided and decimated. As a result, the church leaders enquired if the Alliance could send them a pastor suited to heal the wounds.[78]

Thus it was that Watson summoned Lorimer with the words, "You wanted a hard job. Here it is. Report to Belleville immediately." He resigned his Methodist ministry and preached his first sermon in Belleville on September 16, 1923, to 30 people, reporting to Watson,

---

* The old church building where Edgar Lorimer first preached is now displayed in Black Creek Pioneer Village, North York.

"I don't know whether they think I am the man they want or need, but I do know that this is the hard job I have been praying for (harder than I thought it would be). . . ."[79] By the following spring, many of the problems had been sorted out, and the congregation had doubled. Under the impact of a convention featuring the Cleveland Coloured Quintette, Roffe organized the Belleville church into an official Alliance branch on March 23, 1924. The founding officers were: H. W. Baragar, E. G. Brown, Charles Elvins (treasurer), O. Latchford (secretary), B. A. Sandford and Seth Wheeler. Today, the church is known as Quinte Alliance Church.

Another recruit to the Alliance ministry was Frederick William Hollinrake, born of Methodist parents in Milton, Ontario, in 1866. Converted in Sunday school, at 22 he left his job as clerk in his father's store and, believing he was called to the ministry, he attended Albert College in Belleville (Methodist) and later Victoria College in Cobourg and Toronto. After 29 years of ministry in six locations, he resigned in 1920 from Barton Street Methodist Church, Hamilton (now Livingston United Church), "because I find myself out of harmony with the policy and teachings." He cited his convictions regarding the pre-millennial return of Christ and the divine inspiration and authority of Scripture. "For the truth I hold dear," he said, "I step out of the Methodist Church. God is leading me apart from all denominations . . . in the formation of an independent church in Hamilton."[80] Accordingly, in July of that year he founded Ebenezer Tabernacle, on Gage Avenue.

The 1921 Bosworth campaign brought to Hollinrake's attention the official message of the Alliance, which he embraced. Soon he became a friend of Roffe and Smith. As a result, Alliance missionary conventions became a regular feature of Ebenezer Tabernacle and Hollinrake was frequently invited to attend district committee meetings as an observer. However, Hollinrake's preference for denominational independence kept his church and the Alliance at arm's length in official matters as long as he remained its pastor.

In July 1924, the Ebenezer congregation undertook the construction of a larger building at the corner of King Street and Rosslyn Avenue, to be named Delta Tabernacle. Four cornerstones, each proclaiming a facet of the Fourfold Gospel, were laid during a ceremony conducted by Pastor Smith of Christie Street Tabernacle. Charles Duff laid the stone inscribed "Christ our Saviour"; John Lindsay, "Christ our Sanctifier"; Charles Grobb of Christie Street, "Christ our Healer"; and A. M. Shaver, "Christ our Coming King."

The Aura of Uncertainty | 77

3.15
3.15 The Cleveland Coloured Quintette was a great attraction at the Christie Tabernacle.

3.16 Rev. Edgar Lorimer was one of several long-service pastors to join the Alliance during the early 1920s. He was largely responsible for bringing the Belleville work into the Alliance fold.

3.17 Rev. Elmer B. Fitch was the first pastor of the Ottawa Gospel Tabernacle from 1924 to 1927. He then served the Winnipeg Gospel Tabernacle until 1930.

3.16

3.17

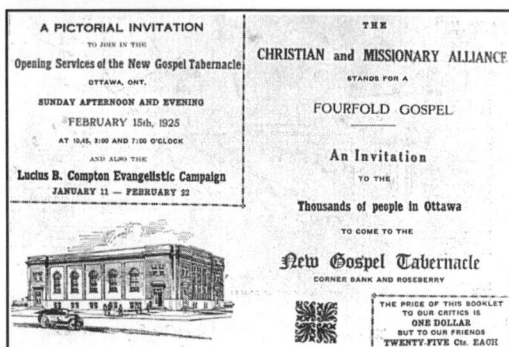

3.18

3.18 A pictorial invitation to the opening of the Ottawa Gospel Tabernacle.

3.19
3.19 For many years John Patton was an outstanding lay leader in the Ottawa Gospel Tabernacle and in the affairs of the Eastern and Central Canadian District

78 / *The Aura of Uncertainty*

3.20 The first General Council of the Alliance ever to meet in Canada, convened in the Christie Street Tabernacle in 1924. Here, the delegates pose in Willowvale Park. In the front row, centre, are A. C. Snead, O. J. Smith, A. W. Roffe, F. H. Senft and J. D. Williams.

3.21 Huge crowds attended the Ottawa Bosworth campaign in April and May 1924. As a result, the Gospel Tabernacle was erected immediately.

The Aura of Uncertainty / 79

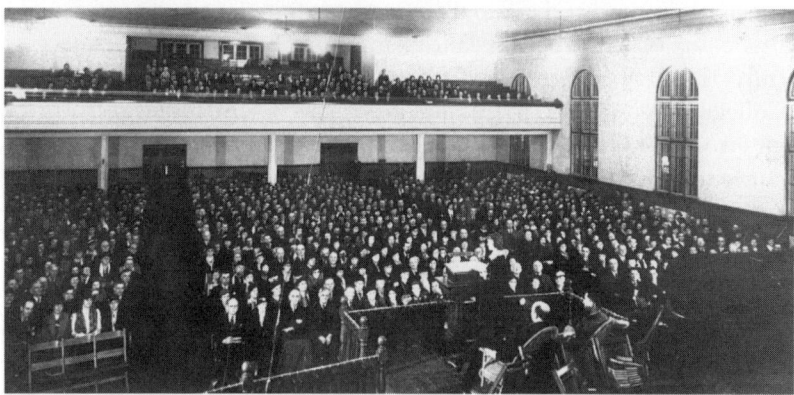

3.22

3.23

3.22 The Ottawa Gospel Tabernacle, as it appeared in 1925.

3.23 Large crowds in the Ottawa Gospel Tabernacle, under the ministry of Rev. Elmer Fitch.

3.24 Delta Tabernacle, located at the junction of King Street and Rosslyn Avenue in Hamilton, was dedicated on February 8, 1925.

3.25 In 1921, Rev. F. W. Hollinrake brought independent Ebenezer (later Delta) Tabernacle, Hamilton, into close cooperation with the Alliance. The congregation became an official affiliate in 1939.

3.25

3.24

The new tabernacle was dedicated on February 8, 1925.[81] In 1937 Hollinrake retired from the pastorate of Delta Tabernacle, becoming an official worker of the district and assistant pastor of Christie Street Tabernacle in Toronto.[82] In March 1939, Delta Tabernacle cautiously entered the Alliance fellowship as an affiliated church, the district entry reading, "After fourteen years of lonely life, they are now part of the Alliance family."[83]* Over the years, Delta Tabernacle produced many outstanding missionaries and pastors. In 1987 the church relocated and is now known as Paramount Drive Alliance Church.

A third recruit was George Milton Blackett, born into a Congregational home in London, England, in 1891. Converted at thirteen, he sensed a pronounced call to the ministry at nineteen and commenced preaching on street corners and in mission halls. He tried unsuccessfully to enter Spurgeon's College but, hearing of Toronto Bible College, he emigrated to Canada in 1912 with the express purpose of entering that institution. While there, he became a friend of another student, Ivory Jeffrey (a member of Parkdale Tabernacle and future Alliance missionary statesman), who offered to board Blackett at his parental home in Parkdale. There he was introduced to Alliance doctrines and Alliance missions—and to Jeffrey's cousin, Lucy Jeffrey.

As a freshman at Toronto Bible College, George Blackett came to know a senior student by the name of Oswald J. Smith, then an ardent Presbyterian. Together they edited a college paper.

Upon graduation in 1915, Blackett joined the Congregational Union of Canada and accepted a call to the pastorate of Pine Grove and Humber Summit churches, near Woodbridge, Ontario, which he served for eight years. It was in Pine Grove Congregational Church in 1917 that Blackett married Lucy Jeffrey, the Rev. Oswald J. Smith officiating.

Branch Expansion

From 1920 onwards, the acrimony associated with the issue of church union mounted steadily, often dividing congregations and separating clergy from the laity and from fellow clergy. Coupled with these conditions, Blackett felt keenly the inroads of modernism within the Congregational ministry. He found encouragement in his stand for evangelical truth by getting into Toronto as often as possible to

---

* In May 1983, the church finally adopted the Alliance constitution.

hear some of the great visiting speakers at the Christie Street Tabernacle. Coincident with these developments, a group of Owen Sound laymen met in January 1924 to pray for revival in their city. Someone mentioned the Alliance and the meeting concluded with a request being sent to District Superintendent Roffe to hold an Alliance convention in Owen Sound. The convention, April 4-18, featured the Cleveland Coloured Quintette, Nellie Jones of China, Rev. O. J. Smith and Rev. A. W. Roffe. The 800-seat city hall was packed to capacity each night, and large numbers professed salvation, many Christians sought the fullness of Christ in their lives and a missionary offering of $4,500 was received. A steering group was formed on April 26 which immediately requested Roffe to "send us a man" to organize and lead an Alliance branch in Owen Sound.[84]

Roffe had to reply, "We have no man to send," and he reported the sad situation publicly at the Annual Council meeting in Toronto in May. In the audience were George and Lucy Blackett. They felt that God was leading him into an Alliance ministry. After the service, Blackett searched out Roffe to volunteer, and Roffe accepted him on the spot with the words, "I have been praying for four years that you would come into the Alliance."[85] Blackett was appointed to the Owen Sound project on June 16 but by the time he had settled his affairs in Pinegrove he had no money and the move was to cost $40. Just before they were due to leave with their furniture, someone gave them $41.50. The extra $1.50 provided them with something to eat on the way, and they arrived in Owen Sound with ten cents to spare! There he preached his first sermon on July 6.[86]

An official branch in Owen Sound was organized on October 13. Among the elected officials were H. W. Howell, treasurer; J. Williams, assistant treasurer; William Leavens, secretary; and A. Nelson, assistant secretary.

As for George Blackett, after serving in Owen Sound and at the Christie Street Tabernacle for ten years, he became a most influential Alliance leader in western Canada, where he served for an additional 25 years.

Perhaps the most interesting church birth during 1923 and 1924 was that of Ottawa. Although that city had been named among the four founding fraternal branches of the Dominion Auxiliary in February 1889, its leader, Mr. Hobbs, had been unable to organize a branch at that time. In June 1891 the Dominion Auxiliary, under John Salmon, held its first convention in the capital, featuring A. B.

Simpson and other speakers. In September of that same year, a branch was organized, under the presidency of John Lucy. Inspired by conventions in 1909 and 1910, attempts were made to organize a church, but proved unsuccessful.[87]

In September 1911, Rev. Louis J. Long was appointed superintendent of the Canadian District. At the same time he accepted a call from the Ottawa branch to form and to pastor a church, with the intent of moving district headquarters to the capital. However, before he moved, Pastor Salmon retired from Bethany Church, Toronto, and Long was persuaded to accept the vacated pastorate. The Ottawa branch would have to wait another twelve years for a church.

As part of a convention tour in November 1923, Roffe, accompanied by Smith and the Cleveland Coloured Quintette, held a convention in Ottawa at St. George's Hall and the Imperial Theatre, which, on occasions, was attended by more than 1,000 persons. "Scores" professed conversion, and "hundreds were deeply stirred."[88] It appeared that perhaps the time had come to start a church. Roffe appointed an interim local committee, consisting of John Patton, Dr. L. L. Darby, William Lamb, J. S. Milne and R. S. Reid. As a result of the committee's recommendation, Rev. Elmer B. Fitch, pastor of the Gospel Tabernacle in New York, was asked to visit Ottawa and subsequently accepted their call, preaching his first sermon there on January 6, 1924. Seventy attended that first service, 75 attended afternoon Sunday school and 200 attended the evening service.[89]

Four weeks later, Roffe returned with Smith, Nellie Jones, the Quintette, and Roffe's daughter, Ethel, for another missionary convention. This time, Loew's Theatre was packed with 2,800 people, while others were turned away. Six thousand dollars in cash and pledges were received, by far the largest missionary offering yet received from the capital.[90]

The Bosworths Return

Meanwhile, the year 1924 brought a major change to the direction of the Alliance. In January, President Paul Rader resigned. Roffe now felt free to arrange a full-scale Bosworth campaign in Ottawa for seven weeks commencing on April 6, hoping that this occasion would rival the first Bosworth visit to Toronto three years previously.* It

---

* The Bosworths had appeared for the second time in Toronto for ten days during the spring of 1923. However, they were confined to the tabernacle with a low key campaign which received relatively little publicity.

proved to be even greater. By the end of three weeks, the 3,000-seat Horticultural Building in Lansdown Park was filled every night. Although the services frequently lasted until midnight, many seemed reluctant to go home. A week later, the meetings were moved to the newly built Auditorium, on O'Connor Street at Argyle, seating 8,500. Within two weeks, hundreds were being turned away from the services. According to one reporter, "men and women are being saved by hundreds at each service, and scores are being healed."[91]

By the end of the campaign, it was reported that 12,000 had made professions of salvation. In three services a total of 925 were baptized. Nearly 6,000 had been anointed for healing and some 1,500 testimonials of healing had been received in writing alone.[92]

Evangelist Bosworth had once again preached the Simpsonian doctrines of the Fourfold Gospel. He had placed the primary emphasis on salvation for all, by faith, without works and on sanctification as the will of God for all who are saved. "It is the Christian's privilege," he emphasized, "to receive the baptism of the Holy Spirit." The absence of clear teaching on the divine command to "be ye filled with the Spirit" has robbed millions of Christians of a happy Christian life, said Bosworth.[93] As for divine healing, Bosworth continued, "Christ has provided this blessing for all Christians, by faith." Paraphrasing one of Dr. Simpson's early writings he said, "Jesus nailed to the cross our sicknesses as well as our sins."[94]

With such a strong emphasis on free grace and sanctification, it was not surprising that Bishop Warren of the Holiness Movement Church, Rev. Peter Wiseman of the Fifth Avenue Holiness Church and Rev. A. J. Shea (father of gospel singer Bev Shea) of the Methodist Church in Ottawa South, openly identified with the campaign, assisting on the platform. It was also not surprising that the Bosworths were denounced by some leaders of the Roman and Reformed traditions.[95]

Nevertheless, many thousands of Ottawanians believed that God had met their needs, both spiritual and physical, as never before. One newspaper reporter saw the campaign as "one of the most stirring religious movements ever seen here. Beginning in a small way in a hall seating only a few hundred," he continued, "it grew to a huge campaign in seven short weeks, eclipsing everything of its kind held here, and shaking the City to its foundations."[98]

Among those who responded were two youths. Edwin T. Holt was a frail nineteen-year-old who was born in England of Congregational parents and came to Ottawa when two years of age. Rheumatic fever damaged his heart and left him severely handicapped. At one of the Bosworth meetings he was saved and instantly healed. After graduating from Bible college he began a 53-year career as an Alliance pastor in eastern Canada. The second youth was eighteen-year-old Richard G. Simpson. Born into a Presbyterian home in nearby Bell's Corners and orphaned at twelve, he attended one of the Bosworth meetings and came under conviction. After experiencing conversion and sanctification, he graduated from the Missionary Training Institute and was ordained in 1933. His 41-year career as pastor and evangelist was served in eastern Canada, New England and Saskatchewan.

At the conclusion of the final service, 6,000 people packed Union Station "in one solid mass of humanity, with hats, handkerchiefs and small flags, waving frantically their good wishes."[97] The evangelists were carried shoulder high through the crowd in the station concourse to the platform gates, as "God Be with You 'till We Meet Again" and other hymns were sung. Early in the Bosworth campaign, as the rising response was observed, the interim committee decided to proceed immediately with the establishment of a gospel centre along the lines of Smith's work in Toronto. A similar corporation was formed, with the interim committee members, augmented by J. T. Beattie, A. W. Clark, William Frazier and W. J. Hill becoming the board of directors. There was no church membership, the directors being the government of all affairs, both temporal and spiritual. Half way through the Bosworth campaign it was announced that a tabernacle would be erected as quickly as possible on the corner of Bank Street and Roseberry.[98]

As soon as the campaign ended, a large tent at Bourke and Carling Avenue served as a temporary home for the congregation. Ground was broken on August 31, and the cornerstones laid on October 11 in a ceremony conducted by Roffe and attended by a crowd in excess of 1,500. The building was dedicated on February 15, 1925, the dedicatory sermon being preached by Rev. F. H. Senft, president of the Alliance.[99]

The new Gospel Tabernacle seated 2,200 on theatre seats. It was a comfortable, well-designed and well-constructed building. Like its Toronto counterpart, the Ottawa tabernacle was for many years a key factor in the supply of both personnel and money for the Alliance missionary enterprise.*

---

* The famous Gospel Tabernacle building still stands, but is no longer connected with the Alliance.

A Pastor is Lost

Not all developments during 1924 were happy ones. Rev. Oliver Crockford, founder and pastor of the Cedarvale Tabernacle in Toronto, had first encountered Alliance teaching through the Bosworths and had been pointed to Simpson's books for further information on doctrinal matters. These he read avidly and agreed with, and both he and his congregation swung into the Alliance orb. In January 1922 he became a member of the district committee and within a year concluded that Simpson's doctrines of sanctification and divine healing were not shared by many on the committee, nor were the policies of "special attractions and programs to induce missionary giving" in conformity with Simpson's expressed views. Then came a letter from an Alliance missionary in Ecuador, stating that he regularly used quinine as a treatment for malaria. This was clearly not consistent with Simpson's published views. Crockford wrote a lengthy letter to Roffe expressing his deep concerns, who passed it on to Foreign Secretary Rev. A. C. Snead who replied, quite correctly, that from early days Alliance missionaries had not been required to believe in divine healing.* He conceded that, with very few exceptions, missionaries in Africa took quinine regularly, yet many of them believed they firmly stood for divine healing. The Foreign Secretary insisted that Crockford and his church could continue to support Alliance missions with the full assurance that there were some missionaries who "stand firmly and truly for the full truth of Divine healing."[100]

Crockford was not satisfied with such an explanation. He wrote to Roffe, "When I entered into fellowship with the Alliance I understood they really practised what they professed to believe, but I find I was mistaken." Crockford believed that it was inconsistent to claim that forgiveness of sin and healing for the body had been provided jointly through the meritorious grace of Christ's atonement, the first obtained by faith without works, the second by works (doctors and medicines) plus faith. This position, he said, would place the truth of the Alliance belief in sanctification in doubt, because if sanctification meant that Christ "was all, in all," he must be Lord of the body as well as the soul. If He could not purify the body without our assistance, how could we believe that He alone could or would purify the soul?

---

* In 1892 Simpson wrote, "We do not require missionaries of the International Missionary Alliance to believe in Divine healing." But, "a missionary will be much stronger and better off for believing in Divine healing. . . . We believe that the majority of our missionaries will be found dispensing with remedies."[101]

"These inconsistencies," he said, "leave me no alternative but to resign."[102] And with him went his congregation and tabernacle.*

Crockford's points were valid but his schismatic action precluded any constructive effect. Had he remained within the Alliance he might have succeeded in prodding other leaders to re-examine their faith. When his resignation was read to the district committee, several acknowledged that many of the members in the older branches still stood for the positions originally taught by Simpson.[103] However, the committee believed that Crockford was over-concerned about the doctrine of healing, and they hoped he might return to a "more balanced view."[104]

The withdrawal of Crockford and the Cedarvale Tabernacle on April 3, 1924,[105] terminated all further discussion about clarification of Alliance doctrines. However, fifteen persons from Crockford's congregation decided to remain loyal to the Alliance and requested Roffe to immediately open a new Alliance work in the east end of Toronto.[106] The district committee supported the request, but Roffe decided that no such action would be attempted until passions had cooled. Meanwhile, the group of fifteen commenced holding their own prayer meetings in various homes, requesting the Alliance Tabernacle (Christie Street) to adopt them as a daughter church. The tabernacle accepted and the district committee brought pressure on the superintendent to "press the development as vigorously as possible."[107]

Early in October Roffe organized the East End Alliance branch. Elton Beal was elected treasurer; W. J. Laughlin, missionary treasurer; and Mr. Foley, secretary. A 300-seat hall on Gerrard at Redwood was rented and services commenced October 19. For several months the Alliance Tabernacle assisted financially and in providing speakers. The first pastor, Rev. C. L. Whitman, a former missionary in Africa, arrived on the scene in January 1925.[108] After several moves, the congregation dedicated a renovated fire hall on Greenwood Avenue on December 4, 1927, the work becoming known as the Greenwood Avenue Tabernacle.[109] In 1962 the church property was

---

* Oliver Crockford pursued his independent ministry for twenty years. Then he went into business and eventually into municipal politics. In 1946 he was elected reeve (mayor) of Scarborough. Known as "Mr. Scarborough," he was credited with pushing the borough into the twentieth century. During his eight years in office, municipal assessment rose from $11 to $220 million. The Golden Mile commercial and industrial complex and the Scarborough General Hospital owe their existence to his initiatives. In 1970 a new wing of the hospital was named the Oliver E. Crockford Pavilion. He died in 1986.

expropriated and the church corporately terminated. However, many of the former members formed the nucleus of a new church known today as Brimley Road Alliance Church.

In Midland, Ontario, a small group seceded from a Baptist church in March 1922, and formed the New Testament Baptist Church. However, the members could not agree on several doctrinal issues. In the spring of 1924, still without a pastor, they asked Roffe to conduct an Alliance convention. Roffe obliged, with the assistance of Rev. William Hay, a former Baptist minister from Winnipeg, and the Cleveland Coloured Quintette. This convention made a deep impression on the congregation, and on June 20 they voted to affiliate with the Alliance. Among the twenty church leaders present on that occasion were Mr. and Mrs. Herman Brooks (parents of Rev. Willis Brooks), Mr. and Mrs. R. Webb, Mr. and Mrs. W. J. Brownlee, and Mr. A. Griffith. As a result, on July 28, Roffe organized the branch with founding officers A. Griffith, W. J. Brownlee, H. Broad and Mr. Shutz.[110] Services commenced in the Orange Hall in September, with Rev. William Hay as pastor.[111] The church is known today as the Alliance Church, Midland.

District Leadership Challenges

The question of district incorporation had first arisen in 1912, when the Lappin Avenue Church (Toronto) became the first in Canada to adopt the Alliance constitution, but the district had been unable to obtain legal ownership of the property without becoming an incorporated body.[112] In 1921, in reaction to Pastor Smith's purchase of the Christie Street property in his own name, Roffe enquired about district ownership, and it was reaffirmed that the district could not own property unless it was incorporated. As a result, Roffe was authorized by the district committee to proceed with "incorporation of the Alliance in Canada."[113] However, no action was taken.

Early in June 1923 a dispute arose regarding the responsibilities and authorities of the district superintendent and the district committee. There had been no formal district organization, the committee members being selected by the superintendent "to consult with and advise the superintendent in the work." The frequent and lengthy absences of the superintendent had often forced the other committee members to make decisions on their own, for which they had no authority. Complicating the situation, four or five of the committee members associated with the Christie Street Tabernacle had formed a sort of unofficial cabinet, which often swayed the opinion of the other members.[114]

On their part, the committee members complained that even when the superintendent was in town, they had no influence on policy, but were simply informed of the superintendent's decisions after the fact. They further contended that the superintendent reported receipts and disbursements only in rounded figures,* and that by "holding aloof," he was alienating himself from the branches as well as his committee.[115] Conceding that "a great deal of the difficulty is due to the district being unorganized and having no basis laid down on which its business should be conducted," they urged that "no new member be added to the committee without some proper recognized procedure being observed"; that a district organization and constitution be drawn up immediately; that all "branches which are strong enough" be allowed to "handle their own conventions independently, the superintendent confining himself to pioneer or outside conventions";[116] and that the Alliance in Canada have its own official magazine, to be known as the *Alliance World*, edited by Pastor Smith and published by the Alliance Tabernacle.[117]

As Lionel Watson saw it, the committee members from the Tabernacle were "a little intoxicated with success."[118] Roffe's concern was "the danger of a tendency growing, to think of this district as a Canadian Alliance."[119]

Home Secretary E. J. Richards and Financial Secretary W. S. Poling came to Toronto to investigate. As a result, effective July 31, 1923, the "Canadian Office" became a branch office of the New York Finance Department. Lionel Watson was created office manager and assistant treasurer for Canadian funds under the direct oversight of the financial secretary. In addition, Lionel Watson officially became assistant district superintendent under Roffe.[120] Both the superintendent and his assistant seemed content with these changes, but the other members of the committee continued to press for organization and incorporation.[121]

When during the spring of 1924, Pastor Crockford and his Cedarvale Tabernacle seceded from the Alliance, taking with them the property, the committee insisted that Lionel Watson obtain

---

* The committee made no insinuations of misuse of funds, but were solely concerned with acceptable accountability procedures.

approval from the board of managers in New York to prepare a draft proposal for a district constitution, to be followed as quickly as possible by full district organization and incorporation.[122] Approval was obtained and the first annual district prayer and business conference called to convene on May 28, 1924.[123] The constitution, patterned after the American model, was adopted and the following became the first elected officials of the Canadian District:[124]

District Superintendent	A. W. Roffe
Asst. District Superintendent	Lionel Watson
Secretary	E. T. Young
Treasurer	Lionel Watson
District Executive Committee	E. B. Fitch, H. S. Hallman, O. J. Smith, J. B. Snider, J. H. Woodward
Trustees	John Patton, J. J. Thompson, W. C. Willis

Organization of the district paved the way for a petition of incorporation under the laws of Ontario, and after several months of delay the bill received Royal Assent on April 8.[125] At last, "The Christian and Missionary Alliance in Canada" was authorized to own property. However, it would be a long, slow process to convince existing church trustees to turn over their properties to the Alliance.

ROFFE'S FINAL DAYS

The year 1924 was important to the Canadian District in terms of its image being formed in the minds of its American brethren. The phenomenal success of the Bosworths in Toronto and Ottawa and the emergence of the two great tabernacles were much publicized in the *Alliance Weekly*. The huge missionary collections taken up in both centres were of special interest to the Alliance.

In May 1924, Annual Council convened for the first time in Canada at Toronto. Massey Hall was secured for the Sunday service, while other meetings were held in "the spacious tabernacle auditorium." President Frederick Senft paid tribute to Pastor Salmon, Mayor Howland, Dr. Zimmerman and other Canadians who had been intimately involved in the work of the Alliance during its earliest days.[126]

The year 1924 marked the climax and the end of the great church opening work of Roffe.* By that time, Methodist, Presbyterian and Congregational churches were too involved in combat over the issue of unionism to be interested in accommodating the Alliance in its widespread missionary conventions and collections. Moreover, by then, the Alliance was recognized for what it really was—a competing denomination. Generally, it was no longer welcome in the other churches. From then on, the high cost of hall rentals and the increased administrative work required would greatly inhibit the convention program, especially in new locations. This added to Roffe's burdens in attending to his far-flung district. In an attempt to provide some relief to the ailing superintendent, the Home Secretary appointed John Woodward as assistant superintendent for western Canada. However, the help was too little and too late. Early in March 1925, Roffe suffered a major nervous collapse and was able to contribute very little to the work from then on.

News of Roffe's condition brought decisive action from New York. The Home Secretary became convinced that the District of Canada was too large and too complex for one superintendent to administer. He conceived a plan to divide Canada into three districts—Western, Central and Eastern.

Richards immediately visited Roffe in Toronto to discuss his plans. He found his Canadian superintendent "in a very serious condition, suffering intensely." Roffe was persuaded that the responsibilities for all Canada were too much for him. Explaining his plan to divide the country into three districts, Richards offered Roffe the superintendency of a new Western Canada District. Roffe turned down the offer for health and family reasons and because he believed that the potential of the west demanded a youthful and vigorous man. He did, however, accept an alternative offer to become a "field evangelist."[127]

In May, Richards presented his plan to the district prayer and business conference meeting in Toronto. The Western Canadian District was to run from Fort William to the Rockies, the Central Canadian District from Fort William to the Quebec-New Brunswick border, and the Eastern Canadian District to comprise the maritime provinces.[128] The conference delegates were enthusiastic. Lionel Watson saw the formation of the Eastern Canadian District as the only way to effectively develop the maritimes. From his experience it had

---

* Additional works opened by Roffe were: Galt and Wallaceburg (1922); Forest Hill, Lake, London and Mimico (1924). None of these has survived.

been more difficult to administer a program in Toronto for the maritimes than one for the prairies.* Watson was nominated for the superintendency of the Central Canadian District, but the vote was not unanimous. He therefore declined and as no other nomination was forthcoming, Home Secretary E. J. Richards became superintendent pro tem and Watson continued as assistant superintendent.[129]

Thus ended the superintendency of Alfred W. Roffe. His New York superiors may not always have been content with his reluctance to thrust an Alliance presence into the territory of the major denominations, the district committee may have been critical of his concept of committee participation, and the branches may have felt neglected by their superintendent. Yet he had been largely responsible for making known the Alliance cause in dozens of locations and on hundreds of occasions. His efforts resulted in the giving of hundreds of thousands of missionary dollars, and the sending forth of some twenty or more missionaries. He had spent his diminishing strength in the cause. When he took office in 1919 there were only eight active branches in existence. When he laid down his burdens in 1925 there were 23 in existence. The Alliance in Canada had not been revived: it had been reborn!

Roffe closed his final report to the Home Department and to Council with a tribute to those who had helped him in the work:

> I have it on my heart at this time to refer to the noble band of workers (some thirty in all) with which God has blessed the Canadian District. For the most part they stand on virgin soil, seeking to pray their way into the confidence of those who greatly need, but who are not very enthusiastic about receiving, the testimony we have to present.... They need our prayers, while the paramount need of the work is an increase of workers of like vision, of like faith and like passion.[130]

REFERENCES

1. Arthur Bryant, *The Lion and the Unicorn* (London: Collins Press, 1969), p. 21.
2. S. D. Clark, *Church and Sect in Canada* (Toronto: University of Toronto Press, 1965), p. 431; John Webster Grant, *The Church in the Canadian Era* (Toronto: McGraw Hill Ryerson Ltd., 1972), pp. 106, 107.
3. N. Keith Clifford, *The Resistance to Church Union in Canada* (Vancouver: University of British Columbia Press, 1985), pp. 6, 17, 18.

---

* Approval to divide Canada was obtained from Council one week later.

92 / *The Aura of Uncertainty*

4. Ibid., p. 2.
5. H. M. Gwatkin, *The Arian Controversy* (London: Longmans, Green, and Co., 1914), pp. 110, 111.
6. *The Christian and Missionary Alliance*, 10 Oct 1910, p. 57.
7. *The Alliance Weekly*, 23 Oct 1957, p. 7.
8. *The Toronto Globe*, 18 Jan 1919, p. 14; ibid., 30 Jan 1919, p. 6; ibid., 31 Jan 1919, p. 6; ibid., 1 Feb 1919, p. 8; ibid., 3 Feb 1919, p. 8; ibid., 4 Feb 1919, p. 8; ibid., 5 Feb 1919, p. 6; ibid., 6 Feb 1919, p. 6
9. Ibid., 14 Jun 1919, p. 8; *The Toronto Star*, 7 Jun 1919, p. 25; ibid., 14 Jun 1919, p. 30; *The Alliance Weekly*, 28 Jun 1919, editorial.
10. Board of Managers, Minutes, 22 Jul 1919.
11. Ibid., 16 Sep 1919; *Alliance Weekly*, 18 Oct 1919, p. 50.
12. A. E. Thompson, *The Life of A.B. Simpson* (Harrisburg: Christian Publications Inc., 1920), pp. 215, 219, 220.
13. Board of Managers, 5 Nov 1919.
14. *Alliance Weekly*, 29 May 1920, p. 134.
15. *Life of A.B. Simpson*, p. 222.
16. *Toronto Globe*, 31 Oct 1919, p. 6.
17. *Life of A.B. Simpson*, pp. 222, 223.
18. *The Evangelical Christian* (Toronto), Dec 1919, p. 367.
19. Annual Report of the C&MA, May 1918, pp. 55, 56.
20. Ibid., May 1921, p. 1; District of Canada, Minutes, Feb 1921.
21. Ibid., Report of the Canadian District 1921/22, pp. 1, 2.
22. *Toronto Globe*, 21 Apr 1920, p. 9.
23. Ibid., 29 Apr 1920, p. 9.
24. *Life of A. B. Simpson*, pp. 105, 106; *Toronto Globe*, 24 May 1920, p. 9.
25. *Alliance Weekly*, 29 May 1920, pp. 131, 132.
26. Board of Managers, 16 May 1921.
27. Ibid., 20-25 Sep 1922.
28. Manual of the C&MA, 1924, pp. 51, 52.
29. *The Ottawa Citizen*, 2 Feb 1920, p. 3; ibid., 4 Feb 1920, p. 2; ibid., 7 Feb 1920, p. 11.
30. The Kingston *British Whig*, 25 Jan 1921, p. 2; ibid., 27 Jan 1921, p. 2; ibid., 29 Jan 1921, p. 2.
31. *The Moncton Daily Times*, 14 Mar 1921, p. 8; ibid., 15 Mar 1921, p. 8; ibid., 17 Mar 1921, p. 8; *The Moncton Transcript*, 14 Mar 1921, p. 8; ibid., 16 Mar 1921, p. 5; ibid., 19 Mar 1921, p. 5; ibid., 21 Mar 1921, p. 6.
32. *St. John Evening Times Star*, 28 Feb 1921.
33. Annual Report, May 1921, p. 84.
34. *Alliance Witness*, 12 Feb 1921, p. 736.
35. District of Canada, Minutes, 1 Oct 1920; Board of Managers, 4 Oct 1920, pp. 2, 3.
36. O. J. Smith, *What Hath God Wrought* (Toronto: The Peoples Press, 1947), p. 57; Lois Neely, *Fire in His Bones* (Wheaton: Tyndale House Publishing Co., 1982), p. 127.

37. Parkdale Tabernacle Church, Records, p. 47; District of Canada, correspondence, Watson to Roffe, 24 Dec 1920; *The Toronto Star*, 31 Dec 1920, p. 19.
38. *The Alliance World* (Toronto), Dec 1923, p. 15; *The Word of Life* (Toronto), Oct 1923, p. 17.
39. O. J. Smith, *Can Organized Religion Survive?* (Toronto: Tabernacle Publishers, 1932), p. 27.
40. Parkdale Tabernacle, p. 47.
41. *Alliance Weekly*, 23 Apr 1921, p. 93.
42. District of Canada, Minutes, 12, 20 Jan; 1, 7, 22 Feb 1921.
43. *Toronto Star*, 4 Jun 1921, p. 14
44. *Toronto Globe*, 25 Apr 1921, p. 13.
45. Ibid.
46. Ibid., 26 Apr 1921, p. 11.
47. *Alliance Weekly*, 4 Jun 1921, p. 186.
48. *Evangelical Christian*, Jul 1921, pp. 199, 200, 218; *Toronto Star*, 16 May 1921, p. 20; ibid., 18 May 1921, p. 3; *Toronto Globe*, 18 May 1921, p. 13; *The Toronto Telegram*, 17 May 1921, p. 10.
49. *Alliance Weekly*, 23 Feb 1924, p. 840; ibid., 22 Mar 1924, p. 56; *The Prophet* (Toronto), Apr 1924, p. 18.
50. District of Canada, Cedarvale file, 11 Jun 1921.
51. *The News of News*, Parkdale Tabernacle, Aug-Dec 1921.
52. *Alliance Witness*, 22 Oct 1921, pp. 506, 510; 5 Nov 1921, p. 591.
53. *Toronto Telegram*, 31 Dec 1921, p. 14.
54. *Prophet*, Jul 1923, p. 13; ibid., Jan 1924, pp. 14, 15; *What Hath God Wrought*, pp. 53, 54, 61.
55. *Prophet*, Jan 1924, p. 14.
56. Ibid., Jan 1924, p. 15; *What Hath God Wrought*, p. 59; *Toronto Star*, 2 Jul 1921, p. 18.
57. *Toronto Globe*, 15 May 1922, p. 13.
58. *Can Organized Religion Survive?*, p. 27; *Prophet*, "Our Home Policy," May-Jun 1924; *Alliance Witness*, 9 Feb 1924, p. 804.
59. *Can Organized Religion Survive?*, p. 20.
60. Ibid., pp. 37, 38.
61. District of Canada, Minutes, 10 Oct 1921.
62. Board of Managers, 12 Oct 1921.
63. Annual Report, May 1922, pp. 65, 66.
64. *Alliance Weekly*, 28 May 1921, p. 171; 26 Nov 1921, p. 586.
65. Ibid., 7 Apr 1923, p. 94.
66. Ibid., 10 Jun 1922, p. 197.
67. Ibid., 12 Jun 1920, p. 171.
68. *Alliance Witness*, 15 Apr 1922, p. 76; Annual Report, May 1922, p. 3.
69. *Alliance Witness*, 15 Apr 1922, p. 76; ibid., 30 Sep 1922, pp. 458, 463.
70. Ibid., 5 Aug 1922, p. 334.

94 / The Aura of Uncertainty

71. Ibid., 7 Oct 1922, p. 479.
72. District of Canada, Minutes, 2 Feb 1923; ibid., Chatham file, 22 Dec 1922.
73. Ibid., Minutes, 7 Apr 1923, p. 94.
74. Ibid., 7 Apr 1923, p. 94; 15 Sep 1923, p. 466.
75. Ibid., 19 May 1923, p. 198.
76. Ibid.
77. *The Canadian Alliance* (Toronto), Aug 1924, p. 14; Annual Report, May 1922, pp. 5, 6.
78. District of Canada, Minutes, 18 Sep 1923.
79. Ibid., Correspondence, Belleville file, Lorimer to Watson, 17 Sep 1923; 27 Oct 1923.
80. F. W. Hollinrake, *Reasons Why I Retired from the Methodist Church*, no date; ibid., "Statement of Pastor Hollinrake to his People of Delta Tabernacle," pamphlet, 11 Jan 1937; Delta Tabernacle, *A History of the First Fifty Years of Delta Tabernacle*, pp. 5, 6.
81. *A History of the First Fifty Years of Delta Tabernacle*, p. 5.
82. Eastern and Central Canadian District Prayer Conference, Minutes, 1937; The Alliance Tabernacle (Toronto), Minutes, 17 Sep 1937.
83. Eastern and Central Canadian District Prayer Conference, Minutes, 1937.
84. *Canadian Alliance*, Aug 1924, p. 8; *Alliance Weekly*, 17 May 1924, p. 198.
85. District of Canada, Minutes, 16 Jun 1924.
86. *Canadian Alliance*, Aug 1924, p. 15.
87. Lindsay Reynolds, *Footprints* (Toronto: The C&MA in Canada, 1983), pp. 112, 276, 277.
88. *Alliance World*, Dec 1923, p. 4; A. W. Roffe, "Twelve Months of Miracles," Report to District Conference, 1925; Herman Grierson, "Fifty Years in Retrospect" (Ottawa: unpublished, 1974), pp. 12, 13.
89. "Twelve Months of Miracles."
90. *Alliance Weekly*, 12 Apr 1924, p. 106; *Prophet*, Jan 1924, p. 3.
91. *Alliance Weekly*, 24 May 1924, p. 215.
92. *Ottawa Citizen*, 27 May 1924, p. 18; *Alliance Witness*, 14 Jun 1924, p. 270.
93. *Ottawa Citizen*, 24 Apr 1924, p. 16.
94. Ibid.; ibid., 21 May 1924, p. 13; ibid., 26 May 1924, p. 19.
95. Ibid., 21 May 1924, p. 13; ibid., 23 May 1924, p. 28; ibid., 26 May 1924, p. 19.
96. Ibid., 27 May 1924, p. 18.
97. Ibid.
98. Ibid., 16 May 1924, p. 5.
99. *Fifty Years in Retrospect*, pp. 23-26.
100. District of Canada, Correspondence, Cedarvale Tabernacle file, Sneed to Crockford, 12 Mar 1924.
101. *Christian Alliance*, 1 Apr 1892, p. 210; District of Canada, Minutes, 4 Feb 1924.
102. Ibid., Crockford to Roffe, 6 Nov 1923.

The Aura of Uncertainty / 95

103. Ibid., Watson to Crockford, 5 Dec 1923.
104. Ibid., Minutes, 3 Dec 1923.
105. Ibid., Correspondence, Cedarvale Tabernacle file, Crockford to Roffe, 3 Apr 1924.
106. Ibid., Minutes, 31 May 1924.
107. Ibid., 14 Jul 1924; ibid., 2 Sep 1924.
108. *Himself* (Toronto), Jan 1925, p. 18.
109. Eastern and Central Canadian District, Minutes, 6 Dec 1927.
110. *Canadian Alliance*, Aug 1924, p. 9; *Alliance Weekly*, 4 Oct 1924, p. 230.
111. District of Canada, Minutes, 2 Sep 1924; *Canadian Alliance*, Oct. 1924, p. 4.
112. *Footprints*, p. 357.
113. District of Canada, Minutes, 10 Oct 1921.
114. Ibid., Correspondence, Home Dept. file, Watson to Richards, 7 Nov 1923.
115. Ibid., Richards to Watson, 25 Jan 1924.
116. Ibid., Watson to Richards, 8 Nov 1923.
117. Ibid., Minutes, 2 Nov 1923.
118. Ibid., Correspondence, Home Dept. file, Watson to Richards, 7 Nov 1923.
119. Ibid., 19 Jun 1923.
120. Ibid., Correspondence, Richards to Roffe, 25 Jun 1923; Board of Managers, 31 Jul 1923.
121. District of Canada, Minutes, 3 Dec 1923; 7 Jan 1924; 4 Feb 1924.
122. Ibid., 3 Mar 1924; 5 May 1924.
123. Ibid., 3 Mar 1924.
124. Canadian District Annual Conference, Minutes, 1924.
125. Canadian District Executive Committee, Minutes, 2 Sep 1924.
126. *Alliance Weekly*, 7 Jun 1924, p. 247.
127. Board of Managers, attachment Richards to "My dear brother," 16 Mar 1924.
128. Canadian District, 20 May 1925.
129. Ibid.
130. Annual Report to Council, May 1925, pp. 157, 158.

CHAPTER FOUR

The Vision of Need

"The dominant motive in the religious life of Canada," wrote Dr. E. H. Oliver, "has been the winning of the frontier. Frontiers are not always geographical. They are spiritual and cultural as well."[1]

For the Alliance in Canada, the frontier was spiritual. In the over-churched east, the frontier had been the propagation and experience of the deeper life truths. In the under-churched west, the frontier would be the evangelization of neglected prairie settlers.

The nineteenth-century American policy of "Manifest Destiny," by which divine sanction was claimed for republican overspread of the continent, instilled fear and mistrust in the hearts of Canadians. Motivated by thoughts of self-defence, the eastern provinces entered into unification talks which culminated with Confederation in 1867. In 1870, Manitoba joined, followed by British Columbia a year later, with the proviso that a transcontinental railway be built as a tangible linkage between east and west. The railroad was completed in 1885, and would serve the prairies even more than British Columbia.

Settlement of the West

Immediately following the opening of the railway, settlers began to arrive on the prairies, first from Ontario and then from Europe and the United States. During the decade before the completion of the railroad 1,629 immigrants came to Canada, settling chiefly in Ontario. In the next decade, ending in 1891, 80,000 came and nearly all settled in the prairie provinces. By 1901 another 100,000 had arrived, by 1911 a further 445,000, and by 1921 still another 420,000.

Thus, in less than 40 years, more than one million immigrants had made a new home on the Canadian prairies.

These new Canadians settled along the ever-increasing network of railway lines in numbers far in excess of the capabilities of all the churches combined to reach them with the gospel. Settlements sprang up almost overnight and vast areas of thousands of square miles became dotted with homesteads, often separated by several miles. These settlers were preoccupied with physical survival and showed little or no concern for spiritual or moral values. By 1921, a whole new Canadian-born adult generation existed on the prairies that knew little or nothing about Christ.

The inability of the churches to meet the spiritual needs of the immigrants opened the floodgates to every kind of sect and cult imaginable. According to William E. Mann, in Alberta alone between 1900 and 1920 eighteen sects and twelve cults became entrenched. Such profusion and confusion of teachings had never been experienced in the east.[2]

The churches worked vigorously to combat the new teachings. They found that in many places three or even four struggling denominational churches existed almost side by side in small towns or even in the open country, while increasing areas had no witness at all. As a result, a western cooperative movement developed whereby a "united" church began to take the place of several competing denominational churches. In time, this trend, supported by economic considerations, developed into a swell for the church union movement. Despite these developments the urgent needs remained overwhelming. The superintendent of Methodist missions lamented that when the summer student missionary workers returned to college, he was left with 40 vacant stations. He claimed that all the Protestant churches together were not contacting more than 50 per cent of the territory and that the Methodists alone had 26 vacant mission stations in Alberta.[3]

A Call for Help

Such was the situation when in July 1921 A. W. Roffe, superintendent of the Alliance District of Canada, received a letter from a small unorganized group in Edmonton calling itself Beulah Mission. In part, the letter read, "We feel that a Christian and Missionary Alliance work would be what Edmonton ought to have. We would like someone to come."[4] Roffe passed the letter on to John H.

Woodward, a recent graduate of the Missionary Training Institute, living in Hamilton, with instructions to "think it over."

Beulah Mission was the remains of a work started around 1910, known as Beulah Home and Mission, a home for unwed mothers and a rescue mission for men. During World War I, most of the unemployed men that had frequented the mission enlisted in the army, so the work of the mission was virtually brought to an end. Although the home continued to exist independently for several more years, by 1919 the mission was reduced to a small group of evangelical Christians without a pastor, meeting weekly in private homes. By the time they wrote the letter to Roffe the group was renting a small clapboard church building at 10822-98th Street, which they shared with the Swedish Baptist Church.* What prompted their desire to become part of the Alliance is not certain. Some believe that A. M. Loptson, a member of the group who that year was appointed an Alliance missionary to the Philippines, had suggested the Alliance to them. Mary Parker recalled hearing her mother say that there were a few families who had read about the Alliance. In any event, the work and nature of the Alliance had been well publicized in Edmonton some years previously. In the summer of 1912, John J. Thompson of Orillia, Ontario (brother of Dr. Simpson's biographer), held special meetings in Edmonton at which time he succeeded in arousing considerable public interest. Some four months later, a team consisting of Alliance Foreign Secretary Dr. R. H. Glover and Home Secretary E. J. Richards held meetings for four days in McDougal Methodist, First Presbyterian, Westminster Presbyterian churches and the YMCA, featuring both "missionary" and "spiritual life" topics.[6]

Moreover, when Roffe received the letter from Edmonton, the Bosworth meetings in Toronto had terminated just a few weeks previously and had been given coverage in the Edmonton media. In addition, the proceedings of the Methodist Conference in Orillia, in June, had been featured in Edmonton newspapers and contained the following quotation from a report submitted on divine healing.

> The ministry of Jesus was a ministry to the ailing body as well as to the ailing soul. Recent happenings seem to

---

* The Swedish Baptist Church building remained the home of the Beulah congregation until late 1923, when a property at the corner of 107th Avenue and 98th Street was purchased. At the same time, a disused Anglican building on Jasper Avenue was acquired and moved to the new location, and on December 2 the new church home was opened.[5]

indicate that multitudes will flock to the church as they flocked to Jesus, if the church seeks to recover this ministry of healing. If there was more teaching on the subject, on the part of the Christian Church, and it was given its place in the preaching of the Gospel, it could not fail to exercise a beneficial effect on the church membership.

The article continued, "In the discussion that followed the moving of the adoption of the report, was heard an echo of the recent Bosworth healing mission in Toronto."[7]

Perhaps the Toronto Bosworth campaign had a part in establishing the first Alliance church in western Canada!

John Henry Woodward was born in Aldershot, England, on April 18, 1895, the son of a British army sergeant major. His mother was so convinced that the baby would be a girl that she had picked out "her" name. When his father arrived home to find that a boy had been born, he turned to his wife and said, "Well, it's not a girl. What's his 'John Henry' to be?" The distraught wife replied, "That's as good as any other. Let's take that." So, he became John Henry Woodward!

As a boy, Woodward attended the Colchester Primitive Methodist Church where Charles Hadden Spurgeon had been converted. When he was about fifteen, the family relocated to Hamilton, Ontario. The story of his conversion is told by himself.

> The most outstanding event of my life was when I was saved. When I left England I had been sowing wild oats. I recall on board ship when we arrived at Montreal, I looked out over the coastline of Canada and said, "A new land and a new life." In my heart I wanted a new life, but when I got to Hamilton I found that sin in Canada was the same as sin in England. One Sunday evening I walked down the street and came to Barton Street Methodist Church. I had never been inside a church in Canada, but that evening I had a lonely heart. I could see the bright lights inside and hear the people singing heartily. Suddenly, I found myself turning into the church. I heard Rev. H. G. Livingston* preach. . . . I saw my empty, wasted life and where I was headed. In

---

*Rev. Henry Gilbert Livingston served the Barton Street Methodist Church from 1904-1916. The church was renamed in his honour and is today known as Livingston United Church.

the seat, (nobody else knew anything about it), I asked God to save me. The Lord did it right there.[8]

When Rev. F. W. Hollinrake resigned from Barton Street Methodist Church, Hamilton (see page 76), and opened Ebenezer Tabernacle, Woodward also left the Methodist Church and became a charter member of what would become Delta Tabernacle.

Woodward took the Edmonton letter home, discussed it with his wife and prayed about it. He had received an offer of appointment with the South Africa General Mission. In addition, Dr. P. W. Philpott wanted him to accept the pastorate of one of his Christian Workers Churches in Belleville. As they prayed about it, western Canada under the Alliance seemed to be the divine answer. So in August 1921, able to afford no more than his own fare on a "harvest special," he left for Edmonton. It would be seven months before his wife and baby could follow. When Woodward stepped off the train in Edmonton, he was greeted by a small group,* "but," said he, "they were the cream of the crop, godly people."[9] He preached his first sermon on August 21 from the text, "There went with him a band of men whose hearts God had touched" (1 Samuel 10:26). Twenty-five to 30 people were in attendance for the worship service and 25 at Sunday school.

Woodward tells of some of the difficulties experienced during those early days of the Beulah work.

> As we rented the church building from the Swedish Baptists, we could not plan for special meetings. If their itinerant minister was coming in for Sunday, we could only hold one service that day. We had a Beulah Mission sign on one side of the door and the Swedish Baptist sign on the other side. Their sign was larger, so more people came to their services! The people wanted to give me a salary of $100 a month, but when I learned that some of them were out of work, I turned down all salary and said that I should take a step of faith. We placed three boxes near the door, one marked "missions," one "church," and the third "pastor." Needless to say, during the first winter

---

* In his "History of Beulah Church," J. H. Woodward names fourteen people who met him on the Edmonton platform and says they constituted his new congregation. However, in his "History of the Western Canadian District" he states that he was met by three or four people, and that the congregation consisted of four men and three ladies.

when the blizzards blew and the snow fell, there were no people in the pews and no money in the boxes. We simply had to pray things through, which we gladly did.[10]

On one occasion we came the closest we ever did to having nothing. We had some butter and some tea, but no bread. However, we sat around the table and thanked God for the meal we were about to enjoy. Suddenly, I heard the noise of someone approaching the door. I got up and opened it, and saw a lady setting down a basket of food. She said, "God told me that the pastor and his family needed something to eat." So we had hot chicken, cranberries, mashed potatoes and pumpkin pie. It wasn't Thanksgiving Day, but it was thanksgiving day![11]

An Urgent Need

Within a few days of arrival in Edmonton, Woodward commenced visiting the surrounding areas and was shocked to discover the dearth of Christian knowledge. Many had never even heard the name of Jesus, and community after community were without a church or Sunday school. Asking some children if they knew of Jesus, he was told, "No sir, he doesn't live around these parts." When he told a woman, "I want to talk to you about Jesus," she replied, "Never heard of him," and hurried on.[12] Woodward's subsequent research revealed that there were more than 2,500 prairie school districts in which there was no Sunday school or religious activity of any kind.[13]

Soon, a lengthy report of the western tragedy reached District Superintendent Roffe. In his almost two years in office, Roffe had not visited the western half of his constituency. He immediately laid plans to make an extensive tour of the west, and on October 11, Roffe, accompanied by his wife, set out on his historic 62-day fact finding tour. He wrote, "We started out from Toronto with the feeling that we were going, we knew not where, we were to be entertained by we knew not whom, and the expenses of the trip were to be met, we knew not how." He held meetings in Winnipeg, Regina, Medicine Hat, Calgary, Innisfail, Edmonton and Vancouver, during which he preached 74 times.[14] In addition, he preached on numerous occasions to small groups in country locations. Mrs. Roffe, who possessed a good solo voice, used her gift to great acceptance throughout the tour.

On November 20, Roffe had the joy of organizing Beulah Mission into an official Alliance branch, which was renamed Beulah Tabernacle of The Christian and Missionary Alliance, the first church to be organized in western Canada. There were thirteen charter members. Among the first executive board members were H. B. Johnston, secretary and A. Whitelaw, treasurer. The first Sunday school superintendent was Roger Chapman.

Woodward had arranged for the Roffes to experience a little of the life of a prairie worker in the winter time! Roffe's own account is revealing.

> It was about 5.00 p.m. when we alighted from the train, only to learn that our services were being held many miles away. It was a bitter cold night, and we were met by a young man with a sleigh. With rough roads and but little snow we started to bump our way on a ten mile drive across the windswept prairie. It soon grew dark and on and on we journeyed for the longest and coldest ten miles I could remember. Eventually we turned in and across the great fields towards a lonely light which guided us to a log house where we threw off our wraps and hastily partook of refreshments kindly prepared by our waiting hostess. Then, another stretched out mile and a half to a school house, where less than two dozen persons had gathered, and where our meeting started a little after nine o'clock.
>
> Needless to say, it was a late hour when our service closed, after which the missionary pastor, his wife and child, Mrs. Roffe and the writer all bundled into the old sleigh, and were off again for another six mile drive across the snow. We eventually turned from the road into a trail and stopped in front of a queer little house which was to be our home during our stay in those parts.
>
> Not being accustomed to life in the west, and the zero mark [°F] having been passed considerably, we reached our destination suffering from extreme cold, only to find the fires all out. By the time the preacher had his horses stabled, the fire going and we had partaken of light refreshments, it was time to settle down for the night, or rather the morning, for it was then 1.00 a.m.

The following day the program included another cold drive of six miles to a farm house for dinner, and where we conducted a service with ten persons present. One felt it was worth all the inconvenience, if not hardship, to see the appreciation of those dear prairie friends, with their limited privileges and hungry hearts. "Please sing it again," they asked Mrs. Roffe, and as she sang, they wept and were blessed.

Six miles back to our little prairie home, a hasty repast and then, we were off to a school house, where our meeting got under way about half past eight. One more bitter cold drive and we were through for the day.[15]

However, the chief value of Roffe's first western tour lay in quite another direction. At the beginning of his visit, Woodward had taken him to see the great stretches of prairie land, dotted with homesteads and small communities. What Woodward had told him about the poverty of spiritual knowledge he found was all too true. One day they stopped to watch a harvesting scene. As Roffe gazed across the fields of waving grain, he was captivated by the sheer immensity of the panorama before him. He watched the multitude of harvesters, labouring to reap the golden treasure before it would be lost to a cruel prairie winter, and he thought of another harvest of far greater value, also ready for reaping, but for which there were no reapers. As he dwelt upon this tragedy, the mournful monotone of the wind passing through the standing stalks of grain added a haunting note of sadness to the prairie scene. In his imagination he could see the west beckoning to the east for help, but there was no response. The east was absorbed in its own affairs.

The words of John O. Thompson's missionary hymn had never held deeper meaning for Roffe than they had that autumn day in 1921:

> Far and near the fields are teeming with the waves of ripened grain;
> Far and near their gold is gleaming o'er the sunny slope and plain.
> Lord of harvest, send forth reapers! Hear us, Lord, to Thee we cry;
> Send them now the sheaves to gather, ere the harvest-time pass by.

The Vision of Need / 105

4.1

Courtesy Public Archives of Canada

4.1 A train from the east unloads its burden of settlers on the western prairies.

4.2 Rev. and Mrs. John H. Woodward, as they appeared during their early days in the west.

4.3 The first workers of the Great West Mission obtain their horses in May 1922, and pose with the management. From left to right: Pastor Woodward, Safara Witmer, District Superintendent Roffe, Robert Gillies and Hugh Middleton. George Bell arrived shortly thereafter.

4.2

4.3

106 / The Vision of Need

4.4 A western harvest scene like this, in 1921, gave birth to a "vision of need," in the mind of District Superintendent Roffe. Courtesy Public Archives of Canada

Such thoughts gave birth to what Roffe termed "A Vision of Need." In that vision, western Canada was as much a mission field as darkest Africa.

One of Roffe's favourite preaching themes was Spiritual Vision, which he divided into three parts, A Vision of Need, A Vision of Self, and A Vision of God (see page 58). True to form, Roffe's "Vision of Need" for western Canada would be just the first step in his mind towards a practical plan to meet that need.

On his return to Toronto on December 11, Roffe reported his western trip, emphasizing the "Vision of Need," and calling for a "Vision of Self," which he hoped would result in a practical response from the east. It is to the credit of Parkdale Tabernacle Church, under the leadership of Rev. O. J. Smith, that just ten days later it formed the Wayside Mission as a subsidiary home missions outreach, and made its founding announcement:

The Wayside Mission

Need: There are scores of lonely, neglected settlements in Canada, where no missionary work is being carried on. Small villages and isolated farming communities in northern Ontario and the far west have no opportunity of attending religious services of any kind. Children, in places where Sunday Schools are unknown, are growing up in total ignorance of the Bible and its teaching.

Method: Workers will go out two by two, to proclaim the message of Salvation, and to distribute gospels and tracts in the territory assigned to them. Both men and women will be accepted.

Support: The Wayside Mission will be carried on by faith in God, each worker and the Tabernacle depending upon Him for the supply of both temporal and spiritual needs.

The Wayside Mission was the first Alliance attempt during the 1920s to meet the challenge of Canadian home missions.[16] Its weakness was that its workers would be far removed from their patron church, and were effectively a law unto themselves. Its strength was that it was a year round evangelistic thrust. A total of five missionaries carried a witness chiefly to northern Alberta and northern Ontario for three years.*

THE GREAT WEST MISSION

Pastor Smith's initiative was not well received by John Woodward. He believed that missionary work in the west should be directed from the west. Three months later he advanced his own plan "to carry on a campaign in the summer months only, by having men visit the individual ranches and farms." They would not be concerned with lumbercamps, trappers and Indian villages, but would "bring a personal gospel message to every homestead on the prairies."[17] Students at Nyack and other Alliance schools would be urged to give a summer or two to spread the gospel in western Canada, and it should be presented to them as part of their training to become "pioneer missionaries." The district committee approved Woodward's project as an addition to the Wayside Mission project. However, the committee expressed concern with how to meet the expenses of the Bible school students in the absence of a sponsoring church.[18]

Thus, the Great West Mission, as it became known, was launched in the spring of 1922 under the direction of John Woodward. The Missionary Training Institute agreed to present the proposal to the student body. By the end of the school year, four men students had volunteered for western Canada service, and obtained transportation to Edmonton. They were George Bell, Robert Gillies, Safara A. Witmer and Hugh Middleton.**

Woodward found sufficient money to purchase a horse, harness and blanket for each student missionary. Then, after copying his own area from a larger map, each man was expected to "mount his steed

---

* The five missionaries sent out by Parkdale Tabernacle under the auspices of the Wayside Mission were: Louis Butcher, John Henderson, Charles Malicky, Charles Melindy, and Douglas Noseworthy.

** Robert Gillies was born in Scotland in 1902, and immigrated to Canada as a boy. Converted at the age of fifteen, he became a member of the Gospel Tabernacle (Alliance) at Brantford, Ontario. His desire was to become a missionary in China or India, but being lame in one leg, he was not accepted after graduation from Nyack. Safara A. Witmer studied in Fort Wayne Bible College, Taylor University, Winona Lake School of Theology, and the University of Chicago, where he earned a Ph.D. degree in education and psychology. He then served Fort Wayne Bible College for 27 years as instructor, registrar, dean and lastly, president. In 1958 he was appointed executive secretary of the Accrediting Association of Bible Colleges, a post he held until his death in 1962. A lucid writer of several books, he authored a classic on the history and significance of the Bible college movement entitled, *The Bible College Story: Education with Dimension*.

and away, not knowing where he will lie down at night or in what direction he must look for his next meal." His objective was to reach every family in his prescribed area of service, to hold services in the open, in a barnyard, or in a schoolhouse. There would be no salary. Each worker would have to pray in his own requirements, eat where and when people were kind enough to feed him, and sleep where given a bed. If no bed was given, he had a blanket, and, rain or shine, he would have to sleep with his horse under the stars. The strength of the project was that each student quickly learned what trusting God meant, and hundreds of homesteads heard of Christ for the first time. But with no plan to follow up professed conversions or other contacts one may wonder how many came to know saving grace. On rare occasions a Sunday school was started and perhaps several services held at a particular location. Within three weeks one worker covered every homestead within a 40 square mile area. By mid-summer about 100 square miles had been covered.[19]

Beulah Tabernacle held its first annual missionary convention from July 2-9, 1922. Among the speakers were Rev. and Mrs. William Finlay of West Africa, District Superintendent Roffe and four student workers of the Great West Mission. Through the courtesy of one of the Edmonton newspapers, Roffe was able to broadcast several of his messages on the "radiophone," "reaching hundreds of homesteads scattered through vast prairies." These were the first radio broadcasts of Alliance messages anywhere in Canada. The missionary offering at this first convention amounted to $2,800.[20]

At the end of the summer, the students were each handed $5 by Woodward "to help with the train fare back to Nyack," and Woodward, with some local help, continued to visit settlements close to Edmonton. He gives the following account:

> Work during the winter called for a dog team and sled. A team of trained huskies would have cost more than we could afford, so we settled for one fully trained husky, as the lead dog. On our first trip, the second and third dogs refused to do their share of the pulling. After a while the lead dog got tired of having to do more than his share. Suddenly he stopped, turned around, looked at the other dogs, decided who the culprits were and then walked over and bit the ears of the second and third dogs. We had no more trouble after that. I thought how nice it would be if some churches had an officer whose job it would be to spot

church members who were not pulling their weight, and bring them into line—somehow![21]

Apart from the pastoral ministry in Edmonton, the western work was almost entirely evangelistic, with little thought of establishing churches. Two small preaching stations existed in schools in Shaunavon, Saskatchewan, under a Mr. Gordon, and at Ravenscrag, Alberta, under a Fred Wicks, the local CPR station agent. Both these men had been converted under Woodward's rural program. The Edmonton church progressed slowly, "labouring under the difficulty of being in a building poorly situated and with unfortunate associations," according to Roffe.[22] Both Roffe and Woodward believed that Winnipeg, the largest city in the west, would one day prove to be "the great strategic centre" in the evangelization of Manitoba.[23] Calgary was regarded as the future centre for an Alberta ministry.

The Dr. Morris campaign in Toronto, featuring the Alliance Coloured Quintette, was due to close on August 31. On July 31, the district committee decided, with the consent of Dr. Morris and the quintette, to conduct three months of meetings in the west, commencing September 10. O. J. Smith was dispatched to the west three weeks in advance to make the arrangements. Meetings were held in Edmonton, Calgary, Regina, Saskatoon, Brandon and Winnipeg. These meetings gave great prominence to the Alliance, particularly in Calgary and Winnipeg.[24] As a result, a few old friends of the Alliance in Calgary wrote Roffe, asking if it would be possible to reopen the church in Calgary, but no bona fide pastors were available.[25]* Thus, it was recognized as an urgent need, to have "thoroughly trained Alliance men, brought up in the Alliance fellowship" available "for beginning works in Winnipeg and Calgary."[28]

MORE SUMMER RECRUITS

By the spring of 1923, Woodward was laying plans for the second summer of Great West Mission activities. Louis J. Butcher

---

* These friends were remnants of a former Alliance work in Calgary, which had commenced on August 9, 1908, under the direction of Rev. Joseph Baker.[26] A large tent was erected on the corner of Eighth Avenue and Second Street and in October a large campaign began with Rev. Harold Stephens and Rev. W. F. Menninger. Late in January the church services were moved, "owing to the extreme cold," to a rented hall at 707 Second Avenue West. In spring of 1909 the work was closed down "due to insufficient support." Although it never attained organized status, the Calgary church was the first Alliance church venture in western Canada.[27]

and Charles Malicky, missionaries of the Wayside Mission, were planning to work among the Indians and trappers at Fort Chipewyan in northern Alberta, and Woodward cooperatively offered to outfit them. At first, he had intended to accompany Butcher and Malicky, but due to the need for someone to oversee the student missionaries, he decided not to go north, a decision he may have regretted later. In any event, he proceeded to Nyack to present the urgent need of western Canada to the students, as his own account describes.

> I had almost no money. I collected all I could get my hands on, and spent it all on a ticket that would take me as far as Winnipeg. When I got off the train there, I had but twenty-five cents in my pocket, and I knew no one in the city. The train arrived during the morning and my connection was to leave at six p.m. I walked up and down the platform all day, pleading the promises of God. Shortly before my train arrived, I sat down in a seat, and noticed another man across from me. I kept looking at the clock—a quarter to six! Then the train arrived. I still sat there. Then the man came over and asked me if I was a stranger. "Yes, sir," I answered, "Don't know a person." "How long are you staying?" "I expect to go out on this train." "Well, they are loading now." I said, "Yes," but made no move. He asked, "Have you got your ticket?" I replied, "No, sir." He asked me what kind of work I did, and I told him. To cut my story short, he bought my ticket to Toronto, sleeper and all — what a luxury![29]

Once he was in Toronto, friends at the Tabernacle bought his ticket to New York. Then at Nyack, Woodward made an urgent appeal for summer workers, and of some twenty volunteers, he selected four women and six men: Sadie Klopfenstein, Catherine McCoy, Muriel Owen, Elizabeth Ritchie, George Bell, Edward Cross, Walter Jones, George Moffat, Clarence Sanger and Thomas Van Plew. Among these, four are of particular interest to Canadians.

Muriel Owen was born and brought up in Toronto. When in her teens, she became a Christian Scientist with her mother, who had health problems. In September 1921, at the age of 24, she visited an aunt, Olive Chapman, who lived in Edmonton and attended Beulah Mission. At first, the gospel preaching of Pastor Woodward was very strange to her, but within a month, as her account reveals, she came under deep conviction:

> On October 16, 1921, the Lord spoke strongly to me, but I was reluctant to go forward in front of the people. My aunt, sensing the situation, took me by the arm and literally dragged me to the altar.... I attended every service and grew in the Lord. Pastor Woodward, full of love for missions, both home and foreign, was faithful in keeping this theme before us. So it was that, within a year of my conversion, I entered the Missionary Training Institute, to become a missionary.

At Nyack, she met George Moffat, whom she later married. Together they served as Alliance missionaries in Ecuador. Widowed on the field in 1972, she retired at the age of 76, after 49 years of missionary service.

George O. Moffat was born near Duns, Berwickshire, Scotland, in 1896. After serving in the British army during the war and suffering severe wounds, he emigrated to Canada in 1920, settling in Toronto. In August 1921, he attended one of O. J. Smith's tent meetings that followed the Bosworth campaign (see page 66) and was converted. Three weeks later, he heard Walter Turnbull, then dean of Nyack, plead for young men, preferably those who had served in the war, to do hard pioneer work in the jungles of South America. For Moffat, that meant him, and within six weeks of his conversion, he was studying at Nyack. There he met fellow student Muriel Owen, got to know her better during their summer on the prairies, married her and served the Lord in Ecuador for 48 years.

George Bell was born in Ireland and came to Philadelphia, Pennsylvania, as a boy. He fought under the Stars and Stripes in World War I and was severely wounded in one leg. After graduation from Nyack, he was appointed an Alliance missionary in the French Sudan. Later he married Ethel Roffe. Bell was killed in a bus accident in 1936 while on furlough.

Edward (Ed) Cross was born in 1900 near Stamford–Welland County, Ontario. At the age of four, he suffered a fall which left him lame and continuously in pain. At age twenty, his ailment was diagnosed as tuberculosis of the hip. He went forward during a gospel service at Zion Methodist Church, Toronto, but, receiving poor counselling, he continued to yearn for peace with God. Through his own study of the Scriptures, at twenty years of age, he found peace and joy in trusting Christ as Saviour, Sanctifier and Healer, and dedicated his life to God's service. A year later he enrolled at Nyack. During the summer of 1922 he worked with the Shantymen's Christian Association in the lumber camps, and during the summer of 1923 with the Great West Mission.

The district committee believed that it was wrong to expect the Nyack students to pay their own way to the prairies but all Woodward could put together for this purpose was $325, enough for five fares to Edmonton. The other five paid their own way to Toronto, appeared at the Dominion Convention "in their riding clothes," and received financial assistance for the trip west.[30]

It cost Woodward $1,000 for horses, saddles, blankets, and a buggy for general use. As Muriel Owen remembered:

> Each of us was given a horse, saddle, and blanket with $5 and sent off in different directions. We were totally responsible for our own horse. This was especially difficult for me, as I was a city girl and had never learned to ride or care for a horse. I quickly became acquainted with my horse, and he with me. On many occasions it seemed to me that he was my only earthly friend. Indeed, we became so attached that by the end of the summer, I hated to say "goodbye" to him. When we left Edmonton, we were told to visit every home and wherever possible, to hold public services in schoolhouses, and to report back to Edmonton on a certain date each month for an all day prayer session, at which times we gave accounts of our experiences. Those sessions were so refreshing and the fellowship was so sweet.

Asked if she was ever fearful, Mrs. Moffat recalled:

> The homesteads were sometimes separated by such great distances that one might ride for hours on end without seeing anything but vast stretches of prairie. On occasions I was very lonely, and even fearful. I had to learn, step by step, to trust my heavenly Father. I recall one day it was late afternoon, and seeing nothing, I began to fear that I would

have to spend the night in an open field, without shelter of any kind. I rode on, trying to exercise a faltering faith. In a short while I spotted a windmill in the distance, and I knew that I would soon see a farm house. By the time I reached it, darkness had fallen. I knocked on the door timidly. It opened and I was greeted by a cheerful German lady, who spoke good English. Having introduced myself and my mission, she invited me in and made me feel "at home." She said I could spend two or three days there to rest, if I wished to. It turned out that the family were devout Christians. Then the table was loaded with all sorts of food. Thanks were given in German, which I did not understand, but I felt the Holy Spirit's presence right there. It was a happy, relaxing time, and I learned that I needn't have worried.[31]

On one occasion that year, Woodward took several workers with him across the border into Montana to a community of one hundred families where there was no gospel witness. One of the workers remained for several weeks, and over a dozen conversions were reported.[32]

At the end of the summer, Woodward prepared fearlessly blunt appraisals of each student, listing weaknesses as well as strengths. In view of what actually became of them, the following extracts display Woodward's ability to judge those working under him:

> Muriel Owen: She was not afraid of difficulty, and entered into her labours with zeal and energy. She has an ideal spirit and would be a good worker for some new field.
>
> George Moffat: His work was exceedingly well done and much appreciated by the communities in which he laboured. He won his way into the hearts of people and considered no hardship too great to reach people with the gospel. He will make a first class missionary.
>
> Ed Cross: He was markedly spiritual and did admirable work. He has sympathy and love for the people, particularly in cases of suffering, which gave him ready access to their hearts. Possessed of a pioneer spirit, he chooses the

hard places, because of their hardship. If his physical affliction is removed, he would be an admirable pioneer for any field.

George Bell: We sent him into the hardest of places. Fearing neither man or beast, he ploughed his way into the hearts of the people and produced results. He will break through anything for God and find joy in doing it. Kind, sympathetic and courteous to women, he will make an admirable pioneer missionary.[33]

The summer's work was judged successful, but because of concerns for the personal safety of the women it was decided that only men would be sent in the future.

VISION FOR THE CITIES

Pursuant to Roffe's and Woodward's dream of having Alliance works in Winnipeg and Calgary, Roffe planned huge conventions for these two cities and Edmonton. President Paul Rader agreed to come as the chief speaker. Not only was the tour intended to launch local works in Winnipeg and Calgary, but it would be the first time that the west would really be "tapped for missions." But if Roffe had visions of western denominationalists emptying their pockets for Alliance foreign missions as they had done in the east whenever Paul Rader spoke, he would be disappointed.

An "intensive" convention was scheduled for Edmonton, September 16-23, in McDougal Methodist Church. The Calgary convention, September 24-30 in Grace Presbyterian Church and the 4,000-seat Victoria Pavilion was to be followed by one in Winnipeg, October 2-7, with weekday meetings in Zion Methodist Church and the Sunday finale in the Trade Pavilion. On the assumption that local groups would request Alliance branches to be opened, agreement was obtained from Rev. E. W. Davis of Vermillion, Ohio, to be prepared to move to Calgary and Walter Turnbull agreed to provide another man to be ready to enter Winnipeg.[34]

Two weeks before the campaign began, President Rader cancelled out in order to be present at some function of his independent church, the Gospel Tabernacle, in Chicago. This embarrassing development was taken most seriously by Roffe, who might well have cancelled the whole campaign if financial arrangements had not been so far advanced.*

The western Canadian campaign proceeded without the president but with his brother, Luke Rader, as a fill-in. The complement included the Coloured Quintette, Thomas Moseley from Tibet, Mrs. Cutler from India, Louis Butcher from the Northern Alberta Indians, Roffe and Woodward.

At the climax of the Edmonton convention on September 22, 1923, Roffe, assisted by a group of local clergymen, examined and ordained John Woodward to the Christian ministry. He had proven himself to be a faithful, energetic, capable and dependable pastor and leader, richly deserving the honour of being the first person to be ordained in western Canada under the auspices of the Alliance.

Another significant event took place during convention days in Edmonton. Roffe received a request to meet with a frail, grey-haired lady by the name of Miss Margaret Connor. He immediately recognized the name and the meeting was quickly arranged.

Margaret Connor was born in Donegal, Ireland, in 1876. Her father died when she was young and the family immigrated to Toronto around the turn of the century. Margaret managed the family tailoring business. They made Roffe's Christian Workers Bathurst Street Tabernacle their church home.

At 35, Margaret Connor felt called to be a missionary and began training at Nyack. However, discovering that her age and frailty would disqualify her as an Alliance missionary, she returned to Toronto to work as a practical nurse with the Toronto Mission Union until she enlisted at the Moody Bible Institute in 1916 for further training. Although her assessments in scholastics, practical Christian work and personal characteristics were consistently high, her health was considered to be a drawback for employment in Christian work even in the homeland. After spending some months back home in Toronto, she heard an appeal for "workers willing to give their lives in the preaching of the gospel in the west." Undaunted, Margaret

---

* This incident marked the beginning of the end of a workable relationship between the board of managers and the president. Among several misgivings, the board advised Rader that his outside interests were preventing him from giving himself to the duties of president of the Alliance, because of his unavailability to lead. In the board's view, Rader had not been giving "due regard to the Alliance men who are making heroic sacrificial efforts to extend the Alliance work throughout the districts." The board cited "the most recent campaign in Canada as an illustration of your failure to give the desired leadership in the proper character, to the extension work."[35] Rader's presidency terminated a few weeks later.

The Vision of Need / 117

4.5

4.5 District Superintendent Roffe tries out John Woodward's six dog-power sleigh.

4.6 Walter Jones, John Woodward and George Bell in 1923.

4.6

4.7 Ed Cross rides the prairies, during the summer of 1923.

4.7

118 / The Vision of Need

4.8

4.8 Sadie Klopfenstein, Muriel Owen and Catherine McCoy, three of the only four women ever to be members of the "Alliance Cavalry," pose with their mounts during the summer of 1923.

4.9 Margaret Connor, an outstanding pioneer worker in western Canada, joined the Alliance in September 1923.

4.10 Alliance workers attend the Dominion Convention of May 1924, in Toronto, Ontario. John Woodward and Gordon Skitch are at the left of the second row. Over Skitch's right shoulder is Ed Cross. On this occasion Woodward received a gift and approval to purchase a gospel car.

4.9

4.10

went out on her own to the vicinity of Denzil, Saskatchewan, preaching her first message in December 1918 in the Allenbach school house. During the first winter, when influenza swept the area, Margaret Connor endeared herself by visiting from home to home, nursing the sick and encouraging the worried. In 1919, she organized a church at Allenbach. This was followed by others at Elk and Major, Saskatchewan, as well as several preaching stations. Two graduates of Moody Bible Institute, the sisters Elva and Clysta Stephenson, of Grandview, Manitoba, became her fast friends. They sang well together and became a great attraction in Miss Connor's widening ministry. By the summer of 1923 she was preaching to a group at Greenvale, when Catherine McCoy, the Nyack summer student, "happened along" and assisted Margaret in starting a church there. These four churches now occupied Margaret Connor's full time, so that she could range no further afield.[36]

In September 1923, this frail and faithful worker of 47 met with her old pastor who was by then superintendent of the Alliance in Canada. She offered to unite her four churches with the Alliance provided that a young man could be sent to completely take them off her hands, thus allowing her to be free to start new churches! One can imagine the emotion of the situation. Roffe accepted her offer on the spot. Woodward was sent a few weeks later to hold missionary conventions among these new Alliance works and an honest attempt was made to locate a suitable young man to pastor them. Thus, Miss Connor became an important Alliance worker.[37]

In retrospect, the Rader campaign was viewed with considerable disappointment. Luke Rader had proven to be "difficult." Moreover, although the meetings had been well attended in all three locations, a serious financial problem had resulted. Expenses had amounted to $3,700, but offerings for expenses totalled only $3,100. Fortunately, some members of the Alliance Tabernacle in Toronto made up the difference.

Missionary offerings were also disappointing. At Winnipeg, by far the largest centre, only $2,400 had been received. At Edmonton, the smallest city, $3,900 had been given for foreign missions, undoubtedly much of it coming from the members of Beulah Tabernacle. Calgary made the largest offering of $4,700. The total of $11,000 from the three centres was particularly disappointing to Roffe. Western denominationalists of those days considered the prairies of Canada to be their greatest missionary challenge and responsibility.[38] He concluded that the west could not be taken for granted with the east. "The Canadian east and the Canadian west are not alike, to say the least," wrote Roffe, "and it looks as if they never will be."[39]

Despite these negative features of the Rader conventions, there were two very positive consequences. The first involved a new leader. Rev. William Hay (see page 87) had been president of the Baptist Union and Missionary Society of New Zealand.[40] In 1921 he came to Canada, and, being impressed with the spiritual needs of western Canada, settled in Winnipeg and commenced holding services in the Furby Theatre on Portage Avenue.[41]

In December of that year, Roffe first visited western Canada and held meetings in Winnipeg, at which time the two men met. Roffe was much impressed with "the high type of Christian leader" he found in Hay. On his part, Hay found he was "Alliance in doctrine," especially in the matters of divine healing and pre-millennialism.[42]

In October 1923, one month after the completion of the Rader Winnipeg meetings, Hay offered to bring himself and his small Winnipeg work into the Alliance. However, Roffe and the district committee considered that the Alliance was not yet ready to have a work in Winnipeg and that it would be wise for both Hay and the Alliance to learn more about each other before taking such a step. Hay agreed to suspend his struggling work in Winnipeg, to come east and take part in conventions, tent meetings, and to assist in other ways, with the understanding (at least on his part) that he would return to Winnipeg to head up an Alliance work.[43]

The second positive consequence of the Rader conventions was the establishing of a second western church. During the Rader meetings in Calgary, Roffe received an urgent request to reopen the work in that city. An interim committee was appointed, of which Thomas Hughes was treasurer and Dr. Elmer Wright was recording secretary and missionary treasurer. Rev. E. W. Davis of Vermillion, Ohio, accepted a pastoral call and preached his first sermon on October 7, in the Variety Theatre on Eighth Avenue at Second Street East. The new church services were advertised as "undenominational in character, which affords a great field for fellowship among all Christians."[44] In January 1924, the new Calgary congregation relocated to The Basement Tabernacle at 310 Eighth Avenue East.[45] Sunday services were attended by 250 in the morning and up to 500 at night.[46]

Early Western Crises

Back in the spring of 1923, Woodward had intended to accompany Louis Butcher and Charles Malicky, missionaries of the Wayside Mission, on their expedition to the Indians and trappers around Fort Chipewyan. He had not gone with them because of his Edmonton pastoral duties and because of the need for someone to oversee the summer student missionaries about to arrive. During the Rader conventions in September, Butcher related stirring accounts of the work and hardships of missionaries of the "far north."[47] When some questions arose regarding his accountability, Butcher appeared before the district committee in Toronto on October 16, and the Wayside Mission was merged with the Great West Mission, placing Woodward in charge of all missionary work in western Canada. However, as Butcher's plans for the following winter were complete and he had been re-equipped by the Alliance Tabernacle, it was decided that he should leave at once for Fort Chipewyan, with all future plans to be approved by Woodward.[48]

Early in January 1924, Anglican Bishop J. R. Lucas, of the Diocese of Mackenzie River, complained about some pamphlets distributed in the diocese by Butcher, under the name of The Great West Bible Mission of The Christian and Missionary Alliance.* The pamphlets contained criticism of Anglican missions.[49] The incident proved to be a great embarrassment to both Roffe and the Alliance and an official apology was sent to and accepted by Bishop Lucas.[50] However, ensuing investigation into Butcher's conduct raised questions of integrity, and Butcher was dismissed from all connection with the Alliance and the Alliance Tabernacle in Toronto.[51]

Coincident with this situation was another crisis, centred in the new Calgary church. Pastor E. W. Davis and the interim board were unable to resolve deep-seated differences. With Roffe almost constantly on the road directing missionary conventions and Davis refusing to deal with Roffe's assistant, Lionel Watson, communications between the trouble spot and district headquarters broke down and John Woodward was given pro tempore authority to take whatever action he felt was necessary on behalf of the superintendent.

---

* Prior to becoming a missionary of the Wayside Mission, Louis Butcher had taught parochial school at Fort Chipewyan under Bishop Lucas. The two had experienced sharp disagreements.[52]

The result was that Davis's resignation was received and accepted on February 24.[53]

In an attempt to save the church from fragmentation, Woodward called a congregational meeting and officially organized it on February 26. Thomas Hughes was elected chairman of the board, R. Young as recording secretary, and five others as members of the new board.[54]

However, the congregation was still torn by competing loyalties and mistrust. Public meetings ceased. Then half of the congregation declared itself independent of the Alliance and, calling disaffected Butcher as its pastor, began holding services in the hall previously used by the Alliance. Moreover, it used the Alliance name, The Great West Mission. During May and June, unsuccessful attempts were made to install a Rev. Rickard, "a suitable pastor for that difficult place," and then a Rev. R. C. Rodger.[55] But the Calgary situation was beyond redemption. By October, both halves of the original congregation had permanently dissolved. Thus ended Roffe's and Woodward's dream of a Calgary work to spearhead Alliance development in Alberta.

The heart-breaking losses associated with the Butcher and Davis crises and other mounting district pressures caused Roffe to suffer a severe nervous collapse, and his health was never regained during his final year of office. The barriers of distance and time in communication between east and west had become abundantly clear, underlining the necessity of managing western affairs, as far as possible, in the west. As early as May 1924, the district executive committee suggested that "Mr. Woodward be given the office of assistant superintendent for the West," but no action was taken.[56] Six weeks later, the committee requested the district superintendent to pursue the matter with haste.[57] Roffe did present the request to Home Secretary Rev. E. J. Richards, but it was not until December 2 that the board of managers approved the appointment of John Woodward as Assistant Superintendent, West, for the Canadian District.[58]

A New Methodology

Back in the spring of that year, Woodward had pressed on with his plans for expansion in the west. The Great West Mission endeavour had been almost entirely an evangelistic outreach to the homesteaders of the prairies. However needful this work, it was not likely to result in new churches which would in turn evangelize surrounding areas and provide volunteers and money for Alliance missions. It was for these reasons that Roffe and Woodward hoped and prayed for the establishment of churches in the cities and towns. The Alliance was not alone in its interest; indeed, the need to reach cities and towns before the cults did was frequently expressed in western newspapers of those days. As one writer saw it, the cities were Christianity's greatest challenge, as they were the centres of population that would produce the leaders of tomorrow and influence education, politics and commerce.[59]

For some months Woodward had been pondering the best method to reach the towns. Saddlebag preachers, who had proven their worth in evangelizing the homesteaders, were not well suited for town and city evangelism. Perhaps a gospel car was the answer. It could cover distances between towns quickly, carry a tent and other supplies and even provide sleeping accommodations in a pinch.

The idea of a gospel car was not novel to Woodward. Three years previously, Anglican Archdeacon McElheran recommended the use of "motor vans" in country areas "for administering rites," as the homesteaders often lacked church buildings. Four vans were subsequently constructed and from time to time the use of these vans was reported in Edmonton newspapers.[60] Moreover, during the summer of 1923, the Salvation Army commissioned their first "motor chariot" for work on the prairies. Woodward's intent for a gospel car was specifically to evangelize and form churches in the towns. Determining the cost of a one-ton Ford truck chassis, and obtaining a bid to construct the body, he found that $1,060 would provide such a vehicle. Woodward explained his plan to the district committee and publicly presented his financial need on the last night of the Dominion Convention in Toronto. The $400 given was seen as "evidence of [God's] approval," so Woodward decided to "proceed to purchase the car, believing God will send in all funds as required."[61]

Woodward returned to Edmonton and immediately ordered the gospel car, for delivery in six weeks' time. The district tried unsuccessfully to have the balance met from the Home Department extension fund.[62] However, Woodward had more success in his own church. A man came to the Sunday morning service and said, "I've heard about this Gospel Car. Tell me about it." On receiving the details, he wrote out a cheque for $500![63]

The gospel car was delivered on Saturday, July 12, and displayed in front of Beulah Tabernacle. It was announced in the newspapers that the car would be dedicated following the 3 p.m. Sunday service. The ceremony commenced and a large crowd gathered, when Woodward announced that $160 was still required in order to pay in full for the car on the Monday morning. He added that the car must be free of debt before it could be dedicated. An offering which followed amounted to $200, enough to clear the debt, fill the tank and send two young missionaries on their way.[64]

That summer, the six students from Nyack who joined the Great West Mission included Ed Cross and Gordon Skitch. Cross, who had served the previous summer, had just graduated from Nyack and had applied to be a missionary to Ecuador. Gordon Arnold Skitch, born in Gravenhurst, Ontario, in 1900, was converted at the age of 22 in the old Bloor Street Methodist Church in Toronto. He entered Alberta College (Methodist) in Edmonton in 1922. Following his first year, he set out with a party of boys on a boating trip. The venture ended in disaster, with one of the boys being drowned. As a result, Skitch suffered a nervous breakdown. Convalescing in an Edmonton hospital, he was nursed by his future wife, Mabel Railton, from Smithville, Ontario. Both young people had become disillusioned with Methodism, and Mabel suggested they visit Beulah Tabernacle. A lasting bond was formed between Skitch and Woodward. That fall, Gordon Skitch began attending Nyack. On completion of his first year, he attended Council and prayer conference in Toronto, heard Woodward's plea for funds to purchase the gospel car, and returned to Edmonton to work under the Great West Mission.

Cross and Skitch were appointed to be the first crew of the gospel car. On Monday morning, July 14, car and crew were dispatched on a projected 1,200-mile missionary circuit into Saskatchewan, with intended stopovers of one night in each town. By mid-afternoon of the first day, the party arrived in Gwynne, some 45 miles south of Edmonton. The town, consisting of a railway station, grain elevator, general store, pool room, dance hall, community centre and a few houses, had a reputation of being "a centre for a moonshine gang," where it was unsafe for women and girls to venture out after sundown. There seemed to be little hope for a successful gospel service. Nevertheless, the outdoor service commenced with Gordon Skitch mounting the little platform that unfolded from the side of the van and starting to sing gospel hymns. People began to emerge from the stores and houses to listen. Then Ed Cross preached "in no uncertain manner, the story of the cross." There was no heckling, and the townspeople urged the two missionaries to preach again the next day in the community hall. At the close of that second service, several people openly wept their way to the platform for salvation. Again the students were urged to stay, and night after night people came to the Lord.[65]

One man was so deeply convicted of sin that he came back to the car one night, and, wakening the missionaries, asked them to pray with him for forgiveness and salvation. He was gloriously saved, and the following week his wife came to the Lord. A rejoicing storekeeper handed the missionaries the key to his store and told them to help themselves to whatever they wanted.[66]

Instead of staying for only one night, as planned, the gospel team stayed for six weeks—until Skitch had to return to Nyack. Three great baptismal services were held on the banks of the river. At the first, more than sixty autos, besides democrats, buggies and saddle horses arrived and several hundred people witnessed a great Sunday afternoon confession of faith from over 50 baptismal candidates.[67] So great was the impact of their testimonies that another 50 people professed salvation on the spot.

One of those baptized that day was a young man by the name of Reuben Pearson. He told John Woodward after the service that he liked to tinker with electronic equipment and planned to pursue studies in radio. Woodward, himself interested in the possibilities of broadcasting the gospel, gave Pearson a room in his Edmonton basement for a "radio workshop." Within three years, Pearson's technical skills enabled Woodward to commence broadcasting, a most significant factor in Alliance development in the west during the next twenty years.[68]

Halfway through the Gwynne revival, Woodward wrote Roffe that "the Gospel Car is just what I had believed God for," and described the town's response.

> At the first town, Gwynne, the Lord broke up the people on the first night. Some of the hardest men and a good number of young people have come to the Lord. The owner of the dance hall has been saved and will no longer rent his hall for dances. The owner of the pool room is under deep conviction but hesitates because he knows he will have to close his pool room.[69]

To the Canadian Alliance, he reported:

> The itinerary mapped out for the Gospel Car has been cancelled. Recently I paid a visit to Gwynne and literally cried as we drove into the town and saw the autos lined right across the streets, buggies, democrats and saddle horses hitched up, and the people singing the praises of

God in the open air, with the young people forming the choir. I preached one night when it was pouring rain. At the close of the meeting, while some seekers were being dealt with, it was suggested that I give another message. It was by then 10 o'clock, but the people took their seats again and we delivered the second message of the night.[70]

WESTERN CHURCHES ARE BORN

Following the Gwynne revival, Ed Cross, by then having been rejected for missionary service in Ecuador, was persuaded by Woodward to become a full-time worker in western Canada. His assignment was to "consolidate the work at Gwynne on weekends," and to "render valuable assistance in Edmonton" during the week.[71]

The other four Nyack students enlisted during the summer of 1924 continued in the traditional work of the "Alliance cavalry." John Cunningham and Ben Barton covered large areas on horseback. George Moffat started a work at Thorhild, some 50 miles north of Edmonton. When he left for Ecuador in the late summer, the work was put in charge of a Rev. F. W. Williams. In January 1925, Robert Moynan, a son-in-law of the great Presbyterian missionary Jonathan Goforth, took over this work, which in addition to the church at Thorhild, had preaching stations at Teawoods, Goldsboro, Moose Hill and Abee, all within a twelve-mile radius. Raymond Francisco worked an area 50 to 60 miles northeast of Thorhild. He was instrumental in bringing into the Alliance fold an existing small church at Lac LaBiche, with two preaching stations at Grandon and Big Bay. When he returned to Nyack, a Miss A. B. Rose was left in charge.

That summer the Great West Mission also sent out George H. Sinderson, an inexperienced young man from Winnipeg, to Vegreville, 60 miles east of Edmonton. Meetings were held in the town hall, crowned with a missionary convention. "One experience I vividly remember," Sinderson wrote later, "was that I baptized a baby. The parents were anxious to have their baby christened so I obliged. This was my first and last." Sinderson stayed on at Vegreville until December, and as a result, an Alliance church was opened. Mr. and Mrs. R. P. Spies were the mainstays of the work for several years.*

---

* The church at Vegreville continued for seven years. In the Great Depression, when the area had become semi-abandoned, the work was closed. As for George Sinderson, after attending and graduating from the Winnipeg Bible Training School and language study in France, he became a Baptist missionary in Chad for more than 35 years.

In October 1924, Roffe made an attempt to "Canadianize" the jurisdiction of the province of British Columbia, which had been placed under the U.S. Pacific Northwest District since 1914. That province had originally been an important part of the Canadian North-West District formed by Dr. Zimmerman in 1906, headquartered in Vancouver. After Zimmerman returned to Toronto, the affairs of the west were, to at least some extent, looked after by Travelling Superintendent Harold Stephens until his resignation in 1911. Thereafter, New York headquarters and indeed Rev. Simpson personally made a determined but unsuccessful attempt to secure a superintendent for Canada's west, culminating with another unsuccessful plan in 1914 to relieve District Superintendent L. J. Long of local pastoral duties so that he could give some attention to the west. It was at that point that British Columbia came under the jurisdiction of the Pacific Northwest District. Now, some ten years later, although the District of Canada made an attempt to reunite the westernmost province with the rest of Canada, the board of managers ruled against the change, believing that it could be more efficiently administered from Seattle than from Toronto.[72]

Notwithstanding the successes of the summer of 1924, Woodward's heart remained heavy for the cities of western Canada, including Regina. "I would like to see some attempt made with an evangelistic party to get into Regina," he said in a letter to Roffe. "My faith has been rising for that city."

A Foothold is Gained

On October 15, Roffe and Miss Butterfield of Palestine commenced an eight-week missionary convention tour of western Canada. For Roffe it would be an especially unforgettable visit. As events would turn out, it would be his last official visit to the great west land. He was again captivated with the "vision of need" that had sparked the western work in 1921:

> This is our fifth visit to this wonderful Canadian west land and we are once again catching a glimpse of what it costs to glean a harvest. No one thinks of anything but gathering in the wheat. The hum of perhaps two dozen threshers can be heard. Before dawn the whistles sound out their shrill summons and the great work continues on into the night, by the light of great blazing stacks of straw. It is HARVEST

TIME, and all else must give way, while both men and women apply themselves to the one supreme task of gathering in the treasure. Little wonder that we seem as two pygmies before such a scene. The harvest of golden grain calls forth the very best in Canadian farmers. Why, then, is the church guilty of wasting time in frolic and fun, with an even greater harvest on her hands? Western farmers, their wives and their neighbours have a vision of need to harvest grain, but, alas, the church lacks a vision of need to harvest perishing souls.[73]

Roffe and Miss Butterfield conducted eleven conventions, as well as numerous individual meetings. Among the small centres visited was Gwynne. Roffe reports:

There stood Mr. Cross, one of the heroes of the revival, as our train pulled into the small Albertan centre. By 9 o'clock, our meeting was under way. The portable organ played its part, and song sheets sent out from Toronto, helped out. The people, with a look of expectancy, sat on backless benches and eagerly drank in the messages. We thank God for the power of the Holy Ghost, that can revolutionize such a place, hitherto noted for its hardness and opposition to the Gospel. Without doubt this is a miracle performed before our eyes. The missionary offering, something quite new to these babes in Christ, amounted to $291. Already, three young people have commenced Bible school training. We are tempted to ask, can anything in the East produce such a record?

Among the cities, Winnipeg was carefully avoided because of a recent successful Penecostal convention. However, Woodward felt it wise not to ignore Calgary. The Calgary Gospel Mission, under former Alliance missionary to Jamaica Mrs. David McKillop, was host. Although both the accommodation and attendance were small, one important result of the convention was an agreement for an all day meeting to be held monthly in the mission under the direction of Woodward.[74]

As might have been expected, the Third Annual Missionary Convention, convening in Beulah Church, Edmonton, November 9-16, 1924, was the greatest of all the conventions in terms of a

The Vision of Need / 129

4.11
4.11 Gordon Skitch and Ed Cross enact how the gospel will be preached by means of the gospel car, before leaving on their historic first assignment.

4.12
4.12 During a visit to Gwynne, Alberta, John Woodward enjoys lunch with the crew of the gospel car.

130 / *The Vision of Need*

4.13 A large crowd gathers for a baptismal service near Gwynne, Alberta, during the summer of 1924.

4.14 Ed Cross makes a point from the pulpit of Beulah Tabernacle, Edmonton, Alberta, during the autumn of 1924.

4.15 A former Anglican building, moved to the corner of 107th Avenue and 98th Street, Edmonton, was, with additions, the home of the Beulah congregation from December 1923 until April 1956.

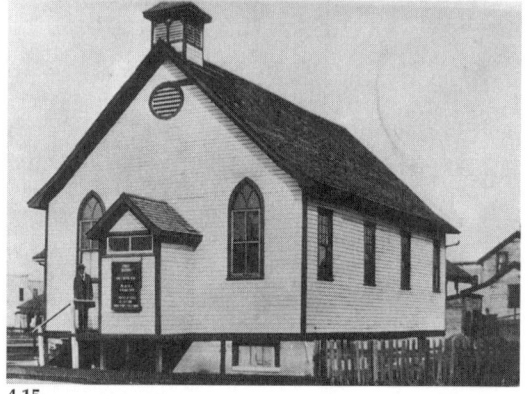

missionary collection of $2,033. Home Secretary E. J. Richards was present for two days and special music was supplied by the Stephenson sisters. Of historic significance, the First Western Workers Prayer Conference was held during the missionary convention.[75]*

Without doubt, the most significant western convention in the fall of 1924 was held in Regina. For three years Roffe had tried to find a nucleus of interest in that city and to make arrangements with some friendly church to use its sanctuary for an Alliance convention. Slowly but slowly word had spread through prairie cities and towns that the Alliance was collecting money for the support of foreign missions. Westerners were convinced that the most urgent missionary need of all lay at western doorsteps, and that, morally, money raised in the west for missions should be spent to alleviate the desperate spiritual need of the settlers. Secondly, the issue of church union was then at its crisis stage and was consuming denominational attention. Any group that might be viewed as a possible threat to the dream of a national union church was either ignored or treated with contempt. Lastly, as modernism continued to replace evangelicalism in the denominations, a cleavage with external "fundamentalist" groups became inevitable. By the summer of 1924, Woodward reported to Roffe that even in Edmonton, an icy curtain of isolation had descended. "We are no longer welcome in either McDougal Methodist or First Presbyterian churches," he wrote.[76]

It was therefore a matter of rejoicing when Roffe received a letter from Central Church of Christ at the corner of 15th Avenue and Retallack Street, Regina, to say that the Alliance was welcome to hold its proposed one-week convention in their sanctuary. The services were held three times each Sunday and twice on each weekday. The opening Sunday, November 30, brought attendances of 55 in the morning, 35 in the afternoon and 75 at night. The small numbers left Roffe somewhat dubious after the first day, but his hopes mounted as he reported that at least one man, F. M. Still, and his wife, were solidly behind the idea of forming a permanent Alliance work in Regina. Throughout the week, attendance and interest grew, and Roffe was able to write that people were "beginning to make inquiries regarding the future." Then came the special news: "A spiritually minded brother has just come in from about 90 miles away to attend the meetings and to talk about an Alliance work in Regina. He and two

---

* This First Western Workers Prayer Conference should not be confused with the First Western Canadian District Workers' Prayer Conference, of October 1-4, 1925.

other laymen are holding meetings in three other points in the country. If we had a man in Regina, he would be able to visit [these places]." The "spiritually-minded brother" was Joseph C. Spratt of Sprattsville and Girvin. He would prove to be a great co-worker for several years to come.

As the convention moved toward its closing Sunday, Roffe became convinced "that Sunday will be the test day, when we put on our full missionary program."[77] He later reported on that closing service:

> For some hours before the closing day, at which we had decided to have a full missionary program we became conscious of approaching conflict. The closing Sunday morning service had not advanced far when one sensed a spirit of prejudice. Principalities and powers were engaged in conflict and ere long we were facing a wall of opposition against our blessed missionary propaganda. One experienced a strong impulse to dispose of the idea of a missionary offering. However, prayer was answered and the pledge cards distributed. Then, we became joyfully conscious that the cold icy feeling was melting before our eyes, prejudice was giving way to sympathetic interest, and lo, an up-to-date miracle was performed on this the occasion of our first convention in the City of Regina, by an offering for world evangelization amounting to $1782 [second only to Edmonton]. The vision had come and the vision was honoured. When the result was finally announced, the congregation stood and sang with deeply stirred hearts, "Praise God from whom all blessings flow."[78]

Before the convention team left Regina, the little group of Alliance devotees, which by then included Duncan Campbell and his wife, was formed into a prayer committee to pray together, work together and maintain together a growing Alliance testimony in Regina.[79] Just three months later, the prayer committee felt strong enough to launch out with a full program of church services. On Sunday, March 8, 1925, the first regular church services commenced meeting on Victoria Avenue opposite the Sherwood Building. Various laymen, including Joe Spratt, spoke at the services, augmented occasionally with a visiting clergyman or missionary. In April, the fledgling church became the Alliance Mission, and when Woodward visited in May, he organized it into an official branch of the Alliance. In August, the Alliance Mission relocated to 1829 Rose Street.

At the close of the first Regina convention, Roffe returned to his desk in Toronto. As he bid farewell to the prairies officially for the last time, he was firmly convinced of the wisdom of striving to obtain more workers, so that the burgeoning opportunities of the west might be grasped before they were lost. But where, he mused, could the needed workers be found? That was his sad concern as he left the west. Writing down his impressions, he stated:

> We are persuaded beyond all questioning that The Christian and Missionary Alliance possesses a spiritual gold mine in this great Canadian North-West land. But, where are the men to work it? The ordinary type of worker will never fit into the situation. Men prepared to rough it for the Master's sake are greatly needed—none other need apply.[80]

Shortly after his return to Toronto, District Superintendent Roffe suffered another major nervous collapse and Home Secretary E. J. Richards tried to persuade him that the task of being superintendent for all Canada was too much for him. Richards informed Roffe of his intention to divide Canada into three districts, and offered him the superintendency of the new Western Canadian District, because "that is the area about which he has talked and written with such enthusiasm." Roffe turned down the offer because of family commitments in Gravenhurst, his poor health which would not permit him to care for a district that was 72 hours away from his home, and because he was too old a man to do justice to the tremendous possibilities of the western prairies.[81]

In his final report to the Home Secretary, Roffe was pleased to report that in western Canada, in 1924, four new branches and eight out-stations had been established.

Roffe had played a major role in the rebirth of the Alliance in western Canada and his vision of evangelistic need would characterize the new district for many years to come.

REFERENCES

1. Edmund H. Oliver, *His Dominion of Canada* (Toronto: The United Church of Canada, 1932), p. XII.
2. William E. Mann, *Sect, Cult and Church in Alberta* (Toronto: University of Toronto Press, 1955), pp. 9-26.

3. *Christian Guardian*, Toronto, 26 Dec 1923, p. 7.
4. J.W. Woodward, "History of the Western Canadian District of The Christian and Missionary Alliance" (taped, 1971), The Call.
5. *Edmonton Journal*, 27 Oct 1923, p. 12; 1 Dec, p. 23.
6. Ibid., 23 Nov 1912, p. 20; 25 Nov, p. 15; 27 Nov, p. 10.
7. Ibid., 25 Jun 1921, p. 8.
8. J. W. Woodward, "Interview with Mrs. Pearl Eckert" (taped 12 Jun 1978).
9. "History of the Western Canadian District," The Call.
10. J. H. Woodward, "History of Beulah Church," undated.
11. "History of the Western Canadian District," The Call.
12. Ibid.
13. Ibid.
14. *Alliance Weekly*, 14 Jan 1922, p. 693.
15. Ibid., pp. 699, 702.
16. *The News of News* (Parkdale Tabernacle), Dec 1921, p. 3.
17. District of Canada, Minutes, 24 Mar 1922.
18. Ibid.
19. *Alliance Weekly*, 26 Aug 1922, p. 378.
20. Ibid., 5 Aug 1922, p. 332.
21. "History of the Western Canadian District," The Methods.
22. District of Canada, Minutes, 2 Feb 1923.
23. "History of the Western Canadian District," The Message.
24. *Alliance Weekly*, 20 Jan 1923, p. 702.
25. District of Canada, Minutes, 2 Feb 1923.
26. *Footprints*, p. 326.
27. *Calgary Herald*, 8 Aug 1908, p. 8; 26 Sep, p. 2; 10 Oct, p. 2; 5 Dec, p. 7; 28 Jan 1909, p. 11.
28. District of Canada, Minutes, 2 Feb 1923.
29. The Word of Life (Toronto), Sep 1923, p. 9; *Alliance Weekly*, 12 May 1923, p. 182.
30. *Alliance Weekly*, 7 Jul 1923, p. 311.
31. Memoirs of Mrs. Muriel Moffat, Jul 1984.
32. *Alliance Weekly*, 8 Sep 1923, p. 454.
33. District of Canada files, 1923.
34. District of Canada, Minutes, 31 Aug 1923, p. 2.
35. Board of Managers, Minutes, 30 Nov 1923.
36. District of Canada, Minutes, 16 Oct 1923; 1 Nov 1923; *Alliance Weekly*, 15 Dec 1923, p. 690.
37. District of Canada, Minutes, 16 Oct 1923; 2 Nov 1923; S.G. Keller "The Gospel on the Prairies," booklet.
38. District of Canada, Minutes, 16 Oct 1923; *Edmonton Journal*, 18 Sep 1923, p. 8; 19 Sep, p. 7; 20 Sep, p. 20; 21 Sep, p. 6; 22 Sep, p. 6; *Calgary Herald*, 22 Sep 1923, p. 6;

29 Sep, p. 20; *Winnipeg Tribune*, 29 Sep 1923, p. 11; 6 Oct, p. 10; *Alliance Weekly*, 20 Oct 1923, p. 538; 10 Nov, p. 586; 24 Nov, p. 628.
39. *Alliance Weekly*, 22 Mar 1924, p. 58.
40. *Alliance Weekly*, 13 Mar 1926, p. 179; *Prophet*, Jan 1924, p. 4.
41. *Winnipeg Tribune*, 3 Dec 1921, p. 18.
42. Ibid.
43. District of Canada, Minutes, 1 Nov 1923, p. 3; *Winnipeg Tribune*, 10 Nov 1923, p. 17.
44. *Calgary Herald*, 6 Oct 1923, p. 16; 13 Oct 1923, p. 5; 22 Oct 1923, p. 10; 24 Oct 1923, p. 6; *Alliance Weekly*, 10 Nov 1923, p. 586; 22 Dec 1923, p. 7.
45. *Calgary Herald*, 5 Jan 1924, p. 5; 2 Feb 1924, p. 16.
46. *Alliance Weekly*, 15 Mar 1924, p. 42.
47. Ibid., 1 Sep 1923, p. 434.
48. District of Canada, Minutes, 16 Oct 1923; ibid., Correspondence, Roffe to Lucas, 6 Feb 1924.
49. Ibid., Lucas to O'Meara, 12 Jan 1924; ibid., Lucas to Richardson, 4 Feb 1924; ibid., Lucas to Roffe, 27 Feb 1924.
50. Ibid., Woodward to Roffe, 1 Mar 1924; ibid., Roffe to Lucas, 4 Apr 1924; ibid., Minutes, 4 Feb 1924.
51. Ibid., Correspondence, Watson to H.B. Co., 4 Apr 1924; ibid., Roffe to Lucas, 4 Apr 1924; ibid., Watson to Woodward, 4 Apr 1924; ibid., Watson to Butcher, 9 Apr 1924.
52. Ibid., Lucas to Richardson, 4 Feb 1924.
53. Ibid., Correspondence, Davis to Roffe, 8 Feb 1924; ibid., Woodward to Watson, 10 Feb 1924; ibid., Davis to Roffe, 12 Feb 1924; ibid., Davis to Woodward, 20 Feb 1924; 21 Feb 1924; ibid., Davis to Roffe, 22 Feb 1924; ibid., Woodward to Watson, 27 Feb 1924.
54. Ibid., Woodward to Davis, 21 Feb 1924; ibid., Woodward to Roffe, 22 Feb 1924; ibid., Woodward to Watson, 27 Feb 1924.
55. Ibid., Watson to Wright, 2 May 1924; ibid., Minutes, 16 Jun 1924.
56. Ibid., 31 May 1924.
57. Ibid., 14 Jul 1924.
58. Home Department, 2 Dec 1924; Board of Managers, 2 Dec 1924.
59. *Edmonton Journal*, 27 May 1928, p. 8.
60. Ibid., 18 Jun 1921, p. 15.
61. *The Canadian Alliance*, Jul 1924, p. 10; District Records, 14 Jul 1924, p. 5.
62. Ibid., 16 Jun 1924.
63. Reminiscences of J. H. Woodward, 1971.
64. Ibid.
65. *The Canadian Alliance*, Sep 1924, pp. 2, 3.
66. Ibid.
67. A. W. Roffe, "Five Thousand Miles in Answer to Prayer," 1924, pp. 22, 23; *Alliance Weekly*, 24 Jun 1925, p. 62.

68. "History of Western Canadian District," The Method, The Finances, The Message.
69. District of Canada, Correspondence, Woodward to Roffe, 19 Aug 1924.
70. *The Canadian Alliance*, Sep 1924, p. 3.
71. District of Canada, Correspondence, Woodward to Roffe, 19 Aug 1924.
72. District of Canada, Records, 30 Oct 1924.
73. A. W. Roffe, "Five Thousand Miles in Answer to Prayer," 1924, pp. 7, 17.
74. *The Alliance Weekly*, 7 Feb 1925, p. 94.
75. Ibid., 24 Jan 1925, p. 62; *Edmonton Journal*, 8 Nov 1924, p. 8.
76. District of Canada, Correspondence, Woodward to Watson, 17 Jul 1924.
77. Ibid., Roffe to Woodward, 4 Dec 1924; *The Alliance Weekly*, 7 Feb 1925, p. 94; *Regina Leader Post*, 29 Nov 1924, p. 20; 6 Dec 1924, p. 18.
78. A. W. Roffe, "Five Thousand Miles in Answer to Prayer," 1924, pp. 32, 33.
79. *The Alliance Witness*, 7 Feb 1925, p. 94.
80. A. W. Roffe, "Five Thousand Miles in Answer to Prayer," 1924, p. 35; Annual Report, May 1925, p. 158.
81. Board of Managers, Correspondence, Richards to "My dear brother," 16 Mar 1925; District of Canada, Correspondence, Watson to Woodward, 11 Apr 1925.

CHAPTER FIVE

Conflict of Interest

Exactly three weeks after the District of Canada was divided in three, the great Canadian controversy over church union reached its climax on June 10, 1925. On that day, the United Church of Canada came into being. To unionist Dr. George C. Pigeon, it was "the greatest spiritual enterprise of one hundred years."[1] To dissident Dr. Ephraim Scott, it was "our Country's greatest national crime."[2]

At the height of the turbulent negotiations, the unionists had expressed the hope that the spirit of unity might "take shape in a church which may fittingly be described as national."[3] This thought was echoed in a resolution adopted at the first Council of the United Church, expressing the desire "that the present union . . . may under the Providence of God pave the way for further unions of the churches of Christ."[4] Canada was hailed by the media and from many pulpits as a sort of morning star of world cross-confessional church union.[5] However, to many thousands of denominationalists it was the evening star of their hopes, as they now found themselves disinherited of their distinctive faiths and church polities.

The Aftermath of Union

Since 1925, the persistence of divergent views within denominations and the continuing emergence of new sects and cults has seemingly negated all serious hope of reversing the fragmentation of Protestant Christianity in Canada. Nor do church historians continue to refer to the "spirit of 1925" in lofty terms. S. D. Clark, writing in 1948, saw the union as "a reflection of the growing dominance of secular values associated with politics and big business."[6] N. Keith Clifford, writing in 1985, described the union as a "rift between theological liberals and conservatives"[7]—a view long held by non-ecumenical conservatives. In any event, there has been little disagreement about the immediate results of the union of 1925. As C. E. Silcox wrote, the union left a "legacy of bitterness which separated friends and broke churches, communities and the nation at large into fighting factions."[8]

Ultimately, about one third of the Presbyterians, some 154,000 of them, refused to become part of the United Church. Believing that it was beyond the powers of the federal government to legislate their church out of existence, they championed a claim to a continuing Presbyterian Church. Losing more than 80 percent of their church buildings and an overwhelming proportion of their clergy, theirs was no small task to regroup and rebuild. The challenge required their utmost devotion. As a result, during the first decade following 1925, Presbyterians became ingrown, paying little attention to external theological and ecclesiastical currents. Fourteen years later they were rewarded for their persistence. The United Church of Canada Act was altered to permit the continuing Presbyterians to legally call themselves the Presbyterian Church of Canada.

Among the Congregational churches, only eight rejected union.* However, within the uniting Congregational churches there were dissenting members who in time would find new church homes, usually among independent churches holding to Reformed doctrines.

All Methodist churches entered the union. Opposition was never very visible or threatening during the years of negotiation, as Methodist polities were such as to make it difficult to organize collective resistance. From a unionist perspective, historians of the United Church of Canada, almost without exception, have regarded Methodist losses associated with the union issue hardly worth mentioning.** However, there were significant numbers of former Meth-

---

* Of the eight Congregational churches that refused to enter the union, it is interesting to note that Olivet Church, Toronto (formerly Hazelton Avenue Church), had sat under the ministry of Rev. John Salmon, while Pine Grove and Humber Summit churches had been ministered to by Rev. George Blackett. In addition, Bethel Church, Kingston, had been strongly influenced by Salmon, and many of its members had formed an Alliance fraternal branch a quarter of a century earlier.

** Dr. S. D. Chown, the final general superintendent of the Methodist Church, viewed Methodist opposition to union as being significant only in its provision of "interesting material for a psychological study of the contagion of prejudice."[9]

odists who viewed the union as a fatal compromise with truth, that could only lead to the loss of a precious Methodist heritage. C. E. Silcox has cautiously admitted that "querulous voices" were sometimes raised to protest the demise of distinctive Methodist doctrines, and that "a certain leakage... to Pentecostal and allied movements" had occurred.[10] Nevertheless, former Methodists would not lightly sever their historic ties. There would be few mass or even group withdrawals. Most of the unhappy former Methodists would remain in their United Churches to be the "salt," until, one by one, family by family, over the next decade or so, they would find new church homes among the Salvationist, Pentecostal, Alliance, Nazarene, Free Methodist and other sects of the holiness tradition. Describing the sects that did, in fact, provide new church homes for post-union discontents, Rev. A. C. Forrest of the United Church of Canada wrote:

> Like our forefathers, the sects may be narrow and puritanical, fundamentalist, pharisaic... but they use, often with clear understanding, the great old theological terms of salvation, atonement, sanctification, plus a few rather new and obscure ones.... And they have standards, which although negative, set their followers apart from the world.[11]

Missed Opportunity

Such, then, was the ecclesiastical environment in which the three new Canadian districts of The Christian and Missionary Alliance began to function in May 1925. Home Secretary E. J. Richards, residing in New York, was technically superintendent of the Central Canadian District, and Lionel Watson, in Toronto, was his assistant. It was impossible for Richards, travelling around the continent most of the time, to function as district superintendent. Lionel Watson had proved himself to be an able administrator. But he was not a preacher, and he could not possibly be expected to conduct the missionary conventions as Roffe had done, which were so vital to the prevailing Alliance character. The work in Ontario alone was large enough to keep him occupied with administrative duties. By the decision of the Home Department to create an Eastern Canadian District, the burden of trying to develop the potential of the maritime provinces had been lifted from his shoulders. But not for long!

In June, Home Secretary Richards advised Watson that on closer scrutiny of the records it had been noted that current missionary offerings from the maritimes would not justify the appointment of a separate superintendent for the eastern provinces. Until such offerings increased, the concept of an Eastern Canadian District was to be held intact, but work in the maritimes would have to be carried out by the Central Canadian District. The combined operation would be known as "The Eastern and Central Canadian Districts."*

The news was devastating to Watson. In an impassioned response to Richards, he pleaded for the Alliance cause in Central and Eastern Canada. Two full-time superintendents were needed, he said, if the uniquely developing opportunities were not to be lost to other denominations. If two superintendents were impossible, then one full-time aggressive superintendent was imperative. "If I see things correctly," he wrote, "the area needs an exceptionally strong man who will go about and put new life and energy into the branches. . . . I want to see a definite program of advance, which, under present arrangements I can not see." Watson continued,

> In view of this situation, do you not think it possible to assign Mr. Jago** as temporary superintendent? . . . He is quite willing to consider the question. Among the advantages are his energy and perseverance, and the fact that he comes from the Maritime Provinces and would understand Easterners would be of great help to us. . . . I do not know any other man who could fill the bill. . . . I know, of course, that he is pastor of a small church in the United States, but it seems to me that for the sake of the Alliance as a whole, it is vastly more important that he should be handling an important district like this, rather than a little church. . . . When all the circumstances are considered, there is no place as important to the Alliance or its missionary work than here in Canada at the present time. . . . If the Board wants to receive [missionary] support from Canada, it had better consider us as special, this time. Otherwise Canada will fall down badly in the missionary end of it.[12]

---

* For three or four years the title of "Eastern and Central Canadian Districts" was rigorously maintained. By then it became plain to all that there would be no separate Eastern Canadian District, and the "s" was dropped.

** Rev. E. O. Jago, a former missionary to Argentina, was married to Mary E. Thompson of Avening, Ontario, sister of Rev. A. E. Thompson, Dr. Simpson's biographer.

As Lionel Watson saw it, in heavily over-churched eastern and central Canada, emerging from a national ecclesiastical upheaval, Alliance policy was out-of-tune with the circumstances. For some time to come, the chief source of new Alliance members would be from those leaving their denominational churches. They would not be content to simply belong to a supply base for Alliance foreign missions, but would be looking for new church homes, where homeland as well as foreign responsibilities were recognized, and where doctrinal emphases were compatible with their own. Watson described the situation as "the churchianity of Canadians which does not obtain in the United States."[13]

Watson's advice and warning went unheeded. No one was appointed to be resident superintendent of central or eastern Canada for the next year. Thus, the maritimes were totally neglected and central Canada was inadequately covered at a time of greatest need and greatest opportunity for the Alliance to become a significant force in Canadian church life.

A QUESTION OF PRIORITIES

The apparent lack of interest or understanding for the Canadian situation stemmed from a conflict of interest regarding priorities. During its early years, the Alliance had held that its "primary objective" was an every member experience in the truths of salvation and the deeper spiritual life. This was considered to be basic and causative in the pursuit of the "ultimate objective" of evangelism at home and abroad. In the course of years, foreign missions had, for many, become the primary and causative objective. The fraternal branch, unhampered by church responsibilities and eminently suited to leading its membership into the experience of the deeper spiritual life, had become the church branch, better suited to raising missionary support. However, of necessity, the advent of the church branch brought with it church responsibilities which the Alliance was reticent to accept.

The following minute, entered six months before the United Church of Canada came into being, indicates the reaction of the Home Department to the plight of Canadian church people.

> It is impossible to overestimate the wide open doors that are before us in Canada at this time. The church union is going to leave hundreds of vacant church buildings as well

as thousands of people hungry for full gospel truth, and with no church home. The opportunities are simply boundless. With the right kind of men available for deputational work, hundreds of these [opportunities] are open before us, and our missionary appeal never fails to bring a hearty response. We covet the prayers of the Board of Managers that suitable workers may be secured to tour this great Dominion, to bring in resources for our missionary enterprise.[14]

Among those opposing this widespread tendency of the early 1920s to see only foreign opportunity in domestic need was the editor of the *Alliance Weekly*, who in 1924 wrote, "The pioneer vision of the Alliance applies to the home field as well as the foreign. There is much virgin soil to be occupied in the homeland, and it should be the purpose and plan of every worker to push out into new territory."[15]

The aura of uncertainty surrounding Alliance priorities characteristic of the presidencies of Paul Rader and Frederick Senft came to an end in May 1926 with the election of Harry Shuman to the top Alliance position. A quiet and hard-working man, Shuman was possessed of firm convictions and the ability to express them unambiguously. Henceforth it would be made crystal clear that the first and causative Alliance priority would be foreign missions. In his address to the Council of 1928 President Shuman stated, "The task of the Home Department is to enlarge the home base so as to provide missionary funds in such an amount that no call for reinforcements shall go unanswered."[16] One year later he reinforced this policy by telling Council, "The work at home, both in its general administration and in the ministry of districts and branches should be planned with a view to contributing in the largest possible way to the all-important work of spreading the gospel in the regions beyond."[17] Neither of these statements indicated any concern for the experience of deeper life truths in the lives of the supporters of Alliance foreign missions, or for the witness of the gospel of salvation at home, or for Alliance responsibility for the nurture of the homeland church.

Rev. G. Vernor Brown became Home Secretary in 1929, and in a letter to all district conferences, he echoed the president's first priority of foreign missions and coined the slogan, "When missionary effort thrives, the home work thrives with it." He then urged all districts to recognize and apply "this vital principle." As a warning to any who might think otherwise, he added, "The enlargement and stability of our home base will be measured by the breadth and sacrificial character of our missionary vision."

The Alliance of the 1920s wanted to enjoy the benefits without accepting the responsibilities of a supporting homeland church. The views of Shuman and Brown regarding the subservience of homeland to foreign work constituted a critical departure from Simpson's early concept of the objectives and priorities for his movement (see pages 15 and 16). Some years later, President Shuman modified his earlier bias, stating that the development of the home work was of major importance, that the teaching and experience of Fourfold Gospel truth should be basic, and that every department of the society should perpetuate the movement's true characteristics of message and mission.[18] However, the earlier unbalanced emphasis on foreign missions that had been expressed on many occasions by many protagonists had, by that time, become entrenched in Alliance thought and continued to dominate Alliance strategy throughout the United States and eastern Canada, stunting homeland growth. For eastern Canada, from the consummation of church union until after the end of World War II (except for a brief interlude during the superintendency of J. D. Williams), the growth of Alliance churches virtually stagnated in a period of unparalleled opportunity for churches of the holiness tradition.*

Some groups, particularly the Pentecostals, initiated programs to increase the number of their churches and spread their doctrines, together with a full missions program. They would reap most of the fruits of the church union fall-out during the inter-war period.

MONTREAL INITIATIVES

In May 1925, Watson and Pastor Fitch of the Ottawa Gospel Tabernacle obtained the services of ten students from the Missionary Training Institute in Nyack to participate in a series of meetings throughout the Ottawa Valley. The group ministered to an estimated

---

* In the United States, between 1919 and 1929, the Alliance experienced substantial growth. However, from 1929 to 1939 the number of Alliance churches remained almost static. In the Eastern and Central Canadian District, the number of churches actually decreased from 23 to 22 between 1930 and 1947. During the same period in the Western Canadian District, where high priority was given to evangelization of the thinly churched population, the number of churches increased from 12 to 64. For the Pentecostals, who gave top priority to church planting, the number of their churches throughout Canada rose from 70 to 475 for the same period.

total of 12,000 people, chiefly through public meetings.[19] Many in these meetings enquired about Alliance doctrines and activities and where the nearest Alliance church was located or was planned.

Of particular interest was a development in Montreal. The reestablishment of an annual Montreal convention in 1922 had rekindled the interest of former fraternal branch members. As the church union crisis approached, the convention also attracted the interest of unhappy denominationalists. One of the principal reasons for church union was to decrease church competition, thus effecting an economy of church buildings and operating costs. On the very birthday of the United Church of Canada, what had been Dominion Square Methodist Church* and Douglas Methodist Church officially amalgamated and relocated to Westmount, becoming Dominion-Douglas United Church. Several of their downtown members, dissatisfied over church union and not prepared to make the move to Westmount, began to look for a new church home. A group of these former Methodists asked district headquarters for information about Alliance doctrines and enquired if the Alliance was prepared to open a church in downtown Montreal. Watson's reply is not extant but early in July George and Ruth Beach of Akron, Ohio, were pulled out of the Ottawa Valley group and dispatched to Montreal to look into the situation.

On July 15 a meeting of interested parties was held in the Friendly Home (Rene Levesque Boulevard near Guy Street). Some came from Onward Mission in Verdun, some from churches in Notre Dame de Grace (west end), some from downtown churches and one or two from the north end of the city. The big question asked of Beach was, "Is The Christian and Missionary Alliance really going to back a church in Montreal at this time?"[20] Beach was assured that if the Alliance really meant business this time, he could expect to receive the backing of John Fraser, superintendent of Welcome Hall Mission; Hannah Smith, matron of the Friendly Home (both in downtown Montreal); and M. R. Middleton, superintendent of Onward Mission in Verdun. There was even talk of Onward Mission being "run under the auspices of The Christian and Missionary Alliance."[21]

Divergent views on the location of an Alliance church were evident. However, on that date, Beach organized an official branch of

---

* It was in the Dominion Square Methodist Church that in September 1891 the first Alliance convention in Montreal was held. On that occasion, a fraternal branch was organized.

the Alliance, with a charter membership of 25 and an executive committee of six. William McEwan was elected secretary and Fred Sparke treasurer, and Beach became the pastor.[22]

The problem of location for the new work could not be resolved by democratic means. It appears that Beach finally made the decision where to locate downtown. The old Douglas Methodist Church building at the corner of St. Catherine and Chomedy Streets was rented "for a very reasonable fee" and became the home of the first church of the Alliance in Quebec.

The need to secure the work by a series of special meetings with popular speakers was recognized by both Beach and Watson. In September, Beach appealed to Watson, "I request a loan of $200 to start the work in Montreal. I must have a strong Bible teacher for one week of services, to be followed with a strong evangelistic campaign, if we are to establish this work." The loan was granted, several campaigns were planned and even advertised, but, for various reasons, the speakers backed out, leaving Beach to his own devices.[23] The congregation did not grow and operational debts increased. Of much concern was the fact that the Pentecostals were conducting a thriving work a few blocks away on Drummond Street, under Pastor Charles Baker, a dynamic pulpiteer and former popular Methodist lay preacher.

In November of that year (1925) Beach lamented to Watson, "The people here have supported the foreign work of the Alliance for years. Now, they feel that a little interest and help is due them in starting a local work in Montreal."[24] The small congregation could do little more than pay the rent for the church building. David J. Fant, the railroad engineer from Atlanta, addressed some meetings in Montreal and reported his observations to both the Home Secretary and Watson:

> They have a fine young man and his wife in charge of the work, and a splendid committee. The old Methodist church building is in first class repair and is located on one of the most public thoroughfares in the city. They could not possibly obtain a location like this elsewhere for anything like what they are paying. However, they are unable to support Mr. Beach with the other expenses. During the two weeks I was there, he received no support at all, from any source. It is absolutely impossible for him to continue

unless he gets a little financial help. It seems to me that it is now or never for Montreal. While I know the C. & M.A. is pressed for funds, I believe that an investment of a little money for just a few months would bring back a hundredfold in missionary money.[25]

The Pentecostal people are flourishing a short distance away, and we can do it too if the work is pressed at this time. We can not depend on the people who will turn up for special meetings. We must build with those people who are committed to the regular services.[26]

David Fant had put his finger on the crux of a general problem. The people who showed up for conventions provided most of the money received for Alliance missions, but the burden of church establishment and support had to be borne by the faithful who were committed to the regular church functions. Especially during the formative period of a new work, expenses sometimes exceeded means. However, the Alliance, which was telling itself that it was first and foremost a foreign missions society, was reluctant to divert monies received for missions to assist struggling new congregations, even at a time of unparalleled opportunity to expand the home base.

The downtown work in Montreal struggled on with little encouragement and no further financial assistance from the district or the Home Department. In May 1926, unable to put bread on the table or pay his rent, Beach resigned his charge. When Watson's attempts to obtain another pastor failed, some of the members switched to the Pentecostal work, and the lease on the Methodist church building had to be terminated.[27]

Over the next 31 years of stops and starts the Montreal Central work found temporary havens in the Friendly Home, downtown; in a house on University Street, downtown; in a store on Victoria Avenue, Westmount; in a store on Sherbrooke Street in the Notre Dame de Grace district of the west end; and finally in the YMCA on Drummond Street, downtown. The heroic effort was officially terminated in 1957. Outstanding among all others in terms of faithful persistence and undimmed vision of a central work in Montreal was Marjorie Webster, the indefatigable branch secretary for 25 years.

The gloomy procession of events in connection with the Montreal Central work did not end Alliance opportunities for the city. At the very time that Beach resigned his downtown charge, a new drama was unfolding in the north end.

Church union had left the former Methodist congregation of Shaw Memorial United Church much divided and without a minister. On February 1, 1926, the Rev. Albert Hinton arrived and preached his first sermon to his new charge.* A kindly and friendly man, Hinton gave great promise of being able to bind up congregational wounds, especially those of the evangelical minority. However, one of his first sermons clearly revealed his commitment to Darwinian theories, prompting some twenty members to "come out from among them." Prominent among these seceders were the families of William Duckworth, John (Jack) Richards, P. Dobie, and John Meadows. Within a few days a group of fourteen adults met in the Duckworth home to discuss what they should do about a new church. The general preference was to become a new Methodist church, but this was clearly no longer possible. It was resolved that the group must remain together and that they would seek the Lord's will in the matter. To this end, Duckworth was asked to determine if a certain Fred Sparke would agree to conduct weekly prayer and Bible study meetings.

Born in 1895 in Plymouth, England, of Methodist parents, Frederick W. Sparke was converted at his mother's knee, when eleven years of age. The family emigrated in 1912, settling in the north end of Montreal and becoming members of the Delorimier Street Methodist Church. Fred became an accountant. He also became a leader in the Epworth League,** and a lay preacher. By the early 1920s, Canadian Methodism was fast succumbing to modernism, and this, together with the rising controversy over church union caused Sparke to feel increasingly alienated from the denomination of his heritage. He began to look elsewhere for opportunities of Christian service which brought him in contact with John Fraser, superintendent of Welcome Hall Mission. Roffe commenced holding annual missionary conventions in Montreal in 1922, and it was to one of these early annual conventions that Fraser invited Sparke and at which Sparke made his first contacts with the Alliance.

At the third annual conference in February 1924, Sparke's attention was riveted by Ethel Roffe's convincing testimony of healing from advanced tuberculosis. As Sparke saw it, here was a new emphasis on God's purposes for His church. As a result of that

---

* Born in England, Albert Hinton had been a stone mason in his early years. He is said to have done some fine work in connection with a restoration of part of Windsor Castle.

** The Epworth League was a society of young people in the Methodist Church. Its purpose was to "promote intelligent and loyal piety in the youth of the church; to aid them in attaining purity of heart and growth in grace; to train them in works of mercy and help."

testimony, Sparke immediately examined Simpson's published works, and compared his doctrine with that once espoused by his Methodist tradition. He concluded that the Fourfold Gospel was the answer to decaying Methodism. When Beach called a meeting for all those interested in founding an Alliance church in Montreal, Sparke was present. He not only became a member of the Alliance and its Montreal Central branch, but was elected as its first treasurer. Now, in the spring of 1926, Beach was leaving and it looked like the downtown work was collapsing. While pondering these uncertainties William Duckworth asked him to lead the weekly prayer and Bible study meetings in his north end home. Sparke believed that this was God's opportunity for him and he accepted the challenge.[28]

Sparke was no stranger among his little class, as he and his relatives had often attended services in the Shaw Memorial Church. He recommended affiliation with the Alliance, and a letter to district headquarters brought Lionel Watson to Montreal. A hall over a garage on Beaubien Street near Christophe Colombe Avenue was rented and the first church services commenced on May 1, 1926, with 35 in attendance at morning worship, 18 at Sunday school and 100 at the evening service. In the afternoon, the Alliance Gospel Hall was organized with 25 charter members. Fred Sparke was called as its first pastor (unpaid); P. Dobie was elected treasurer; Harold Meadows, secretary; and William Duckworth, chairman of the board and Sunday school superintendent. That autumn, the church held its first missionary convention and $700 was received to outfit Miss Beuler (later Mrs. Schelander) for work in India. By that time, Sunday morning attendance had grown to 85 and Sunday school to 72. Thus was a "permanent" Alliance work established in Montreal.[29] While there were many other locations in eastern Canada where erstwhile Methodists joined Alliance ranks, the two Montreal churches were unique. In particular, the north end work was the only case where, as a result of the church union controversies, a core of former Methodists formed an independent church, which then affiliated with the Alliance.

TURMOIL ON CHRISTIE STREET

The flow of former Methodists into the Alliance churches of central and eastern Canada implanted a Methodistic quality to the district. As membership grew more by transfer than by conversion, an emphasis developed for holiness teaching and living. High standards for Christian conduct tended to set Alliance churches apart from some other evangelical churches. These characteristics, together with conservative tastes for the conduct of public services, would be noted by visiting evangelists for some twenty years. As Lionel Watson reported to Council, "In Canada, men of other denominations are looking to The Christian and Missionary Alliance to see if it can supply that real spiritual life and fellowship for which their hearts are hungry."[30]

In Toronto, the tension between Pastor Oswald J. Smith and his tabernacle congregation, which initially had become evident following the first Bosworth campaign, increased markedly towards the end of 1925. The original cause of tension had centred around the fact that the Christie Street work had grown out of a Parkdale nucleus committed to the original Alliance objective of first, the experience of the deeper spiritual life by its members, to be followed by the ultimate objective of world evangelism. To effect this program, the church had committed itself to the New Testament principles of self-government, as interpreted by the Alliance constitution for local churches.

As things had turned out, the ministry under Smith consisted almost exclusively of continuous evangelistic and missionary campaigns. Moreover, church government had ceased to be in any sense democratic but was entirely in the hands of the pastor and his "chosen few."

By 1925, the unhappy segment of the congregation had become more numerous and more vocal. They disagreed with their pastor that a tabernacle "must remain an evangelistic centre and nothing else." They were tired of a spiritual diet of milk, and clamoured for meat. As they saw it, Simon the fisherman must also be Simon the shepherd. Moreover, they believed that Pastor Smith's program "drew an irresponsible following of sermon tasters . . . unbalanced, undisciplined, enthusiastic, strongly personal in their attachments, increasingly unable to appreciate the simpler and less spectacular operations of the Spirit,"[31] for whom emotion rather than spirituality was the motivation for missionary support. Furthermore, they contended that "the lack of an organized church fellowship opens the door to unchristian bickering and fighting for power; while the lack of organized [response] leaves the congregation vulnerable to division and spiritual decline."[32] Disavowing such views was a majority of the adherents and perhaps half the members of the committee. Just who were the leaders of the opposition by 1925 is not clear. Pastor Smith attributed the opposition to "Methodists who [sic] I had unwisely taken into the committee."[33]

On May 13, 1926, the annual district conference elected Smith as district superintendent.[34] Eight days later the board of managers gave their approval,[35] and the pastor tendered his resignation from the tabernacle ministry, effective at the end of June. "In view of Mr. Smith's unique relation to the founding and establishing of the Alliance Tabernacle," he was created Pastor Emeritus.[36]

Over the next two years, Smith maintained hope for a return to the Christie Street ministry.[37] A majority of the committee wanted him back, but it could not bring itself to issue a recall. Lionel Watson, who proved himself to be Smith's lifelong friend, has left us with a remarkable analysis of what he termed "this most mystifying enigma." As Watson saw it, the problem was not just to find an acceptable balance between evangelism and nurture in church ministry and between autocracy and democracy in church government. There was a third problem—the perception by some of a changed and perhaps still changing pastoral personality. In the minds of this faction there were "two Oswald Smiths." There was the one of early days—humble, trustful and approachable, whom everyone had loved. However, they claimed, there had emerged a different Oswald Smith, boastful and opinionated, who was both the product and the victim of his own sudden success and popularity. According to Watson, the committee would have welcomed back the Oswald Smith of former days but they did not know which Smith would respond. Eventually, a recall was extended in November 1926 which "lacked a wholehearted enthusiasm." Smith accepted the call on the condition that the "troublemakers" of the committee be removed, a requirement which, according to Watson, "shocked the committee from the youngest to the oldest," and closed the door to any further negotiation. In frustration and disappointment, Smith resigned the superintendency and accepted a call to Los Angeles, effective February 1, 1927.[38]

Two months later Dr. Ira E. David became pastor of the tabernacle. Widely acclaimed for his deep biblical knowledge, his sermons are still remembered for their contribution to the armoury of defensive theology. The old guard of the tabernacle was greatly elated with a return to a teaching ministry. However, a majority of the adherents were only interested in a continuous campaign ministry, and without the restraints of committed membership soon found their satisfaction elsewhere.

In December of that year, two former members of the tabernacle committee wrote letters to the board of managers in New York, urging that the current members of the committee and Dr. David be asked to resign, and Smith be re-installed as pastor. It was an uneasy Dr. David who was summoned to New York to discuss "conditions prevailing at the Tabernacle." The effect of this meddlesome action was fourfold: it reopened the pastoral issue within the committee and congregation; it greatly discouraged and upset Dr. David; it sensitized the board of managers to a situation that might become shattering; and it encouraged former pastor Smith to believe that if he returned to Toronto he would be recalled to the tabernacle ministry.[39]

With high expectations Smith resigned his Los Angeles pulpit and returned to Toronto.[40] On the invitation of Dr. David he preached in his old pulpit on the evening of June 3 to an overflowing audience. Clearly, some decision had to be made and made quickly, but the committee remained paralyzed.

On July 12 President Harry M. Shuman and Vice-President Walter M. Turnbull came to Toronto to meet with the committee, Lionel Watson and Pastor Ira David. Assuming the chair, Shuman made it clear that he had come armed with the "wishes of the Board of Managers." First, Pastor David would be "released from the pastorate" and appointed "travelling evangelist," effective August 31. Second, as the tabernacle was in fact an independent work, it was clearly possible that at any time a leader might appear "who could secure a majority vote of the Committee to completely alienate the work and property from the Society." In order to prevent the possible loss of the building for Alliance use, the board wished "to place the Corporation of the Alliance Tabernacle Willowvale Park into the hands of the men at Headquarters." Third, the board wished "that the work be organized into a regular Alliance branch as set forth in the Constitution of The Christian and Missionary Alliance and that the board of managers appoint an interim committee to have charge of the work until a charter membership has been obtained and a new executive committee elected by the members."[41]

It was a difficult meeting, during which much personal hurt was sustained. In the end, the board's "wishes" prevailed. Dr. David tendered his resignation effective August 31, the committee resigned, and an interim committee was appointed to act under the authority of the board of managers and the district superintendent. A tentative date for the completion of a charter membership and the election of officers was set for October 28. Nine new members were appointed to the committee of the holding corporation of Alliance Tabernacle

Willowvale Park, all of them members of the board of managers in New York. President Shuman, Rev. J. D. Williams (district superintendent elect), and Lionel Watson (recently appointed assistant treasurer in New York) were created directors.[42]

Within ten days Rev. F. Noel Palmer, associate pastor of the Gospel Tabernacle in New York, would preach in Toronto as a pastoral candidate, with a view to commencing a tabernacle ministry on September 1.* Thus, there would be no lapse in the ministry of the tabernacle between the pastorates of Dr. David and Noel Palmer.

News of these developments soon reached the ears of Smith. His reactions could not have been surprising. He resigned from the board of managers and from being a field evangelist and credentialed worker of the Alliance. His resignation was accepted and acknowledged by the board through its secretary, Rev. D. J. Fant. It is to the credit of both Smith and Fant that these two documents are the epitome of cordiality. In his resignation Smith stated that recent developments at the tabernacle had convinced him that it would be impossible for him to carry out his vision for Toronto through the Alliance. Then he added,

> The burden is upon me to get the message out and I must be true to my convictions. Already I have prayed and waited for over two years and I dare not longer delay. God called me to Toronto; it is my city . . . my work in Toronto is not yet done, and I trust that my new effort will not be looked upon as in any way competitive, for I wish the Alliance every possible blessing. It has been a great joy to serve with such a spiritual movement in the past and I will be glad to co-operate whenever possible in the future.[43]

In his response Fant wrote:

> We are pleased with the spirit of your letter and your expressed desire to continue in fellowship and to cooperate whenever possible in the future. We join with you in this desire and trust, whatever may be your field of service in the future, that you may realize constantly that you are in the will of God and that God's blessing is resting

---

* Rev. F. Noel Palmer was a founder of the Inter-Varsity Fellowship in England. His wife was a granddaughter of General Booth of the Salvation Army.

upon you. Trusting that the Lord will definitely guide you for much fruit in His service. . . .[44]

And so the Peoples Church was founded in Toronto by Rev. Oswald J. Smith on September 9, just one week after Palmer commenced his ministry at the Alliance Tabernacle.

Despite his great pulpit eloquence, Palmer was unable to persuade the former crowds to return to the tabernacle. Two years later he accepted a call to his old colleagues, the Inter-Varsity Christian Fellowship. Tabernacle leaders who had not been able to get along with Smith had by then found it equally difficult to get along without him. They began to wonder if the time had come to forget the past and to consider if Smith might yet be the man who could rebuild the tabernacle fortunes. A special sub-committee of the executive board of the tabernacle, which included District Superintendent Williams, opened negotiations and found that Smith was quite prepared to "offer his assistance to the Toronto Tabernacle in any capacity in which he could serve them."[45]

A series of tripartite communications between the district superintendent, the tabernacle executive committee and the board of managers in New York ensued in rapid succession. The resulting tangle of misconceptions and misunderstandings caused the board, and particularly the president, to believe that the committee was trying to assume the "role of an umpire," which was "full of implications not too respectful." When passions subsided, it was generally concluded that "insurmountable difficulties" existed and the issue was forever dropped.[46]

There are many lessons to be learned from the recital of these difficult episodes.

It will be recalled that when, in May 1925, the District of Canada was divided into three districts, Lionel Watson was nominated for the superintendency of the new Central Canadian District. However, the vote was not unanimous in his favour. He therefore declined, and Home Secretary E. J. Richards became titular superintendent, pro tem, while Watson continued as resident assistant superintendent and administrator. The Eastern Canadian District was, in effect, strangled in its crib and Watson had to superintend the affairs of the combined Eastern and Central Canadian Districts, without title. In May 1926 Rev. O. J. Smith became superintendent of the combined districts, but eight months later he resigned. Richards again assumed the title, leaving Watson to carry on with the burden. However, three months later, Watson finally came into his own, when the annual district conference unanimously elected him their superintendent, which action was approved by the board of managers one week later. Watson proved to be one of the ablest administrators the district ever had, but his lack of preaching skill and the fact that he had not been ordained were hindrances to his overall effectiveness. He had to bear with a latent resistance on the part of some of his pastors. Watson served officially as district superintendent for only one year, at which time he was appointed assistant treasurer of the Alliance in New York,* and Rev. J. D. Williams became district superintendent.

New Leaders Emerge

Rev. William Hay resigned his Midland charge in April 1925. The congregation unanimously called Gordon Skitch, who graduated from the Missionary Training Institute in Nyack that spring. Skitch soon proved to be a very hard working and able pastor, and quickly earned the love of his little congregation. In September 1926, a party consisting of District Superintendent Smith, Rev. D. N. Cameron of Bedford Park Baptist Church in Toronto, Dr. E. Ralph Hooper and Lionel Watson conducted special meetings in Midland, and at the closing service, Skitch was ordained.[47]

A series of services held earlier that year in February featured Gipsy John Hawkins and Norman G. Loveless.[48] Many conversions were reported, but of particular importance to the Alliance in Canada was the conversion of a sixteen-year-old youth by the name of Willis Herman Brooks. About the time he became a teenager, his nominally Anglican parents were converted in the little Baptist church that became the Alliance church in Midland. It was a different home after that, but the youth was fun-loving and found it difficult to think seriously about spiritual matters. Although he had been urged by his parents to attend the Hawkins meetings, he put off going until, at last, he "ran out of excuses" and went along. As Willis Brooks recalled:

> I remember exactly where I sat listening to Evangelist Gipsy John Hawkins. It was the first time that I really

---

* After serving as assistant treasurer for several years, Lionel Watson returned to Toronto to become advertising manager of Evangelical Publishers. He then worked for Peoples Church in various administrative capacities until his sudden death in 1939 at the age of 59.

understood the Gospel and of my need of a saviour. I had no intention of going forward when the altar call was given. However, during the invitation, I noticed the song leader of the team, Norman Loveless, leave the platform and walk down the aisle on my side. To my utter dismay he turned into the seat where I was sitting, and, putting his hand upon my shoulder he said, "Young man, wouldn't you like to give your heart to Christ?" I guess it was that touch that broke my resistance—I was not accustomed to that sort of thing. I just followed him to the altar. One of the elders of the church came with me. After a few words from the evangelist, the elder took me into the little side room. I was somewhat bewildered about how I was to give my heart to Christ. In one sentence the elder made it clear. "Willis," he said, "just tell God that you are a sinner and need His forgiveness, and ask Jesus to come into your life." And that is what I did.[49]

Pastor Skitch believed that new Christians should be put to work immediately, and so he asked Brooks to join him in his open air meetings. Midland was a small town and anything done in public soon became widely known. Young Brooks shrank from the prospect. But, as he wrote, "You don't say 'no' to Gordon Skitch, so I found myself the next Saturday night on a corner of the main street singing gospel songs. Then, to my horror he said, 'Here is a young man who wants to give his testimony.' I certainly did not want to, but I had to tell the people about my conversion."[50]

Two months later, Skitch invited Brooks to accompany him to the graduation exercises of the Canadian Bible Institute in Toronto. Brooks had no money and he knew that his pastor could not afford to pay for him, so he sold his bicycle to provide for the trip. During the program, Brooks felt that God was calling him into His service and that he should attend that school. That fall he enrolled.

Upon graduation two years later, Brooks became an Alliance worker at Kingscote, near Hopeville. In the summer of 1929, he was sent to Wallaceburg to revive a dying work. The church had been founded in December 1922, following some meetings conducted by C. J. Wallace of Detroit. S. B. McCalden had become the first pastor. Five years later, Harry G. Muir, who was pastoring on a weekend basis, asked the Alliance to take over the work, and provide "a real good young man" as resident full-time pastor. Two recent graduates of Canadian Bible Institute, Della Carstead and Grace Johns, were sent, and the work appeared to prosper until the issue of tongues became a focal point. The ensuing concern for truth degenerated into a spectacle of invective. As a result, most of the congregation separated to form another church, and for several weeks even the remaining fragment was alienated from the district. Into these decimated and desperate conditions was sent the twenty-year-old Willis Brooks. "It was tough," he said. "There were only three or four families that could be counted on. I just about starved." A year later the work was closed.[51]

This painful experience left its mark on Brooks. Then in 1930 he was sent to Alliston to shepherd a small work started the previous year by Firm Sauvé, the future missionary.[52] Despite his efforts, attendance remained pitifully small. Late that year Brooks was told that he would be reassigned. At this point his determination failed. Lonely, discouraged and now uncertain of his call to the ministry, he returned to Midland and to secular employment. However, God had evidently kept His eye on His discouraged servant. Another graduate of the Canadian Bible Institute, Earl Whitmore, was working at a place called Lake Post Office, near Bancroft, at an outreach project of the Faith Mission in Trenton.* Late in 1931, Whitmore invited Brooks to join him in his itinerant ministry to five widely separated preaching stations. It was wintertime and bitterly cold, and the only means of transportation between the points was by horse and cutter. Brooks recalled that this experience was the best thing that could have happened to him. It got the blood circulating in his veins and his mind off his concerns. Moreover, he found that the urge to preach had come back and with it his confidence returned.

Next spring, Whitmore became pastor of Faith Mission,[53] leaving Brooks to look after the Lake circuit by himself. In January 1934, Brooks became Whitmore's assistant in Trenton. The mission congregation consisted of elements of several holiness groups—Methodist, Free Methodist, Pentecostal, Holiness, Standard and Nazarene. With such a strong holiness emphasis, it was forcibly driven home to Brooks that there was more to the Christian experience than being forgiven. The life must be redirected and empowered for sanctified service by the Holy Spirit.

---

* Faith Mission, Trenton, was founded in 1903 by Mrs. Mary Gainforth. In 1895 she had been healed of advanced tuberculosis, through the ministry of Dr. R. J. Zimmerman, in Peterborough. The work became an Alliance affiliate in 1914.

Conflict of Interest / 157

5.2 Rev. Harry M. Shuman was president of the Alliance from 1925 to 1954.

5.1 Lionel Watson, an able administrator, was effectively superintendent of the Eastern and Central Canadian Districts from May 1925 until May 1928, although he held the title for only the last year. He was the only layman ever to fill this role in Canada.

5.3 William Duckworth, the leading seceder from Shaw Memorial United Church, stands in front of his home, where the first independent meetings in the north end of Montreal were held early in 1926.

5.4 Fred Sparke led the north end seceders into the Alliance fellowship and became their first pastor. With Alliance incorporation in Quebec in 1930, he became the first Alliance pastor qualified to conduct acts of civil status.

5.5 Pastor Edwin T. Holt in his Lappin Avenue (Toronto) pulpit in 1929.

158 / *Conflict of Interest*

5.6 Montreal and Ottawa attendees of the Dominion convention of 1927 pose at the Knowlton Conference Grounds. The tallest man in the back row is Fred Sparke, and in the same row, the man with the moustache is William Duckworth, both of Montreal. Second from the left in the second seated row is John Patton of Ottawa and fourth from the left is District Superintendent Lionel Watson.

Not surprisingly, the mission meetings were on the noisy side. Far from being distracting, Brooks found them to be helpful.

> We had some unbelievable meetings in that church. Those people, by their Amens and Hallelujahs would just pull the preach right out of you. So, I think that in some measure I developed as a preacher in that Spirit-blessed atmosphere of the Trenton mission.[54]

Thus, by the early summer of 1934, Willis Brooks was confident once more of God's call to the ministry, and he was ready to step forward on his next assignment—as is related in the next chapter.

A CLIMATE OF CHANGE

During the spring of 1926, the King's Messengers, from the Gospel Tabernacle in Ottawa, held a meeting in the village of Overbrook, and several families petitioned the tabernacle to open a Sunday school there. Frank Spain undertook the work, and three years later, an old church property was purchased and the Overbrook Gospel Tabernacle was organized. Destroyed by fire in March 1949, the first building was replaced by a new structure two years later, at which time the church was renamed the Riverview Community Church of the C&MA. In 1965, most of the remaining members joined with the Gospel Tabernacle in downtown Ottawa, and the building was sold.

The city of London had long been an Alliance centre. In 1896 John Salmon held the city's first annual Alliance convention in an overflowing St. Andrew's Presbyterian Church. That was the only occasion that Simpson preached in London. During the convention an Alliance fraternal branch was organized. Three years later, the annual convention was held in the Christian Workers' Church, at the corner of Ottaway and Adelaide Streets. From then on, this church was the home of the local Alliance branch, until its demise in 1914.[55] After 1914, the Alliance showed no further interest in fraternal branches. In 1924, Rev. Archibald G. Doner, who had a ministry in Bethany Church, Peterborough, a few months previously, gathered together a small group interested in the Alliance, and commenced holding services in a hall on Pall Mall Street. The first annual missionary convention of this new Alliance generation in London was held that year. Two years later, Doner accepted a call to the Gospel Tabernacle, Brantford, and was replaced in London by Rev. J. B. Snider, who relocated the work to a new hall in Richmond Street. Under Snider's ministry, the work was organized as an Alliance branch in 1926, with Edmund Geiger elected as secretary, Reginald Wigglesworth as treasurer, R. Dickenson as Sunday school superintendent and Firmin J. Sauvé, Sr., as missionary treasurer.[56]

Later that same year, the work was again relocated to the old Christian Workers' church building that had been the home of the fraternal branch 30 years previously and renamed the Alliance Tabernacle. In 1930, the congregation purchased the building and permanency appeared to be assured. However, just four years later, the work rapidly declined and ended its days. Eighteen years would pass before London would again have an Alliance testimony.

During the late 1920s, the fast growing appeal of Pentecostal teaching and experience coupled with the aggressive national organization of the Pentecostal Assemblies of Canada impacted heavily on the Alliance. In downtown Montreal, the lure of Pastor Baker's Pentecostal meetings on Drummond Street had been at least partly the cause of the rapid defection of most of the pastorless Central Alliance congregation in 1926. In Toronto that same year, the congregation of the tabernacle dissipated rapidly after the resignation of Smith, many finding a new church home in the Evangel Temple (Pentecostal).*

In January 1927, Fred Sparke, pastor of the Alliance Gospel Hall in the north end of Montreal reported to District Superintendent Lionel Watson, "We are in need of your prayers. The Pentecostal people have opened a branch about a stone's throw from the hall and they are not hesitating to approach our people in order to get them to their meetings.** We have lost some who had leanings to their doctrines."[57] Reporting one year later, Sparke mentions "a feeling of despondency" due to "a break away of a large number of those holding to Pentecostal doctrines."[58] That same year, Lionel Watson reported to the annual conference that despite a series of missionary conventions in St. John, Truro and Halifax, "no advance" had been made

---

* The committee formed to explore the possibility of Smith's return to the tabernacle in 1928 reported him saying that he had come back to Toronto "with a view to conserving our Alliance constituency that was scattering to Pentecostalism."

** Doubtless this refers to the work of Pastor Swan on St. Hubert Street, about a quarter of a mile away.

because "the Pentecostal movement had interfered seriously with our work." Many old friends had joined the new Pentecostal churches in those cities.[59]

The Alliance in eastern Canada in the 1920s experienced something similar with respect to the Pentecostal movement as the Alliance in the United States had experienced twenty years earlier. Nevertheless, the loss of members from the north end branch in Montreal had some good effects. It jolted both pastor and people into taking action to promote viability and permanency.

In October 1927, the Alliance Gospel Hall decided that the work needed a full-time pastor. Part-time pastor Sparke gave up his secular employment, trusting God to enable the little church to support him.[60] Seven months later he was ordained.[61] Up to this point in time, the Alliance in Quebec had not been allowed to own property, celebrate marriages, administer baptism (christen or register births) or to perform the rite of burial. Only ordained clergymen of authorized denominations, who were British subjects, were permitted to keep registers of civil status, and the general law of the province recognized only the Roman Catholic Church, the Church of England and, since 1925, the United Church of Canada. However, provision had been made for other denominations and independent churches by special legislative enactment for each particular congregation—an expensive requirement. Ontario lawyers advised that the existing Ontario corporation of the Alliance be merged into a "Dominion" corporation enactment by the federal government, then, inasmuch as matters of property and civil rights, as well as the solemnization of marriages belonged to the jurisdiction of the provinces, to have the Province of Quebec confer relevant rights upon the Dominion corporation. However, Quebec lawyers urged a separate Quebec incorporation. Fortunately their wise counsel was heeded, and on January 15, 1929, the district executive committee authorized a "petition of incorporation in Quebec."[62]

Meanwhile, the Alliance Gospel Hall in the north end of Montreal became impatient with Pastor Sparke's inability to keep a register and perform acts of civil status. In October 1928 they dispatched an urgent request to the district office, pleading for immediate action to obtain authority to conduct acts of civil status, adding that if such action were not taken immediately, the church would "seriously contemplate the desirability of securing other denominational affiliation." The district paid additional fees to accelerate the legal process, and the Quebec legal firm did a masterful job. On March 20, 1930, "An Act to Incorporate The Christian and Missionary Alliance in Quebec" received royal assent. It was an historic Act, because not only was a minor denomination given authority to perform marriages through its ordained clergymen, but, for the first time, the ordained clergymen did not need to be British subjects.* This was a privilege not granted to the Anglican Church or the United Church of Canada.[63]

In return for this privilege, the Alliance in Quebec was required to appoint a superintendent and deputy superintendent, both residents of Quebec and British subjects, who would be held responsible for the care and use of the registers of civil status. Thus it was that William McEwan of the Montreal Central work and John (Jack) Richards of the Alliance Gospel Hall in the north end of Montreal, became the first titular superintendent and deputy superintendent, respectively, of the Alliance in Quebec, and Rev. Fred Sparke became the first Alliance pastor in Quebec authorized to perform acts of civil status.[64]

The acquisition of such a charter at that time would be a most valuable asset for the Alliance in years to come.

RENEWAL OF HOME MISSIONS

As mentioned previously, Rev. J. D. Williams became district superintendent in September 1928. Without doubt, he was among the most highly qualified of all superintendents. Born in Bakerstown, Pennsylvania, in 1870, Williams taught school after graduation from Curry University in Pittsburg, before attending Nyack. He then served as pastor for ten years and as district superintendent of three different American districts for nineteen years. For three years he was principal of Fort Wayne Bible Institute and was founder and dean of St. Paul Bible Institute for eight years. During a brief stay in the Philippines, he founded the Ebenezer Bible Institute and for seven years was secretary of the Education Department in New York. After coming to Canada in 1928, he continued to serve on the board of managers, of which he had been a member for 28 years.

Arriving in Toronto on the heels of the sudden departure of Lionel Watson and Dr. Ira David, and the sudden return of Rev.

---

* One single church, but not a denomination, had previously obtained this privilege.

Oswald Smith, Williams found that many of his new district's affairs were somewhat disturbed. His well-balanced views of overall Alliance responsibilities, together with his qualities of dignity, fairness, friendliness and efficiency, often resolved a knotty situation. He was once described as "a breath of fresh air," which fanned new life into the district.

By 1928, the Alliance homeland of the United States and Canada consisted of fourteen districts, each with its own district superintendent, except for the Eastern and Central Canadian Districts which shared a single superintendent between them. In that year, following Council's request that attention be given to extension work, the board of managers grouped the districts into five "fields" and appointed five of the district superintendents as field secretaries.[65]

Williams was proclaimed "Field Secretary for Canada, exclusive of British Columbia," over his own two districts and that of Western Canada, which was under John Woodward. Even before Williams became a field secretary, he had shown a marked interest in home-land evangelism, as an intrinsic part of the work of the Great Commission, quite apart from any resulting benefit that might accrue to foreign missions. Indeed, he had made a study of homeland evangelism and had written a booklet entitled "Alliance Pioneer Bands," in which he took the view that Christ's Great Commission was addressed to the whole church in the whole world. This meant that evangelization of the homeland for its own sake was as much the will of Christ as was the evangelization of foreign countries.

At his first district conference in November 1929, despite the view specifically expressed by the home secretary that the "vital principle" for Alliance homeland endeavour was that "when the missionary effort thrives, the home work thrives with it," Williams was not reticent to express his own views on the need of home evangelism and home missions for their own sake. From a long list of reasons for these vital ministries, he emphasized the following:

1. The increasing ignorance of Christ and the gospel.
2. The need to make known the evangelical gospel to counteract the incoming tide of infidelity, rationalism and false cultism.
3. The need to establish Sunday Schools where children can be catechised in the doctrines of Christianity.
4. The need to put out Bible school students to work

during the summer in areas where they can develop the gifts required to pastor, to preach, to teach and to evangelize, all in one, and thereby determine their calling before graduation.
5. The need to demonstrate an unselfish, non-sectarian missionary spirit in reaching the otherwise unreached at home; working with other Christians of other denominations, and endeavouring to set before such neglected communities the world-wide concern of the Alliance.
6. The need to "lengthen the cords" and "strengthen the stakes" in the homeland, in balance with our pursuits in the foreign fields.
7. The need for greater effort to remove prejudice and inspire confidence in the Alliance by making friends with other Christian groups.

The district superintendent then called for the formation of a permanent "Committee of Evangelism." Under the chairmanship of Gilbert Johnson, the future education secretary, the committee endorsed Williams's plans, urging "that every branch or church be regarded as a centre of evangelism utilizing its own forces to evangelize its outlying areas, that laymen take up many of the pastoral duties in the churches, thus freeing pastors to lead other laymen (bands) into the work of rural evangelism." Lastly, the committee recommended the appointment of a district evangelist, under the direction of the district superintendent. The conference approved all recommendations of the committee and established a district extension fund.[66]

Reports of the new district initiative on home missions were taken back to the churches by the returning delegates. The larger churches were, perhaps, in the best position to respond quickly and effectively. The Alliance Tabernacle in Toronto, through its "Fishers of Men Band" visited rural areas by car on weekends, holding evangelistic services wherever they found interest. E. D. (Ed) Simmons, their lay leader, was a vigorous worker and outdoor preacher for many years and he had the voice to match his calling.[67]

In his earliest extant report to the district superintendent on the work of the Fishers of Men Band, Simmons wrote, "During the last six months we have travelled 2,500 miles, visited fifteen locations, held thirty-five services and distributed thousands of tracts. Best of all a number of souls have been saved and many Christians encouraged to press on." From the many reports of visits the following are gleaned:

"Frequently we started out on Saturday afternoon and returned to our homes perhaps as late as 4:30 am Monday morning. As we start work at 8:30 am you will agree that we have a man's job. . . ." "At Musselman's Lake we had three open air meetings on Sunday. Most of our audience wore bathing suits, but thank God, they listened and some forgot to go swimming. . . . Last February we visited Castleton [92 miles east of Toronto]. On part of the journey we covered only seven miles in seven hours, spending most of our time digging the car out of snow drifts. But we got there and held a gospel service—the first they had in ten years. The people were hungry for truth, so a building was purchased and today they are an Alliance congregation. . . . On August 4th, eight were baptized in the creek, followed by the Lord's Supper."[68]

In Ottawa, the King's Messengers of the Gospel Tabernacle distributed tracts and literature, witnessing when doors were opened, and holding meetings in homes and schoolhouses.[69]

In Peterborough, the idea of evangelistic outreach into the homeland "regions beyond" was not new. Several years earlier, under the leadership of Pastor R. K. Mills, daughter churches had been started in Lindsay and South Lake, and during the summer of 1926, 60 meetings had been held in surrounding Indian villages. Thousands of tracts had been handed out and several conversions were reported. Nevertheless, under the impetus of this new and additional evangelism thrust, Pastor Gilbert Johnson opened a new preaching station at nearby Drummer Centre. A year later, after he had transferred to Owen Sound, he started rural ministries in Rockford, Ottewell and Kepple.

Even in small works such as the Alliance Gospel Hall in Montreal, the spreading flame of home evangelism took hold. Under Pastor T. J. Spier, a French Canadian worker was subsidized by the English-speaking congregation to distribute French tracts and New Testaments door to door. The first French-language public services under Alliance auspices were conducted in Montreal by this worker.*

In his report to the Home Secretary for 1930, Williams reported that 31 evangelistic campaigns had been conducted by fifteen evangelists, including himself and Mrs. Williams. Delegates to the conference of 1931 expressed their appreciation for "the high spiritual

---

* The first French language public services are discussed more fully in Chapter 9.

character of District Superintendent and Mrs. Williams in their aggressive policy of evangelization for the great unreached territories of our District, especially those of Quebec, the maritimes and rural Ontario." Nor did interest in foreign missions slump as interest in home missions expanded. In 1929, the Eastern and Central District sent more than $62,000 to the general fund in New York. The district was the third largest giver of all eleven Alliance districts in North America, providing ten percent of all foreign missionary funds.

About this time, President Shuman modified his earlier stance on the supremacy of foreign missions. In his letter to the district conferences of 1934, he stated:

> There are some matters regarding our work that are ever upon my heart. One is that we, as workers, shall know, love, and experience the real Fourfold Gospel message as taught by Dr. Simpson. There are multitudes of hungry and confused people who need the truth of the reality and fullness of Christ. The things which are truly characteristic of our movement are its message, its spirit, and its missionary vision and passion. Every department of our work should be of such a nature that these shall be fully maintained and perpetuated.*

This was not a call to return to the original Alliance concept of a causative faith and experience as a prerequisite to world evangelism, but it was a call to Alliance workers to return to an emphasis of distinctive Alliance teaching, experience and practice. Similar statements were to come from the president for several years, but many subordinate leaders were slow to share in this more balanced presentation of Alliance priorities. However, the Eastern and Central Canadian District under the vigorous leadership of Williams, embraced this renewal of distinctive Alliance teaching and emphasis, which was more in keeping with what many conservative Canadian Christians wanted in an emerging denomination of the inter-war period.

EFFORTS FOR EXPANSION

One of the first commitments that District Superintendent Williams had to keep was one made for him by his predecessor, Lionel

---

* This 1934 statement of President Shuman should be compared with those he made in 1928 and 1929, quoted on page 142.

Watson. During the spring of 1928, Watson had agreed to hold meetings in the Prince Edward Street Church of St. John, New Brunswick, with a view to accepting the church into the Alliance fold. Accordingly, Williams held meetings in St. John, from September 24-26.[70]

The history of the St. John church starts considerably before Williams's first visit. In 1849 the Baptists erected a brick church building, seating 800, on Brussels Street, in downtown St. John. Seventy years later the congregation united with another Baptist church and relocated to a more affluent section of the city.

In 1917, a group of businessmen, including fruit and vegetable wholesaler John G. Willett, burdened for the souls of the poor and debauched of St. John, opened the City Mission. The converts were reluctant to travel long distances to the suburban churches, which for the most part did not welcome them. When, in 1919, the old Baptist church building on Brussels Street was offered for sale, Willett and his friend Charles Robinson purchased it as a church home for the converts and a centre for the mission work. On May 20, 1920, the Brussels Street Church was organized, with Willett and Robinson as elders and the Rev. O. P. Brown as pastor. The new church covenanted "to provide for the poor; to labour for the salvation of the unsaved and the spread of the Gospel at home and abroad; to be prayerful, believing and benevolent; to minister one to another as occasion may demand, without regard to any return; to maintain devout lives in our homes; to separate ourselves from the world in pursuit of service and pleasure; to avoid tattling and to seek to preserve among us the Spirit of unity."[71] Thus was cast the character and purpose of the Brussels Street Church.

In February 1921, the church invited the Alliance to hold its first convention in St. John since the days of John Salmon. These conventions became an annual event and forged an ever strengthening bond between the church and the Alliance. It seemed to the members of the Brussels Street Church* that the goals and beliefs of both organisms were coincident and that a closer association was opportune.

On September 16, 1928, agreement was reached to admit the church into the Alliance. James E. Davey,** a recent graduate of

---

* In 1922 Brussels Street became Prince Edward Street and the name of the church was changed accordingly.

** Before his conversion, James E. Davey was a tug boat operator in Chesapeake Bay. He served the Alliance in various pastoral and district superintendency appointments for 39 years. His son, Rev. James A. Davey, is currently Vice President, General Services, of the Alliance in Colorado Springs headquarters.

Nyack College, began his ministry there on October 28. On January 26, 1929, the church became an official branch of the Alliance, with a charter membership of sixteen persons, to be known as the Gospel Tabernacle of the C&MA. A congregational equity in the building was transferred to the Alliance "in trust." (The Alliance as yet held no New Brunswick charter.) Willett maintained controlling financial interest in the building and granted the congregation rent-free occupancy.[72]

And so, after 33 years of struggle, the Alliance gained a toe-hold of permanency in the maritime provinces.

The year 1929 also saw the establishment of an Alliance branch in Windsor, although that city's earliest connections with the Alliance extend back at least another three years. Local tradition credits a Mrs. Norman Barr of the Central Alliance Church in Detroit with the formation of an Alliance-minded nucleus in the Canadian border city. By December 1925 a regular prayer meeting was being conducted by Detroit friends in a hall on Erie Street "with the concurrence" of the district office.[73] In May 1926, the Windsor group started Sunday services as the Gospel Tabernacle of The Christian and Missionary Alliance, and relocated to 112 Sandwich Street. The first Sunday services were conducted by John Woodward, on his way back west after recruiting summer students at the Canadian Bible Institute in Toronto.[74]

Without a pastor, the Gospel Tabernacle was supplied by visiting preachers of various persuasions.[75] More and more the work took on the characteristics of a Pentecostal church. From October 1926 onwards, the Alliance connection was dropped from their advertising, and the work became known as the Full Gospel Tabernacle.[76]

In November 1926, another work, the Full Gospel Church, located on London Street at the corner of Bruce Avenue, together with its pastor, the Rev. A. G. Philpotts, joined the Pentecostal Assemblies of Canada. The church was renamed Elim Tabernacle. However, Philpotts soon became alienated from his denomination over doctrinal matters, and in February 1928, was "repudiated" by the Assemblies.[77] Taking most of his congregation with him, he relocated Elim Tabernacle to Wyandotte Street[78] and advertised the church as "an evangelistic enterprise on undenominational lines," "fundamental but not fanatical."[79]

This was the signal for the struggling Full Gospel Tabernacle, the former Alliance work, to close down, and for some of its former members to make Elim Tabernacle their new church home. Three months later, Philpotts visited District Superintendent Watson in

Toronto to discuss the possibility of an Alliance ministry for himself and an Alliance affiliation for his church. His proposals were not enthusiastically received.[80]

In July, Watson and his successor-to-be, J. D. Williams, visited Windsor. They agreed that in view of the strained relationships with the evangelical community of Windsor, Alliance affiliation for the church and full accreditation for Philpotts would be premature. However, one month later, the district executive committee approved a temporary evangelist's certificate for Philpotts.[81]

In December, during an eight-day Alliance convention in Elim Tabernacle, Rev. S. M. Gerow, a former pastor of the Central Alliance Church in Detroit, acquainted the congregation with "Alliance beliefs and practices." The convention ended with an offering for the support of Alliance missions.[82] Five months later, on May 1, 1929, Elim Tabernacle officially became affiliated with the Alliance and was renamed the Alliance Tabernacle. The church was reorganized as an Alliance branch with H. O. Sweet as secretary, John Courtney as treasurer, F. B. Size as financial secretary and D. Cooper as member-at-large on the executive board. On that same day, Philpotts became its fully credentialed Alliance pastor.[83] After several relocations, the Windsor church is known today as Heritage Park Alliance Church.

During the conference of November 1930, a new worker was introduced to the delegates. Born in Glasgow, Scotland, William McArthur settled in Hespeler, Ontario, with his family and they made their spiritual home with the local Baptist church. After attending Toronto Bible College and graduating from Toronto Baptist Seminary, he pastored Westboro (Ottawa) Baptist Church for a year, at which time he "felt called into fellowship with the Alliance." He attended Nyack College briefly before receiving his first Alliance charge in Windsor in 1932. McArthur ministered in the east for fourteen years and then served on the faculty of Canadian Bible College for twelve years, including four years as president. His final six years of ministry were in the U.S. Pacific Northwest District.

At this time, another well-known, long service worker entered the Alliance ranks. The son of a Primitive Methodist lay preacher, Charles Victor Freeman was born in Loughborough, Leicestershire, England, in 1907. When he was thirteen, his family immigrated to Montreal before moving to Hamilton. In a 1927 campaign of Dr. Charles Price, held in Hamilton Arena, Victor Freeman was converted and committed to the service of Christ. He was baptized on

Easter Sunday, became a member of Delta Tabernacle, and a year later enrolled in the Canadian Bible Institute, Toronto. After his first year, he co-pastored the church at Castleton and then attended the Toronto Bible College, graduating three years later. Ordained under the Alliance on December 22, 1932, he served ten churches during a career of 47 years, and was also district secretary for 21 years.

Annual Council convened for the second time in Canada in 1930, in the Gospel Tabernacle in Ottawa. The Hon. A. M. Carmichael, M.P.* brought words of welcome on behalf of Parliament. In response to his invitation, Council devoted an entire afternoon to a visit of the Parliament Buildings. Motorcycle police organized a long line of automobiles and led the procession from the tabernacle in the sightseeing drive through the capital city. Arriving at Parliament Hill, the delegates assembled in the Hall of Fame, where they were addressed by the Speaker of the House, the Hon. Rudolphe Lemieux. After a tour of the buildings, the delegates had their official picture taken in front of the Parliament Buildings. Of that Thirty-third Annual Council, the *Alliance Weekly* reported, "Not in years have our annual council sessions been conducted on such a high order of Christian deportment, coupled with quiet holy dignity."[84]

The Gospel Tabernacle of Ottawa suffered a severe division in 1931. When, in 1924, at the height of the first Ottawa Bosworth campaign, it had been decided to build a large tabernacle, a corporation was formed to safeguard the interests of those lending money for the project. The original corporation members consisted chiefly of those who were willing and able to personally guarantee the bank loans. As there existed neither a church membership nor elders, all authority centred in the self-perpetuating members of the corporation. Had the debts been paid quickly, as at the Toronto Alliance Tabernacle (two years), trouble might never have arisen. However, the work had been built largely around the ministry of its first pastor,

---

* Born in Smithdale and raised in Bradford, Ontario, Archibald M. Carmichael joined the Progressive Party at its inception in 1921, and was elected in the Kindersley, Saskatchewan, riding that year and for fourteen years represented Kindersley in Parliament. During the first Ottawa Bosworth campaign in 1924 Carmichael came in touch with the Alliance. He threw his lot in with the Gospel Tabernacle, and served on the board of managers in New York. After retirement from politics, he was ordained under the Alliance, serving first in Glendale, California. From 1937-1939 he was pastor of Beulah Tabernacle in Edmonton. The Progressive Party won 65 seats in 1921, but in 1932 its more radical members left to form the Cooperative Commonwealth Federation (which later became the New Democratic Party), while the more conservative members linked up with the Conservative Party to form the Progressive Conservative Party.

the Rev. Elmer B. Fitch. His continuous campaign policy came to a close with his resignation in 1927, and was replaced by a series of short teaching ministries. Attendance decreased, debt payments fell behind, and the congregation began to clamour for a voice in the election of officers, the calling of a pastor and the setting of policies.

In 1931, mounting disagreement resulted in a disastrous schism, in which the recalcitrants departed to form the Metropolitan Tabernacle, now the Metropolitan Bible Church of the Associated Gospel Churches of Canada. Although the Gospel Tabernacle was subsequently reorganized along more conventional lines and for many years was a model in missionary giving, the congregation never again reached its former size or prestige within the district.

"Making Do" in the Thirties

The stock market collapse of October 1929 initiated a worldwide economic depression that persisted until the threats of deprivation were overshadowed by the threats of obliteration some six or seven years later. Canada felt the effects with particular severity, because its export-dependent economy was especially vulnerable to the whims of world markets. Between 1929 and 1932, wages fell by 42 percent, and by 1933 more than 25 percent of the work force was unemployed. Churches, like all other segments of society, had to learn to get by on less. The exercise of faith in divine provision for need had to be tempered with practicality in spending. Pastoral salaries fell anywhere from 30 to 50 percent. One denomination reported that appropriations for foreign missions fell by more than half between 1928 and 1935. The Alliance fared somewhat better; receipts for the general fund fell 35 percent between 1928 and 1933.

Some idea of the hardships can be imagined from the action taken by the executive board of the Christie Street Tabernacle, Toronto, in January 1933.

1. Sunday services will be confined to the chapel to conserve heat.
2. Sunday services will be dismissed not later than 8:30 pm to conserve light.
3. The pastor's salary will be reduced from $40 to $30 per week.
4. The janitor's salary will be reduced from $22 to $18 per week.

At the Alliance Gospel Hall in Montreal, Pastor T. J. Spier's salary was $15 per week. It happened that the city was paving a lane behind the house of a founder of the church, retired William Duckworth, who went out to observe the progress of the work. Who should he see wheeling a barrow load of concrete, but "my own pastor." Apparently, it nearly broke the old man's heart to see what his pastor had to do on his "day off" in order to keep bread on the table.

In 1929, the board of managers and the Home Department took action to match outflow with income. Six of the nine Bible schools were closed, including the two Canadian schools at Toronto and Edmonton. The total elimination of Canadian schools caused severe damage to Alliance progress in Canada, which would not be assuaged in eastern Canada until 1956. (This is discussed fully in Chapter 8.) Once again Canadians felt they were coming off second best.

Four years later, on the recommendation of the board of managers, the Council of 1933 elected Williams superintendent of the Western Canadian District in addition to the Eastern and Central Canadian Districts.[85] The territory which just seven years previously had been judged to require three superintendents was now allotted one. It was a return to pre-1925 days, except that this time there would not even be a part-time assistant in the district office.

Williams met the challenge of home evangelism in the west with enthusiasm. However, the more mundane affairs of the east were not so vigorously pursued as formerly. The superintending of all Canada (except British Columbia) was simply too great a task for one man to carry out.

In May 1934, Williams was appointed superintendent of the Pacific Northwest District,[86] without replacement for Eastern and Central Canada. Eastern Canadians viewed this action as district favouritism, and they expressed their views clearly. The outburst of resentment brought President Shuman and Home Secretary Brown to Toronto to face eight unhappy members of the district executive committee on July 10. The two visitors did their best to explain the action taken but apparently the committee members remained unimpressed. Towards the end of the meeting, the visitors offered to appoint Rev. James F. Brabazon, a sixteen-year missionary to India presently in the United States on furlough, as "temporary district superintendent." Brabazon arrived in Toronto the following month to take up his charge.[87]

Brabazon's term of service lasted for one year and ten days. He could do little in that time to leave his image on the affairs of the district. However, it was soon evident that his concept of home work hinged on the advance of foreign missions, rather than the salvation and nurture of Canadian souls. At his only district conference, which convened in October 1934, he stated:

> If we could press into the nearby centres of our Central and Eastern Districts we might definitely reduce the number of needy fields in the dark corners of the earth. We have unlimited resources for the furtherance of the missionary enterprize in these unoccupied centres.[88]

Attending that conference was Rev. David Mason,* a veteran of ten years of missionary service in the Belgian Congo (Zaire), and at that time serving as co-secretary with Rev. A. C. Snead in the Foreign Department.

In May 1935, Brabazon tendered his resignation, effective August 31, in order to return to India.[89] President Shuman met with the district executive committee on June 3, and presented a recommendation of the board of managers that Rev. David Mason be appointed district superintendent. Aware of Mason's acumen in the affairs of the Foreign Department and his wide popularity as a missionary speaker, the committee members were apprehensive of the proposal. After discussion, a motion was passed "that we accept the Board's recommendation provided that the new superintendent be free to give his undivided attention to the work of the District."[90] On June 19 the board of managers made the appointment official, effective September 1.

Meanwhile, the Christie Street Tabernacle had been without a pastor for eleven months. Early in July their most recent pastoral call

---

* David Mason was born "of pious parents, near the banks of the Firth of Forth," in Fifeshire, Scotland, in 1883. In his youth he became a sailor, and, by his own testimony, indulged in the sins usually attributed to the ways of the sea. Narrow escapes and seeming disaster overtook him time and again, which eventually aroused his conscience. When 27, he attended a Gospel Hall service in Cleveland, Ohio, where he was soundly converted. A few months later, after hearing a missionary address by A. B. Simpson at Beulah Beach Park, and believing he had received a divine call to be a missionary, he left the sea and entered the Missionary Training Institute in Nyack. In 1913 he sailed for his first term in the Belgian Congo. Ten years later, the Masons returned to the United States, to provide "a suitable home and education" for their children, at which time he joined the staff of the Foreign Department.

was rejected.[91] The board of managers saw an opportunity to meet an urgent pastoral need and at the same time reduce the cost of maintaining a district superintendent. President Shuman requested the tabernacle executive committee to vote on the board's proposal of a dual ministry for Mason. "After a lengthy discussion and careful consideration" they turned down the proposition by majority vote.[92]

This decision brought Home Secretary Verner Brown to Toronto on August 2 to press his point with both the district executive committee and the tabernacle executive committee.[93] As an incentive to accept the board proposal, Brown offered to send furloughed Rev. E. Frank Irwin, missionary to French Indo China (Vietnam), to help out with district matters for a few months.[94]

The district executive committee refrained from taking any action, but the tabernacle executive committee, after discussing "the question thoroughly from all points," by majority vote agreed to accept Rev. David Mason as "acting pastor without any stated time."[95] Mason arrived in Toronto to take up his dual functions on September 1.

HOMELAND POLICY AND PRACTICE

It would be difficult to conceive of a district superintendent more dedicated to Alliance missions than was Rev. David Mason. A former missionary himself, this resolute Scot was in full sympathy with the Alliance philosophy of operation that prevailed during the 1910s and the 1920s. For him, the determinative task of the Alliance was to spread the gospel in the regions beyond the homeland borders, and the home work existed as a supply base for personnel and money.

However, after 1930, Alliance leadership came to realize that such a policy was stagnating homeland work. They began to remind themselves that the Alliance had not come into existence as a foreign missionary society, but rather as a spiritual agency for the teaching and experience of the Spirit-filled life, whose members, thus divinely guided and empowered, would reach out to both the homeland and in the regions beyond. If the Alliance was to direct the affairs of homeland churches, Alliance leadership had to recognize its homeland responsibilities in the areas of nurture and evangelism.

By the mid-1930s President Shuman no longer viewed missions as the determinative factor in all Alliance interests. In 1935 he told the district conferences,

Never have I been more thoroughly convinced of the importance of knowing the Alliance message and of faithfully proclaiming it.

In 1937 he told them,

Two great objectives should be clearly before us in making our plans for the future—the building of a church at home ... and a vigorous prosecution of our missionary program.

The next year he added,

It is important that we consider well the factors that are essential to our Alliance ministry. These include systematic instruction in the Scriptures and especially in deeper truths of God's Word, constructive evangelism, intercessory prayer, and worldwide missions.

Addressing the Eastern and Central Canadian District Conference in September 1938, Shuman urged them to "seek to lead people into a personal experience of sanctification and healing."[96]

The district superintendents' conference of December 1940 reached a consensus regarding a new homeland policy. The Alliance, stated the report, had been raised up of God and given a divine message to propagate and a divine mission to fulfill. It continued,

In the course of years we have through prevailing prayer and detailed planning, developed our work abroad with greater rapidity than we have extended the work at home. It is now evidently in the will of God that we give increasing emphasis, attention and planning to the development and extension of the home work.

Referring to the fact that rejected candidates for foreign work were usually placed in home work, the conference added,

Only those with a rugged, pioneering spirit should be selected—men and women with a God-given call and a God-given passion for souls, ready to pray, plod and sacrifice, and go anywhere, under any conditions, whenever God may call them.

One year later, in 1941, President Shuman would make his historic pronouncement that the Alliance was both "a missionary movement and a partial denomination."[97]

The Alliance had at least officially recognized its homeland responsibilities in their own right, regardless of the consequence or benefit to foreign missions. More important than the rhetoric was the action taken by Council and the board from the late 1930s on, to enact legislation aimed at revitalizing home work and establishing a healthier and more responsible balance in Alliance worldwide responsibilities.

It would appear that District Superintendent David Mason had difficulty in identifying with the shift in homeland policy. In any event, his eleven-year superintendency was characterized by the old policies of the previous two decades. As a result, during a period when the country had regained a healthy economy, when the Alliance south of the border was expanding numerically and financially, and when the Alliance in western Canada together with other holiness groups across Canada were experiencing unprecedented growth rates, the Eastern and Central Canadian District showed zero growth in the number of churches. District contributions to Alliance missions grew from $31,000 in 1934 to $63,000 in 1946. However, as inflation during this period was at least 100 percent, the growth in purchasing power of the contributions remained essentially static.

Shortly after taking office, Mason explained his strategy for district advance to be first "the building up of existing works ... and then from the strengthened churches to branch out into nearby towns."[98] It seemed to make good sense because many churches were indeed struggling to keep alive. However, the success of the policy depended on what was meant by "building up" the existing works. The Committee of Evangelism became the Committee of Home Work and instead of devoting its time to developing opportunities for pioneer evangelism and new churches, was mostly occupied with planning and implementing a program of missionary conventions for existing churches. Uneasy with the virtual collapse of the former pioneer evangelism program, and apparently attributing the reason to an obviously overworked district superintendent, the Home Work Committee in September 1936 urged the Christie Street Tabernacle to provide its own full-time pastor or at least assistant pastor, "thus releasing our district superintendent for more district work."[99]

One year later, Rev. F. W. Hollinrake retired from the pastorate of Delta Tabernacle and was taken on as assistant pastor of Christie

Street Tabernacle. However, due to his failing health, this arrangement lasted only fifteen months. Not until February 1940 did Rev. William H. Lewellan accept a call and was Mason released for full-time district work.

District Superintendent Mason had been in Toronto less than two weeks when, in September 1935, Rev. Oswald Smith of the Peoples Church made an offer to pay the cost of sending out five new Alliance missionary couples. During the ensuing interview, David Mason and his assistant, Frank Irwin, faced three former Alliance colleagues, Oswald Smith, Lionel Watson and William Willis (formerly committee vice-chairman and treasurer of the Alliance Tabernacle). The meeting was cordial. All agreed to forget the past and concentrate on present and future possibilities. Watson wanted assurance that the Alliance was prepared to cooperate.

The Peoples Church leaders explained that their offer rested on the fact that money could be raised more easily for new ventures than for the support of existing programs—a sad but candid observation. They agreed that other "appealing" projects would be considered. Pastor Smith's old Bible college friend, Alliance missionary Rev. Ivory Jeffrey, had acquainted him with the need for a building in which to train pastors in French Indo China. The upshot of the meeting was that Mason attended a Peoples Church evangelistic service two days later, at which he and Alliance missions were introduced, as only Pastor Smith could do, and the Alliance, through Ivory Jeffrey, received a substantial gift for the work in Indo China.[100]

Six months later, in the spring of 1936, District Superintendent Mason, Rev. W. E. Pressman of the Netherlands East Indies, Rev. Frank Irwin of French Indo China and Rev. E. P. Howard of French West Africa, together with missionaries and officials of other missionary societies participated in an eight-day missionary convention in the Peoples Church. At the close of the convention, the Alliance received a substantial contribution for its missionary program.[101]

In March 1938, Smith advised Mason that other missionary societies were sending their presidents to his conventions. He therefore requested that President Shuman address the next Peoples Church missionary convention.[102] It appears that Shuman decided against participation. Almost certainly, if he had participated, it would have bred resentment among Alliance churches, unless he was prepared to take the time to participate in their missionary conventions as well. It is probable that Shuman's decision was interpreted as a lack of cooperation on the part of the Alliance. In any event, Alliance participation in Peoples Church conventions dwindled thereafter, and the arrangement came to an end a few years later.

Perhaps the support for Alliance missions from the independent Peoples Church (or a fear of losing it), inspired Mason to have a new vision for Alliance advance in Canada. At any rate, during the annual district conference of September 1939, he shocked the delegates with the words:

> I feel that perhaps the time is ripe for development along other lines, such as are used by other faith missionary organizations. It might be well, if Conference considers it wise, to ask the Board of Managers to allow us in Canada to function as a missionary society, rather than just another district. This might entail a missionary headquarters with a definite program of missionary propaganda (in churches outside the Alliance fellowship) as well as a caring for existing works.[103]

Not wanting to be rushed into such a novel scheme, conference adopted a motion that the district executive committee study the details of the superintendent's suggestion. After consultation with the Home Department, the committee advised the conference of September 1940 against the adoption of the plan.[104] Rather, it recommended that more effort be made to develop the district along conventional lines. Reinforcing this opinion, the Home Work Committee recommended that in view of the large amount of money lying dormant in the extension fund, the district superintendent and executive committee take action to "open one or more new places for our work this coming year."[105] However, in his annual report, the district superintendent did little to encourage home work progress. He expressed "regret that there have been no new places opened for our work in the district during the past year." A number of possibilities had been considered "but circumstances, etc., seemed to render any fruitful effort unavailing."[106]

The period 1936 to 1939 was a sad epoch for the Alliance Gospel Tabernacle in St. John, New Brunswick. The work had been founded specifically to meet the spiritual needs of a poor section of the city, and for this reason, although missionary interest had remained good, especially during conventions, contributions had never been re-

Conflict of Interest / 179

5.7 The delegates of the General Council of May 1930 pose in front of the Parliament Buildings in Ottawa.

5.8 During the 1930s E. W. (Ed) Simmons was a vigorous lay evangelist, under the extensive home evangelism policy of District Superintendent J. D. Williams.

5.9 Rev. J. D. Williams was superintendent of the Eastern and Central Canadian District from 1928 to 1934 and of the Western Canadian District from 1933 to 1936.

5.10 Rev. James F. Brabazon, a furloughed missionary to India, served as interim superintendent from August 1934 to August 1935.

5.11 Pastor C. V. Freeman of Montreal enjoys a relaxing afternoon during a Laurentian speaking engagement.

5.12 The Prayer Conference of 1934 meets at the Owen Sound Tabernacle.

5.13 Rev. David Mason was superintendent from 1935 to 1946.

garded as high. After the conclusion of the ministry of Rev. James E. Davey in 1930, Rev. A. G. Philpotts became pastor. A decline set in four years later and by 1936, both attendance and missionary giving were at an all-time low.[107] As far as Philpotts and Mason were concerned, relocation to a more affluent section of town was the answer.

The older members of the congregation, who lived in the vicinity of the Prince Edward Street building and had founded the work as a ministry to the city's poor, resisted relocation to an area that would serve a different social class. The newer members were anxious to relocate to affluent areas closer to where they lived. To justify his decision for relocation, District Superintendent Mason stated, "The Alliance endeavors to reach principally the better middle-class as its first objective in any city."[108] In protest, Head Elder John Willett wrote,

> Are there no lost souls to be reached in the immediate vicinity of the church? Have we forgotten that God is no respecter of locations as well as persons? This church was dedicated twenty years ago to the service of God in a ministry to the poor and neglected of St. John. If some of our number wish to go out and reach after the upper classes, we say "God speed" but let us carry on the work in which we were engaged when the Alliance was pleased to receive us nine years ago.[109]

Mason responded:

> It is not that we do not feel the necessity of home mission work.... But, as an Alliance movement we have another mission and in order to accomplish our mission another location would be more suitable.[110]

These and many other polemic pronouncements polarized the church. The result of a congregational vote taken on June 30 convinced Philpotts that a solid majority would follow him to a new location, and the first service in temporary premises on King Street was conducted on August 15, 1937, against the strong protests of John Willett and his followers.[111] Difficulties with the landlord necessitated a second move two months later to another area on Cobourg Street.[112] Less than half the original congregation accompanied Philpotts on the first move and fewer still went with him to the second location. The work struggled on for twenty months and was officially closed on March 31, 1939.[113]

Meanwhile, the segment of the congregation which refused to move organized as a new independent church, meeting in the chapel of the Prince Edward Street building and retaining the old name of the Gospel Tabernacle. Its first pastor, Rev. Professor J. W. Hill, of Baptist connection, ministered until the fall of 1939. In November of that year, Rev. Lawrence J. Pyne, district evangelist, was invited to hold an evangelistic campaign at the Gospel Tabernacle.* So great was the response that the 1,400-seat sanctuary, unused for three years, quickly had to be prepared for use and was soon filled. At the conclusion of the campaign on December 1, Pyne received and accepted a call to the pastorate of this independent church. He served the Gospel Tabernacle in St. John for one year, and is credited with bringing it into the Alliance fold again—this time as an affiliate.[114]

On March 29, 1944, during the ministry of Rev. Ernest J. Bailey,** the church was reorganized as an official Alliance branch.[115] Today, located on McLaughlin Crescent in East St. John, the church is known as the St. John Alliance Church.

THE WAR YEARS

The 1930s were characterized not only by economic hardship but by a growing threat of a new and even more terrible world war.

---

* Born in Saco, Maine, in 1912, Lawrence J. Pyne grew up in St. John and attended Sunday school in the Prince Edward (Brussels) Street Church. After attending Nyack and Toronto Bible Colleges, he entered the Alliance ministry in 1934, serving in both eastern and western Canada for fourteen years before returning to the United States in 1948.

** Ernest J. Bailey was born into a Methodist home in Listowell, Ontario, in 1912. He was converted at Stratford at the age of nine under the ministry of Scottish evangelist Joseph C. McCauley. The family moved to Owen Sound and came into fellowship with the Alliance. At the time of his graduation from Nyack College in 1937, when asked where he might serve, he replied, "Only my Saviour knows, but my heart is in the Country I love—Canada." His first charge was a pioneer work in Lindsay, Ontario, where he ministered "with high hopes, unbounded enthusiasm and faith in God." He served a total of 29 years in Canadian churches and ten years in the New England District. For several years he was a member of the Home Department and the board of managers, where he earned a reputation for "spiritual fervency and intellectual honesty." Among other activities he worked with the Reorganization Committee in 1970, was chairman of the Sunday School Curriculum Committee, a member of the Committee on Publications and the Board of Directors of Christian Publications, Inc. For a while he was secretary of the Alliance Corporation in Canada and played a significant role in the early deliberations that led to autonomy for the Alliance in Canada.

The fear of such a catastrophe gave birth to a widespread attitude of pacifism throughout Britain, the Commonwealth, and the United States. After Hitler was appointed chancellor of Germany in 1933 and the death of President Field Marshal von Hindenburg a year later, war became a certainty. In Canada, pacifism gave way to a determination to prepare for an ugly task that could not be prevented.

Britain and most of the Commonwealth went to war with Nazi Germany on September 3, and Canada issued its own declaration of war on September 10. Most Canadians were convinced that Hitler was an incorrigible tyrant and aggressor, who had to be put down. Quebec, still smarting from World War I memories of conscription, viewed the war of 1939 somewhat differently from the rest of the nation. Nevertheless, the country was remarkably united. Young men and women from across the nation, including Quebec, began to enlist and Alliance young people played their full part.

Conditions in the United States affecting Alliance attitudes toward the war in 1939 were considerably different from those in Canada. President Franklin D. Roosevelt moved cautiously because his nation was deeply divided on the issues of neutrality and intervention. More than that, the United States was anything but united in matters of blood ties and national friendships. Robert L. Niklaus has fairly expressed the American dilemma in the Alliance publication *All for Jesus*, as follows:

> Arguments did not always rest on logic or biblical principles. Americans of German, Italian or Irish descent wanted to see England and France take a beating. Jews saw Hitler as evil personified. Anglo-Saxons generally supported the Allied cause, while Catholics sympathized with Franco's Spain and followed the Pope's contention that Communism was the world's worst enemy.[116]

Alliance leaders in the United States were divided in their views of the drama unfolding in Europe. One month after the war began, an *Alliance Weekly* editorial found little reason to favour one side over the other and complained about "the offensive and misleading" propaganda put forth by both Britain and Germany, which would only serve to "hinder feelings of sympathy." "Let us, who are Christian," concluded the editor, "maintain open minds as the inspired miasma of international hate spreads widely, creating bitter feelings of contempt and misjudgment."[117]

Such a view, expressed by the official organ of the Alliance, could not be expected to be understood or accepted by Canadian members, engaged in a life and death struggle to preserve, in their view, the very same freedoms and rights held to be basic in the American dream.

In May 1940, a third of a million British troops were trapped on the Dunkerque beaches between the advancing German forces and the sea. When it seemed nothing could save them, hundreds of small private craft put to sea from ports in southeastern England, and for three days and nights kept up a shuttle in a daring and determined effort to save their kin. Surprisingly, the weather remained fair and the seas calm. A mysterious fog settled and persisted over the beaches, protecting rescuer and rescued from airborne extermination. In the end, almost all the British Expeditionary Force was rescued.

To the world at large it was the "luck of the British," but to many Christians in the Commonwealth it was the "miracle of Dunkerque." In Toronto, the Christie Street Tabernacle went on public record as ascribing the deliverance to the grace of God, in the provision of the protecting fog and calm seas. Notices were inserted in Toronto newspapers and a copy of the "resolution of thanks" was sent to the editor of the *Alliance Weekly*. The resolution was published—without comment.[118] Members of the Alliance in Canada had hoped for an indication that their American brethren had stood with them in their time of desperate need, or at least joined with them in rejoicing.

The Japanese attack on Pearl Harbour in December dispelled American neutrality. Americans soon found themselves at war, not only with Japan, but also with the Axis powers in Europe. Together with other denominations, the Alliance supplied chaplains, and lay members joined the forces in ever increasing numbers. Suddenly, the war became necessary and even noble in the eyes of the writers in the *Alliance Weekly*. Local churches were urged to minister to servicemen and women and the conducting of meetings in military installations became a common item of note.[119] The names and sometimes the photographs of those enlisting began to appear in serialized "Honour Rolls." Finally, after some prodding from Canadian sources, a much belated, incomplete "All Canadian Honour Roll" appeared in December 1943—more than four years after Canadian Alliance members had joined in the fray and indeed not a few had laid down their lives in the defence of freedom.[120]

If nothing more, these incidents serve to illustrate some of the difficulties of publishing an official organ of an international denomination. It is an almost impossible task to be all things to all men.

Almost immediately following Canada's entry into the war in September 1939, in an attempt to avoid running out of convertible currency reserves, the federal government restricted the transfer of Canadian funds to the United States to $100 per month. Until then, all Canadian contributions to Alliance missions were transmitted monthly by local treasurers to New York headquarters, which issued receipts to the donors. Now headquarters established a branch treasury office in Toronto to handle all Canadian contributions and receipts, and appointed District Superintendent David Mason as manager. Permission was obtained to transmit drafts in sterling to India, "thus absorbing all Canadian contributions." The Toronto office functioned until after the conclusion of hostilities. Although the arrangement was no doubt much to the liking of Mason, it must have constituted a further distraction from normal district responsibilities.[121]

The year 1944 saw the second branch of the Alliance in the maritime provinces permanently established in Truro, Nova Scotia. Fourteen years previously, on June 16, 1930, at the close of a campaign by D. J. Fant, Sr., District Superintendent J. D. Williams chaired a meeting which resulted in the formation of a branch with fourteen charter members. Paul R. Roffe, a recent graduate of Nyack College and future Alliance missionary to Peru, acted as secretary, pro tem. At the first congregational meeting two weeks later, W. P. Carter was elected secretary-treasurer, along with three other executive committee members. Paul Roffe served as pastor until he left for Peru in August of the following year.[122]

Services were held in a hall at 619 Prince Street for one year, after which the congregation moved to the auditorium of the old YMCA building at the corner of Pleasant and Prince Streets. Unfortunately, the work was plagued by short pastorates—nine in six years. Rev. John A. MacMillen,* a former Alliance missionary to China

---

* From October 1932 to May 1934, Rev. John A. MacMillen, temporarily residing in Toronto, served on the district executive and assisted in district affairs. Born in Toronto of Presbyterian parents, MacMillen learned the printing trade and founded a printing press. From his youth he was interested in missionary work, serving on the boards of the Canadian Mission to India and the Chinese Christian Institute of Toronto. In 1923 he went to Wuchow, South China, to direct Alliance Publications and three years later he was sent to the Philippines as chairman of the field, where he organized the Ebenezer Bible Institute. After his wife's death in 1929, he returned to Canada. Later he would serve as assistant editor of the *Alliance Weekly* and teach at Nyack College for 16 years.

and the Philippines, served as pastor for nine months in 1932. Writing to District Superintendent Williams, MacMillen put his finger on the historic problem for new denominations trying to penetrate the maritimes. "Truro," he wrote, "is over-churched and over-missioned. Indeed, I have never been in a town of this size with so many places of worship." MacMillen explained that the churches were highly competitive and suspicious of each other, so that goodwill and cooperation were almost impossible. Wistfully he added, "But now that we have entered, it would be a pity to allow it to go down."[123]

MacMillen's words were ominous. Without more developed ministries to provide a semblance of security and commitment, the work steadily declined and finally closed its doors in late 1936.

In January 1944, Rev. A. W. Roffe, the former district superintendent, received a letter from Louise H. McCully, superintendent of the Berachah Mission in Truro. That work had been started by Louise McCully and her sister Elizabeth in 1885, following a gospel campaign by William Meikle. As a result, children were brought in from homes where parents seldom if ever attended churches, in a section of town known as "Hell's Half-Acre." Three years later, through the gifts of interested friends, a permanent mission hall was built on Waddell Street, near Queen Street.

In 1896, Elizabeth took full charge of Berachah Mission when Louise left to attend Simpson's Missionary Training Institute in New York. Upon graduation two years later, Louise and her fellow graduate Margaret Quinn of Listowell, Ontario, sailed for their first term as Alliance missionaries to Central China. When, two years later, the Boxer rebellion temporarily drove out the missionaries from China, Louise McCully went to Korea under the Presbyterian Mission Board of Canada. There she founded the Bible Institute for Women, of which she was principal for many years. In 1909, Elizabeth joined her sister in Korea, and the work at Berachah Mission came under the superintendency of Thomas Edwards, an early convert of the mission.

In 1943, after 45 years of missionary service in the Orient, Louise McCully returned to her native Truro. Edwards, who had been superintendent for 34 years, retired, and Louise McCully, at the age of 79, again became superintendent of the mission. Although she felt well able to carry out the administrative and preaching duties, she soon concluded (not surprisingly) that she was no longer able to tramp the streets and climb the stairs required for the visitation part of the work.

Louise McCully had not lost her love for the "Alliance message," nor had she lost her propensity for Presbyterian independence. Her letter to Roffe enquired if the Alliance would send "an Alliance trained man who will preach a full gospel and will work to reach some of the spiritually hungry folk. . . . A young married man and his wife would seem quite ideal." To ensure that there would be no misunderstanding, Louise McCully added, "We do not propose to ask you to start a church here."[124] Roffe forwarded the letter to Mason who opened communications with Miss McCully. Mason explained that the Alliance did not send their men to independent works unless they would agree to hold an annual Alliance missionary convention and pledge. However, he did send Pastor Ernest J. Bailey of St. John to explore Truro possibilities.[125]

The result was that an Alliance missionary convention was held the following October, attended by Mason. At the conclusion, Pastor G. Robert Gray of Kemptville received and accepted a call to Berachah Mission. Happily, a few of the families that had formed the first Alliance venture in Truro joined the work at Berachah Mission.

In January 1945, the aged and ailing Louise McCully stepped down and Gray became superintendent as well as preacher and worker. At the same time, the name Berachah Mission was changed to The Christian and Missionary Alliance. On June 29, 1946, the work was "partially organized" as an Alliance branch, with the faithful Thomas Edwards, Elmer Johnson and Mrs. Boyd as an executive committee. A year later, the property was turned over to the district. In 1961 the old building was condemned and razed. For the next four years, a remnant of the congregation met in a variety of ill-suited locations. During the ministry of Rev. W. Cyril Troyer, a lot at 29 Philip Street was purchased in 1964 and on April 1 of the following year the first service was held in the partially completed sanctuary. This historic congregation continues today in the same quarters and is known as Truro Alliance Church.

An estimated 35 million people directly or indirectly lost their lives in World War II, the most destructive war in human history. Apart from the loss of life, unknown millions suffered injury, deprivation and mental anguish. The Alliance family was not spared. Scarcely a family did not lose a loved one or close friend. Unfortunately, no one seems to have compiled a complete list of the names of Alliance laity who lost their lives in the defence of cherished freedoms.

Among the official Alliance workers, many accounts have survived of perils and hardships sustained as a result of the conflict. One of the most dramatic incidents of suffering was that of missionary Ethel Bell (Roffe) of French West Africa (see page 64). Widowed and returning to Canada on furlough in 1942 with her two children, their ship was torpedoed in the South Atlantic and sank within one minute. Only fourteen survived, including Ethel Bell and her children, she, a lone woman among eleven men and two children, on a raft for twenty days! Burned by day and chilled by night, they were never dry. With little food or water, men died one by one, Ethel conducting the funeral services, and committing each victim to the shark-infested waters. When first spotted by an American destroyer, they were mistaken for a U-boat and shelled. Providentially, they were not injured and the destroyer finally rescued them.

Four Alliance missionaries suffered death by violence. Four died in Japanese prison camps, and two died after release, from afflictions that were either caused or aggravated by prison conditions. Three of these missionaries were from the Eastern and Central Canadian District. Rev. Franklin Grobb developed acute appendicitis while in a Japanese camp. Delays in carrying out an operation resulted in death from peritonitis, two months before the end of the war. Veteran missionary statesman Dr. Robert Jaffray, a diabetic, succumbed to the effects of inadequate and inappropriate prison diet, one month before the armistice. Rev. Ernest Presswood survived prison camp in a weakened condition. Six months later, in Borneo, he died of pneumonia.

DISTRICT DISSENTION

As the war neared its conclusion, David Mason reached his tenth anniversary as district superintendent. Undoubtedly, he hoped to end his Canadian days in peace, and with goodwill to all. However, his final months would be largely absorbed with a sad debacle involving four churches, including historic Bethany Tabernacle of Peterborough, and a family of pastors that he had hastily and unwisely admitted to the district pastoral team.

The work in Peterborough had its origin in 1889, when Rev. John Salmon formed the Peterborough branch, and three years later opened Bethany Mission. After a few months, the branch united with the mission, and, under the aegis of Salmon, Bethany Church (Tabernacle) was founded.[126]

True to Salmon's Congregational convictions, all churches formed by him were "entirely separate from and independent of any outside ecclesiastical control."[127] They were officially united only by subscription to the Bethany Constitution, which affirmed a commitment to the doctrines of the Fourfold Gospel.

When, in 1910, the Home Department brought pressure on district superintendents to persuade the churches to commit their properties to the Alliance, Salmon resigned.[128] His successor, Rev. Harold Stephens, took up the task, but all the churches committed to the Bethany Constitution refused to budge on the issue. Two years later, District Superintendent Long made a similar attempt which met with similar refusal. Over the years, many unsuccessful attempts were made by district superintendents and the Home Secretary to persuade the Peterborough church to scrap its Bethany Constitution and to adopt the Alliance Constitution with its "reversion clause."[129]

Notwithstanding, agreement was reached a year later to reorganize the church along the Alliance pattern and to abide by certain articles of the Alliance Constitution, notably the holding of an Alliance annual missionary convention and pledge, the role of the district superintendent in the calling or dismissal of a pastor and in the overall spiritual supervision of the church.[130]

In 1931, a heated disagreement between the church board and the district superintendent regarding the calling of a pastor polarized the congregation into two sections—the "old" members, who would struggle to draw the work closer to the Alliance, and the "new" members, who would work to make the church entirely independent.[131]

Meanwhile, Walter S. Crone, founder and pastor of the independent Evangelistic Centre in Niagara Falls, was working very hard with an evangelistic outreach program among the Indians in the surrounding countryside. After reading the Alliance Manual, which not only contained a statement of faith with which he could identify, but also indicated an Alliance concern for pioneer missions, Crone concluded that he and his church would fit well into the Alliance organization and program.[132] In December 1940, Crone dispatched a letter to District Superintendent Mason. As a result, the Evangelistic Centre was reorganized as an Alliance branch and Crone was ordained to the Alliance ministry.[133]

A year later, Crone, assisted by his brother-in-law, Harold Edwards, opened a daughter church in Fort Erie, Edwards becoming its first pastor. Within a few months, the work became an Alliance branch and Edwards became an official Alliance worker.[134]

The renewal of home evangelism concern as a fundamental plank in the Alliance program continued to make progress, despite the inhibitions of world depression and world war. In his annual letter to all district conferences in 1941, Home Secretary Nelson urged steps to be taken to extend the home work. One year later, he stated that "Each District should seek to develop a definite and clearly defined extension program," and if needed "set up permanent District extension funds." Lest the districts think only in terms of large urban centres, he added that their programs should keep in mind "a wide range of types and sizes of churches." This policy interested Crone, who, during a talk with Mason, urged that the district become involved in rural evangelism. According to Mason, Crone was told that "we didn't have a proper set-up in the Alliance for home mission work."[135] However, according to Crone, he was told that "home mission work was not in line with Alliance policy and would have to be organized outside the Alliance."[136]

As for the conference of September 1942, its sole reaction to the reading of the Home Secretary's encyclical was to appoint a Sunday on which "a sermon be preached on the theme of home evangelism."[137]

The pulpit of Bethany Tabernacle became vacant in December 1942 and was filled by Crone a month later. Before leaving Niagara Falls, he arranged for another brother-in-law, Norman H. Street, to take over the Evangelistic Centre, and he was ordained during the Conference of August 1943. At the same time Crone introduced his father, H. W. Crone, to the district executive committee, which appointed him to the ministry of the Lappin Avenue Church, in the west end of Toronto.[138]

During the short interval between the Peterborough ministries, the issue of the constitution surfaced again. The church board decided that this time "something definite should be done to have the issue permanently settled."[139] It was discovered that the property deeds referred to the Bethany Constitution. Legal counsel advised that the property could not be turned over to the Alliance or anyone else, unless and until the Bethany Constitution was superceded. There was obviously no possibility of achieving that with the present membership, but by the same token, neither was there any way to agree on a definition of "outside ecclesiastical control" favourable to the Alliance exercising any authority in the affairs of the church. This meant that only the lowest grade of affiliation was possible. The implications of this situation caused the slumbering antagonists of the "old" and the "new" member groups to awake to full vitality and vehemence.

Into this unhappy quarrel came the new pastor, Walter Crone. He plunged into the extensive local program of evangelism among the

Indians of the Rice Lake Reserve. If the district was not going to do anything about it, he reasoned, he would do something himself. Accordingly, in May 1943, he organized Canadian Pioneer Evangelism, a society "to carry the Gospel of Jesus Christ the Saviour, Sanctifier, Healer and Coming King, into the regions of our country which are not being reached by any other Gospel work." The society had a board of directors and an ordaining council, whose members were pastors and leading laymen from an assortment of churches, including two Alliance churches. All this was in place before Mason was advised.[140]

Understandably, this development embarrassed and even angered Mason. He stated that he could not permit "an accredited Alliance worker to project an organization, which in many ways will have the same function as the Alliance."[141] Crone seemed to see the point and offered to disband his society if the district would pursue home evangelism with vigour. However, the district executive committee decided that Crone's objective "does not come within the scope of our extension program, as this district is not set up to properly support home mission work," adding that Alliance responsibility is "primarily the propagation of the Gospel in the lands where Christ has not been named."[142]

Meanwhile, differences between Crone and Mason continued to erode relationships between Bethany Tabernacle and Mason. The "old" members sided with the district superintendent, while the "new" members sided with their pastor.[143]

In July 1943, Crone sent letters to other Alliance pastors in the district, soliciting support for his home missions. Once more tensions mounted.[144] Again Crone offered to dissolve his society, if the district "will immediately set up machinery" for the development of home missions, this time offering his own services in "a responsible position in this department of the District work."[145]

Again the district executive committee turned down the offer, this time giving its reason as a preference for "extension in urban centres rather than rural."[146]

In an attempt to stem the tide of dissention, the district executive committee reexamined its former stand, but again decided "that it is not the Lord's will for us as a District to assume responsibility for the work of Canadian Pioneer Evangelism."[147]

The impasse prevailed throughout the year 1944. In December, Crone resigned from the pastorate of Bethany Tabernacle on the grounds that the district was not in compliance with Alliance policy. He defended his claim by quoting from the Alliance Manual the stated policy to evangelize "the neglected areas at home" and to "prosecute mission work in the home field."[148]

The congregation was faced with either losing its pastor or severing connections with the Alliance.[149] "After a very lengthy discussion" a large majority of the members expressed the view that if the pastor could no longer fellowship with the district, neither could the congregation, and they asked their board to find some means to achieve complete independence.[150]

However, the board decided to try again to persuade the district to "implement the policies stated in the Alliance Manual concerning home missions."[151]

On December 27, the board and Crone met with David Mason and Nathan Bailey. Crone agreed to withdraw his resignation and the board agreed to take no further action regarding separation from the Alliance, in return for the district agreeing to bring up the matter of a district policy for home evangelism at the conference of September 1945.[152] An uneasy calm prevailed during the nine-month interval.

District Superintendent Mason did bring before conference the request of Bethany Tabernacle for the district to initiate a "program of Home Mission work in the rural sections of our District."[153] The Home Work Committee, under the leadership of Nathan Bailey, expressed its conviction for the urgent need for "a definite Home Mission effort of a pioneer nature to reach out to the rural and unevangelized sections of the District, where souls can be reached for Christ." It recommended the appointment of Crone to the position of full-time Rural Field Secretary. Conference adopted the recommendation.[154]

It looked like a solution had been found to the gnawing problem at Peterborough. However, Crone turned down the offer.[155]

Two weeks later, Crone surrendered his Alliance credentials, but this time he did not resign as pastor of Bethany Tabernacle. There then ensued numerous meetings regarding the severing of Alliance ties. Acrimony and discourtesy characterized many of these meetings. In April 1946, Pastor Crone and a committee of three drafted a proposed constitution for a completely independent church.[156]

A week or two later, Council elected David Mason as treasurer of the Alliance. Undoubtedly, he was glad to be rid of the turmoil of the Eastern and Central Canadian District. He left Toronto three weeks later, turning over district affairs to Rev. Nathan Bailey, on an interim basis. That same month, Bailey and Home Secretary Nelson made a last attempt to hold on to Bethany Tabernacle by two lengthy discussions in Peterborough—all to no avail.[157]

On June 26, Bethany Tabernacle members voted 73 per cent in favour of complete independence.[158] So, Bethany Tabernacle, the second oldest church in Canada to be associated with the Alliance, severed its connections of 57 years.*

Nor was that the end of the problem. Pastor H. W. Crone of the Lappin Avenue Church was instrumental in the rupture of his congregation. He was dismissed from the Alliance but filed suit for wrongful dismissal.[159] Fortunately, the matter was settled out of court, at some cost. The decimated congregation was able to hold on to its property and its existence within the Alliance because it was committed to the Alliance Constitution.

Pastor Edwards of the Fort Erie church found he would be more comfortable outside the Alliance, and his church broke its Alliance affiliation "so as to be free to assist in any good work, home or foreign."[160]

The Evangelistic Centre in Niagara Falls was broken apart. Pastor Street, although ordained by the Alliance, had never felt comfortable with its doctrines of sanctification and divine healing. He surrendered his credentials and resigned from the pastorate of the centre. When he left, at least three-quarters of the congregation went with him to found the Church of the Redeemer (Independent). Some of the seceders demanded repayment of their capital loans against the centre. Fortunately, the remnant of the congregation, at great personal sacrifice and with generous assistance from the district revolving fund, were able to pay off their creditors and retain the building for the Alliance. Slowly the faithful rallied around the leadership of Pastor H. C. Harris. In March 1969, under the ministry of Rev. Henry Hiebert, a new church building was erected and the name of the church became Glengate Alliance Church.

Thus, of the four churches and four pastors of the Crone connection that became involved in the controversy about home missions, two churches were salvaged and two were lost, along with all four pastors. One may wonder why such catastrophes occurred. There were many contributing factors. Undoubtedly, the place of home missions within the district program was a major issue. Despite

---

* Bethany Tabernacle exists today as The Church of the Open Bible, a member of the Associated Gospel Churches of Canada.

the change in Alliance policy of the early 1930s, urging a vigorous pursuit of both urban and rural home evangelism for its own sake, Mason clung to the concept of a determinative foreign missions program, the economics of which precluded any serious attempt to invest in home evangelism, particularly in economically costly rural evangelism. His tunnel vision in this matter was at the root of much of the unpopularity he experienced throughout his superintendency. Nor can the members of the district executive committee hide in the shadow of the determined Scot.

Reporting the final details of the Peterborough loss to Home Secretary Nelson, Rev. Nathan Bailey concluded, "I feel we are reaping the fruit of the past few years of District management."[161] It is doubtful Bailey meant to imply that all blame should be laid at the feet of "District management." Given the facts, many of the actions of the dissidents cannot be excused. Nevertheless, failure to pursue a denomination's homeland responsibility, perfunctory accreditations and intransigent attitudes on the part of district leadership also played their part.

REFERENCES

1. *The Presbyterian Witness*, Toronto, 1 Mar 1923.
2. *The Toronto Star*, 11 Jan 1925.
3. Basis of Union (Toronto, 1922), p. 18.
4. Records of Proceedings of the First Council (Toronto, 1925), p. 214.
5. John S. Moir, *The Cross in Canada* (Toronto: The Ryerson Press, 1966), p. 226.
6. S. D. Clark, *Church and Sect in Canada* (Toronto: University of Toronto Press, 1948), p. 431.
7. N. Keith Clifford, *The Resistance to Church Union in Canada 1904-1939* (Vancouver: University of B.C. Press, 1985), p. 184.
8. C. E. Silcox, *Church Union in Canada* (New York: Institute of Social and Religious Research, 1933), p. 463.
9. S. D. Chown, *The Study of Church Union in Canada* (Toronto: The Ryerson Press, 1930), p. 80.
10. *Church Union in Canada*, pp. 55, 464.
11. A. C. Forrest, *Why the Sects?* (Toronto: The United Church Publishing House, 1946), p. 12.
12. Eastern and Central Canadian Districts, Letters, Home Department., Watson to Richards, 2 Dec 1925; ibid., Minutes, 15 Dec 1925.
13. Eastern, Minutes, 27 Dec 1926.
14. Home Department, Minutes, 2 Dec 1924, p. 114.

15. *Alliance Weekly*, 6 Dec 1924, p. 395.
16. Annual Report, 1927-1928, p. 118.
17. Ibid., 1928-1929, pp. 8, 9.
18. Ibid., 1932-1933, p. 12; Eastern, Conference Records, President's letter, 7 Sep 1934.
19. *Alliance Weekly*, 2 May 1925, p. 303; 5 Sep 1925, p. 614; 19 Sep 1925, p. 642.
20. Eastern, Letters, Montreal, Beach to Watson, 14 Sep 1925.
21. Ibid.
22. Ibid.; *Alliance Weekly*, 22 May 1926, p. 342.
23. Eastern, Letters, Montreal, Beach to Watson, 2 Oct 1925.
24. Ibid., 1 Nov 1925.
25. Ibid., Fant to Richards/Watson, 4 Nov 1925.
26. Ibid.
27. Eastern, Minutes, 14 May; 15 Jul 1926.
28. Reminiscences of Rev. and Mrs. F. W. Sparke.
29. Eastern, Reports of the Branches, Montreal, 1926 and 1927; ibid., Conference Records, 18 May 1927.
30. Annual Report, 1925-1926, p. 131.
31. Eastern, Letters, Smith, Report to Elders, Jan 1930.
32. Ibid.
33. Author's interview with Dr. O. J. Smith, 11 Aug 1977; Lois Neely, *Fire in His Bones* (Wheaton: Tyndale House Publishers Inc., 1982), pp. 148, 149.
34. Eastern, Conference Records, 13 May 1926.
35. *Alliance Weekly*, 5 Jun 1926, p. 375.
36. Alliance Tabernacle Willowvale Park Corp., Minutes, 17 May 1926.
37. Eastern, Letters, Smith, Smith to Board of Managers, 27 Jul 1928.
38. Ibid., Watson to Smith, 30 Jan 1927.
39. Willowvale, Minutes, 19, 29 Dec 1927; *Fire in His Bones*, p. 155.
40. Ibid.
41. Willowvale, Minutes, 5, 12 Jul; 12 Aug 1928; Home Department, Minutes, 4 Sep 1928, p. 200.
42. Ibid.
43. Eastern, Letters, Smith, Smith to Board of Managers, 27 Jul 1928.
44. Ibid., Fant to Smith, 2 Aug 1928.
45. Ibid., Report of Committee to meet Rev. O. J. Smith, 6 Oct 1930; ibid., Williams to Christie, 10 Oct 1930.
46. Ibid., Resolution of Board of Alliance Tabernacle, 1 Nov 1930; ibid., Fant to Executive Committee of Alliance Tabernacle, 7 Nov 1930; ibid., Christie to Williams, 18 Nov 1930; ibid., Fant to Williams, 25 Nov 1930.
47. *Alliance Weekly*, 9 Oct 1926, p. 664.
48. Ibid., 20 Feb 1926, p. 126; 13 Mar 1926, p. 179.

196 / *Conflict of Interest*

49. Author's interview with Rev. W. H. Brooks, 6 Oct 1983.
50. Ibid.
51. Eastern, Minutes, 6 Dec 1927; 5 Mar 1928. Eastern, Conference Records, 1928.
52. *Alliance Weekly*, 9 Aug 1930, p. 517.
53. Ibid., 9 May 1935, p. 305.
54. Author's interview with Rev. W. H. Brooks, 6 Oct 1983.
55. Lindsay Reynolds, *Footprints* (Toronto: The Christian and Missionary Alliance in Canada, 1981), pp. 244, 281, 282.
56. Eastern, Reports of the Branches, London, 1926.
57. Eastern, Letters, Montreal, Sparke to Watson, 11 Jan 1927.
58. Eastern, Reports of the Branches, Montreal, 1927.
59. Eastern, Conference Records, 18 May 1928.
60. Eastern, Minutes, 5 Mar 1928.
61. Ibid., 17 May 1928.
62. Ibid., 15 Jan 1929; Eastern, Letters, Quebec incorporation, Williams to Ross, 16 Jan 1929.
63. Ibid., Ross to Williams, 8 Feb 1930.
64. Eastern, Minutes, 3 Jul 1930.
65. *Alliance Weekly*, 15 Sep 1928, p. 594.
66. Eastern, Conference Records, 29 Nov 1929.
67. *Alliance Witness*, 11 Jan 1930, p. 32.
68. Eastern, Report of District Superintendent to Executive Committee and Conference, 1929.
69. Herman Grierson, "Fifty Years in Retrospect" (Ottawa: unpublished, 1974), p. 35.
70. Eastern, Minutes, 6 Dec 1927; 14 May 1928.
71. Eastern, Letters, St. John, "Our Covenant."
72. Eastern, Minutes, 5 Mar 1928; 18 Oct 1928.
73. Ibid., 15 Dec 1925.
74. *Border Cities Star* (Windsor), 22 May 1926, p. 10.
75. Ibid., 29 May 1926, p. 10; 12 Jun 1926, p. 10.
76. Ibid., 30 Oct 1926, p. 10.
77. Eastern, Minutes, 3 Aug 1928.
78. *Border Cities Star* (Windsor), 11 Feb 1928, p. 10.
79. Ibid., 11 Feb 1928, p. 10; 2 Jun 1928, p. 6.
80. Eastern, Minutes, 29 May 1928.
81. Ibid., 3 Aug 1928.
82. *Border Cities Star* (Windsor), 8 Dec 1928, p. 11; 15 Dec 1928, p. 10.
83. Ibid., 4 May 1929, p. 12; Eastern, Conference Records, Superintendent's Annual Report, 1929.
84. *Alliance Weekly*, 31 May 1930, p. 338; 7 Jun 1930, p. 355.

85. Board of Managers, Minutes, 2 May 1933.
86. *Alliance Weekly*, 7 Jul 1934, p. 428.
87. Eastern, Minutes, 10 Jul 1934; Eastern, Conference Records, 18 Oct 1934; *Alliance Weekly*, 1 Sep 1934, p. 556.
88. Eastern, Conference Records, Report of Acting District Superintendent, Oct 1934.
89. Board of Managers, Minutes, 19 Jun 1935; Annual Report, 1935-1936, p. 133.
90. Eastern, Minutes, 3 Jun 1935.
91. Alliance Tabernacle, Letters, Hyde to Tabernacle, 13 Jul 1935.
92. Ibid., Minutes, 17 Jul 1935.
93. Ibid., Letters, Richards to Tabernacle, 31 Jul 1935.
94. Eastern, Minutes, 2 Aug 1935.
95. Alliance Tabernacle, Minutes, 2 Aug 1935.
96. Eastern, Conference Records, 10 Sep 1935.
97. *Alliance Weekly*, 1 Nov 1941, p. 696.
98. Eastern, Conference Records, Superintendent's Report, Sep 1936.
99. Ibid., Report of Committee on Home Work, Sep 1939; ibid.
100. Eastern, Letters, Smith, memo of interview, 18 Sep 1935.
101. *Alliance Weekly*, 9 May 1936, p. 300.
102. Alliance Tabernacle, Minutes, 1 Mar 1938.
103. Eastern, Conference Records, Superintendent's Report, Sep 1939.
104. Ibid., 29 Sep 1939.
105. Eastern, Minutes, 29 Feb 1940; 1 Mar 1940.
106. Eastern, Conference Records, Superintendent's Report, Sep 1940.
107. Eastern, Letters, St. John, Willett to Mason, 21 Jan 1937.
108. Ibid., Mason to Willett, 3 Jul 1936.
109. Ibid., Willett to Mason, 30 Jun 1937.
110. Ibid., Mason to Willett, 16 Jul 1937.
111. Ibid., Philpotts to Mason, 19 Aug 1937.
112. Ibid., 27 Oct 1937.
113. Ibid., 12 Mar 1939.
114. Eastern, Conference Records, Superintendent's Report, Sep 1940.
115. Ibid., Reports of the Branches, St. John, 1944.
116. Robert Niklaus, et al, *All for Jesus* (Camp Hill: Christian Publications Inc., 1986), p. 184.
117. *Alliance Weekly*, 21 Oct 1939, p. 659.
118. Ibid., 29 Jun 1940, p. 412.
119. Ibid., 10 Jan 1942, p. 28.
120. Ibid., 4 Dec 1943, p. 778.
121. Eastern, Conference Records, 28 Sep 1939; ibid., Superintendent's Report, Sep

1940; Board of Managers, Minutes, 12 Nov 1941; *Alliance Weekly*, 9 May 1942, p. 291.
122. *Alliance Weekly*, 5 Jul 1930, p. 433; 26 Jul 1930, p. 485.
123. Eastern, Letters, Truro, MacMillen to Mason, 16 May 1932.
124. Ibid., McCully to Roffe, 21 Jan 1944.
125. Ibid., Roffe to Mason, 24 Jan 1944; ibid., Mason to McCully, 3,19 Feb 1944; ibid., McCully to Mason, 12 Feb 1944; ibid., Mason to Bailey, 3 Apr 1944.
126. *Footprints*, pp. 122, 124, 125, 173-175, 272, 273.
127. Ibid., p. 518.
128. Ibid., pp. 294, 295.
129. Bethany Tabernacle, Minutes, 28, 29 Sep 1920.
130. Ibid., 5 Jan 1922
131. Bethany Tabernacle, Minutes, 24, 31 Oct 1920.
132. Ibid., 13 Dec 1944.
133. Eastern, Conference Records, Superintendent's Report, Sep 1941.
134. Eastern, Minutes, 30 Jan 1942; *Alliance Weekly*, 18 Apr 1942, p. 253; Eastern, Conference Records, Superintendent's Report, Sep 1942; ibid., Sep 1944.
135. Eastern, Letters, Peterborough, Mason to Crone, 16 June 1943.
136. Ibid., Crone to Mason, 31 May 1943.
137. Eastern, Letters, Peterborough, Memo District Superintendent to Church Board, 12 Jul 1932.
138. Eastern, Minutes, 28 Jan 1943; Eastern, Conference Records, Superintendent's Report, Sep 1942.
139. Bethany Tabernacle, Minutes, 10 Dec 1942.
140. Eastern, Letters, Peterborough, Crone to Mason, 31 May 1943.
141. Ibid., Mason to Crone, 16 June 1943.
142. Eastern, Minutes, 11, 12 Aug 1943.
143. Eastern, Letters, Peterborough, Mason to Crone, 16 June 1943.
144. Ibid., Crone to Turner, 29 Sep 1943.
145. Ibid., Mason to Crone, 30 Sep 1943.
146. Ibid., Mason to Crone, 9 Nov 1943.
147. Ibid., Sparke to Canadian Pioneer Evangelism, 29 Jan 1943.
148. Alliance Manual, 1941, section 4, 7, p. 20; Eastern, Letters, Peterborough, Crone to District Superintendent, 11 Dec 1944; ibid., Crone to Mason, 21 Dec 1944.
149. Bethany Tabernacle, Minutes, 13 Dec 1944.
150. Ibid.; Eastern, Letters, Peterborough, Crone to Mason, 15 Dec 1944.
151. Bethany Tabernacle, Minutes, 14 Dec 1944.
152. Ibid., 27 Dec 1944.
153. Eastern, Conference Records, Superintendent's Report, Sep 1945.

154. Ibid., 27 Sep 1945.
155. Ibid., 28 Sep 1945; Eastern, Minutes, 27 Sep 1945.
156. Ibid., 7 Apr 1946.
157. Ibid., 14 May 1946; Eastern, Letters, Peterborough, Bailey to Nelson, 13 Jun 1946; ibid., Nelson to Bailey, 17 Jun 1946; ibid., Nelson to Bethany Tabernacle, 21 Jun 1946.
158. Ibid., Bailey to Nelson, 27 Jun 1946; Bethany Tabernacle, Minutes, 26 Jun 1946.
159. Eastern, Minutes, 1 Nov 1945; ibid., 9 Apr 1946; ibid., 5 Sep 1946.
160. Eastern, Letters, Fort Erie, Stouffer to Freeman, 2 Aug 1946.
161. Ibid., Peterborough, Bailey to Nelson, 27 Jan 1946.

CHAPTER SIX

Seedtime and Harvest

The Council of May 1925 approved the formation of the Western Canadian District with Rev. John Woodward as its first superintendent. The new district embraced all of Canada west of Fort William, Ontario, including the Northwest Territories, but excluding British Columbia. Thus, for the first time since 1908, most of western Canada officially became a self-administrating district of the Alliance, directly answerable to the Home Secretary in New York. For the first year or two, this technical change of venue made very little difference in the operation of the Alliance in western Canada because, during the previous six months, Woodward, as assistant superintendent for western Canada, had been given a virtually free hand by Rev. A. W. Roffe in the affairs of the west.

The consummation of church union three weeks later affected church conditions in the west for different reasons than it did in the east. In the east the principal concerns associated with union had been doctrinal and political. In the west they had been social and economical. When 1925 dawned, there were already some three thousand prairie churches operating as "united" churches. Thus, when June 10 arrived, the churches of the west, for the most part, slid noiselessly into official union, escaping most of the destructive trauma that beset many of the eastern churches.[1]

However, through an irony of circumstances, the United Church of Canada came into being when the vision that had inspired it in the west was already fading. Almost immediately a reversal of ecumenical devotion began to develop. Previously the cradle of unionist activism, the west soon became the breeding ground of numerous sects and cults.[2]*

By 1925, the requirement of the larger Protestant denominations that their clergy have a university education had influenced most new ministers to adopt the teachings of modernism. This resulted in a shift of emphasis in the churches from personal salvation and personal conversion to social security and social improvement, weakening the general belief in human sinfulness and the need for redemption through the sacrifice of the cross. "The urge toward respectability, modernism, physical expansion and material success," William Mann wrote, "hastened the death of Methodism's evangelistic spirit. The United Church service became formal, dignified, uninspiring, and middle class in appeal."[4]

The abandonment of traditional evangelical teaching left a large residue of unmet spiritual need, as many of the laity of the prairies continued to place great value on the teachings of Scripture. The inundation of new sects offered the disillusioned within the larger denominations many alternative fellowships. Most of the sects were evangelical in nature. They shared a relatively tight code of morality, and a belief in the authority of the Bible, a personal conversion experience, a literal hell and the imminent return of Christ. Their hearty congregational singing, enthusiastic preaching and lay participation appealed to the farming and working classes of a society still emerging from frontier conditions. Thus, they drew support from the disaffected of all the main Protestant churches, and even some from a Roman Catholic background. Those coming from United churches, especially if they were of Methodist stock, usually favoured the Nazarenes, the Alliance, the Pentecostals or the Disciples of Christ. "Sects like the Pentecostals, the Alliance and the Prophetic Baptists," Mann wrote, "were greatly aided in the ultimate assimilation of people of European background by accepting them on equal terms with Anglo-Saxons."[5]

Another factor greatly contributed to sect opportunities in western Canada. For some years before 1925, the number of ministers coming from eastern churches and colleges steadily declined, leaving increasing numbers of western pulpits vacant. In 1926 a United Church report from Calgary and Edmonton stated that "not only is it impossible to expand the church work through the opening of new

---

* William E. Mann counted 35 sects besides numerous cults functioning in Alberta alone by 1946. William G. Smith mentions 100 sects throughout the west during the 1920s.[3]

fields, but even in fields which have long been worked, pastorates are vacant."[6] In 1927, another western report noted a decline in surplus ministers from 270 at union to 20, "and these are not available for Western Canada. The United Church is not even replacing the wastage in ministerial ranks due to death, retirement, and illness."[7] Writing about the vast numbers of new Canadians in Saskatchewan without any Christian witness, Principal E. H. Oliver of St. Andrews College, Saskatoon, stated:

> Neglected, these New Canadians will contribute towards the paganizing of our Country and will themselves suffer moral shipwreck.... I wonder if a voice will rise up against us. "I was a stranger and a New Canadian and you did not visit me. I was a lonely settler and you said, I will make profits out of your wheat, but I will let you eat out your soul in the desolation of the frontier and I will not come to you nor send a messenger of the Word."[8]

However, these and many other warnings went largely unheeded. As a result, the United Church of Canada was forced to withdraw from many rural communities.[9] Into these voids of faith and ministry moved the sects with speed and effect. Thus, the growth of the new denominations lay in large measure in the extent to which they pursued rural evangelism within the frame of the socio-religious needs of the west that prevailed during the 1920s and 1930s.

A NEW DISTRICT'S INFANCY

Against the backdrop of these unique, complicated and perhaps even providential circumstances, John Woodward began the work of the Western Canadian District of the Alliance in May 1925.

Woodward was not primarily an idea man. Although he introduced one or two novel policies, innovation was not his forte. A pragmatist *par excellence*, he made himself knowledgeable of every means being used to spread religion in western Canada. Any means that had proven successful to others, if acceptable in principle might be used. If unproductive, it could and would be dropped.

One might have thought that the organization and strategies of his new district would have been of urgency to Woodward. However, apart from setting the date for the first Western Canadian District

Conference six months off, he turned his immediate attention to the Beulah Tabernacle ministry and the operation of the Great West Mission that summer. Undoubtedly, Woodward was well aware that the full responsibility of the district would progressively encroach on his time. For the present he had pastoral assistant Margaret Connor to share the load at Beulah, and pastor Ed Cross of Gwynne helped out in Edmonton between weekends. It was then the end of May and the seven student missionaries were arriving from Nyack.

It proved to be a disappointing summer for the work of the Great West Mission. "We noted," Woodward wrote, "that the young men from Nyack were too youthful for strenuous work, and we did not obtain from them the fine quality of service which characterized the work of older workers in former years. . . . It was a year of making men, more than accomplishing much for the Lord, as far as visible results were concerned."[10]

The first Western Canadian District Workers' Prayer Conference* convened in Beulah Tabernacle, October 1-5, 1925. During its sessions the new district was organized, its first officers and executive elected and its first policies set forth. Conference expressed its unanimous support of the board of managers' appointment of Woodward as superintendent.** Agnes MacDonald was elected as secretary, and Dr. H. H. S. George as treasurer, both of Edmonton. Members of the executive committee, without portfolio, were Ed Cross of Gwynne, F. M. Still of Regina, H. B. Johnston of Edmonton and B. F. Collins, an unassigned pastor. Rev. E. J. Richards, the Home Secretary, chaired the business sessions until elections were effected.[11]

During the sessions, Richards was pointedly asked to clarify what was meant by "Alliance truth and testimony" and "the Alliance doctrines of salvation, sanctification, divine healing and the Lord's return." According to the minutes, Richards only stated that "Jesus our Saviour, Sanctifier, Healer and Coming again King is our one great message." For the sake of unity he urged that workers be clear "on the necessity of the new birth and preach this truth that gets men from the ranks of the devil to the ranks of God."[12]

---

* Not to be confused with the First Western Workers' Prayer Conference of November 1924. See page 131.

** At the age of 30, John Woodward holds the record of being the youngest ever district superintendent in Canada.

Such a policy certainly was in tune with the outlook of many Alliance leaders during the mid-1920s (see pages 55-57). There were, however, notable exceptions—Woodward often preached on Alliance distinctive beliefs. Nevertheless, the policy stated by Richards would be generally adopted by the district. Throughout the west, the specifics of Alliance teaching would never become the burning issues they were in the east during the inter-war period. According to Canadian church historian John Webster Grant, this distinction between east and west was not restricted to the Alliance:

> The religious ethos of eastern Canada was less easily transplanted than its denominations. . . . Westerners associated churches more with community spirit than with traditional forms of piety. They valued candour and approachability in their ministers more than scholarship or even spirituality, responding warmly to the all-round man who would roll up his sleeves, but suspecting the introvert of pretentious or superior dignity. . . . The widespread employment of students on summer fields may have done more to set a distinctly western pattern of church life than has usually been recognized, . . . a type of ministry that was better adapted to organizing community activities and summer camps than to offering mature spiritual counsel.[13]

The constitution adopted at the 1925 conference included a warning which would reappear in minutes of the board of managers, the Home Department and the annual Councils for several years to come:

> We have observed with much anxiety the drift to large and expensive church buildings, and in some cases the running into debt to the amount of many thousands of dollars. We are firmly convinced that this is contrary to our truth and testimony and we recommend that our workers confine themselves to the simpler tabernacle form of construction.[14]

The conference was also the occasion of the appointment of B. F. Collins to the pastorate of the Alliance work in Regina and of H. Michelfeller to the new work in Vegreville, Alberta.[15] Also listed as workers at this time were John L. Wood of Eildon and Sprattsville, Manitoba, and Fred W. Williams of Egremont, Alberta. George Wade and W. L. Linton McCrae, both students of the Great West Bible Institute in Edmonton, served part-time in the school districts surrounding the city.*

The first annual district conference ran concurrently with the fourth annual missionary conference of Beulah Tabernacle. At an October 4 service, Ed Cross was ordained—the first ordination under the authority of Woodward and the Western Canadian District.[16]

During the conference, Woodward emphasized the vital need to establish churches and urged that everyone interested in the spread of the gospel in western Canada should make this the goal and centre of his or her prayer life. "After all," said Woodward, "God comes upon men, not methods."[17]

Agnes MacDonald, the new district secretary, wrote in the *Alliance Weekly*:

> A deep longing took possession of all the members of the district to sink humbly before God into the centre of His will, that revival fires might break out through this land. ... The new district covets the prayers of the older districts, as it begins to feel its way under the new responsibility.[18]

Winnipeg Developments

Early in 1926, Woodward received an invitation from Rev. Harry L. Turner of Winnipeg to preach in his church on January 31. Born in Campbellford, Ontario, in 1886, Harry Lester Turner was the son of a well-to-do Methodist store keeper. When still a youth he left home and lived a life of profligacy for three years, during which time he contracted tuberculosis. Despairing of life, he tells us, he cried to God for mercy and forgiveness and was immediately converted, healed and called to prepare for a career as a Methodist missionary.[19]

He entered Albert College in Belleville, Ontario (a Methodist collegiate), but realizing it would take many years of education to

---

* During the first western Canadian district conference, Home Secretary Richards sounded an appropriate "word of counsel" concerning the importance of keeping meaningful conference records. Conferences in both western and eastern Canada maintained excellent records until about the end of World War II. Thereafter, progressive curtailment of details and background information have rendered the records increasingly less useful for interpretive purposes. The same phenomenon applies to district executive and local church records.

become a Methodist missionary, he reset his sights on an Alliance missionary career and entered the Missionary Training Institute at Nyack. There, he tells us, he experienced the filling of the Spirit.

In 1913, short of graduation and still impatient, he determined to go to Argentina immediately, convinced that some sponsor would send him as he was. The board of managers examined him, and apparently impressed with his determination and sense of urgency, appointed him an Alliance missionary to his chosen field.[20]

In 1916, Turner became chairman of the Argentine field. Shortly afterwards, he embraced Pentecostal teaching and, as a result, the field became embroiled in contention and incrimination. In 1918 he resigned from all Alliance connections.[21] Happily, personal (though not official) relationships were restored before he departed for Canada with the expressed intention of returning to Argentina under the Pentecostals.[22]

Once back in Canada, Harry Turner joined the Pentecostal Assemblies of Canada, but the declining health of his wife precluded his appointment as a missionary.[23] In 1922 he became pastor of the Pentecostal Assembly of God in Winnipeg (now known as Calvary Temple). This ministry ended in schism in 1924, with half the congregation joining Turner to form the independent Glad Tidings Assembly.

Turner's evening Bible class at Glad Tidings was well attended, indicating a need in Winnipeg for Bible instruction on a systematic basis. Realization of this, coupled with a deep concern for the need of trained workers to carry the gospel to the prairie settlers, caused Turner to conclude, "The Lord has laid it upon my heart to open a Bible School." A vacant Anglican hall was rented, and on January 4, 1925, the Winnipeg Bible Training School* opened its doors to its first 26 students. Among them was George H. Sinderson, whose recently completed ministry in Vegreville was resulting in the opening of an Alliance church in that town (see page 126), and George M. Magnus, originally of Elba, Ontario, who would become a quiet but effective Alliance worker. Turner was the first principal of the school, and together with a Baptist preacher and a Canadian Sunday School Mission worker, formed the founding faculty.[24]

One may imagine that Woodward was perplexed at Turner's invitation to preach in his church. Turner explained that he had "experienced some unexpected problems" which involved him in

---

* The school later became Winnipeg Bible College and Theological Seminary, which in 1991 were renamed Providence College and Providence Theological Seminary.

personal criticism. As a result he planned to resign his pastorate and principalship and leave Winnipeg.[25] He had acquainted his church with the Alliance and he expected they would decide to become identified with it.[26]

For several years Woodward had believed that one day Winnipeg would become "the great strategic centre" from which the Alliance message would "go out into the prairies of Manitoba."[27] Thinking that perhaps this was the Lord's time, he accepted the invitation. The text of his sermon was 1 Corinthians 2:2, "I was determined not to know anything among you but Jesus Christ."[28]

The next night, February 1, 1926, the members voted to join the Alliance and Woodward immediately organized them into an official branch, with a charter membership of 80.[29] The church, located at Simcoe and St. Matthews Streets, was re-named the Christian and Missionary Alliance Church, and Turner agreed to stay on for four months.

New Western Workers

In May of that year, Woodward resigned from Beulah Tabernacle to devote his full attention to the affairs of the superintendency. Increasing demands on his time and opportunities to conduct evangelistic campaigns underlined the critical need for more pastors. "Our single greatest need in the district," Woodward told the Home Department, "is for more and more well-trained and experienced workers." That same month he reported to Council:

> Western Canada is a distinctly pioneer field, with few cities but hundreds of villages and thousands of school districts without any Gospel witness whatever.... When organized last September we had only two works organized. Now we have four.... [In the last eight months] six permanent workers have been added and fourteen young men from our schools are being put to work this summer. ... The problem of using women students has been largely solved by establishing Summer Vacation Bible Schools for children. Two of these schools were held last year and there are to be twenty-five this year. Two young women take charge of each of these schools.... In looking forward, our hearts leap within us at the prospect. Denominational

doors are opening up and many persons not satisfied with the great church union are looking our way. Given a few leaders of experience to man our cities and help to develop our young men, God will give us the whole country.[30]

Late in March, Ed Cross married Selma Anderson of Gwynne. On the honeymoon couple's return to Edmonton from Toronto in April, they were accompanied by seven student workers from the Canadian Bible Institute, in Toronto, heading west for summer work with the Great West Mission. Three of the students, Gordon Wishart, Robert Lennox, and Sid Pugh, were already fast friends and would have significant ministries in the days that lay ahead.

Born in Banbridge, Northern Ireland, in 1904, J. V. Gordon Wishart settled in Toronto with his parents some ten years later. By 1923, nineteen-year-old Gordon was a member of the Danforth Avenue Methodist Church (now Eastminster United Church) where his family attended, although he had not yet experienced conversion. On Tuesday, May 22, he reluctantly accompanied his sister to the Christie Street Tabernacle to attend a service of the annual Dominion Alliance convention at which Luke Rader, brother of the Alliance president, was preaching. Wishart insisted they sit at the back, as close to the door as possible, so that in the event of an altar call, he could make a hasty exit. As Wishart feared, Rader gave an invitation, while the congregation sang "Let the Tide Come In." Wishart came under deep conviction of his sin, and made his way down the full length of the long aisle to the platform. There, he was led by the tabernacle treasurer, W. C. Willis, to confess his need of a saviour and to claim the forgiveness and acceptance of God through Christ.

Some time later, Pastor Oswald J. Smith appointed him to be president of the Young People's Society. A campaign with youth evangelist D. J. Fant (son of the railroad engineer from Atlanta) was planned and the first service got under way with Wishart in charge, supported by the presence of Pastor Smith, but with no sign of Fant. As Wishart recounted:

> We got on the platform and I leaned over to the pastor and said, "I notice that the evangelist hasn't arrived." He said, "Well, have some singing." So, I had some singing and then I said to him, "He isn't here yet." He answered, "Have some testimonies." So, I called for some testimonies. Then

he said, "Have some choruses." We did, and then I stepped back and said to him, "What are we going to do? The evangelist hasn't arrived yet." "Have some more singing," he said. So, we sang another number, and then I said to the pastor, "What will we do?" He said, "Have one more hymn or chorus, and if he hasn't arrived, give the address yourself." And that is how I got started as a preacher.[31]

During the summer of 1925, Wishart visited Alliance pastor John L. Wood at Sprattsville, Manitoba, and there preached his first sermon to a western congregation. And so a most unusual preaching ministry across Canada and into the United States commenced, which lasted for more than 65 years.

Upon his return to Toronto in September, Wishart enrolled as a student at the Canadian Bible Institute.

Just seventeen days junior to Wishart, Robert Lennox was born in Bellshill (near Glasgow), Scotland, but grew up in Belfast, Northern Ireland, where he received a fifth grade education. During his early teens he attended some meetings in a Baptist church featuring an American evangelist. As he later testified, "I made my profession of faith in Christ, was baptized, became a member of that church, and commenced participating in its various ministries. It was under the influence of that evangelist that I made up my mind to one day become a missionary."[32]

Lennox and his family moved to Ottawa in 1923 and identified with a local Baptist church. The following year he attended the first great Bosworth campaign in that city, which resulted in the formation of the Gospel Tabernacle. "More and more," said Lennox, "we got going to The Christian and Missionary Alliance. . . . [Soon] we had become identified with the Alliance and had severed our connection with the Baptists. Later that year I heard about the classes being offered by the Alliance in Toronto. I was much interested in overseas missions and it was with that in mind that I went to the Canadian Bible Institute in September 1925."[33]

Perhaps because of the limitations imposed by his grade five schooling, Lennox was, to use his own words, "one of the poorest students" among the 25 who attended that year. "Somehow," he said, "I managed to get through that one year, but I don't think I learned very much." He concluded that he could never qualify as a candidate for foreign missions, so he volunteered to work with the Great West Mission.[34]

The third member of the trio of friends from the Canadian Bible Institute to accompany Ed and Selma Cross back west was Sidney Tobias Pugh. Born in Pickering Township, Ontario, in 1892, he and his four brothers and sisters were orphaned when quite young and dispersed to various aunts and uncles. Sidney was brought up in Whitby. One sister, Effie, who lived in Birmingham, Michigan, was converted under an Alliance ministry. Through her witness, Sidney (Sid) was converted and pointed to the Alliance. In 1923, Sid, his wife, and sister Effie moved to Nyack, where Sid and Effie attended the Missionary Training Institute. The following year, disaster struck. Mrs. Pugh died in childbirth. Effie returned to Birmingham with her infant niece and Sid returned to Toronto to find work. In September 1925 he enrolled at the Canadian Bible Institute.

Pioneering Experiences

On their way to Edmonton by train, the Crosses and the students stopped in Winnipeg to spend a Sunday with the new Alliance church and Pastor Harry L. Turner, and to hold an open air service. Once in Edmonton, the summer missionaries were given a blanket and a map, and told what area to "work." Wishart was teamed up with Pugh, the former a bubbling, enthusiastic extrovert of 22, the latter a quiet, reflective introvert of 34. True to character, it was Wishart who asked Woodward, "How will we get to all these places?" The superintendent's answer was, "You will have to either buy a horse at your own expense or walk." A sympathetic horse breeder in Gwynne equipped them with horses for $25 each. "So, we took off, I with forty-six cents in my pocket and my co-worker with fifty-seven cents," said Wishart, who continued:

> Our only instructions were to go out and start preaching wherever and whenever we had an a chance. . . . We were so green that it is a wonder the cows did not eat us for grass!
>
> Now, it was our plan to arrive in a town or settlement every Saturday, where, during the evening we would hold an open air meeting. We would make arrangements to hold a Sunday evening service in the schoolhouse, and then we would visit the surrounding farms and tell them we would be having the service. The people would flock in from all directions. . . .

> I remember that at our first service we were packed out. I said to the people, "How many of you really understand what I am saying about being saved?" Everyone put his hand up. I thought they didn't understand my question, so I said, "Well, if you really want to be saved, then stand up." They all stood up. So, I then said, "If you really mean business with God then get on your knees." They all knelt down. One convert from that meeting, after he graduated from Prairie Bible Institute, became a missionary to China.[35]
>
> I recall another occasion when nine men—big ranchers, came forward for salvation, with tears running down their cheeks. But that single service was all we could give them. . . .
>
> During the week we would visit with the homesteaders, far out on the prairies. If we got permission to use the schoolhouse we would hold an evening meeting. We would sleep there or perhaps in some haystack or barn. On weekends when we visited a town we would get a supply of bread that would do us for a week. When we visited the farms, we would buy some milk. We pretty well lived on bread and milk that summer.[36]

Robert (Bob) Lennox had a different experience:

> I was sent to a little place called Onoway, some forty miles west of Edmonton. . . . It was a widely scattered community where a number of Swedish people had settled on land grants and were breaking ground for the first time. Few of them spoke English and of course I spoke no Swedish. . . . There was an old, disused church building which the Baptist people had put up but had subsequently abandoned. The people were willing to put up with anyone who would conduct a service.[37]
>
> I held services in Onoway and at two other locations several miles away in schoolhouses, but because of the distances involved and my lack of transportation, each location got services only when I was able to be there. . . .[38]
>
> It soon became apparent to all that I had to have transportation. The settlers took up a special collection and pre-

sented me with fifty dollars, with which I set out to buy a horse. I went to a man who sold unbroken horses and he let me have one for the fifty dollars. As the horse had probably never had a previous rider, and I certainly never had a horse before, we had quite a time getting back to Onoway.

Nor was that the end of my troubles. I was trying to make a point some fourteen miles beyond Onoway. I was not familiar with the road and by that time it was growing dark. When we came to a place where a roadway of logs had been thrown over the muskeg, it was quite dark. It was the season when the muskegs were overflowing and I was afraid that I would not be able to keep my wayward steed on the logs. Then I began to hear those awful howls from the bush, and I was sure that the wolves were after me. It turned out that they were only coyotes. I finally made it to my destination where some kindly people gave both me and my horse something to eat and a place to sleep.[39]

One afternoon I was coming home. It was late autumn and the lakes were frozen over. My horse and I picked our way across the ice, at dusk. Some distance before we reached the further bank the ice gave way. The next thing I knew I was up to my hips in ice water. We both made it to shore on our own and after a short ride we came to a house, where the people let me stand before a fire for half an hour or so, to get sort of dried off. Then I got back on my horse and made my way home in the bitter cold. . . . Time and again I had to cast myself on the mercies of God, and I came safely through.[40]

That summer, being free from the pastorate of Beulah Tabernacle, Woodward occasionally was able to accompany some of his summer workers, and he reported their experiences:

Nearly every place we have preached God has given us souls. The other night, while it poured rain, we held a meeting in a schoolhouse. A lady and two boys were our only congregation, but God was as near as though there had been a thousand. It was too dark to read hymn sheets, but, praise God, after we had sung and preached in the dark, both boys gave their hearts to the Lord. In another town we took the hall as God had led us to do. About sixteen were present in a space seating 250. However, God did not lead us there for nothing. He gave us a soul and made us a blessing to a couple who rode several miles to hear God's word preached. The rent of the hall was five dollars and our offering was fifty-five cents. Nevertheless we went home rejoicing because one soul was saved.[41]

You might like to know how we managed about meals. The other day we left a schoolhouse to buy some milk. After explaining to a farmer who we were, he told us we could have all the milk and eggs we wanted, free of charge. As we had been living for days on just bread and milk, we praised God for his goodness.... I am not reporting these things that you might sympathize with us, but that you might praise God with us because He makes our fare taste as good as roast lamb and green peas.[42]

New Work in Winnipeg

At the end of May 1926, Rev. Harry L. Turner bid farewell to the Winnipeg Alliance church and commenced a ministry of independent itinerant evangelism. This paved the way for another important development in Winnipeg.

During the summer and early autumn of 1924, Dr. Charles Price had held a great crusade in Winnipeg. At the time, Roffe and particularly Woodward had wanted to start an Alliance work in that city. To do so, they believed that they needed first to hold an Alliance crusade, featuring perhaps the Bosworths. However, the city-wide acclaim of the Price campaign precluded an Alliance campaign that year. As things turned out, the Price campaign not only proved to be the instrument through which many were brought to conversion, but it also served to point out to many evangelicals in the mainline churches the poverty of evangelical belief and teaching in their churches. As a result of the campaign, the Interdenominational Prayer League was formed to pray for divine guidance of evangelicals of every stamp.[43] Among those forming this ecumenical group were Mr. and Mrs. Sammuel J. Jessop, members of Fort Rouge Methodist Church.

Seedtime and Harvest / 215

6.1
6.1 Having dried out the laundry, Ed Cross poses with some of the locals during the summer of 1925.

6.2
6.2 The first Western Canadian District Conference of October 1925 poses in front of the Great West Bible Institute building. Seated in the front row, centre is Mrs. Woodward, Rev. John Woodward and Home Secretary E. J. Richards. On that occasion Ed Cross (second row, right) was ordained.

216 / *Seedtime and Harvest*

6.3

6.3 Newly-weds Ed and Selma Cross pose with the summer student workers and friends in Winnipeg in 1926. On the truck are Lou Elsher, Gordon Wishart, Bob Lennox and Ross Hammond.

6.4 Gordon Wishart, Wes Edmonds and Bob Lennox enjoy some music at their living quarters. The canine acquaintance remains unidentified.

6.4

6.5 Gordon Wishart in his week-day habit.

6.6 The transformation. Gordon Wishart in his Sunday best.

6.5   6.6

At first, the league met solely for prayer and fellowship on a weeknight. However, by early 1925 a number of the members believed they should leave their denominational churches, and in April they formed the Providence Church (which advertised itself as being "thoroughly evangelical"). One month later, Rev. P. L. Kirkland, D.D., founder of the American Conference of Undenominational Churches, "an orator and writer of unusual ability," became its first pastor and its name was changed to the People's Church. Five months later, Rev. T. M. Sutherland became pastor, but his ministry came to an end in December of that year.[44]

Early in September 1926, the Christian and Missionary Alliance Church (which had been without a pastor for three months) and the People's Church (which had been without a pastor for eight months) were united under the authority of Woodward, and together formed the Winnipeg Gospel Tabernacle of The Christian and Missionary Alliance. The new church first used the old hall at Isabel Street and Bannatyne Avenue formerly occupied by the People's Church.[45] The evident diversities of belief, experience and expressional taste between the two founding bodies made it difficult to reach harmonious compromises. It was clear to Woodward that a pastor with exceptional abilities and qualifications was needed. That need and how it was to be met opened up a further problem.

Back in November 1923, Rev. William Hay had offered to bring himself and his small work in Winnipeg into the Alliance (see page 120). At that time Roffe felt "a little dubious about agreeing to Mr. Hay's desire without first having a chance to know the man a little better." The district executive committee instructed its secretary "to write Mr. Hay, strongly inviting him to come down to Ontario" to take part in campaigns in Ottawa and Toronto.[46]* Ten days later, Hay preached his last sermon in Winnipeg, suspended the work, and announced that he was "leaving for evangelistic campaigns in Ottawa and Toronto with The Christian and Missionary Alliance."[47]

After the conclusion of the campaigns in Ottawa and Toronto, Hay filled in at the Christie Street Tabernacle for a month, during an absence of Pastor Smith. Then, he served consecutively as pastor of Alliance churches in Midland, Mimico and Greenwood Avenue in Toronto, and also as a member of the district executive committee. On one occasion he was consulted by the committee as to the "best

---

* The letter from the secretary to Hay is not available for examination, so that whatever may have been promised or implied is unknown.

methods of launching a work in Winnipeg," at which time he "showed a strong desire to return to Winnipeg to resume work under the Alliance." On another occasion he pointedly told the committee that he was "called to Winnipeg." Clearly, Hay was anticipating an Alliance ministry for himself in Winnipeg some day.[48]

However, by 1926, the district headquarters in Toronto no longer held jurisdiction over affairs in western Canada. Hay had come into the Alliance as a Baptist minister, and Woodward perhaps could not conceive of a Baptist being sympathetic to Pentecostal and Methodistic quirks. In any event, he did not believe that Hay was the right man for the job in Winnipeg.

During the latter half of 1926, discontentment arose in the Ottawa Gospel Tabernacle (see page 170), and it became known that Pastor Elmer B. Fitch was interested in a ministry elsewhere. As far as Woodward was concerned, Fitch was the ideal man for Winnipeg. However, Hay's aspirations were widely known and Fitch was reluctant to consider Winnipeg for himself.

The Winnipeg problem dragged on throughout the last four months of 1926 and was at last resolved by the action of Hay. Finally convinced that he would never be given a Winnipeg ministry under the Alliance, he resigned from the pastorate of the Greenwood Avenue Church and from all Alliance connection, as of the end of December. Thus were the services of this cultured and accomplished man lost to the Alliance—a loss that could ill be afforded by either the Western Canadian or the Eastern and Central Canadian Districts.

Arrangements with Fitch were then concluded. Receiving and accepting a call from the Winnipeg Gospel Tabernacle, he preached his last sermon in the Ottawa Gospel Tabernacle on Palm Sunday, April 10, 1927, was farewelled by the congregation and the district on Wednesday, was elected a member of the Western Canadian District on Saturday, conducted his first service at his new church on Easter Sunday, and was installed as pastor three days later.[49]

Tragedy and Challenge

A shocking loss to the west occurred during the summer of 1926. On August 25, Rev. Ed Cross died in the Royal Alexandra Hospital in Edmonton from what was diagnosed as "tuberculosis of the kidneys." That summer, in order to help meet some of the urgent evangelistic opportunities, Cross had turned over his pastorate at

Gwynne to graduating student Lynton McCrae, and commenced an extensive itinerant evangelistic ministry. While conducting services in the town of Blackfalds in July, he collapsed and was taken to the hospital in Edmonton.[50] The loss was keenly felt by all the district, particularly by his wife of just five months, and his family in Toronto.*

At the end of the summer, most of the student missionaries of the Great West Mission went back to their Bible colleges, but Lennox and Pugh had given up any thought of returning to Bible college and decided to winter in Edmonton. There they became friends with Randall Harris. Walking along one of the city's main streets one day, the three friends noticed a great number of vagrant men on the sidewalks. "Someone needs to start a city mission for these poor fellows," commented Harris. Later that day Lennox said to Pugh, "What about that idea of Randall's? Why don't you and I start a mission for the homeless men of Edmonton?" Thus inspired, Lennox and Pugh opened the Jasper Avenue Mission. Several concerned acquaintances among the Beulah Tabernacle congregation and others of Baptist connection assisted with the project. Lennox recalled:

> The chief jeweller in Edmonton, a Mr. Ash, became very interested, in fact he was the chief financial backer of the venture.... We found people and businesses that would donate food. Then, we cooked up meat and vegetables and made soup for the boys getting off the trains in Edmonton. We had a large basement, and obtaining some blankets, we laid them out on the basement floor. We gave each man a bowl of soup and a slice or two of bread. Then, after a little service, we put them to bed downstairs. This we did all through the winter.... Sid Pugh was a great singer with a wonderful voice. He could sing and I could play the piano a bit. So, I rattled off the Gospel hymns and Sid would lead them in singing. The place was filled night after night. Some were in awful condition. We would talk with them personally, and as we had opportunity or they showed inclination, we took advantage of every interest they had. Some made a profession of faith in Jesus Christ.[51]

---

* The body of Ed Cross was interred in Mount Pleasant Cemetery, Toronto. Mrs. Selma Cross lived on in widowhood for 58 years, passing away in Calgary on May 2, 1984.

Although the Western Canadian District had come into existence in May 1925, missionary giving from the west was lumped in with eastern contributions as "Canadian receipts" until late in 1926. When western contributions began to be listed separately, the board of managers noted with alarm that western giving was "very low." Although Woodward pointed out that the work of pioneer evangelism could not possibly be expected to yield large returns in missionary receipts, he resolved to increase interest in missionary giving and to focus on the establishment of city churches where there would be the potential to significantly increase missionary offerings. In his report to the April 1927 conference, he made a strong plea for increased interest in foreign missions:

> During the past year we were unable to hold missionary conventions in many of the cities but four were conducted in smaller points. Less than $500 was pledged. The amount is fair for the points toured but is poor for the district [as a whole].
>
> We strongly urge each worker to place in our hands a note stating when he wants his next [missionary] convention. We would also urge each worker to seek to open up as many outstations as possible and to have a missionary convention in each of them.
>
> We believe it would be very pleasing to God and conducive to unprecedented blessing if every branch sought to give more to the regions beyond that it retains for the work at home each year. This will require strict economy at home with great liberality towards the fields abroad.

The loss of Woodward from Beulah Tabernacle proved to be a difficult adjustment for the congregation, especially since pastoral assistant Margaret Connor was on an extended leave of absence due to the illness of her brother in Hamilton. The process of finding a satisfactory new senior pastor dragged on.

By the end of December 1926, Gordon Wishart decided to terminate his studies at the Canadian Bible Institute in Toronto. Early in January 1927 he returned to the west and became a full-time worker. His first assignment was to preach at Beulah Tabernacle for ten Sundays.[52]

RADIO MINISTRY BEGINNINGS

In the summer of 1924, John Woodward had provided Reuben Pearson with a "radio workshop" in his basement because of his interest in broadcasting the gospel to the isolated prairie dwellers (see page 125). The prospects of reaching so many by the work of so few appealed to his sense of economy and practicality. However, with still nothing accomplished in Woodward's basement, in 1925, a Baptist layman in Calgary, William Aberhart, started the first religious broadcast in western Canada, using commercial facilities.[53]* By 1927, cult broadcasts had caused public resentment and opposition to all new religious broadcasts, making it almost impossible to buy time from commercial stations. Eager to delay no longer, and with still little encouragement from Pearson's development work, Woodward decided that the Alliance must purchase commercial equipment for its own station.[54] And so plans were approved, prices obtained and contributions collected from interested and generous friends to cover the purchase price of the equipment needed. As Woodward recalled:

> We ordered our equipment from Cleveland, Ohio. Then we applied for a license, and got our first rejection. We called a half night of prayer, applied the second time and got a second rejection. Then we called another half night of prayer and applied the third time and received a third rejection. One day, while we were still reading the morning mail, a telegram arrived from Ottawa which read, "YOU ARE AUTHORIZED TO PROCEED WITH THE PURCHASE OF YOUR EQUIPMENT STOP LICENSE WILL BE ISSUED SHORTLY." So, God in the face of all the resistance, gave us the green light.[55]

What Woodward did not mention was that God used the influence of the Hon. A. M. Carmichael, M.P. for Kindersley, Saskatchewan, to obtain that license.[56]

---

* Aberhart began teaching a Sunday afternoon Bible class in 1918 at the Westbourne Baptist Church. In 1925 he commenced broadcasting his teaching over station CFCN in a program which became known as the Calgary Prophetic Bible Institute. For some time his soloist and song leader was Lemuel Fowler, who was the father of Alliance leaders, Rev. Gerald and Rev. Gordon Fowler. In time, Aberhart became the founder of the Social Credit Party and was elected Premier of Alberta in 1935.

When the equipment arrived at customs in Edmonton, Woodward discovered that the duty to be paid amounted to about 50 percent of the purchase price. "You have forty-eight hours, Mr. Woodward, to get the money or we ship it back," advised the clerk. Attempting to persuade the clerk to allow more time, Woodward mentioned that his men were all ready to install the equipment in the Great West Bible Institute building. "Do they teach geography in that institute?" quizzed the clerk. "Yes." "Do they teach English?" "Yes." "Then you are a school," the clerk declared. "This is educational equipment. You don't have to pay any duty."

The transmitter and a broadcasting studio were located in one of the rooms of the Bible institute building. The station, using the call letters CHMA, had a transmission power of only 125 watts. Four Edmonton stations shared the same frequency of 580 K.C., each station being allotted specific times. On Easter Sunday, April 17, 1927, the first morning church service was broadcast from Beulah Tabernacle at which the new station was dedicated, the first licensed all religious radio station in Canada. In addition to the Sunday morning worship service, programs featuring "Sunday School," "Current Events in the light of prophecy," "Hospital Hour of sacred music" and "At the Fireside" rounded out each Sunday's broadcasts. In addition, a devotional broadcast was featured Tuesday and Thursday evenings. For many years to come, the radio ministry served thousands of people not only across the prairies and British Columbia but also in parts of Alaska, the Yukon and the northwestern United States. Beulah Tabernacle, a relatively small and heretofore unknown church, became the "radio church home" for thousands of people without a church: the lonely and isolated homesteader, the rancher out on the plains, the lumberjack, the trapper, and the Royal Canadian Mounted Police officer at some remote post.

The following are excerpts from letters received from "persons scattered through the prairies":

1. We enjoy your talks and singing Sunday night. Amidst all the confusion on religious matters that come to us over the radio, there are some we know have the root of the Gospel and know Christ as their Saviour.

   I have been listening to your broadcasts on Sunday afternoons and have enjoyed them very much. I am greatly interested in Mr. Ambrose's talks opening up a fresh vista on current events so exemplified by the Jews, and would like some literature on the subject.

2. I want to thank you for all the good things you broadcast. I do enjoy them so much. God seems so near and I get such a blessing.

   Please put our names on your Radio Sunday School roll. We enjoy your school so much. [Signed by a family of six.]

3. We enjoy your broadcasting very much. It surely is a great blessing to people placed as we are, because we only have a church a few months in the summer time.

   We want to acknowledge your programs. Mother greets you and thanks you for your services over the air. She enjoys them very much, being shut in all winter and can't hear the Gospel in any other way.[57]

The peculiar topographical and atmospheric conditions of the prairies, especially under winter night time conditions, made it possible for broadcasts to be picked up at astonishing distances. A woman in Bangor, Maine (2,000 miles), heard a program and became a regular contributor. The radio operator on a ship crossing the equator in the Pacific Ocean (5,000 miles) listened to a gospel message, fell under conviction and found Christ as his Saviour. He then sent a letter, telling of his experience, enclosing a gift.[58]

In 1930, after closure of the institute, land was purchased and a new 250-watt transmitter with its own building and tower were located in Jasper Place. Four years later, when regulations demanded new, more powerful and high precision transmission equipment, it became financially impossible to continue on a non-commercial, part-time basis. The station was sold and became CFRN, which by contract provided time for the Alliance. The Alliance kept time for its own broadcasts and sold the rest at a small profit to other religious bodies.

There seems to be little doubt that the use of radio, first in Edmonton and later in Saskatoon, Regina and Moose Jaw, was one of the most significant factors in the development of an Alliance presence and influence in western Canada. Reporting the effects to Home Secretary Rev. E. J. Richards five months after the Edmonton broadcasts began, Woodward stated, "We are creating goodwill, and a new respect has come from the public for our work, as a result of the increased publicity."[59] In more recent years, Rev. Willis Brooks stated, "It [radio broadcasting] had a very dramatic effect. First, many people were converted and then many joined our fellowship."[60]

Nor were these views restricted to those with vested interests in the success of the Alliance. Anglican historian W. E. Mann wrote in 1955:

> The growth of the Alliance in the period 1930-46 was closely linked to the policy of continuous radio broadcasting.... Other sectarian leaders became alert to the success of Aberhart and the Alliance, and rushed to get air time. The Pentecostal Assemblies of Canada, the Nazarenes, the Alberta Bible Academy of Swedish Baptists at Wetaskiwin and two Lutheran colleges bought Alliance radio time on station CFRN.... It is significant that it was these sects which were among the fastest growing religious bodies in the province.[61]

M. P. Pierson, an engineer of station CFRN, was of the opinion that "ninety percent of the success of the Alliance in Alberta is due to its long continuous and clever use of radio."[62]

The mainline denominations were not entirely pleased with the gospel radio programs. A worker of the United Church expressed a genuine concern:

> It is a fact that radio preaching is reaching hundreds of thousands of people who otherwise would hear no preaching at all. It is also a fact that some who have hitherto been church attendants are today satisfying themselves with these radio messages. Is radio preaching extending the reach of the pulpit and at the same time hurting the church?... The difference between listening to a radio sermon and going to church is the same as the difference between calling a girl on the telephone and spending the evening with her.... The Bible does not say that God so loved the world that He telephoned down the good news. He sent His only begotten Son.[63]

The Great West Mission resumed its itinerant operations in the summer of 1927, at which time Bob Lennox temporarily left the work of the Jasper Avenue Mission in Edmonton to Sid Pugh and again joined the contingent of students. Gordon Wishart also, who had been engaged for several months in pastoral and evangelistic preaching, rejoined the force. That summer, Wishart, Lennox and Ross Hammond were assigned to the gospel car. The team conducted numerous tent meetings throughout Alberta and Saskatchewan. They were joined in many locations by Elva and Clysta Stephenson, whose singing was the chief musical attraction. Almost everywhere the team stopped, people responded heartily. The Alliance name and message had become associated with the needs and tastes of westerners. In particular, the camp meeting air and free expression of emotions appealed to the prairie audiences. As historian William Mann expressed it, "Conditions of social isolation common up to 1925 and still existing in certain outlying districts in 1946 favoured those teachings and sects which came to grips with the needs of the lonely and the isolated."[64]

During the busy summer months of 1927, Woodward had not forgotten the strong nudge he had received from the board of managers some months previously about the low missionary givings from the district. Nor had he forgotten his resolve to establish city churches which could be expected to raise the level of missionary giving.

"Our western people," he wrote to Home Secretary Richards later that year, "are not educated to missions and therefore must be stirred up." He pled for "a strong missionary" to tour the district, and promised that if one were sent, "a much greater work could be done." Woodward had reason to be confident that missionary offerings would increase. "Western Canada this year has the second greatest harvest in history. Alberta has the greatest," he wrote. "The farmers will be wealthy. The missionary opportunity is immense."

Then he added, "My great burden is that I have not been able to turn the school [the Great West Bible Institute, of which he was principal] over to other shoulders and take advantage of the opportunity as I desire." He would have occasion to regret that admission a year later.

Woodward expressed his hope to the board of managers "to be able to reach our larger points" in the spring of 1928. "In Calgary," he wrote, "a number of our old friends are showing favour again. We can probably re-open Calgary if we can put on a real campaign."[65]

As for Regina, that work had been heavy on Woodward's heart since Pastor Collins had resigned early in 1926 and no suitable replacement had been found. The work had dwindled, necessitating the closure of the hall on Victoria Avenue. However, a core of "devoted friends" continued to meet in homes and whenever special meetings were arranged, "a goodly number of hungry persons gather." What was needed to rejuvenate the work in that city, Woodward said, was a large campaign by a popular evangelist, to be followed immediately by a strong and sustained ministry.[66]

A Victoria Development

Although no new city churches were opened in the prairie provinces in 1927, it was in Victoria, which fell within the jurisdiction of the Pacific Northwest District, that Canada's most westerly province was to have its first permanent Alliance church in that year.

Back in April 1923, the Victoria Ministerial Association brought to their city Pentecostal evangelist Dr. Charles S. Price of Seattle for a three-week campaign. Dr. Price emphasized evangelism, the "fuller life," divine healing and the return of Christ. His ministry and the effects it produced were in many ways similar to that of F. F. Bosworth of the Alliance.

The campaign began in the 2,500-seat Metropolitan Methodist Church, but by the third service, "hundreds were turned away," and thereafter the Willows Arena, seating 7,000, was used. As the campaign progressed, 9,000 were crammed into the arena while "many others could not be accommodated."[67]

Various ministers of the six or seven supporting denominations took their turns on the platform. Among these were Rev. Daniel Walker of Erskine Presbyterian Church, Rev. John F. Dimmick of Wesley Methodist Church, and Rev. Thomas J. McCrossan, visiting from the United Presbyterian Church in Albany, Oregon (where Price had just completed a similar campaign).[68] Twelve days into the campaign, Dimmick and his daughter, Ruby, sat in the audience. Eight years previously, infantile paralysis (polio) had left this young woman with a paralyzed and under-developed leg. She walked with the aid of a brace, an extension boot and a crutch. While Price was talking she said to her father, "Take off my brace and boot. The Lord has just healed me." He did so, and found his daughter possessed of two normal legs.[69]

According to one reporter, this and other healings "caused a tremendous stir throughout the city." He continued, "In the history of concerted Christian effort in the evangelistic way, there has never before been the tremendous interest around as was manifested in this campaign."[70]

The effects on the churches persisted for some time, and denominational barriers seemed less formidable than before the Price campaign. Walker reported, "The prayer meetings have gone up by leaps and bounds, and the people are praising the blessing God." Rev. Dr. W. S. Sipprell of Metropolitan Methodist Church wrote, "The spiritual results have been wonderful.... I think there must have been 1200 at our prayer meeting on Wednesday last (it used to be 40)." Rev. Dr. Arthur de B. Owen of the Reformed Episcopal Church said, "I have tried to hold a prayer meeting for eight years. Sometimes we had five people, generally less. Last Saturday we had 425."[71]

Dimmick would never be the same after his daughter's healing. Ordained under the Methodist Episcopal Church, he had served churches in British Columbia since 1910. After the church union of 1925 he continued with the new United Church of Canada for one year, then resigned, joined the Alliance and pastored churches in the United States until his retirement fourteen years later.

Walker, born in Glasgow, Scotland, emigrated to Canada in 1908. For five years he had been superintendent of the Central City Mission in Vancouver. Then, for two and one-half years he had done missionary work in Ashcroft. Ordained a Presbyterian minister in 1917, he had held a succession of pastorates in Victoria. In 1925 he and his church opposed church union and identified with the continuing Presbyterians. However, he maintained contacts with many beyond his denomination who, like himself, had been touched by the Price meetings.

McCrossan had many Canadian connections. Born of Methodist parents in Chatham, Ontario, in 1868, he graduated from Victoria University in Toronto, and was ordained to the Methodist ministry in 1892. Commencing his ministry as a missionary along the shores of James Bay in Ontario, he later held charges in and around Winnipeg, Prince Albert, Indian Head and Victoria. During his Winnipeg ministry he also taught Greek at the University of Manitoba. In 1902 he joined the Presbyterians in the United States, serving in Minneapolis and Oregon. Following the Price campaigns in Albany and Victoria, he came into the Alliance and was pastor of the Gospel Tabernacle in Seattle.

By 1927, in Victoria, church union controversies and the inroads of modernism had produced a growing number of dissatisfied church members. Perhaps McCrossan's contacts in Victoria had kept him advised of the malaise and vacuum of evangelical preaching in their city. In any event, on Saturday, July 9, he announced in the Victoria newspaper that he would deliver three lectures on Bible topics on Saturday evening, Sunday afternoon and evening at King's Hall on Lower Yates Street. "All welcome," ended the notice. "Bring your needs and Tabernacle book—and the kiddies."[72]

The little hall was filled, largely by those who longed for the Christianity expressed during the Price campaign four years previously. Into his Bible studies McCrossan wove the themes of Alliance teaching. By early December the people decided to start their own Alliance church. District Superintendent Rev. W. W. Newberry was contacted and Walker was invited to become an Alliance pastor.

On December 16, Walker resigned from the Presbyterian church. Representatives of his former churches paid Walker "a high tribute to his services and unselfish earnestness in the conduct of his charge," and it appears that he embarked on his new ministry with the blessing and good will of his old comrades.[73]

A few days later, a branch of the Alliance was organized in Victoria, and Walker accepted a unanimous call to its pastorate.[74] The first service was held at King's Hall on Sunday morning, New Year's Day, 1928.[75] Six months later, the congregation purchased and renovated King's Hall, and the building was renamed the Gospel Tabernacle. The first officials were Messrs. Waind, English, Low and McDonald. At special services marking the event, Rev. John Dimmick and his daughter Ruby testified to the truth of the doctrine of divine healing and Ruby demonstrated with her once crippled leg. Having graduated from Simpson Bible Institute (Alliance), she was engaged in Christian work. She said various reports had claimed her healing was fraudulent. One report had said that she had died. "But," said Ruby Dimmick with a smile, "here I am, and the last year has been the happiest in my life."[76]

So the Alliance in Victoria traces its founding impulse to the Price campaign of 1923.* Its early days were characterized by a very strong emphasis on healing, which was probably unique for an Alliance church in western Canada. Walker served the congregation for ten years and then retired.

---

* Rev. Harold Stephens and his wife, the former May Agnew, conducted a large Alliance convention in Harmony Hall, on View Street, Victoria, in 1908. However, no fraternal branch or church appears to have resulted from that endeavour.[77]

In 1940, a 400-seat building was erected on Yates Street between Vancouver and Cooke Streets and remained the church home until the present Victoria Alliance Church building on Townley Street was erected thirty years later.

THE PRAIRIE CITY CAMPAIGN

By January 1928 Woodward was completing arrangements for his promised city campaign tour. He had secured the services of the popular Welsh Nazarene evangelist, Rev. John Thomas, and his associate, Edson Crosby (related to the famous hymnwriter, Fanny Crosby) with his "silver bells and musical saw." The campaign tour was to cover Edmonton, Calgary, Regina and Winnipeg, for eight weeks starting on March 25. The length of the tour made it impossible for Woodward to accompany it for more than a fraction of the time. What was needed was a tour manager to chair the services, lead the singing and ensure that an Alliance character and presence was maintained throughout. Woodward wrote to Rev. Gordon Skitch, his former summer student worker, who for the past 32 months had been pastor of the Alliance church in Midland, Ontario, to enquire if the church would release their pastor for this special assignment. The opportunity appealed greatly to Skitch but believing it too much to ask for a leave of eight or more weeks, he submitted his resignation. However, the local committee refused to accept their pastor's resignation, offering instead to "grant Rev. Skitch a temporary release to conduct a ten or eleven week mission in the West."[78]

Skitch proceeded to Edmonton, and the ten-day Thomas campaign got under way in the Capitol Theatre on March 25 with Skitch as campaign manager and song leader. Edmontonians were pleased with the team. A newspaper reporter commented, "Large audiences greeted the famous Welsh revivalist, Rev. John Thomas.... Seldom is it the lot of a speaker to win the esteem of an audience in one meeting, but this, the evangelist seems to have accomplished. Edson Crosby captivated the audiences by playing the silver bells and musical saw." As for the song leading, the reporter stated, "Rev. Gordon Skitch of Midland, Ontario, a former student of Alberta College, led the singing most acceptably."[79]

The interest of the Beulah executive committee seemed to be largely focused on the song leader. Almost two years had passed since Woodward had left the ministry of Beulah Church, and the congregation was becoming discouraged. Now they were convinced that Skitch could be the solution to their problem of finding a pastor. Before the end of the campaign they issued him a call. Skitch felt drawn to the congregation that had meant so much to him during the time of his distress five years previously (see page 124). He accepted the call on an "acting" basis, until his resignation could be accepted by the Midland church committee. The committee in Midland again proved reluctant to accept their pastor's resignation and it was not until May 14 that it bowed to the inevitability and irreversibility of Skitch's departure.[80]

The Third Annual Conference (1928) of the Western Canadian District followed on the heels of the Thomas campaign meetings in Edmonton, April 4-8.[81] During this conference the issue of ordination for women was first raised in the recorded history of the Alliance in Canada. The sensitive matter arose in the context of an appeal by Home Secretary E. J. Richards to "go very slowly in setting apart men for the work of the ministry," allowing candidates to first "prove their call by their work." This suggested the question, could a woman who had proved her call by her work be ordained to the ministry? Richards referred to the "Alliance position" that recognizes the ministry of women "by setting them apart as deaconesses," but "does not ordain them as ministers of the gospel." Accordingly, pastor Fred W. Williams and evangelist Gordon Wishart were ordained, while assistant pastor Margaret Connor was "set apart as a deaconess."[82]

Rev. Gordon Wishart was appointed to replace Skitch as campaign manager and song leader for the remaining Thomas meetings in Calgary, Regina and Winnipeg. It was in Calgary, where the Thomas campaign began April 4, that Woodward hoped to make the greatest impact and establish a permanent Alliance work. For some reason, he teamed up with the Interdenominational Prayer and Evangelistic League of Calgary to sponsor the campaign. The local Nazarene church loaned their building for weeknights and the Alazhar Temple was rented for weekend use. Since Wishart remained in Edmonton for the district conference, the Calgary meetings had been in progress for four or five days before the Alliance representative arrived. By that time, the meetings were being advertised daily as being sponsored by the League with the assistance of the Church of the Nazarene. The sixteen days of meetings were well attended but do not appear to have made much impact on the city for the Alliance. It would take another ten years of missionary conventions and evange-

Seedtime and Harvest / 231

6.7 John Woodward, assisted by Gordon Wishart, conducts a baptismal service at Gwynne, Alberta.

6.8 The singing team of Clysta and Elva Stephenson made a major musical contribution to many Alliance prairie meetings.

6.9 Rev. Thomas J. McCrossan held services in Victoria in July 1927, which led to the founding of the Victoria Alliance Church.

232 / *Seedtime and Harvest*

6.10
6.11

6.10 Newlyweds Gordon and Myrtle Wishart in December 1928.

6.11 During the late 1920s and 1930s, Rev. and Mrs. Fred Williams were effective Alliance workers in western Canada.

6.12

6.12 Student workers Firm Sauvé, Robert McConachie and Ray Clemmer start out from Regina with the gospel car, in July 1930.

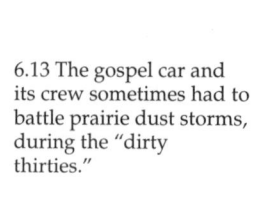

6.13 The gospel car and its crew sometimes had to battle prairie dust storms, during the "dirty thirties."

6.13

listic campaigns before the Alliance would be able to establish a church in that important city.

While in Calgary, Thomas received notice in the mail of some meetings in Lima, Ohio. The evangelist was a Miss Myrtle Bradley of Sandusky, Ohio. Of Baptist connection, she had been converted through an Alliance missionary. Addressing Wishart, Thomas exclaimed, "Say, here is the girl you ought to bring to Canada. You should hear her preach." Thomas passed on his recommendation to District Superintendent Woodward. Meanwhile, the team wound up its affairs in Calgary and proceeded to Regina.

The "devoted friends" who formed the Alliance church in Regina just 28 months previously were much excited at the prospects of the Thomas campaign. The Canadian Legion Hall at the corner of Albert Street and Eleventh Avenue had been rented, and the campaign started on April 22. Thomas preached, Crosby "played on the musical saw and silver bells," the Stephenson sisters "sang gospel songs," and the newly-ordained "Rev. Gordon Wishart led the singing." A local newspaper reported, "The gathering occupied every chair in the hall and left a number of those attending standing around the edges of the hall."[83]

Services throughout the twelve-day campaign were filled, and the reports brought Woodward to see for himself. Drawing Wishart aside he exclaimed, "These meetings must not stop. This is our chance. John Thomas recommends a girl evangelist by the name of Myrtle Bradley. Many give her a high recommendation. Let's send her an invitation by telegram." At Wishart's urging, the invitation ended with the words, "This is a faith venture."[84]

Myrtle Bradley began preaching in Regina just ten days after the Thomas campaign ended. "Miss Bradley is a vigorous preacher and is winning the hearts of all who hear her. Come early. Bring a friend," read the announcement of her first service.[85]

At the end of May, Wishart left Regina to supply the North Side Tabernacle in Chicago. A meeting was called to reorganize the Regina church with F. M. Still again elected chairman and Duncan Campbell, secretary. Charles Dibden became treasurer, and Myrtle Bradley accepted a call to be "pastor, evangelist."[86] Services were held in the Legion Hall until August, at which time, the hall being "too large and too costly," the congregation moved to Moose Hall on Eleventh Avenue. Converts were won and new families began to attach themselves to the work. Within five months the congregation had grown to over a hundred.[87]

On November 11, Myrtle Bradley preached her farewell message and returned to Sandusky, Ohio. She recommended that the church call Wishart as its pastor. It did so and he accepted the call. On Christmas Day, Gordon Wishart and Myrtle Bradley were married in Sandusky, and the couple returned to Regina and commenced a team ministry on January 6, 1929.[88]

The Thomas campaign in Winnipeg ran for fifteen days, May 6-20, followed immediately by a five-day missionary convention. Having exhausted his supply of song leaders, Woodward and Fitch had to lead the singing themselves. The meetings were held in St. Stephen's Hall (Anglican) and it was reported that attendance was good.

SETBACKS AND GROWTH

The Thomas campaign re-established the church in Regina and brought blessing to the Edmonton and Winnipeg churches. But it failed to open a single new city church or bring about immediate improvement in missionary giving, which was the primary goal. Despite Woodward's high hopes, the bumper wheat harvest of 1927 had not resulted in a substantial increase in missionary giving, which that year totalled $3,800. Even worse, 1928 gifts amounted to $3,100, with expenses of $4,100 (which included the district superintendent's stipend and the costs of transporting officials and missionaries in connection with conference and missionary conventions). Alarmed, the board of managers reminded Woodward of his admission the previous year that he had not been able to find a replacement for himself in his capacity of principal of the Great West Bible Institute. The board had a solution for the problem. It urged that since there were good Bible schools in both Toronto and St. Paul, "it would be best for all concerned if the Great West Bible Institute could be discontinued."[89]

Convinced that western students would not travel to attend eastern schools, but would attend western schools of other denominations and not return to Alliance service, Woodward delayed acting upon the recommendation of his superiors in New York.*[90]

Despite low missionary offerings and the apparent inability to establish new churches in the prairie cities, other evidences pointed

---

* This is discussed more fully in Chapter 8.

to divine favour upon the work of the district. George Magnus commenced his Alliance career with pioneer work at Dauphin, Manitoba, and then started a work at Wimborne, Alberta. Robert C. Hess and his wife, fresh from Nyack, headed for Regina but on the way heard of the dearth of gospel preaching at Neidpath, Saskatchewan. Pitching a small tent close to the town, they began to visit the people. Hess helped the farmers with their harvest and soon won their hearts. In three months he had a congregation of over one hundred, plus two outstations.[91]

After a visit of the gospel car to Denzil, Saskatchewan, residents became so excited about having a permanent Christian centre in their community that they collected enough money to immediately erect their own church building. Rev. James Gibson, a former Methodist "field worker," joined the Alliance and took charge of this new work. At Cactus Lake, Saskatchewan, a struggling Alliance work of four years suddenly sprang to life under the ministry of Margaret Connor, and as a result, it too erected "a beautiful but simple church building on rising ground that commands a view for many miles in every direction." Appropriately, it was named the Prairie Gospel Tabernacle.[92]

Not everyone looked on the rural successes of the sects with approval. A United Church minister wrote, "Sectarianism is rife upon the plains. All sorts of religionists are scattering literature and broadcasting messages.... With profound fervour and the shallowest of theology, they preach 'four-square' and other geometrical types of Gospel, and seriously divide the religious life of the sparsely settled frontier."[93]*

During the spring of 1928, the Western Canadian District was incorporated under the Alberta Benevolent Societies Act, and on August 13, the name of "The Christian and Missionary Alliance, Western Canada District" was duly entered. The following were the first registered officials of the corporation.

District Superintendent	J. H. Woodward
Assistant District Superintendent	G. A. Skitch
Secretary	J. L. Wood
Treasurer	H. B. Johnston

---

* Aimee Semple McPherson preached a "Four-square Gospel." It is likely that the writer of this article meant to include the Fourfold Gospel of the Alliance in his reference.

| District Executive Committee | F. W. Williams, Miss S. O. Gardiner, F. M. Still, J. C. Spratt, J. R. Archibald, Miss M. Connor, E. B. Fitch, H. F. Leadley, Mrs. B. Tinkler |
| Trustees | J. R. Ross, Dr. H. H. S. George, F. M. Still, J. C. Spratt, H. F. Leadley |

The first district conference to convene beyond Edmonton was held May 1929 in Winnipeg.[94] At that conference, the district was divided into three provincial sections, each headed by a "sectional Superintendent." Skitch represented Alberta; Wishart, Saskatchewan; and Fitch, Manitoba. Woodward reported to Council his hope that this arrangement would result "in a fuller knowledge of conditions throughout the district, enabling us to formulate plans for the more efficient development of the work."[95] He instructed the three sectional superintendents to comb their respective sections, and report every opportunity to hold evangelistic campaigns, missionary conventions or possibilities of starting new works. Perhaps the new thrust contributed to the increased missionary giving, which that year amounted to $4,100. However, costs increased to $4,300 so that the net result was still a deficit of $200.

Death of Western Dreams

However, that year the Foreign Department had more to worry about than a deficit of $200 incurred in western Canada. By then it had become clear that the policy of forcing the homeland work into a subsidiary position had resulted in the stagnation of homeland growth (see page 143). Indeed, since 1927 (fully two years prior to the onset of the Great Depression) stagnation had become declination. To maintain support of foreign work, the board of managers looked for ways to reduce homeland costs. In response to the urging of Council in 1920, there were by 1929 seven regional Bible schools operating in the United States besides the two in Canada. During that summer, the board closed both Canadian schools and two in the United States.[96]* Canadians in general viewed this action with shock, but for westerners and particularly John Woodward, the closure of the Great West Bible Institute was a disaster. He had always maintained that its continued operation was absolutely necessary for the supply of workers for the Canadian west.

---

* By 1935 two more schools in the United States were closed.

Not only was the Edmonton school ordered closed, but its property was to be sold immediately and the district executive committee advised to "wait for clear leading from God for the future."[97] However, for two years the committee refused to admit that the institution was permanently closed. From time to time it schemed for a re-opening.[98]

One of these schemes developed so far as to choose a new dean, set a date for reopening and formally request the board's approval to proceed. The board refused,[99] and the Home Department advised Woodward not "to re-open the school until the question of the basis on which the district will operate be fully determined and approval of the Board be granted."[100] Approval would not be granted for another fourteen years.

Other matters played upon the mind of the distraught district superintendent. After the closure of the school in 1929, the Home Department advised Woodward that in view of the shortage of funds, he should abandon rural extension work in the Canadian west. Now that he had been released from the Bible school in Edmonton, he should relocate the district office to Calgary, where he could concentrate on starting a new Calgary church and on opening new city works in Manitoba and Saskatchewan.[101] Compliance with this request would have meant the complete disruption of the work about to begin with the Great West Mission that summer. Woodward remained in Edmonton for another year, and when he did move, it was not to Calgary.

Depression Devastation

The year 1929 was important for the Alliance in Saskatoon. Following a healing campaign in 1927, charismatic evangelist J. A. Erickson organized a small fellowship which met in an old Presbyterian building on Spadina Crescent, calling itself the Old Knox Apostolic Church. A year later, Erickson left and Rev. Harry L. Turner, formerly of Winnipeg and more recently an independent evangelist, became its pastor. Soon his church became a spiritual oasis for Woodward's equestrian and motorized itinerant workers in southern Saskatchewan.[102]

In April 1929, Woodward, with the assistance of Turner, held the first Alliance missionary convention in Saskatoon, at the Old Knox Apostolic Church. The week-long convention, featuring four Alliance missionaries, the Stephenson sisters, Woodward and Turner was given good media coverage. Suddenly, the Alliance name became known throughout the city, and some of Turner's congregation began to show interest in the program of the Alliance.[103]

A few weeks later, the summer work of the Great West Mission got under way. Bob Lennox, completing another season with the Jasper Avenue Mission, was assigned to an area near Denzil, Saskatchewan. For several days Lennox boarded with a farming family whose son had been studying at the University of Saskatchewan. Lennox reported:

> This young man attended my meetings regularly, night after night. Then, we would go back to his home, but instead of going to bed, we would sit down and he would ply me with questions. I gave him the pat answers I had been taught but they failed to satisfy him. He was genuinely seeking light—answers to his questions about the articles of the Christian faith, but I, with my limited knowledge, could not help him.[104]

Some time later, Lennox conducted a week of meetings at Turner's church in Saskatoon. According to Lennox:

> I made some faux pas in my Biblical interpretations, which Mr. Turner was quick to correct. He was a very competent and eloquent preacher. As I look back, I blush to think I took a series of messages under the scrutiny of a man like that. These two experiences convinced me that I was not equipped to be preaching to thinking people. Then and there I made up my mind to do something about my education. That was the turning point of my life. I resigned from the work of the Great West Mission and returned to Ottawa.[105]*

---

* Among his many subsequent achievements and ministries, Lennox earned B.A. and M.A. degrees from McGill (while doubling as superintendent of the Alliance branch in downtown Montreal), B.Th. and Ph.D. degrees from Princeton and an honourary degree of D.D. from Knox College, Toronto. For two years he held the chair of Old Testament Literature and Exegesis at Presbyterian College, Montreal, and for seven years held the chair of Old Testament Language and Literature at Knox College, Toronto. For 22 years he was principal of Presbyterian College and also served a term as Moderator of the General Assembly of the Presbyterian Church in Canada.

When interviewed by the author in 1984, he remarked, "I want you to know that my conversion experience as a teenager is just as real to me today as it was to me then." Dr. Lennox passed on to his reward in 1987 at the age of 83.

Women students had participated in the early work of the Great West Mission, but due to a growing concern for their safety, applications were later accepted only from men (see chapter four). Two or three years after that decision, women were again accepted but only when they could be placed in settlements, usually in the care of resident friends, where they served in the work of evangelistic campaigns or summer Bible schools. During the summer of 1929, Mabel Bailey and Muriel Dougall, students of Nyack, were sent to Teulon, Manitoba (about 40 miles west of Winnipeg), to conduct children's meetings. Mabel Bailey wrote:

> We found open doors everywhere; people just begged us to come, saying, "It doesn't matter about ourselves if only our children have something." There was no place in town where we could stay, but one lady offered her unfinished attic to us. The people were wonderful to us. One lady did our baking; another gave us milk; another brought us fruit and vegetables. One lady went to almost everyone in town, from the mayor to the janitor of the school, saying, "These girls are from the pioneer missionary school of The Christian and Missionary Alliance. They get no money for coming out here; they just come to bring us the Gospel. They live by faith." Thus, the message was spread. We were there just a week. It was so hard to leave. The cry was, "Won't you come back, or send someone else?"[106]

That same summer, students Ray Clemmer and Merle Bennett brought the message of the gospel by horseback to the homesteads of Manitoba.

The relative prosperity of the "roaring twenties" came to a sudden end on Black Thursday, October 24, 1929. On that day the stock market crash in New York triggered a worldwide economic depression that would persist for six years, until the threats to world order gave birth to a world rearmament program that brought new life to world economies. While Canada as a whole felt the effects of the depression severely, the prairie provinces, almost totally dependent on the world grain market, were the hardest hit. Added to the problem of dwindling markets was the need to meet debt interest payments on farm machinery purchased during the period of the expanding markets of the mid-twenties, and the prevalence of prolonged dust storms and insect infestations. The result was that western wheat production fell from 321 million bushels in 1928 to only 37 million in 1937. While for all Canada wages fell 42 percent and unemployment rose to 25 percent, on the prairies both measurements approximated 50 percent.

Alliance pastors suffered along with their congregations. Some western pastors subsisted on freewill offerings that averaged as little as $6 per week. Reporting the situation to Council, Woodward stated:

> Western Canada is passing through the most serious crisis in its history.... The resulting distress is most acute, and the suffering of the people most pitiful. In some sections the schools cannot remain open through lack of funds.... The Lord's work has suffered severely [but] the workers are giving themselves unsparingly to ministering to the people, sharing suffering with them, and the blessing of the Lord has been manifest throughout the whole District.[107]

Woodward ended his annual report to the district conference of April 1930 with high tribute for his faithful workers:

> In the face of almost insurmountable difficulties the workers have gone forward without complaint; sacrifices have been made cheerfully and a love for each other and the work has been noticeable throughout the year. Your superintendent takes no credit for any progress made, but gives it where it rightfully belongs, under the Lord, to the faithful and loyal district workers. [108]

Many stories have been told concerning the ministry during those dark days. If that of the late Gordon Skitch is not indicative of all, it is certainly typical of many. When asked to relate some incidents of her husband's ministry in Edmonton, Mrs. Mabel Skitch answered:

> Every day was both a crisis and a miracle. I think that the two outstanding characteristics of my husband were his great trust in God and his great love for people. These qualities showed up almost every day. One day I took every cent we had and asked Gordon to go to the store and buy some meat and bread. Some time later he returned home—without the meat and bread or the money. When

> I asked him about it, he told me that on the way home he had met a poor man who had nothing with which to feed his family, so he had given him our meat and bread. "Don't worry," said Gordon to me, tenderly, "I know God will supply our needs too."
>
> Another day he visited a family and found them shivering in a cold house, unable to afford any coal for the stove. So, Gordon came home and took most of our little bit of coal over to the poor family.
>
> Then, there was the time he left the house on a cold day, bundled up in his overcoat. When he returned he had no coat, and it was biting cold. Somewhere along the way he had come across a man without a coat and had given him his.
>
> As I look back, I think it was so wonderful living in those days. Gordon just rejoiced all the time. He never thought there was any problem that God was not going to solve. And God always did![109]

As a visitor from the east reported, "Brother Skitch is beloved of his people, justly so, for he has a heart that is as large as the local area over which he has the oversight."[110]

Between 1928 and 1935, Alliance people throughout the homeland cut back their foreign missions giving by 35 percent and missionary allowances were cut by as much as 35 percent. The ensuing drive to increase missionary giving, and the ever-tightening squeeze on homeland expenditures, impaired homeland expansion. The decision to expand the missionary force in the face of declining resources has been hailed as a step of faith on the part of leadership. Nevertheless, it is to the missionaries, the homeland pastors and their smitten constituents (most of whom were not consulted but who were called upon to make most of the sacrifices) that much credit is due.

By the end of 1929, Woodward had not yet acted on the Home Department's advice of the previous May to relocate the district headquarters to Calgary. In January 1930, he received fresh instructions that the Western Canadian District was to "operate upon a program looking toward establishing the superintendent in a pastorate, thus eventually obviating the necessity of superintendent's allowance."[111]

However devastating the decision, at least the reason was made abundantly clear. The closure of the Bible school and other forced economies had not succeeded in placing the district in the black, in terms of missionary contributions.

Four months later, Woodward dutifully relocated—not to Calgary but to Winnipeg, with a view to taking over the pulpit of the Winnipeg Gospel Tabernacle, whose pastor, the Rev. Elmer B. Fitch would be leaving in September.[112] For Woodward, Winnipeg was always the "great strategic centre"— but this time there was more to his move to that city.

When, in 1923, plans were approved by the board of managers for a national Canadian Bible school in Toronto, Woodward had protested that westerners would not travel to the east for training, but would attend non-Alliance western schools and would be lost to Alliance ministries. Roffe had acquiesced and Woodward had been allowed to open "study classes" which became the Great West Bible Institute.

Despite the contribution of the school, "spirit-filled workers, indoctrinated with Alliance truth" had remained the critical need for western expansion. By 1929, without a western or eastern school, Woodward despaired of being able to meet the need. Shortly after his arrival in Winnipeg, he was appointed a part-time instructor at the Winnipeg Bible Training Institute. In this capacity he taught "Alliance doctrine" and was able to steer several graduates into the Alliance orb over the next few years. Nevertheless, Woodward's duties in both church and school took time that should have been spent to great advantage in district matters at a critical point of time.

Relocation of the district headquarters necessitated incorporation in Manitoba. At the same time, application was filed for incorporation in Saskatchewan. Both incorporations became effective on June 6, 1930.

SASKATCHEWAN STRUGGLES

Towards the end of 1929, Rev. Harry L. Turner's Old Knox Apostolic Church in Saskatoon became deeply divided. One part of the congregation, following the lead of its pastor, was drawing closer to the Alliance, but the other part remained highly charismatic in character and independent in outlook. To complicate the situation, the city decided to take over the church property to erect a new high school. Turner viewed these developments as an appropriate occasion to resign and seek reinstatement in the Alliance. In January 1930, the board of managers approved the re-issue of full Alliance credentials, and appointed their former missionary to Argentina a field evangelist, effective April 1.[113] Thus, Rev. Harry L. Turner officially returned to the Alliance fold.*

With the completion of Turner's ministry in Saskatoon at the end of March, the Old Knox Apostolic Church became defunct. A segment of the congregation formed the Apostolic Church, and commenced services elsewhere.

Meanwhile, a previously arranged week-long Alliance missionary convention was held early in April in the Old Knox building, attended by those of Turner's former church who were sympathetic to the Alliance. During the convention, on April 14, "in response to a considerable number of requests," Woodward held a public meeting in the auditorium of the public library "for the purpose of considering the establishment of a branch of The Christian and Missionary Alliance in Saskatoon."[114]

"Despite heavy rains," reported Woodward, "over thirty persons were present, of whom twenty-eight voted to become members of the Alliance. We organized the Saskatoon Branch of The Christian and Missionary Alliance, with a temporary committee in charge."[115] Prominent among the charter members was the family of Clifford Broughton. Regular services began July 6 in the Old Knox building under the direction of Woodward, assisted by Turner. It was announced that arrangements were being made to bring to the city "outstanding Bible teachers" during the following fall and winter.[116]

Woodward did most of the preaching until the middle of September, when he began his ministry at the Winnipeg Gospel Tabernacle. After that, it became increasingly difficult to obtain Sunday speakers. In the meantime, the wreckers' hammers had commenced their work on the Old Knox structure, and the congregation relocated to the public library auditorium. These setbacks, coupled with continuing divergent views within the congregation, exacted their toll on the group. Late in December 1930, a visitor reported, "Saskatoon is without a pastor at the present, and the little flock meets together in the mid-week, and wanders to other churches

---

* After 24 years in various Alliance ministries, including seven years as pastor of the Delta Tabernacle in Hamilton, Ontario, Turner served as fifth president of The Christian and Missionary Alliance, from 1954 to 1960.

on the Lord's Day."[117] Early in 1931, the work was suspended, and it would be two and one-half years before the work could be re-established on a permanent footing.

During the summer of 1930, Nyack students Raymond Clemmer,* Firm Sauvé and Robert McConachie served with the Great West Mission. Clemmer reported:

> In the Spring, Mr. Woodward asked me if I would go out in Gospel car work during the summer. This meant that I had to pray for means to get to Edmonton. Needless to say, the Lord undertook and more. He supplied every need to fit up the Gospel car and to send us forth.
>
> The other two boys, who were with me for the summer, I picked up in Regina. (They had come from Nyack on motor cycle). . . . [118]
>
> We started at Scottsburgh, Saskatchewan, with two weeks of special services. The school house seats about seventy-five, but over a hundred were out every night, and not a few nights, a number stood on the outside. A daily vacation Bible school was conducted by two ladies from Regina, and on the closing night 146 people crowded inside the building, while others stood on the outside at the open windows. . . . The Neidpath group has shown a growing interest, with an average Sunday attendance of between seventy-five and a hundred. These two places, together with the Roderickville school house, make a full Sunday's circuit, with about fifty miles of travelling between the appointments. . . .
>
> The hardest problem is to get the minds of the people off the crop failure, which this year has been more drastic and is the third consecutive failure due to drought. Many of our people know not how they will get through the winter, to say nothing of seeding in the Spring.[119]

The deprivations of the western farmers was an almost constant theme in the reports emanating from the prairies during those days. Writing to the *Alliance Weekly* late that year, Woodward stated:

---

*Clemmer became an Alliance missionary, serving in Hong Kong for 17 years and in the Philippines for 23 years. Sauvé served as an Alliance missionary in French West Africa for ten years and then as a pastor in both eastern and western Canada for 21 years.

The workers are suffering as perhaps none have ever been called upon to do in the past. This is the third year in succession in which our people have lost their crops. How they will get through this winter is a problem. Yet, the workers are nobly carrying on in the face of little or no supplies.[120]

About the same time, Rev. John MacMillen made an extensive tour of western Canada, and reported on the effects of widespread crop failure:

> ... money shortage is acute. Many willing workers have nothing to cast into the treasury, and Alliance funds have suffered greatly.... Aggressive work is difficult, and one honours the band of stalwart workers who are bravely facing existing conditions and carrying on under circumstances that involve real sacrifice. No foreign missionaries are working under greater disadvantages, nor are making greater sacrifices than are some of our western pastors....[121]

Undoubtedly, these and other reports convinced many beyond the prairies that western farmers could not maintain their previous level of giving. Indeed, western Canadian missions contributions for 1930 plummeted to $1,700. Although only eight months of salary had been paid to Woodward, this, together with expenses in connection with missionary conventions, resulted in a net deficit of $500, charged to the general fund in New York.

District Stagnation

In March 1931, the board brought the matter to Woodward's attention. The missionary pledge had never been as popular in the west as in the east. Because of the volatile nature of their incomes, western farmers preferred to give when they prospered, and were inclined to be nonchalant when circumstances forced them to reduce their giving. Then, too, the old legacy of western belief, that the evangelization of fellow settlers was the first missionary priority, persisted. These factors had resulted in a "lack of system in the churches as to our missionary obligation." However, it was evident that the board was not interested in theories and excuses. It was convinced that income from the Western Canadian District did not justify the position of a district superintendent, even if a local congregation assumed his entire support. As Woodward could not foresee an early substantial increase in district missionary contributions, he requested the board not to present his name to Council for the coming year.[122]

During the district conference one month later, the nominating committee submitted Woodward's name for re-election to the superintendency. At that point, "Mr. Woodward advised Conference that he had requested the Board not to present his name to Council." In amazement, the delegates turned to Home Secretary G. Verner Brown, the board delegate to the conference that year, for elucidation. He confirmed that "the Board would probably make no appointment in Mr. Woodward's place."

Conference minutes state that "a great deal of discussion" then ensued. Because Woodward was being entirely supported by a local church, western Canadians had great difficulty in imagining what possible benefit could accrue to the general fund by depriving them of their chosen leader and the district of its status among other districts. They might also have argued that it seemed unlikely that even the depressed current level of missionary contributions could be maintained without the sustained urgings of a district superintendent. In the end, the following resolution was adopted:

> Believing strongly that a district superintendent should be in this district, Rev. Gordon A. Skitch is to be sent as a delegate to Annual Council to protest to the Board Mr. Woodward's action. In the event of Council not appointing Mr. Woodward in accordance with his request, Mr. Skitch is to urge that some steps be taken to retain Mr. Woodward's services, if necessary, as a Field Evangelist, devoting the major part of his time to this District work. It was passed that the expenses of the delegate, Mr. Skitch, to Council for this purpose be defrayed from the Great West Bible Institute Funds.[123]

The problem of how to support the field evangelist does not appear to have been faced by conference. In any event, Woodward did not harbour much confidence in Skitch's ability to sway the board or Council. It was probably the saddest and most emotional conference session in the history of the Western Canadian District. Near its close,

Seedtime and Harvest / 247

6.15 Rev. Gordon Skitch was an outstanding home missionary, pastor and district superintendent for 41 years.

6.14

6.15

6.14 The first home of the Saskatoon Gospel Tabernacle was this clapboard structure on University Drive. It served the congregation for six years.

6.16 In 1931, Rev. John Fee, a former Alliance missionary, led his Capital Hill Union Church (Vancouver) into affiliation with the Alliance. This was the first Alliance church on the British Columbia mainland.

6.16

6.17 Rev. George Magnus and family with his highly decorated car, displaying advertising for Alliance services. The car took part in the parade of the 1939 Calgary Stampede.

6.17

248 / *Seedtime and Harvest*

6.18 The famous tabernacle at the corner of 13th Avenue and Osler Street, Regina, erected in 1939, the home of Hillsdale Alliance Church for 28 years. It then served the Chinese Alliance Church for another 21 years.

6.18

6.19

6.19 Haven of Hope choir, Regina, in 1939. Standing, from the left, are Beth Allinger, Kae Johnston, Henry Schroeder and at the far right, Rev. Willis Brooks. Seated at the console is Winnie Cox and beside her Mrs. Florence Brooks.

6.20 Long-service prairie workers Marguerite Railton and Marion Hull, at Denzil, Saskatchewan, in 1939.

6.20

Woodward read his farewell report, from which the following are excerpts:

> The world at large is groaning in almost helpless despair. . . . The brains of all nations are concentrated upon the problem and there is no help in sight apart from God.
>
> The work of the Lord has been greatly handicapped and much anticipated progress has not been made. While it might be a legitimate and proper excuse for lack of development, we see in the present hour the call of God to new steps of faith, for God is still the same. His arm is not shortened that He cannot save, neither is His ear heavy that He cannot hear. On every hand we see God's children suffering and in too many cases losing their faith. We believe it is timely to be reminded that we should be strong in the Lord and in the power of His might.
>
> Never was there an hour when the leaders in God's work needed so much spiritual strength for their personal lives and ministry as they do today, and also there is a crying need for the demonstration of the power of His might in the Holy Ghost. The past is gone. Our successes call us to praise and thanksgiving. Our failures call us to confession and humiliation. . . . With reference to the future, existing conditions necessitate the most serious considerations of the future work in the district. . . . The establishment of Alliance branches in the larger centres is of vital importance to our worldwide work, and it is for this that we must pray and labour. . . .
>
> As this is my last report as superintendent, I wish to express my deep appreciation to you all for your confidence and loyal support. . . .
>
> Finally, my brethren, be strong in the Lord and in the power of His might. The grace of our Lord Jesus Christ be with you all, amen.[124]

So, "Faith Woodward," as he was known, passed from the office of authority in western Canada. He had laboured as superintendent for six years, in addition to four years as the sole or leading Alliance worker in the west. When he first assumed the responsibility in 1925, there were just five churches plus outstations. When he vacated the position in 1931 there were twelve churches plus outstations. Hundreds (perhaps thousands) had heard the gospel preached through the agency of the Great West Mission, and many thousands more through the radio ministry. In addition, several dozen western workers were trained by the Great West Bible Institute. John Woodward never made a name for himself as a preacher, but his outstanding confidence in the promise "my God shall supply all your need" endowed him with a dogged persistence in adversity that enabled him to lay lasting foundations for the Alliance in western Canada. Undoubtedly, he was the right man, in the right place, at the right time.

The results of dispensing with the superintendent in the Western Canadian District were predictable. During the next two years, the district executive committee virtually ceased to function, the sectional superintendents became almost completely absorbed with the affairs of their own churches, and the work of the Great West Mission came to an end. During the summer of 1931, a new Nyack graduate, Wilbert Tinkler, took over the work at Neidpath for two years, until developments at the family farm at Starbuck (near Winnipeg) necessitated his return home.

During the same period, the number of churches in the district decreased by one. Such decline was regrettable and unnecessary, as many other sects of the holiness tradition, especially the Pentecostals, made large gains on the prairies during those years.

Almost without exception, missionary conventions were conducted only in the larger churches. Arranged by the local pastors, the conventions were individualistic rather than coordinated. Surprisingly enough, missionary givings from the district for 1931 and 1932 were about the same as for 1930. Headquarters could take comfort from that statistic and the fact that only insignificant charges were made against the general fund.

Writing about the hardships of those days, the former district superintendent stated:

> With the farming community drawing government relief, the workers have been well nigh destitute, and the New Testament plan of the churches caring for the poor saints has been practiced generally. The Edmonton and Winnipeg churches have carried the burden of the smaller branches, shipping clothing and food to the workers and other needy Christians.[125]

Vancouver Beginnings

During this period of stagnation in the Western Canadian District, the Pacific Northwest District, headquartered in Seattle, Washington, claimed the addition of a Vancouver church. Back in 1913, an Anglican, Minnie Turner, started a Sunday school in her home in the Capitol Hill section of Burnaby. At that time, Burnaby was a new suburb of Vancouver, with few churches, and Miss Turner felt the need of teaching her new neighbours' children something about the Bible. The Sunday school grew rapidly and soon a group of the parents wanted to hold church services. The first services were conducted in Miss Turner's home by the Rev. Gillies, vicar of St. Nicolas Church (Anglican), on October 25, 1914. A week later, the services were relocated to the Howard Avenue schoolhouse.

In 1921, the congregation purchased an old Methodist church building at Hastings Grove, cut it into three sections, and dragged them by sleds to a lot at Hythe and Hastings Streets. The sections were re-joined, a new roof affixed, and the first services held there on November 6. During the weeks that followed, the congregation was ministered to by clergymen of Anglican, Methodist, Baptist, Congregational and Salvation Army connections. No wonder it was named the Capitol Hill Union Church!

In 1923, Rev. John Fee* and his wife, former Alliance missionaries, established a missionary rest home in Burnaby. The church and the Fees became close friends. In 1926, Fee accepted a call to pastor the church in addition to running the rest home. His ministry with the church was, of course, Alliance oriented, and by recommendation of

---

* Born in Camden East, Ontario, in 1866, John Ernest Fee moved to Toronto as a young man to follow a career in the dry goods business. Being shown the way of salvation by a friend, he yielded his heart to Christ, and began to study the Bible and engage in Christian service. When, in 1888, J. Hudson Taylor left Toronto with his first Canadian missionary party for China, Fee was deeply impressed and made up his mind to follow. A year later, he was accepted by the China Inland Mission and went home for a farewell visit with his family and friends. A few days later, his father suddenly died. Being the oldest son, with his two brothers in college preparing for the ministry, Fee turned over his missionary outfit to another candidate and went back into business to help his mother.

Three years later he was able to attend the Missionary Training Institute in New York. In 1894 he sailed for China under the Alliance. In China he met and married Isabella, daughter of Dr. R. H. Glover, who later became Foreign Secretary of the Alliance.

After serving two terms in China and being unable to return, due to ill health, he became pastor of Bethany Church, Peterborough, for four years, and was then called to the Alliance Church in Portland, Oregon, where he served for ten years until 1923.

the church board, the church became affiliated with the Alliance on April 28, 1931.

In 1947, the church was renamed the Capitol Hill Alliance Church. On November 27, 1977, a new building on Delta Avenue was dedicated, and the name once again changed to Brentwood Park Alliance Church, by which name it is known today. It is the second oldest Alliance church in British Columbia and the oldest on the mainland.

Uncertainty Continues

In March 1932, the board of managers recommended to the forthcoming Council that the Western Canadian District be absorbed into the Eastern and Central Canadian District and be administered from Toronto.[126] News of the development sent Woodward scurrying to Minneapolis to meet with Home Secretary Brown to plead for the life of the Western Canadian District. As far as Woodward was concerned, the interests of the west could not be administered properly from the east. Conditions in the two halves of Canada were simply quite different, and communications had proven to be inadequate. Woodward pointed out that in the event of such an arrangement, during an emergency situation there would be no resident in the west who could make a decision on behalf of the Alliance. He received Brown's assurance that the matter would be explored by the Home Department.

The disheartened Western Canadian District pulled itself together enough to hold an annual conference in Edmonton in April. Since there was no one leader, various pastors chaired the sessions and committee meetings. It was the only district conference that ever met in Canada at which no representative from the board of managers or the Home Department was in attendance. Not surprisingly, all business transacted was, to say the least, perfunctory, consisting largely of the reading and accepting of reports from the churches and the approval of minutes. It must have been a depressing occasion.

As promised by Home Secretary Brown, the matter of leadership in western Canada was taken up by the Home Department early in May (before Council met). Based on its opinion that it was "impracticable or disadvantageous to the best interests of the Society" to do otherwise, the Home Department recommended "that Council authorize the Board of Managers to administer the affairs of the

Western Canadian District until next Council" (May 1933).[127] However, during Council of 1932, the board of managers called a special meeting to which "a representative" of the Western Canadian District was invited (presumably Woodward), who gave his views concerning "the conduct of his district." While approving the view that the board should administer the district, the board assured the district representative that it would "give serious consideration to their suggestion that a representative be appointed within the District to meet any emergencies that might arise."[128] Accordingly, the board appointed Woodward to be "Board Representative" for the district.[129] While this arrangement enabled Woodward to act on behalf of the Home Department in an emergency, it failed to provide leadership or direction in day-to-day affairs. In effect, while remaining full-time pastor of the Winnipeg Gospel Tabernacle, it made Woodward resident correspondent for the Home Department, to receive and distribute communications from the department and the board, and to prepare district reports to both bodies.

This arrangement pleased none in western Canada. By the end of the year, the district again began to agitate for the appointment of a superintendent. Again the Home Department was unwilling to burden the general fund with the cost, but it was willing that the Western Canadian District, while maintaining its own district organization, should share in the services of District Superintendent J. D. Williams of the Eastern and Central Canadian District.[130] That district, which had been thriving under the well-balanced policies of its superintendent and whose missionary givings had never been less than $36,000, even in 1932, was appalled when it learned of the plan (see page 172). In contrast, the idea of even a part-time non-resident superintendent with the reputation of Williams held great appeal to westerners, who won the board's approval.

The 1933 district conference convened in Edmonton in April and perhaps a little surprisingly to some was attended by Williams, in anticipation of Council's approval.[131] Resolutions were made "That we acknowledge before God our praise for sending to us as superintendent, Rev. J. D. Williams and that we go on record that our constant prayer shall be for a gracious time of reaping in the whole of Canada"; "That a committee on evangelism and home extension be formed"; and "That a Home Extension Fund be established." In addition, Williams was asked to procure "one of our best evangelists" as a district evangelist.[132] Various Alliance officials might continue to claim that foreign missions was the first priority of the Alliance. Eastern Canadians might insist that the preservation of sound doctrine was their chief concern. However, it was equally clear to western Canadians that their foremost responsibility was to get the gospel message to their unevangelized and largely neglected fellow prairie settlers.

As was taken for granted, Council did subsequently approve the joint superintendency of Williams for both Canadian districts. Considering it inappropriate to remain in the district once Williams took over, Woodward resigned from Winnipeg Gospel Tabernacle and from the Western Canadian District in July, and moved to the United States.*

Signs of Life

The annual conference that year (1933) had been held conjointly with the missionary convention of Beulah Tabernacle. Visitors from Prairie Bible Institute attended and, according to the secretary of the conference, "several graduates sought and obtained credentials to work with us in the home field."[133]

Immediately following the conference and convention, Williams embarked on his first of several in-depth district inspections, advising, encouraging and adjudicating in the affairs of his new constituency. One of the first locations to receive his attention was Saskatoon.

The work in that city, started in July 1930, had been closed down some six or seven months later (see pages 242, 243). In May 1933, Williams met with a small group, including the family of Clifford Broughton, who were still interested in an Alliance church in that city. Williams then asked James M. Murray, one of the graduating students from Prairie Bible Institute, if he would be prepared to lead in "a work of resurrection." Murray agreed, and immediately went to Saskatoon to make arrangements.

An unused clapboard Church of Christ building, seating about 80, stood on the corner of University Drive and Thirteenth Street. This was rented for $15 per month, made possible by gifts passed through

---

* John Woodward ministered to several congregations in Iowa for fifteen years. In 1949 he became an evangelist with the North Eastern District, and from 1955-59 was president of the Arizona Bible Institute. While with that institution, he received an honourary degree of Doctor of Letters from L'Université Internationale, of London, England. Dr. Woodward passed away on April 25, 1979.

the treasury of the Eastern and Central Canadian District, as an expression of eastern concern. Services commenced on August 20, with attendance seldom exceeding 25. Although Murray resigned from the work four months later, Rev. James Gibson of Denzil Church immediately accepted a call to Saskatoon. So, the church known today as Circle Drive Alliance was reborn.

Under the dynamic part-time leadership of Williams, the district appeared to burst into new life. Within two months Edmonton reported 40 conversions within one week. The small town of Provost (150 miles southeast of Edmonton) had 47 conversions and 27 baptisms within a month and even tiny Neidpath reported "a large number of conversions in a recent revival."[134] During his first year, the number of district churches increased from twelve to fifteen and missionary offerings increased from the previous year's $2,000 to $3,400—an all time high![135] By conference the next year, despite the continuing depression, missionary contributions were coming in at an annual rate of $5,000—a figure well in excess of a district superintendent's stipend.

In Regina, pastor Raymond Hess started a daily half-hour radio broadcast. It was not the Haven of Hope broadcast of later years, but it was the start of the Alliance radio ministry in Regina.[136] That same year, the Alliance Gospel Hall in Regina, as it was then known, was once more re-organized. The slate of officers included several well-known names: vice-chairman, Henry Allinger; secretary, Ruby Johnston; treasurer, H. H. Johnston; financial secretary, Jacob Weisbrodt; missionary treasurer, Winnifred Cox; Sunday school superintendent, Duncan Campbell.

Such progress was not always achieved without sacrifice and hardship, especially in the smaller works. Rev. B. A. Jenkin of Ribstone, Alberta, wrote in February 1934:

> I have frozen my feet three times and my face several times.... Very few of our people can afford to buy coal. We are trying to keep our home warm with green poplar wood, together with a few sticks of dry wood now and again. I have to build a fire twice during the night at 2:30 and at 4:30 am, when we retire at 11:30.... No, I am not complaining. I praise God for His goodness to us. But I think the people should know what is involved in our home mission work.[137]

Nevertheless, it was with joy and expectation that conference convened in April 1934. Williams challenged the delegates with the following:

> It is most timely that the Western Canadian District be taking up the new fields of challenge—cities and large towns. We have Calgary in mind, especially. Let us pray for "Great doors and effectual" to be opened.[138]

The delegates responded with loud amens, but their exuberance was soon quelled when Williams announced that he was about to become superintendent of the Pacific Northwest District. A night letter was immediately dispatched to the board of managers "strenuously objecting to the release of Brother Williams from the Western Canadian District ... urging the retention of Brother Williams in this field." Without waiting for a reply from the board, "Rev. J. D. Williams was unanimously nominated as superintendent of the Western Canadian District for the ensuing year."[139]*

New Leaders Emerge

The protest proved ineffective. Both the board and Council approved of the transfer of Williams. However, Williams, with the approval of the board, agreed to again take the Western Canadian District under his wing, on an "as available" time basis.

One of the last official acts of Williams, while still superintendent of both Canadian districts, was to summon to his Toronto office two young preachers. Rev. Lloyd M. Stephens, pastor of the Truro Alliance Hall, and Willis H. Brooks, assistant pastor of the Trenton Faith Mission, entered Williams's office together.

"Young men," began Williams, "I want you both to go to western Canada." Looking Stephens in the eye, he said, "I want you to go to Calgary. We don't have a church there, but prospects are good. We have made arrangements for you to stay in Carseland, just outside the city, with a view to opening a work in Calgary. Already, a weekly cottage meeting is being held there." Turning towards Brooks, the superintendent went on, "I want you to go to Saskatoon. We do not have much there, just a few people. The work is very

---

* It may be recalled that the Eastern and Central Canadian District also protested the transfer of Williams to the American side of the border and that its protest was equally ineffective (see page 172).

discouraging, so if it doesn't work out, don't worry. We have another place called Star City, where we can arrange for you to go."

In late August 1934, Stephens and Brooks started out for the west in Stephens's roadster, as Willis Brooks recalled:

> Arriving in Winnipeg, we spent a weekend at the Alliance church on Furby Street. They were without a pastor, so Lloyd spoke in the morning and I spoke in the evening. We stayed the night with the S. J. Jessop family. Then, we went on to Regina, to the H. H. Johnston home, where all Alliance preachers stayed when passing through Regina. Lloyd stayed overnight, before driving on to Calgary,* but after an evening meal and fellowship I caught the overnight train to Saskatoon. There, on September 2nd, I began holding meetings. We had about eight people, including the Broughton family with whom I stayed, and an elderly gentleman by the name of Jameson.
>
> When I discovered how many, or rather, how few we had in Saskatoon, I began to enquire about Star City. To my horror, I learned that Star City consisted of little more than a grain elevator. The threat of maybe having to go to Star City made me work very hard in Saskatoon! We prayed, planned and worked and God gave us the increase.[142]

Within a few months, Brooks was able to report, "Every department of our work seems to have quickened. Our Sunday School is growing steadily, also our Young People's service. We had a splendid attendance of sixty in our last Sunday morning service."[143]

Then he started a Sunday evening radio broadcast, "Glad Tidings Half Hour," over station CFQC. Soon he reported, "Last night

---

* No Alliance meetings appear to have been held in Calgary since the ill-fated John Thomas evangelistic campaign six years previously until June 1934. At that time a successful three-day missionary convention in Mrs. McKillop's Calgary Gospel Mission was followed up by the decision to send Stephens.[140]

After getting some activities under way, Stephens reported:

> Attendance is keeping up at the Fairplay Sunday night services.... Our prayer meetings in Calgary have been spiritual and we praise the Lord for that little band of souls, holding on to God for a branch in that city. I hope that God will soon indicate His will... so that a work can be established.[141]

Unfortunately, Stephens's hopes were not realized. The project was closed down in November 1935. Three more years would elapse before yet another Calgary venture would prove successful.

our little church was literally packed.... We are continuing our radio work, and it is marvelous the way God has supplied our needs.... Letters have come in from all over the province, telling of blessing received from the programs."[144]

So it was that Willis Brooks began a remarkable career in western Canada which stretched over more than forty years.

In September 1934, Rev. George Blackett resigned from the Alliance Tabernacle in Toronto. One month later, he accepted a call to the Winnipeg Gospel Tabernacle. Thus, yet another stalwart from the east joined the western team. He too was destined to make several notable contributions to the progress of his new district over the next quarter of a century.

Among the several memorable workers joining the western team in 1935 were Marguerite Railton and Marion Hull. A native of New Westminster, Marion Hull graduated from Prairie Bible Institute that spring. Marguerite Railton, a sister of Mrs. Skitch, was born in Smithville, Ontario. A graduate of the Toronto Normal School (teachers' training college), she received training in nursing at the St. Catherine's General Hospital before entering Prairie Bible Institute. There she and Marion Hull met and became life-long friends and partners. "We both felt called to the ministry while in our final year," recalled Marguerite many years later. "We were interviewed by Rev. J. D. Williams, but he told us that the Alliance would not send out girls alone. He asked if we knew of others who were compatible with whom we might work. Each of us suggested the other, so we were accepted and appointed together."[145]

Interestingly, their first assignment was to Denzil, Saskatchewan—the very area where Margaret Connor, another single woman pioneer worker, had founded three prairie churches seventeen years previously, and where, with the help of Nyack student Catherine McCoy, a fourth church had been formed twelve years previously. All these works had been turned over to the Alliance, and by 1935 had been consolidated into two churches, the Denzil Union Church and the Prairie Gospel Tabernacle. It was to the Union Church that Marguerite Railton and Marion Hull were first assigned.

Denzil was a village of about 300 in the middle of the prairie dust bowl, and the two untried young workers had to trust God to supply their needs. "Different families provided a weekly food box, as we had no salary. We never went without," recalled Miss Railton. The highlight of the work at Denzil was the annual summer camp, held since 1933 in a field loaned by E. J. Nedstrud. Forty tents, bunkhouses, granaries and cook cars surrounded the large white tent known as "the Tabernacle." As many as 800 attended annually from across the prairies. Over the years, hundreds were converted and many committed themselves to the ministry at home and abroad.[146]

The two women workers were of true pioneer stock. Their experiences around Denzil included being lost in a blizzard and marooned by a prairie flood. They would remain together throughout a 36-year ministry in five different locations.

Another important worker to join the team of western workers that year was Roy McIntyre, also a new graduate of Prairie Bible Institute. Born in West Guildford, Haliburton Country, Ontario, in 1913, he and his family moved to a homestead in northern Saskatchewan two years later. Converted at seventeen through the ministry of a Prairie Bible Institute team, he enrolled there within a year. After graduation, he became an Alliance worker in Senlac, Saskatchewan, in October 1935. In time he would become district superintendent.

ANOTHER VANCOUVER WORK

What might be termed the first Alliance work in British Columbia was founded in downtown Vancouver in 1906 by Dr. Reuben J. Zimmerman, who at that time was superintendent of the (Canadian) Northwest District. Like all Alliance churches up to that time, it was organized as an independent work. Located for several years on Westminster Avenue at Harris Street, it was known as the Vancouver City Mission.[147]

The Northwest District became defunct a few years later and British Columbia came under the jurisdiction of the Pacific Northwest District. Over the years, the Vancouver City Mission became highly charismatic and eventually entered the Pentecostal fellowship. Even then, it remained friendly to Alliance missionaries in transit to or from the Orient, and for many years District Superintendent W. W. Newberry conducted an annual Alliance missionary convention in the mission. In 1921, Roffe preached there during his first tour of western Canada. However, no determined attempt seems to have been made by the Pacific Northwest District to re-establish a bona fide Alliance work within the core of the province's largest city.

In 1932, Sydney F. Anderson and his wife, Lottie, relocated from Regina to Vancouver. Homesick for the little Gospel Hall on Broad Street and the ministry of Gordon and Myrtle Wishart, the Andersons went from church to church, including the Vancouver City Mission, but could not settle down in any one of them. By 1935 they were friends with several other unsettled Alliance expatriates, including Mr. and Mrs. Bowman from the Alliance Tabernacle in Ottawa and Maude Chatham, the founder of Beulah Mission and Church in Edmonton. The group contacted evangelist Wishart who agreed to give them "two weeks plus a day." District Superintendent Williams was advised, the Fairmount Academy on Eleventh Avenue just west of Main Street was rented and advertising printed. The Wishart campaign commenced on August 11, with Williams assisting. The first service was attended by only 44 persons, but within ten days the services were crowded out with 400 in attendance. Williams devoted a sermon to the topic "What is The Christian and Missionary Alliance?" and a local newspaper reported on the worldwide evangelistic work of the Alliance and its teaching:

> This society believes and teaches all the evangelical doctrines of the Christian Church. It stands uncompromisingly for the authority and inerrancy of the holy scriptures. It seeks to entrench itself behind a splendid orthodoxy.[148]*

At the conclusion of the campaign, it was agreed that prospects for a new church were good and that the meetings must go on. Wishart stayed for four more weeks, then left to fulfil a four-week commitment in Buffalo. During the interval, Williams and various missionaries conducted the services. On his return, Wishart received a call and was inducted on October 27 as first pastor of the Alliance Gospel Hall.[150] Meetings continued in the Fairview Academy until the following year, when they were relocated to the Forresters' Hall, at Broadway and Kingsway.

About a year after the new church was formed, "handsome oak pews" were purchased from a wrecker who was demolishing what had been St. James Church (Anglican), and were placed in storage for the day when the congregation would have a building to go along with them. In April 1936, Chown United Church (formerly Mount Pleasant Presbyterian Church), located at the corner of Tenth Avenue and Ontario Street, burned down to the basement walls, and the

---

* That the reporter was not, apparently, made aware of distinctive Alliance doctrines is not surprising. Many years later, when such incidents were drawn to his attention, Gordon Wishart replied, "I would agree with that, but you must keep in mind . . . that the west and the east were quite different . . . [In the west] the response was mostly on evangelism. In my day, as I think of it, as for putting on deeper life conferences, we didn't hear much of that. But you had it in the east."[149]

remains of the old building and the lot were offered for sale at $4,000. The Alliance congregation had but $825, but the trustees of Chown United Church accepted that as payment in full.

In 1939, during the ministry of Rev. T. William Read, a superstructure seating 400 was erected for $12,000 and was dedicated as the Alliance Tabernacle on November 5. Attending the ceremony were District Superintendent Rev. R. F. C. Schwedler and his predecessor, Williams.[151] The pews purchased two years previously now adorned the interior of "the fine edifice." However, they would not be remembered for their attractiveness, but rather for their "flea-filled, uncomfortable horse hair pads!"

In 1956, adjacent land was purchased, a new 600-seat sanctuary erected, and the original structure transformed into educational facilities. The complex is known today as the Tenth Avenue Alliance Church.

More District Setbacks

In 1935, one year after Williams took charge of the Pacific Northwest District, he found that he could no longer devote adequate time to western Canadian affairs. Soon after his arrival in Seattle, the board authorized re-opening the Simpson Bible Institute in that city, closed five years previously along with both Canadian schools and another American school. In addition to his two district superintendencies, Williams was chosen as the institute's principal and chief instructor. Accordingly, at the conference of April 1935, he asked the delegates to "frankly face" the reality of the situation. While the work in western Canada was, he said, "dear to my heart," he was physically unable to give it the required attention. He would "gladly retire," but if conference insisted he stay, it must be with the understanding that a full-time assistant district superintendent be appointed "to give more immediate attention to the field." Conference responded with a unanimous nomination of Williams as district superintendent and of Rev. Raymond C. Hess of Regina as assistant superintendent.[152] However, the district was unable to pay Hess a salary.[153] Conference therefore, along with the submission of Hess's name as assistant superintendent, dispatched a request to the Home Department:

> That a strong recommendation go to the New York Board urgently requesting that some monthly allowance for an

assistant district superintendent be made, in view of the fact that no remuneration is given to any officer in this Western Canadian District by the New York Board.[154]

The Home Department decided to allow the political hot potato to cool before picking it up. They tabled the urgent request of April until their December meeting.[155] On the tenth of that month, the feisty request was "taken from the table." Carefully avoiding any reference to the explosive subject of payments to the homeland work from the general fund, the department simply recommended to the board "that Rev. Raymond C. Hess of Regina be not appointed to the office of Assistant District Superintendent for the Western Canadian District."[156] It is unlikely that either the district executive committee or the district superintendent was greatly surprised at the response.

Although his conditions were not met, Williams allowed himself to remain as titular head of the district for another year. At that time, late in 1936, he reviewed the results of his tenure. In his first year, when he had worked out of Toronto, western churches had increased from twelve to fifteen and missionary givings had risen from $2,000 to $3,400. During that year, he had made three extensive visits to the district. However, for the next two and a half years, he had been able to make only one brief visit per year, in connection with the annual conference. In that whole period the net growth in the number of churches was just one, and missionary offerings increased by only $300. Williams concluded that in all conscience he could no longer continue to hold the office, so he tendered his resignation, effective at the year end.[157]*

Upon acceptance of Williams's resignation, the Home Department appointed George Blackett of Winnipeg as "Board Representative" for the Western Canadian District, "until the time of Council,"[158] at which time Blackett was re-appointed "without allowance until December 31, 1937."[159] Annual conference found this action unacceptable. The delegates sensed that the old problem of a board representative was being forced on them again. Not willing to be regarded as

---

* Despite the circumstances of his resignation, the loss of Rev. J. D. Williams from the Canadian scene was genuinely lamented by both districts. To be endeared to east and west at that time was in itself a measure of the man. Dr. Paul Rees, of Minneapolis, once said, "To know Brother Williams was to love him. To be with him was a benediction." Canadians from the Atlantic to the Pacific would have agreed with that assessment. Williams left the Pacific Northwest superintendency in 1938, and retired from the principalship of Simpson Bible Institute in 1945. Four years later he died at the age of 79. His blend of spirituality, sympathy and ability would be remembered by Canadians.

Seedtime and Harvest / 263

6.21

6.21 The Tenth Avenue Alliance Church building that was erected in 1939 served as the sanctuary for the Vancouver congregation for sixteen years.

6.22 Thomas Simpson (with his wife), of Regina, the congenial street car driver, ardent Christian witness, and popular Sunday school superintendent.

6.23 Roy and Evelyn McIntyre ready themselves for the Rock of Refuge radio broadcast in Moose Jaw, 1943.

6.23

6.22

264 / *Seedtime and Harvest*

6.24 Nora Bassingthwaighte (Miss "B") was widely known for her widespread western ministry.

6.25 The Brooks family as they appeared in 1944.

6.24

6.26 Marguerite Railton stands in front of the Hythe Church, a typical small prairie church.

6.25

6.26

part of such a plan, Blackett resigned his board appointment. The quiet-spoken Blackett was not disliked by his peers; but he was not their choice. They wanted Skitch to be their leader, and what was more, they wanted him to be a full-time, bona fide district superintendent.

The representative from headquarters at conference was Rev. William Christie, treasurer of the Alliance. Conference must have communicated their views effectively to him. He returned to New York and recommended to the Home Department that Skitch be appointed as district superintendent.[160]

By September the Home Department was convinced. It then recommended to the board that Skitch be appointed district superintendent and evangelist, with a monthly allowance of $110 plus travelling expenses.[161]

News of this development travelled fast from New York to Edmonton, where there was great rejoicing. Skitch immediately resigned from the ministry of Beulah Tabernacle, and prepared to engage himself full-time in the work of district evangelist and superintendent. Within a few months he relocated to Calgary, which from then on became the centre of district operations.

Unfortunately, western enthusiasm was a little ahead of headquarters' deliberation. The board did not approve of the appointment of a superintendent for the Western Canadian District. The Home Department therefore withdrew its original recommendation and recommended instead that Council "authorize the Board to administer the affairs of the Western Canadian District" under a board representative, until a full report regarding "the future administration of Western Canada" could be prepared. This, the board agreed to.[162] The promised report from the Home Department recommended to the board that both Canadian districts be merged under the administration of Rev. David Mason in Toronto.[163]

Perhaps it is providential that the western Canadian response to headquarters on this development has not been preserved for perusal. It is certain, however, that it was sufficiently poignant to cause the Home Department and the board of managers to repeal their former edict. The board approved a new recommendation of the Home Department that:

> In view of the agitation from Western Canada, concerning the action of the last Board Meeting, as to making Canada

a unit, as far as the Alliance work goes, and placing both Districts under one supervision, we recommend that the previous action be rescinded.

We further recommend that the work in Western Canada continue for another year under the supervision of the Board of Managers, in order to give the Home Secretary an opportunity to visit the District and thus be able to bring his own recommendation to the Board concerning the future of the work.[164]

This temporary arrangement would remain in effect for more than four years.

A New Era Begins

Meanwhile, Skitch, with his characteristic optimism, had plunged into the job of leading his district with all the strength he possessed, regardless of title. There can be little doubt that he was the right man for the job. The characteristics that had made him a successful pastor at Beulah Tabernacle now made him a successful western district leader. His great trust in the sovereign purposes of God enabled him to maintain hope and humour, even during periods of severe testing. His love and spirit of self-sacrifice earned him the loyalty and devotion of his constituency. It is interesting to note that the conference of 1938 recommended:

> That our [Board representative] draw all legitimate expenses from the New York Board. (This recommendation in view of the fact that Brother Skitch has been digging into his own slim purse for these expenses.)

Westerners, who valued candour and approachability in their pastors more than sophistication (see page 205), responded warmly to this all-round man who would roll up his sleeves and fork manure or help erect a barn, while discussing starting a new church.

By 1937, western Canada was well on the way to recovery from the Great Depression. For the Alliance family, economic improvement and new district direction gave rise to a decade of unparalleled growth. From 1937 to 1947, during Skitch's leadership, the number of Alliance churches in western Canada increased by 276 percent, and even allowing for inflation, missionary offerings increased by 575 percent.

Back in 1932, letters began coming from the Peace River country in response to radio programs received from Edmonton. During conference that year, it was resolved to "enter the Peace River area as soon as possible." Both Skitch and Turner had held evangelistic meetings at several locations, but the lack of a resident worker precluded any serious attempt to establish a base.

There was another reason for the delay. After the collapse of the (Canadian) Northwest District, even before World War I, the metropolitan areas of Victoria and Vancouver had been annexed to the Pacific Northwest District. Since there were no Alliance works on the prairies, jurisdictional boundaries seemed unimportant.

After Roffe became district superintendent of "all Canada," the demarkation line became of increasing importance. In October 1924, Roffe attempted to "Canadianize" British Columbia, but the board of managers ruled that all of that province fell within the jurisdiction of the Pacific Northwest District (see page 127). However, the 1933 Book of Statutes (Alliance), defined the area of American jurisdiction as "British Columbia to the top of the Rocky Mountain Continental Divide," and the western limit of Canadian jurisdiction as the boundary between Alberta and British Columbia. Thus, either by default or intention, that part of the Peace River country in British Columbia on the eastern side of the continental divide was a no-man's land. In March 1936, the board of managers ruled that henceforth the Western Canadian District would include all of British Columbia "except the cities of Vancouver, Victoria and New Westminster."[165]

Thus the way was opened to the Peace River area of British Columbia, provided, as Gordon Skitch said, "a young man with a vision of God's greatness and willingness to honour those who believe His Word" could be found to pioneer the work.[166] The needed worker came to the fore during the late summer of 1937, when the district executive committee resolved "that Brother Roy McIntyre (late of Senlac) go up through the Peace River district, with a view to establishing a work there."[167] Soon, McIntyre started for Fort St. John, earning the cost of his transportation by harvesting for several weeks. Upon arrival, he tried unsuccessfully for several weeks to open up a work in town, then began visiting homes in and beyond the town. Walter Pomeroy, a farmer who lived some four miles from town, was interested in the message presented by McIntyre, although the Pomeroys were not Christians, at least in the evangelical sense. They invited him to hold services in their home. Soon a growing number were saved, including the Pomeroys, and they continued to meet in the home until an unused Presbyterian church building was offered, rent free, for nearly a year.

On August 12, 1938, an Alliance church with 25 members was organized by Skitch. "Our plan is to make Fort St. John the mother church for the prospective churches in that vast country of more than 80,000 souls," he wrote. "This is the Lord's doing and it is marvelous in our eyes."[168]

E. V. Steele, a new entry to Alliance ranks, took temporary charge of the Fort St. John church, releasing McIntyre for other pioneer opportunities. That same summer, a church was opened at Pouce Coupe (six miles southeast of Dawson Creek) by missionary candidate Fred A. Smith. When he left later that year for Colombia, South America, this infant church was put in charge of new entrant Robert Thomas. Also that summer, John Cunningham, the son of a Hudson's Bay Company fur trader in Fort Resolution, Northwest Territories, and graduate of Prairie Bible Institute, was sent to Hythe (40 miles southeast of Dawson Creek) for pioneer work. Thus commenced the ministry of another long-service pastor.

While the Alliance was gaining a toe-hold in the Peace River area, it also acquired a new friend in the person of Rev. Walter McNaughton, principal and founder of the non-denominational Peace River Bible Institute in Sexsmith (ten miles north of Grande Prairie). Possessed of Alliance credentials, for several years he actively assisted and encouraged the Alliance penetration of the Peace River country.

Also entering Alliance service in western Canada that year was "Alf" H. Orthner. Born in Raymore, Saskatchewan, of Baptist parents, he had been converted in 1935 in Regina, under the ministry of Gordon Wishart. After attending both St. Paul and Simpson Bible Institutes, he commenced his ministry with the Alliance at Kindersley, Saskatchewan.

Nora Bassingthwaighte (later Mrs. Jacob Entz), the former deaconess of the Christie Street Tabernacle, in Toronto, and Alliance missionary to French West Africa, resigned from the tabernacle in June 1938 to accept an invitation to work with Blackett in Winnipeg.[169] A year later, she made Saskatoon and then Regina her headquarters, but in effect became deaconess-at-large for the district as well as youth work secretary and later still, radio assistant and Bible school instructor in church history. Over the next three decades, there was hardly a place in the district which did not benefit from the ministry of "Miss B," as she was affectionately termed.[170]

The Cities Consolidate

The year 1938 also saw the realization of Roffe's dream of a permanent work in Calgary. Early in April, a missionary convention in the Elk's Hall on Seventh Avenue West featured Rev. Percy Green, veteran Alliance missionary to Japan.[171] Skitch was a song leader and Abram Schellenberg, a missionary applicant to Arabia, was soloist. The convention was judged to be unusually successful. Four days later, an evangelistic campaign followed in a hall on Seventh Avenue East which featured Irish evangelist Rev. T. H. Ritchie and singer Schellenberg.

At the conclusion of the campaign it was decided to again attempt to launch a church with Schellenberg as pastor. The first advertisement enjoined the public, "Come and get warmed, cheered and stirred up at The Christian and Missionary Alliance—the home-like church."[172]

Six weeks later, Schellenberg invited George Magnus for two weeks of meetings. Magnus made "a very favourable impression" on the sapling congregation. It was no great surprise, therefore, when in October Schellenberg and his wife were summoned to New York, to proceed to Arabia,* that Magnus accepted a call to Calgary. When Magnus arrived in December, he discovered that the congregation had relocated to smaller and cheaper facilities in the Travellers Building on First Street East, just north of Sixth Avenue. It was "a long, narrow room with many large pillars which quite effectively blocked the view for many of the congregation." A search for more suitable premises was started.

On August 20, 1939, a white clapboard building at 819 13th Avenue West, which had originally been the home of Wesley Meth-

---

* After resigning from his Calgary charge and arriving in New York, Schellenberg was informed that due to the apparent imminence of war in Europe (the September 1938 crisis), his sailing to Arabia was cancelled. Returning to western Canada, he became pastor of the Saskatoon church for two years, and then started an Alliance church in Brandon, Manitoba.

odist Church (now Wesley United Church), was rented from the Mormons. Nine days later, the church was organized as the Alliance Tabernacle from a charter membership of twenty, including Mr. and Mrs. L. B. Fowler, Mr. and Mrs. A. Scheidt and Mr. and Mrs. McKay.

In October 1940, the congregation purchased the old Methodist building.[173] The sanctuary, seating 300, was divided into two sections by what was fondly termed the "guillotine" or "portcullis," a full-width partition that clattered up or down. The congregation first filled the front seats, then the service would be briefly interrupted while the noisy "portcullis" opened, permitting latecomers to enter the rear section.

That same year, Magnus had his car decorated for the Calgary Stampede Parade (see photo, page 247). He recounted:

> The Scripture texts were seen and read by about 70,000 people, gathered to see the parade. It drew quite a number of comments. The CFCN commentator, broadcasting the parade gave it quite a complimentary and elaborate description.[174]

Fifteen years later, under the ministry of John Cunningham, the congregation relocated to a new 700-seat building at 17th Avenue and 1st Street, and changed its name to the Alliance Church. This building served the congregation for another fifteen years. When in 1966, a daughter church was named Foothills Alliance Church, the name of the mother church became First Alliance Church.

Among his many duties, Skitch served as interim pastor in Regina for the first five months of 1938. In March, accompanied by Brooks of Saskatoon and missionary applicant Schellenberg, he conducted a successful evangelistic campaign in Moose Jaw. Although meetings had been conducted almost annually for ten years, interest in the Alliance had not become strong. Now an "Alliance minded nucleus" wanted a church. A store building at 21 High Street was rented and Martin Bowker appointed pastor of what was to be the Alliance Tabernacle. Bowker was replaced a year later by Rev. Roy McIntyre, who remained with the work for nearly ten years. During his ministry, the work grew steadily. A lot at 60 Hochelaga Street was purchased and basement facilities erected which became the church home in 1948. A superstructure was dedicated June 8, 1952, during the ministry of Rev. "Alf" Orthner. The congregation changed its name in

1964 to the Alliance Church, and again in 1981 to the Moose Jaw Alliance Church.

In June 1938, under the urging of Gordon Skitch, Willis Brooks accepted a call to the Alliance Gospel Hall in Regina, and was replaced in Saskatoon by Rev. L. J. Pyne, of Midland, Ontario. Having left behind a vigorous and successful radio broadcast in Saskatoon, Brooks saw no reason why his new board in Regina should not quickly agree to sign a contract for radio time in the Queen City. However, the board flatly turned down the proposal. Three years previously they had been left to pay the bill for pastor Raymond Hess's radio broadcasts when he resigned to become an evangelist.[175]

The board was quite willing for Brooks to have his own radio program, as long as they were not committed to support it. Undaunted, Brooks signed the contract with station CJRM himself. The program grew from one or two broadcasts a week to a daily event, plus an additional half-hour children's program on Saturday, an hour program on Sunday afternoon and a "back home" hour at night. During the winter months, time for ten additional broadcasts was purchased. "It was a continuous evangelistic campaign by radio," commented Brooks.[176] Popular features of these broadcasts were readings and remarks by "Mom Brooks" and music by the Haven of Hope choir and quartet, directed by Henry Schroeder and accompanied by Winnie Cox. Literally thousands of letters were received annually, telling of conversions and other blessings received through the radio ministry. Two of these are reproduced in part:

> 1. I was deep in sin, bound by it as if by heavy chains. I tried for a long time by every possible way to free myself from this terrible octopus of sin, but failed every time. . . . At last I was in such an awful state that Satan whispered suicide to me. Thank God that fear of disgracing my parents kept me from it. . . . One day I came in from choring and as I took off my jacket and rubbers, your voice boomed out of the radio, "If the Son therefore shall make you free, you shall be free indeed." (John 8:36) Without further hesitation, I stole to my bedroom, closed myself in the clothes closet, and took Christ at His own word. Right away I felt a surge of joy that is inexpressible. . . . Praise God for your broadcast and that the Lord caught me before I made a quick end of it all.

2. A couple of weeks ago I went to Norquay to attend the funeral of a young man who had been killed instantly in an accident. He had been unsaved, but just before he left home to go up to where he had the accident, he listened to your program and accepted the Lord and witnessed to several. . . . I know you will appreciate hearing this. It will encourage you.

The radio program soon became a prosperous venture in its own right, and gave the church board cause to regret its decision to have no part in it. However, in many ways the church benefitted indirectly from the broadcasts. The little hall on Victoria Avenue, between Osler and Halifax Streets, quickly became crowded out. The next spring, a lot on the northwest corner of Osler Street and Thirteenth Avenue was purchased and the construction of a tabernacle started. On October 9, 1939, the first service was held in the new building. Seating about 400, the new facilities were soon filled, and two Sunday evening services were required.

Not least among the outstanding lay ministries that contributed to the rapid advancement of the work was that of Thomas Simpson, a personable streetcar driver. His life was a benediction to all he met, and for many years he proved to be a superb Sunday school superintendent.

The Alliance Tabernacle on Osler Street served the congregation for 28 years, until the present Hillsdale Alliance Church building was dedicated on October 1, 1967.

During the annual conference of 1938, "the great need of a worker's news bulletin to keep us in touch with each other" was recognized. In consequence, the bi-monthly *Western Workers Bulletin* was launched under the editorship of Miss Lyle Fewster of Saskatoon. Over the years, this publication would prove to be a major factor in developing a strong district esprit de corps.

By October 1938, Skitch would report:

During the past year, the number of workers in this District has jumped from twenty-nine to fifty-five, and still more are enlisting. God is opening the doors everywhere. . . . Now is the time to strike, while the iron is hot. . . . Western Canada is part of the mission field of the world. It must have the gospel. Foreign missionaries, who have toured these parts . . . have remarked that this is more akin to pioneering in the foreign fields than any [other] home missionary work they have seen in the United States or Canada.[177]

The following May he told Council, "No District in the entire Christian and Missionary Alliance constituency demands more sacrifice than the Lord's work in the neglected areas of western Canada."[178] Then in his impassioned 1940 report to conference, Skitch paraphrased William Carey's famous dictum, "extension or extinction," with his own "evangelize or fossilize."[179] This catchy expression became a sort of district battle cry for the next few years.

Home Secretary S. W. McGarvey, who was present when that fiery report was given, reported on his return to New York, "Rev. Gordon Skitch, the Board's representative in Western Canada is ... a great inspiration to all the workers under his supervision."[180] Also impressed was visiting Alliance missionary Rev. Paul E. Freleigh of French West Africa, who wrote: "Brother Gordon Skitch, the New York Board's representative for this tremendous territory, with his prayerful zeal and optimism, is inspiring the workers to great activity and expectation."[181]

In November 1939, the handsome American evangelist and ex-orchestra leader Rev. J. D. Carlson became pastor of Beulah Tabernacle, Edmonton. Carlson, "a natural stage and radio personality with exceptional musical talent," developed a lively and entertaining program, which regularly filled the newly expanded 900-seat tabernacle.[182]* A new studio and control room permitted the broadcasting of all programs from the tabernacle, including broadcasts every weekday morning, twice on Sunday, and a "Fireside Hour" on Sunday night. Officials of station CFRN stated that these programs rated the highest popularity.[183]

It was not all rhetoric and fanfare. Alliance churches throughout the west were growing in numbers and size at an unprecedented rate.

---

* In 1941, the Baptist evangelistic team of Sawtell and Kelford broke up, and Carlson, although pastor of Beulah Tabernacle in Edmonton, bought over the Calgary radio program, the Sunrise Gospel Hour. He preached in Edmonton on Sundays and spent the rest of the week in Calgary. Not surprisingly, the tabernacle board grew to be less than pleased with this arrangement. In February 1944, Carlson resigned "to devote all his time to the Calgary radio work." However, seven months later he became pastor of the Tenth Avenue Alliance Tabernacle in Vancouver, commuting to Vancouver for Sundays and spending the rest of the week in Calgary. Carlson's "creative planning and music" is credited with filling the pews of the Tenth Avenue Tabernacle on Sundays. However, District Superintendent Schwedler did not approve of Carlson's "novel techniques." Early in 1945 Carlson resigned, sold the Sunrise Gospel Hour and returned to the United States, where he founded the Gospel Lifeline Home and Foreign Mission Society.

Nor was the growth all a result of conversion. As one writer observed, "The plain people wanted a plain gospel, without a lot of novel additions, and if they could not get it in [their own church], they went to those who would give it to them."[184]

Anglican historian William Mann has noted, "After 1935 it [the Alliance] spurted forward, aided by the clever use of Edmonton airwaves."[185] He might have added other factors, including the locations of Saskatoon and Regina and the leadership of Gordon Skitch.

In 1939, Herbert Heppner joined the Alliance team and started a pioneer work in Stony Plain, Alberta. After a period of severe hardship, he reported to conference a "wonderful, glorious, hallelujah time" with his growing congregation. After four years in Stony Plain and another four in Saskatoon he became a missionary under the Spanish Christian Mission.

In 1940, through the urging of a child evangelism worker, Mavis Anderson, John Cunningham started church services in Lethbridge, first in "a dance hall, from there to a fragrant room beneath a restaurant, and then settling in the Y.M.C.A. building." Within two years, Sunday attendances of 60 were reported, a church organized and a radio program started.

Unauthorized Initiative

Perhaps the euphoria of those days was a little too heady for sound decisions to be made at all times. In 1929, the board of managers closed both the national Bible school in Toronto and the regional Bible school in Edmonton (see pages 172, 237). For the next twelve years, easterners longed for the day when permission would be granted to reopen the national school in Toronto, while westerners longed to re-establish a school in the west.* In April 1941, Blackett and Brooks formed a plan to open a Bible school in the basement of the Regina Tabernacle, with Blackett as principal and dean. Skitch was called in and persuaded to allow Blackett to present the plan to conference at the end of May. Blackett told the delegates that God had called him to open an Alliance Bible school in western Canada.[186] The plan was naturally appealing to western ears. Conference approved and the

---

* The subject is discussed fully in chapter eight.

school was organized as Canadian Bible Institute. On October 1, classes commenced.

News of the founding of an Alliance Bible school in Regina filtered through to Toronto and New York, raising both eyebrows and temperatures. For many eastern Canadians, failure to discuss the implications of such a plan with the sister Canadian district was, to say the least, discourteous. Furthermore, the action appeared to be a case of one-upmanship, which to eastern minds suggested a regionalistic and opportunistic spirit. Moreover, the three leaders of the action were former easterners and fellow workers, who knew full well the eastern predicament. It appeared that the east was being stabbed in the back by those it had regarded as native sons. The last straw was that the new school had taken the very name of the Toronto school, which still existed in point of law, waiting only constitutional approval to reopen its doors.

For the men of New York, the western Canadian action was irregular if not illegal and clearly a case of insubordination.* When the Education Department became aware of the situation, it sent a communication to the board as follows:

> The Education Department would report to the Board of Managers that a Bible School has been established in the Western Canadian District without authorization from either Council or the Board of Managers. The Constitution in the last paragraph on page 58 reads: No District School shall be opened without the full approval of Council.[188]

Skitch was summoned to appear before the board, which included David Mason, superintendent of the Eastern and Central Canadian District. What was said at that unhappy meeting is unknown, but it strains common credulity to suppose that Skitch would have defended his actions on the basis of ignorance or innocence. Apparently, he pled for the life of his newborn "baby school," pointing out that to kill it after announcements of its birth had been

---

* Discussing the western action more than forty years later, Willis Brooks recalled:

> We needed a school in western Canada. . . . I felt that if we asked permission of New York to start a school, they would probably say no. . . . My judgment was . . . let's start the school and then see what happens. We found out later that there were very unhappy people in New York.[187]

published and congratulations received in the form of pre-paid tuition fees would be certain to bring disrepute on the Alliance name.*

The outcome was that the new school was allowed to continue, although it had to change its name to Western Canadian Bible Institute and it had to agree to "confine the appeal of the Institute to the Western Canadian District."[190] Moreover, as events turned out, it would be denied official recognition for four years.[191]

Thus, because of abiding by constituted authority, the most heavily populated part of Canada, southern Ontario, was denied a much needed school. By ignoring the rules, the thinly populated prairies, already blessed with twenty other Bible schools, gained yet another. Relationships between the two Canadian districts would not be fully restored until both Skitch and Mason had retired from their superintendencies. That such a division occurred was indeed deplorable, especially since the opening of what would become Canada's only Alliance Bible school should have been a cause for holy celebration from sea to sea. However, there can be little doubt that this precipitative action on the part of the Western Canadian District gave Canada a permanent Alliance Bible school much sooner than if it had been left to the Eastern and Central Canadian District and the New York Headquarters to reach an agreement.

The Skitch Legacy

Meanwhile, Gordon Skitch continued to lead the Western Canadian District in a unique period of growth. He urged his workers "to press forward, never slackening their efforts, until an Alliance branch be established in every large centre, and from those, radiate out to every town in the western provinces."[192]

"What a change in six years!" wrote Firm Sauvé in 1943, on furlough from French West Africa. "Many new works have been started, not only in small towns but also in strategic centres. Today, there is a force of 121 workers.... The growth of the work has been due not only to much prayer as well as hard work on the part of each worker, but also to the able leadership of their district representative, Rev. Gordon A. Skitch."[193]

---

* Mrs. Mabel Skitch recalls hearing that when her subdued husband emerged from the board room, President Shuman said to him, "Come to my office." There he said, "Try not to be too upset. Go home and look after the baby!"[189]

Recognition of the change in district fortunes came also from south of the border. "Mr. Skitch has a passion to evangelize and he is in the field most of the time," wrote Dr. Ira David.[194] President Shuman reported on his return from western Canada, "The work is growing rapidly.... The district is an empire in itself."[195]

Gordon Skitch was equally at home with children as with adults. One day he watched Roy McIntyre of Moose Jaw enticing children to church with treats.[196] From then on, this became Skitch's regular practice. Free candy and his clever bird calls never failed to gain a juvenile audience, which usually remained to hear about God's love for children.

In many cases, independent groups elected to join the Alliance fellowship. In August 1941, Marguerite Railton and Marion Hull were sent to work among a small and scattered group in Hythe, a Peace River village of 300. For the first seven weeks, apparently, it rained incessantly. "Soaked, settled and acclimatized!" they reported. "The roads are absolutely impassable, so we have taken to the fields and stiles to get acquainted with these dear people.... We can't see our way out so we'll pray our way through."[197]

Soon they gathered together a little following and prayed for a meeting place. Funds came in slowly, a lot was acquired and the two women began to dig out the foundation themselves. Finally help came, and the church building was erected, with two living rooms at the rear. Two years later, the work "unanimously voted to link with the Alliance."[198]

In Hanna, Alberta, a small group, started in 1937 and influenced periodically by Alliance preachers including Skitch, elected to "line up" with the Alliance on April 8, 1941, calling Gordon Ferguson as its first Alliance pastor.

In Beaverlodge, a work started in 1940 came into the Alliance in 1943, under pastor N. J. Galbraith. Some of the other better known works that commenced as Alliance churches during this period are:

Brandon, 1941	Rev. Abram Schellenberg
Red Deer, 1943	Rev. Martin Bowker
Medicine Hat, 1944	Rev. T. E. Colley
Revelstoke, 1944	Rev. A. H. Orthner
Kamloops, 1944	Rev. Chester Ansley
Prince George, 1945	Rev. H. B. Persing
Chilliwack, 1945	Rev. Chester Ansley

Another important name to emerge during those invigorating years was that of David T. Anderson. Born in 1917 to a Scottish lay preacher in the employ of the Hudson's Bay Company, he grew up in Yorkton and Winnipeg. Converted at twelve at a Canadian Sunday School Mission camp on the shores of Lake Winnipeg, he graduated from the Winnipeg Bible Institute and the Bethel (Baptist) College and Seminary in St. Paul, Minnesota, and ministered for a few months in a Baptist church in Osceola, Wisconsin. In June 1942, he commenced a long and significant Alliance ministry by becoming pastor of the Alliance Chapel in Vermilion, Alberta.

The district conference of 1942 met at the end of May in Edmonton. "From Winnipeg to the Peace River they came for prayer, praise and fellowship," wrote the editor of the *Western Workers' Witness* (formerly the *Bulletin*).[199]

Every district conference after 1937 unanimously nominated Skitch for "District Superintendent." Each year, the Home Department, the board of managers and Council approved his appointment as "Board Representative." Conference and district executive committee minutes referred to him as "District Superintendent," while national headquarters and Council were careful to use the title of "Board Representative." However, by 1942, statistics dictated that the game of titles had to be drawn to a close. Between 1938 and 1942, the number of churches in the lethargic Eastern and Central Canadian District decreased from 24 to 19, while in the vibrant Western Canadian District they doubled from 22 to 44. By 1942, while western missionary contributions of $15,000 were still far short of the eastern total of $50,000, they were steadily on the increase and were far in excess of costs to the general fund. That western Canada constituted a bona fide district could no longer be denied, nor could an inferior status for its leader be any longer defended.

In June 1942, the Home Department received the annual nomination of Skitch for "District Superintendent," and this time decided to support the nomination, as noted in the minutes:

> A request has again been received from the Conference of the Western Canadian District that a District Superintendent be provided for the district. The Department recommends that a District Superintendent be provided for the Western Canadian District as of January 1, 1943. It is understood that the nomination of the Western Canadian

District Conference for this office will be presented to the December meeting of the Board of Managers.[200]

On December 9, the board gave its historic approval.[201] So, on January 1, 1943, Gordon Skitch at last became superintendent of the Western Canadian District and a fully qualified member of the corps of district superintendents.* Unfortunately, the recognition came late. Just three years later, Skitch's health began to break, which set in motion a train of events that would bring his tenure of office to a premature close at an age when he might have been expected to have been at the peak of his powers.

REFERENCES

1. Edmund H. Oliver, *His Dominion of Canada* (Toronto: United Church of Canada, 1932), pp. 139-141.
2. John Webster Grant, *The Church in the Canadian Era* (Burlington: Welch Publishing Co., 1988), p. 128.
3. William E. Mann, *Sect, Cult and Church in Alberta* (Toronto: University of Toronto Press, 1955), pp. 27, 30; John Webster Grant, ed., *The Churches and the Canadian Experience* (Toronto: Ryerson Press, 1963), p. 129.
4. *Sect, Cult and Church in Alberta*, p. 50.
5. Ibid., pp. 27, 33, 34, 154.
6. "The New Outlook," Toronto, 1 Jan 1926, p. 14.
7. Ibid., 2 Nov 1927, p. 5.
8. Ibid., 2 Nov 1927, p. 4.
9. *Sect, Cult and Church in Alberta*, p. 76.
10. Western Canadian District, Letters, Woodward to Watson, summer 1925.
11. Ibid., Conference Records, Oct 1925.
12. Ibid.
13. *The Church in the Canadian Era*, p. 52.
14. Ibid.; Board of Managers, Minutes, 27 May 1926.
15. Western Canadian District, Conference Records, Oct 1925.
16. *Alliance Weekly*, 14 Nov 1925, p. 778.
17. J. H. Woodward, "History of Western Canada District of The Christian and Missionary Alliance," taped 1971, The Method.
18. *Alliance Weekly*, 14 Nov 1925, p. 778.
19. *Alliance Witness*, 20 Jun 1984, pp. 10, 11.
20. Ibid.

---

* In January 1945, the term of office for district superintendents became three years.

280 / Seedtime and Harvest

21. Missions Evangelica, Olavaria, Letter, Sholin to Turner, 20 Jun 1918.
22. Ibid., Sholin to Glover, 13 Nov 1918; Foreign Department, Letter, Glover to Sholin, 17 Apr 1920.
23. Foreign Department, Letter, Snead to Burman, 4 May 1921.
24. Edward Hildebrandt, "A History of the Winnipeg Bible Institute and College of Theology, 1925-1960" (unpublished, 1965), pp. 21-24.
25. Ibid., p. 24.
26. "History of Western Canada District," The Message.
27. Ibid.
28. Recollections of Wilbert Tinkler, 19 May 1985.
29. *Winnipeg Tribune*, 20 Feb 1926, p. 16.
30. Annual Report of C&MA, May 1926, pp. 129, 130.
31. J. V. Gordon Wishart, Interview by Lindsay Reynolds (taped 29 Aug 1983).
32. Robert Lennox, Interview by Lindsay Reynolds (taped 2 Apr 1984).
33. Ibid.
34. Ibid.
35. J. V. Gordon Wishart, Interview, 29 Aug 1983.
36. Ibid.
37. Robert Lennox, Interview, 2 Apr 1984.
38. Ibid.
39. Ibid.
40. Ibid.
41. *Alliance Weekly*, 26 Oct 1926, p. 689.
42. Ibid.
43. *Winnipeg Tribune*, 2 May 1925, p. 9; 9 May 1925, p. 16; 16 May 1925, p. 11.
44. Ibid., 26 Sep 1925, p. 16; 28 Nov 1925, p. 16.
45. Ibid., 11 Sep 1926, p. 14.
46. District of Canada, Executive Committee Minutes, 1 Nov 1923.
47. *Winnipeg Tribune*, 10 Nov 1923, p. 17.
48. District of Canada, Executive Committee Minutes, 14 Jul 1924; 30 Oct 1924.
49. *Ottawa Citizen*, 2 Apr 1927, p. 15; 9 Apr 1927, p. 18; Western Canadian District, Executive Committee Minutes, 15 Apr 1927, p. 6; *Winnipeg Tribune*, 16 Apr 1927, p. 16; *Alliance Weekly*, 7 May 1927, p. 303; 21 May 1927, p. 334.
50. *Edmonton Journal*, 27 Aug 1926; *Alliance Weekly*, 26 Sep 1926, p. 630.
51. Robert Lennox, Interview, 2 Apr 1984.
52. *Edmonton Journal*, 22 Jan-26 Mar 1927, Saturday church page.
53. *Sect, Cult and Church in Alberta*, p. 22.
54. "History of Western Canada District," The Method.
55. Ibid.
56. *Alliance Weekly*, 21 May 1927, p. 334.

57. District News, Western Canadian District, Mar 1928.
58. "History of Western Canada District," The Message at Work.
59. Board of Managers, Letter, Woodward to Richards, 22 Sep 1927.
60. Willis Brooks, Interview by Lindsay Reynolds, 6 Oct 1983.
61. *Sect, Cult and Church in Alberta*, p. 121.
62. Ibid., p. 122.
63. "New Outlook," Toronto, 9 Apr 1930, p. 347.
64. *Sect, Cult and Church in Alberta*, p. 58.
65. Board of Managers, Letter, Woodward to Richards, 22 Sep 1927.
66. Western Canadian District, Executive Committee Minutes, 15 Apr 1927.
67. *Victoria Colonist*, 7 Apr 1923, p. 6; 10 Apr, p. 6; 13 Apr, p. 16.
68. Ibid., 17 Apr 1923, p. 14; 18 Apr, p. 6; 19 Apr, p. 14; 20 Apr, p. 6.
69. Ibid., 21 Apr 1923, p. 13; 22 Apr, p. 6; 24 Apr, p. 14; 25 Apr, p. 6; 26 Apr, p. 4; 27 Apr, p. 6; 28 Apr, p. 6; T. J. McCrossan, *Christ's Paralyzed Church X-Rayed* (Seattle: Published by the author, 1937), p. 258.
70. *Victoria Colonist*, 1 May 1923, p. 5.
71. Charles Sidney Price, *The Great Physician* (Oakland: Charles S. Price Publishing Co., 1923), pp. 70, 71, 76, 77.
72. *Victoria Daily Times*, 9 July 1927, pp. 10, 11.
73. Ibid., 17 Dec 1927, p. 19.
74. Ibid., 24 Dec 1927, p. 10.
75. Ibid., 31 Dec 1927, p. 10.
76. Ibid., 18 Aug 1928, p. 10.
77. Lindsay Reynolds, *Footprints* (Toronto: The Christian and Missionary Alliance in Canada, 1982), pp. 340, 341.
78. Midland Alliance Church, Executive Committee Minutes, 9 Jan 1928; District News, Western Canadian District, Mar 1928, p. 3.
79. *Edmonton Journal*, 26 Mar 1928, p. 12.
80. Midland Alliance Church, Executive Committee Minutes, 14 May 1928.
81. *Edmonton Journal*, 31 Mar 1928, p. 9.
82. Western Canadian District, Conference Records, Apr 1928; *Alliance Weekly*, 2 Jun 1928, p. 349.
83. *Regina Leader Post*, 23 Apr 1928, p. 8.
84. J. V. Gordon Wishart, Interview, 29 Aug 1983.
85. *Regina Leader Post*, 12 May 1928, p. 34; 4 Aug, p. 16.
86. *Alliance Weekly*, 6 Oct 1928, p. 656.
87. Ibid., 29 Dec 1928, p. 857.
88. *Regina Leader Post*, 10 Nov 1928, p. 30; 5 Jan 1929, p. 26.
89. Board of Managers, Minutes, 2 Mar 1928.
90. *Alliance Weekly*, 2 Jun 1928, p. 349.
91. Ibid., 13 Oct 1928, p. 669.

282 / *Seedtime and Harvest*

92. Ibid., 29 Dec 1928, p. 857, 6 Apr 1929, p. 221.
93. "New Outlook," 2 Nov 1927, p. 9.
94. *Alliance Weekly*, 18 May 1929, p. 320.
95. Annual Report of C&MA, May 1930, p. 126.
96. Home Department of C&MA, Educational Report, 10 Dec 1929.
97. Ibid.
98. Western Canadian District, Conference Records, Apr 1930.
99. Board of Managers, Minutes, 7 May 1930.
100. Home Department of C&MA, Minutes, 3 Jan 1930.
101. Ibid., 2 Oct 1929.
102. *Alliance Weekly*, 29 Dec 1928, p. 856.
103. *Saskatoon Star Phoenix*, 6 Apr 1929.
104. Robert Lennox, Interview, 2 Apr 1984.
105. Ibid.
106. *Alliance Weekly*, 14 Sep 1929, p. 605.
107. Annual Report of C&MA, May 1931, p. 121.
108. Western Canadian District, Conference Records, Apr 1930.
109. Mabel Skitch, Interview by Lindsay Reynolds, 29 Sep 1983.
110. *Alliance Weekly*, 27 Dec 1930, p. 849.
111. Home Department of C&MA, Minutes, 3 Jan 1930.
112. *Alliance Weekly*, 11 Oct 1930, p. 669.
113. Board of Managers, Minutes, 10 Jan 1930; *Saskatoon Star Phoenix*, 25 Jan 1930.
114. *Saskatoon Star Phoenix*, 12 Apr 1930.
115. *Alliance Weekly*, 31 May 1930, p. 352.
116. *Saskatoon Star Phoenix*, 5 Jul 1930.
117. *Alliance Weekly*, 27 Dec 1930, p. 849.
118. Ibid., 5 Jul 1930, p. 433.
119. Ibid., 1 Nov 1930, p. 724.
120. Ibid., 6 Dec 1930, p. 800.
121. Ibid., 27 Dec 1930, pp. 848, 849.
122. Western Canadian District, Conference Records, Apr 1931.
123. Ibid.
124. Ibid.
125. Annual Report of C&MA, May 1932, p. 73.
126. Board of Managers, Minutes, 10 Mar 1932; Western Canadian District, Conference Records, Apr 1932.
127. Home Department of C&MA, Minutes, 3 May 1932, p. 86.
128. Board of Managers, Minutes, 30 May 1932, pp. 106, 107.
129. Ibid., 31 May 1932, p. 108.

130. Ibid., 2 May 1933.
131. *Alliance Weekly*, 17 Jun 1933, p. 380.
132. Western Canadian District, Conference Records, Apr 1933.
133. *Alliance Weekly*, 17 Jun 1933, p. 381.
134. Ibid., p. 380.
135. Ibid., 24 Feb 1934, p. 125.
136. Ibid., 31 Mar 1934, p. 205.
137. Ibid., 24 Feb 1934, p. 125.
138. Western Canadian District, Conference Records, Apr 1934.
139. Ibid.
140. *Alliance Weekly*, 21 Jul 1934, pp. 460, 461.
141. Ibid., 16 Feb 1935, p. 109; 18 May 1935, p. 317.
142. Willis Brooks, Interview, 6 Oct 1983.
143. *Alliance Weekly*, 18 May 1935, p. 318.
144. Ibid., 29 Feb 1936, p. 141.
145. Misses M. Railton and M. Hull, Interview by Lindsay Reynolds, 27 Sep 1983.
146. *Alliance Weekly*, 5 Oct 1940, pp. 636, 637.
147. *Footprints*, pp. 338, 340.
148. *Vancouver Sun*, 24 Aug 1935, p. 8.
149. J. V. Gordon Wishart, Interview 29 Aug 1983.
150. *Vancouver Sun*, 26 Oct 1935, p. 4; *Alliance Weekly*, 2 Nov 1935, p. 708; 21 Dec 1935, p. 820; 19 Sep 1936, pp. 609, 610; 31 Dec 1938, p. 848.
151. *Vancouver Sun*, 4 Nov 1939, p. 8.
152. Western Canadian District, Conference Records, 1935.
153. Ibid., District Superintendent's Report, 1936.
154. Home Department of C&MA, Minutes, 23 Sep 1935.
155. Ibid.
156. Ibid., 10 Dec 1935.
157. Board of Managers, Minutes, 7 Dec 1936; Annual Report of C&MA, May 1938, p. 118.
158. Home Department of C&MA, Minutes, 7 Dec 1936.
159. Ibid., 20 May 1937; Annual Report of C&MA, May 1938, p. 118.
160. Board of Managers, Minutes, 28 Jun 1937.
161. Ibid., 14 Sep 1937; Annual Report of C&MA, May 1938, p. 119.
162. Board of Managers, Minutes, 14 Dec 1937.
163. Ibid., 15 Dec 1938.
164. Ibid., 11 Apr 1939.
165. Ibid., 10 Mar 1936.
166. *Alliance Weekly*, 17 Sep 1938, p. 605.

284 / Seedtime and Harvest

167. Western Canadian District, Executive Committee Minutes, late 1937.
168. *Alliance Weekly*, 17 Sep 1938, p. 605; Annual Report of C&MA, May 1939.
169. *Footprints*, pp. 417, 468.
170. Western Canadian District, Conference Records, May 1939, p. 11; May 1940, p. 6; *Western Workers' Bulletin* , Jun 1939, pp. 6, 8; Sep 1939, pp. 5, 6, 8; Feb 1940, p. 10; Oct 1940, p. 9; Feb 1941, p. 3; *Alliance Weekly*, 5 Oct 1940, p. 637.
171. *Calgary Herald*, 30 Apr 1938, p. 27.
172. Ibid., 11 Jun 1938, p. 25; 2 Jul 1938, p. 25.
173. *Western Workers' Bulletin*, Oct 1940, p. 9; Nov 1940, p. 8.
174. Ibid., Sep 1939, p. 5.
175. *Alliance Weekly*, 31 Mar 1934, p. 205; Western Canadian District, Conference Records, Superintendent's Report, Jun 1936; Willis Brooks, Interview, 6 Oct 1983.
176. Willis Brooks, Interview, 6 Oct 1983.
177. *Western Workers' Bulletin*, Oct 1938, p. 3.
178. Annual Report of C&MA, May 1939, p. 118.
179. Western Canadian District, Conference Records, Superintendent's Report, Jun 1940, p. 3.
180. *Alliance Weekly*, 5 Aug 1939, p. 493.
181. Ibid., 26 Aug 1939, p. 540.
182. *Sect, Cult and Church in Alberta*, pp. 124, 125.
183. *Alliance Weekly*, 17 Feb 1940, p. 108; 14 Mar 1942, p. 172.
184. *Sect, Cult and Church in Alberta*, p. 48.
185. Ibid., p. 20.
186. Western Canadian District, Conference Records, May 1941, pp. 6, 7.
187. Willis Brooks, Interview, 6 Oct 1983.
188. C&MA Education Department, Recommendations to Board of Managers, 10 Sep 1941.
189. Mabel Skitch, Interview, 29 Sep 1983.
190. Home Department of C&MA, Report to Board of Managers, 16 Jun 1942.
191. Board of Managers, Minutes, 21 Mar 1946.
192. Western Canadian District, Conference Records, May 1941, p. 2.
193. *Alliance Weekly*, 23 Oct 1943, p. 685.
194. Ibid., 22 Jan 1944, p. 61.
195. Ibid., 18 Nov 1944, p. 460.
196. Western Canadian District, Conference Records, May 1940, p. 9.
197. *Western Workers' Bulletin*, Nov 1941, p. 5; Jul 1942, p. 5.
198. Western Canadian District, Conference Records, May 1943.
199. *Western Workers' Witness*, Jul 1941, p. 1.
200. Home Department of C&MA, Minutes, 16 Jun 1942.
201. Board of Managers, Minutes, 9 Dec 1942.

PART THREE

From Sea to Sea

CHAPTER SEVEN

Forging a Consensus

On May 8, 1945, Germany surrendered to its enemies. On August 6, the first atomic bomb was dropped on the city of Hiroshima, killing 75,000 persons and permanently maiming at least twice that number. Just eight days later, on August 14, after a second terrifying mushroom cloud rose over what had been Nagasaki, Japan conceded defeat. Thus ended the costliest war in human history.

Among the principal combatants, Germany and much of Russia had been devastated, Japan had been victimized and Britain had become exhausted. Only the United States of America emerged virtuously unscathed and empowered to a degree never before known in history.

Despite the dreams of surviving service men and women to return to what they had held dear, the world could never be the same again. If the first world war had caused worldwide doubt regarding the viability of the church, the second world war brought general rejection. By 1945, throughout most of the world, the church was thrown on the defensive.

However, what happened in Canada and the United States was uniquely different from the rest of the world. As historian John Webster Grant observed, "Men and women, who had shown no more than a perfunctory interest in church before going off to war, demonstrated on their return an enthusiasm that confounded all prognosticators."[1] A boom in religious concern ensued. The returning veterans, who settled down in suburbia to raise the "baby boomers," were eager to preserve for their children an inheritance of Christian values they believed they had fought to preserve. Church and Sunday school attendance doubled and even quadrupled, so that existing facilities could not accommodate the demand. Virtually all denominations embarked on heady church building programs, incurring a degree of debt unheard of before the war. During the period 1945-1966, the United Church of Canada erected 1,500 church buildings.[2]

In many cases, the post-war suburban church building boom was not conducive to spiritual or economic cooperation between denominations. Churches vied for the choicest locations in the developing residential areas. In an attempt to dampen such competition, developers offered specific locations to denominations of their own choice.

Post-war Opportunities

For the Alliance, at least, the homeland boom in church planting was matched by unparalleled opportunity abroad. During the war, Japan had overrun ten of the twenty Alliance mission fields. However, with so many of its Asian fields closed, the Foreign Department turned its attention to South America and Africa.

Back in 1927, sensing a general trend, Council had adopted a policy aimed at accelerating the development of indigenous churches and the progressive transfer of authority from the missionaries to the national churches. However, many missionaries had resisted the implementation of this policy. When the populations of European colonies in Asia emerged from the cruel conditions of Japanese occupation in 1945, many of them refused to submit again to any type of domination. Neither colonialism nor missionary paternalism was any longer acceptable. A post-war spirit of nationalism and independence quickly became a worldwide phenomenon.

After receiving a report on prevailing relationships on the fields, the board of managers concluded that its indigenous church policies of 1927 had been largely ignored or inconsistently applied, and it ordered that immediate steps be taken to implement them. Thus, coincident with the post-war missionary opportunities, the philosophy and character of Alliance foreign missions was drastically altered.

In the homeland, Home Secretary H. E. Nelson grappled with new post-war opportunities. Districts were urged to expand their extension funds. The Home Department established a Key City Project Fund for grants to "New York approved" projects. Minute

Men Clubs were formed within the districts to assist in "district approved" projects. A national Alliance Men's organization with district chapters raised money for additional projects. Home work conventions and pledges, which had tended to be sporadic, became annual events.

The Eastern and Central Canadian District, which contributed regularly to the New York-based extension funds, drew heavily on the Key City Project Fund for assistance in starting or re-starting at least seven churches in Ontario, Quebec and Nova Scotia. The district received more for extension work from New York funds than it contributed. The Western Canadian District preferred to rely on its own schemes for raising money. Astonishingly large amounts were received through the district Minute Men and special congregational appeals.

Home Secretary H. E. Nelson believed that the task of the Home Department was "to afford an ever-widening Christian fellowship" at home and thus "to secure for the worldwide missionary program an expanding measure of interest, prayer and practical support."[3] During his eighteen years in office, the number of Alliance churches in North America increased from 580 to 1,142, and total membership from 38,000 to 64,000.

At the Eastern and Central Canadian District Conference of September 1946, acting superintendent Rev. Nathan Bailey was unanimously elected district superintendent. At the same conference, Nelson announced that the re-establishment of an Alliance work in Peterborough would receive the support of the Home Department, and that in his "candid opinion," the district should own and operate a summer camp or conference ground.[4]

The Peterborough Key City Project got underway immediately.* On September 17, just twelve weeks after the rupture in Bethany Church, a group of 22 of the Alliance faithful met with District Superintendent Bailey and Rev. E. W. Richards, Assistant Home Secretary, in the YMCA building in Peterborough, and the Christian and Missionary Alliance Tabernacle of Peterborough was formed. Predictably, the new church adopted in full the Alliance constitution for local churches. Weekly prayer services commenced immediately in the home of Mrs. Hooey. Rev. R. K. Mills, a former

---

* The first Key City Project for Canada had been the revival of the Montreal–Centre work, in 1944, in the Notre Dame de Grace area, first under Rev. Edgar Lorimer and then under Rev. Firm Sauvé.

pastor of Bethany Church, became interim pastor and preached his first sermon in the Orange Hall on Brock Street on November 3. A large newspaper notice proclaimed, "The Alliance Carries On." Thus, the Alliance witness in Peterborough, started in 1889 by John Salmon as the Peterborough Branch of the Christian Alliance, was re-established 57 years later by Nathan Bailey.[5]*

On January 9, 1947, with a membership of 44, the church was fully organized. Its first officers were Herbert Pullyblank, secretary; Dudley Hewitt, treasurer; Dorothy Hooey, missionary treasurer. One year later, property was purchased and a church building erected, with the help of a loan from New York. The new facilities were dedicated on October 16, 1949, during the ministry of Rev. Ralph Hobson, and the name changed to Park Street Alliance Church.[6] In 1981 the name was again changed to Immanuel Alliance Church, and three years later, under the ministry of Rev. Reid Cook, the congregation erected its present building on Sherbrooke Street West.

A District Conference Grounds

The "candid opinion" of Home Secretary Nelson that the Eastern and Central Canadian District should own its own summer camp or conference ground was all that District Superintendent Bailey needed to proceed vigorously with the project. Ever since the Knowlton (Quebec) Conference Ground had ceased to be the home of the annual district summer conference in 1932 (see pages 72, 73), the district executive committee had struggled annually to make rental arrangements with several conference grounds. During the war years it had become impossible to make satisfactory arrangements.

In 1941, the Christie Street Tabernacle had declined to make further mortgage payments on behalf of the district for the Bible institute property. The district, unable to make its own payments, persuaded the New York trustees to agree to sell off the tabernacle/institute complex, to avoid foreclosure proceedings on the institute property (see page 151). The resulting crisis between the tabernacle and district was resolved by the New York headquarters paying off

---

* The vigorous restoration of an Alliance work in Peterborough was due, in large measure, to the indignation of District Superintendent Bailey. This resulted, at least in part, from his oft-repeated belief in the mistaken tradition that Dr. Simpson had personally started the work in Peterborough. Every recollection of the circumstances of the loss of both church and building was an anathema to him. Even five years later, during a district conference, he referred to Bethany Tabernacle as having been "wrested from us by one who wore our emblem."[7]

the old mortgage and assuming a new mortgage with the district in return for the district gaining full title to the tabernacle property.[8] The crisis passed, but the tabernacle congregation realized that it no longer owned its building and if the institute was not reopened the district would decide to sell the complex and the church would be forced to rebuild and relocate.[9]

In September 1945, the district began to plan towards the purchase of a conference ground "which will offer certain vacation facilities in addition to the usual spiritual ministry of a Bible Conference."[10] A half-hearted search got under way, probably because no one was convinced that money would become available if property was located.* One proposal for providing funds was to convert the institute building into rentable apartments.

Early in 1946, money received from the settlement of an estate enabled the district to pay off the mortgage held by New York headquarters on the institute building and gain clear title to the whole tabernacle/institute complex.[11] During the following summer, Glen Rocks Manor, formerly the summer estate of Lady Eaton, was offered for sale. The fully-equipped and furnished 225-acre property on the northern tip of Lake Rosseau in the Muskoka area could be purchased for $68,000. The Home Work Committee, with a push from District Superintendent Nathan Bailey, recommended its purchase to the conference of September 1946, and with the nod from Home Secretary Nelson, conference approved.

Immediately, the Christie Street Tabernacle was informed that the district intended to sell the tabernacle/institute complex. This time the tabernacle board acquiesced docilely, believing that the time had come to erect a new building better suited to the needs of the congregation. On January 31, 1947, an offer to purchase the complex for $85,000 was accepted by the district. Because the tabernacle property was larger than that of the institute, because the congregation had entirely paid for their tabernacle, and, over the years had paid for more than half the district equity in the institute building, the tabernacle board expected to receive two-thirds of the proceeds of the sale. However, District Superintendent Bailey proposed to award the tabernacle congregation only 38 percent. Rather heated negotiations ensued. In the end, a compromise was reached, and the proceeds were equally divided between church and district.

---

* One property investigated and branded "unsuitable" was an unused race track on the shore of Lake Ontario at Cobourg. Today it is a Pentecostal conference ground.

The purchase of the Glen Rocks property for $67,000 was finalized in December 1947. Had all the district's share of the proceeds of sale of the Christie Street properties been applied against the capital cost of the conference grounds, the venture would have been launched on a sound financial basis. As it was, only slightly more than half was applied. Continuing capital additions, repairs, operating and debt servicing charges plagued the project from the start.

Glen Rocks Bible Conference, "Canada's newest Bible and missionary conference," was dedicated on July 25, 1948, by Home Secretary H. E. Nelson. Featuring an array of the Alliance great, the conference was advertised as "evangelical in faith—interdenominational in fellowship—missionary in spirit." "Here, in this wonderful land of Muskoka," stated a brochure, "one may find inspiration for spirit, soul and body." Indeed, over the years, this was exactly what many found at Glen Rocks. Not a few of the current vintage of Canadian Alliance leaders heard their call to service while at this site of many fond memories.[12]

SEEDS OF CONSENSUS

During the war years, the Eastern and Central District office had served as a collection, receipting, and dispersal centre for all Canadian funds received for Alliance missionary work (see page 185). In this matter the two Canadian districts had shown a will to cooperate. However, the unfortunate circumstances surrounding the opening of the Bible institute in Regina had estranged the two districts (see pages 274-276).

Realizing the need for improved dialogue and relationship between east and west, the Home Department reported to the General Council of 1944, "The day, perhaps, is not far distant when it will be both practical and necessary to establish an official representative agency in the Dominion."[13] Council believed that the day had arrived and took the following action:

> We recommend the establishment of an official representative agency of The Christian and Missionary Alliance in Canada, if and when the Home Department and the Board of Managers deems it advisable.

Four months later, the Home Department dutifully gave its blessing, effective "as soon as the Board of Managers deem it advis-

Forging a Consensus / 293

7.1

7.1 In 1946, the Windsor Alliance Church erected this fine building at the intersection of Goyeau and Tuscarora Street. It would serve the congregation for 36 years.

7.2

7.3

7.2 Mavis Anderson (later Mrs. Weidman), the first full-time district youth secretary in 1947. She is seen here in her Regina office.

7.3 District Superintendent Nathan Bailey visits his Montreal (north-end) congregation in February 1949.

294 | Forging a Consensus

7.4 "Worldwide Missions in Review" in Massey Hall, Toronto, May 7, 1950. Missionaries are on the left, the Preachers' Chorus on the right and Dr. R. R. Brown is at the microphone. This was the last of 74 occasions when Alliance meetings took place in the historic hall.

able."[14] Unfortunately, the board saw no urgency, or perhaps even desirability, for the agency and decided that the "question of the Canadian Agency be laid on the table for the duration" (of the war).[15]

When Nathan Bailey became superintendent, he decided to try again to reach a better understanding with the west through the establishment of a "Canadian Office." He brought the matter to the attention of all the Canadian delegates at the Council of 1947, who, according to Bailey, "agreed that such an office should be established. ... It was agreed that the delegates from western Canada would bring the matter up for consideration at their Conference in June, and that word would then be sent to headquarters, advocating the plan."[16]

However, there is no indication from the records that the matter was addressed at the Regina conference, nor was any reply from the west received by headquarters. The following spring, Bailey brought up the proposal again with the board of managers, which referred the matter to the President's Council. The latter body tabled the proposal "until more information is available."[17] Six months later, the district executive committee petitioned the board for action.[18] In December 1948, with still no indication of western views, the board decided "that a Canadian Office be not established at the present time," the reason given as "because of its effect on the budget."[19]

So the idea of a "Canadian Agency" died. It was historically important as the first serious attempt to coalesce and interpret Canadian needs and aspirations. Twenty-five years would pass before what would generally be referred to as "The Canadian Corporation" would be formed for essentially the same purposes.

On May 4, 1950, the Fifty-Third General Council of The Christian and Missionary Alliance convened in Toronto. It was the third time for a Council to meet in Canada and the second in Toronto. Seven hundred and thirty-four accredited delegates, 222 corresponding delegates and several hundred visitors attended. Council headquarters were located in the King Edward Hotel, business sessions and weekday public services at Cooke's Presbyterian Church* (Queen

---

* During the Council meetings held in Cooke's Church, at least one speaker nostalgically mentioned the Alliance tradition that Cooke's had been the church attended by Dr. Simpson when a student at Knox College, where Mrs. Simpson had been a member, and where the couple had been married. The tradition is in error. We are in possession of Dr. Simpson's own declaration that while at Knox College he attended the Bay Street Presbyterian Church which was close to the Henry residence, where he boarded. Furthermore, the couple was in fact married by Dr. John Jennings, then minister of the Bay Street Church, and the official marriage entry appears in the Bay Street Church records. Not surprisingly, there is no mention of the Simpson-Henry wedding in the records of Cooke's Church.

and Mutual Streets), and Saturday and Sunday services were held in historic Massey Hall. Among the Alliance notables were Dr. H. M. Shuman, president; Dr. R. A. Forrest, president of Toccoa Falls Bible Institute; Dr. A. W. Tozer, vice-president; and Rev. David Mason, treasurer. Guest speakers were Dr. Harold C. Mason of Asbury Theological Seminary in Wilmore, Kentucky, and Dr. Oswald J. Smith of the Peoples Church, Toronto. Rev. William MacRoberts, minister of Cooke's Church, welcomed the Alliance on behalf of his congregation, and Inspector William McAllister of the Toronto police force welcomed the delegates on behalf of the mayor of Toronto and then gave an eloquent testimony of his conversion 25 years previously in the Christie Street Tabernacle. For the first time during a Council in Canada, the Preachers' Chorus, under Dr. R. R. Brown of Omaha, ministered. During the business proceedings, Rev. Harry L. Turner, at that time dean of St. Paul Bible Institute, was elected vice-president of the Alliance.[20]

Before a great audience in Massey Hall on Sunday morning, May 9, Dr. H. M. Shuman delivered his annual address, and the annual missionary rally was held that afternoon. As events turned out, these were the last occasions that the Alliance made use of the famous hall. Between 1919 and 1950, a total of 74 Alliance services were conducted in this Toronto landmark.

A New Toronto Church

The year 1950 saw the entry of another important church into Alliance ranks. Back in 1934, Charles B. Templeton, a nineteen-year-old Toronto newspaper cartoonist, "got religion." One night he came home quite late "heavy with depression." After an earnest talk with his mother, he went to his own room, where "a sense of enormous guilt descended and invaded every part" of him. Templeton wrote:

> Involuntarily, I began to pray . . . "Lord, come down". . . . It may have been some minutes later, or much longer—there was no sense of time—but I found myself, my head in my hands, crouched small on the floor, at the centre of a vast emptiness. The agonizing was past. It had left me numb, speechless, immobilized, alone, tense with a sense of expectancy. In a moment, a weight began to lift. . . . I could have leaped over a wall. An ineffable warmth began to

suffuse every corpuscle. It seemed that a light had turned on in my chest and its refining fire had cleansed me. . . . I heard myself whispering, "Thank you, Lord. Thank you."[21]

Soon Templeton became an itinerant evangelist with the Church of the Nazarene. During a visit home in the summer of 1941, he noticed a church building at Avenue Road and Roxborough Street* which was for sale or rent. Possessed with an urge to preach in this beautiful old building, Templeton signed a lease, effective mid-September.

At first it was planned to call the new venture the Toronto Gospel Tabernacle. For three weeks preceding the opening, notices called for the services of an orchestra and choir leader and musicians, and a few friends cleaned the old building. By the opening service, October 5, the work was known as the Avenue Road Church of the Church of the Nazarene. Their services were advertised as "Old time Wesley Methodism (nothing else), the gospel in word, song and picture." They featured "Charles B. Templeton, former Globe and Mail sports cartoonist and America's outstanding songstress."[22] The first service was attended by 112, in a sanctuary seating 1,200. Within six months, it was impossible to find a seat later than fifteen minutes prior to the service. A second Sunday evening service was commenced. In 1944, the building was purchased and a gallery constructed. Three years later, the church commenced severance proceedings with its denomination, the Church of the Nazarene.

In August 1948, Templeton left to study at Princeton Theological Seminary. One month later, the church called Rev. J. D. Carlson. In March 1949, Avenue Road Church became fully independent, but in September of that year, Carlson applied to have his Alliance credentials re-issued, and was granted "conditional" credentials for one year.[23]

In March 1950, the board of Avenue Road Church met with Templeton present "in an advisory capacity" in order to "consider the desirability of a close bond of connection with a denomination that has included in its fundamental beliefs all the scriptural essentials and expressions of faith for which we stand." The outcome, after a number

---

* Built in 1901, this fine limestone building was the home of Avenue Road Presbyterian Church until 1925, and thereafter of the Avenue Road United Church. From 1934 until 1939 it was used by the Stone Church of the Pentecostal Assemblies, and in 1940 became redundant, except for sporadic, short-term occupants.

of denominations were suggested, was a resolution to enter negotiations with the Alliance, pending congregational consent.[24]

At a congregational meeting a few days later, chaired by Templeton, it was clear that deep divisions existed within the board and the congregation regarding both the ministry and the organization. Templeton urged the church to resolve these difference by joining the Alliance. On a second ballot, the congregation registered a strong approval for this procedure.[25]

During the Council sessions in Cooke's Presbyterian Church, Carlson discussed the possibility of joining the Alliance with Home Secretary Nelson, Superintendent Bailey and the district executive committee. But because of the proximity of the Avenue Road Church to the new Yonge Street Tabernacle (the former Christie Street congregation) and because several of the tabernacle members lived near the Avenue Road Church, the committee feared a critical loss of support for the tabernacle, after a costly and disruptive relocation. Some of the Avenue Road members and the pastor feared the loss of some of the benefits of an independence so recently won. Indeed, the tendencies to independence on the part of some of the members and pastor was another concern of the committee. In the end, the committee insisted on a full acceptance of the Alliance constitution as the price for admission to the Alliance fellowship, and also that Pastor Carlson's undated resignation be submitted and kept on the district file.[26]

The church accepted these and other conditions. On June 25, the Avenue Road Church was received into the Alliance, and subsequently, the church was reorganized as required by the constitution and turned over the deeds of its property to the district.[27]

Not surprisingly, Carlson resigned a year later, and long-time Alliance pastor Rev. Don Shepson was installed on April 6, 1952.[28] Within three years, Avenue Road Church had become the largest congregation in the district and the largest giver to Alliance foreign missions anywhere in Canada.[29]

Western Momentum

The unparalleled growth rate of the Western Canadian District during the war years was sustained into the first few years of peace. Early in 1946, the health of District Superintendent Skitch had begun to break, and soon he was unable to actively attend to district affairs.

Yet, his prevailing influence and remarkable prayer ministry, together with the devotion and affection of his workers, continued to impel the work forward.[30] To add to the superintendent's distress, his colleague Willis Brooks left his church and the Bible school in Regina in October 1946 to assume the pastorate of the Tenth Avenue Church in Vancouver.

In January 1947, the Home Department granted Skitch a leave of absence, "provided he refrain from preaching and give himself to a program of rest."[31] By May, the absence of the superintendent drove the district executive committee to request the Home Department to appoint an "assistant district superintendent."[32] Home Secretary Nelson reported to the board of managers that Skitch was suffering from pernicious anemia and a duodenal ulcer,[33] conditions that had remained undiagnosed and untreated for so long that a partial paralysis of the lower limbs had resulted.[34]

Impatient with the lack of response to their request for an assistant district superintendent, the district executive committee commandeered George Magnus to whittle away at the backlog of work in the district office, with the assistance of "a very small stipend" from the district treasury.[35]

The indomitable spirit of the Western Canadian District during those difficult days is typified by the action of veteran pioneer worker Margaret Connor. At the age of 72, together with a friend, Miss Horne of Edmonton, and assisted by a very old car, she engaged in an itinerant visitation and prayer ministry to workers and residents scattered throughout the Canadian prairies. Counselling, praying and encouraging was her final ministry to her widespread constituency.*

Mavis Anderson also deserves special mention. Having been instrumental in starting a work in Lethbridge seven years previously (see page 274), she returned to western Canada early in 1947, fresh from Moody Bible Institute studies, and was appointed to the newly-created position of full-time District Sunday School and Youth Secretary. Her commission was "to train Sunday School teachers and youth leaders for every Alliance branch." From an office loaned by the college in Regina, she edited two district periodicals, the *Sunday*

---

* Early in the 1950s, Miss Connor purchased a retirement home in Surrey, British Columbia, from where, on May 8, 1962, she passed to her reward in her 86th year. Rev. George Magnus participated in her simple burial service, and Rev. Gordon Fowler was among her pallbearers. Undoubtedly, Margaret Connor ranks with the most outstanding Alliance pioneer workers.

School Booster and the *Compass*, a magazine for youth. Through her work, the idea of the Standard Sunday School emerged, and teacher training was conducted in dozens of locations. The plan was based on a belief that "Where there is no vision of the teaching ministry, the child perishes. Where there is no vision of the child ministry, the church perishes. Where there is no vision of the church ministry, the nation perishes."[36] Within two or three years, many Sunday schools had achieved the new standard for teachers and curriculum and had become "Standard Schools."[37] So impressed was the Home Department with the work of Miss Anderson in western Canada, that five years later, on March 1, 1952, she was appointed National Sunday School Secretary (for Canada and the United States). "Very reluctantly," the Western Canadian District granted her a one-year leave "to set up a National program." Unfortunately for western Canada, the loan became a gift, and Miss Anderson only returned for brief visits.[38*]

By September 1947 the Home Department and the board of managers had decided that "the time is not ripe" for the appointment of an assistant district superintendent.[39] As events turned out, by November 1 Skitch's health appeared to improve so that he attempted, probably unwisely, to resume his duties with the continued assistance of Magnus.[40] However, in January 1948, with only partial control of his limbs, he slipped on some ice and fractured an ankle. Many would have yielded to discouragement, but not Gordon Skitch. Addressing his workers from his hospital bed, he wrote:

> I know that this is part of Romans 8:28, so I accept it with praise in my heart.... This means that I will not be able to get around to help my workers for at least six weeks, but I shall have hours upon hours to remember you all in definite prayer.[41]

However, the setback proved to be more serious than was at first believed. After several months of additional suffering and incapacitation, in June 1948 Skitch tendered his resignation from the superintendency of the Western Canadian District, effective September 30.[42] In his last report to conference that June, Skitch told the delegates:

We are still in need of recognition from New York, of Brother George Magnus to act in the capacity of assistant superintendent. We believe that with the tremendous territory we have, and all the detailed office work, that it would be pleasing to God for us to pray that those responsible in New York will grant our request. . . . [43]

Nevertheless, the New York authorities remained obdurate. Home Secretary H. E. Nelson advised that with only 37 organized and 22 unorganized churches, the Western Canadian District would have to wait until it had at least 80 organized churches before an assistant superintendent would be appointed.[44]

One of the last Alliance churches founded during the superintendency of Gordon Skitch was in Abbotsford, British Columbia. Early in 1948, Rev. Alf Orthner of Chilliwack, with the assistance of Rev. Willis Brooks of Vancouver and other friends, conducted special meetings in various homes. In the fall of that year, Clement Dreger, a recent graduate of the Bible college in Regina, was called as the first pastor, and on September 24, the first services of the Alliance Tabernacle were held in the Eagles' Hall, with 25 in attendance.[45] Before Dreger left in 1952 to become an Alliance missionary, property was purchased on Church Road (later named Alliance Street), and two years later a basement sanctuary was constructed. The church was destined to become Canada's largest Alliance congregation.

As the last day of his superintendency approached, Gordon Skitch wrote a farewell letter to his constituency:

> This is probably one of the most difficult reports that I have been called upon to make as your superintendent. . . . No one but ourselves could possibly know just what a heavy heart Mrs. Skitch and I carry as we even think of that date [September 30] approaching. Our time as God's servants in this capacity has been full of joyful experiences and we both want to thank God unfeignedly for every one connected with this glorious work of the Lord in the Prairies. . . .[46]

And so, at 48, Gordon Skitch laid down his great burden for western Canada. During his eleven years of leadership, with or without appropriate title, the number of churches under his jurisdiction increased from 15 to 64. (An annual growth rate of thirteen percent over a period of eleven years was never before or since achieved anywhere in Canada—see Figure 2.) In the same period, annual district contributions to Alliance missions rose from $4,000 to $46,000. Allowing for inflation of 125 percent, the value of the contributions rose at an annual rate of fifteen per cent—another Canadian record. No doubt, the times were in Gordon Skitch's favour, and the quality of his helpers, such as George Magnus, must not be overlooked. Nevertheless, the achievements of this remarkable man are unique.*

Brooks and Blackett Years

Home Secretary Nelson advised the district executive meeting in October 1948 that the board of managers had approved the names of Rev. Paul H. Hokanson of Oklahoma City and Rev. Willis H. Brooks of Vancouver as candidates for the superintendency.[47] The committee's choice was clearly Brooks. However, Brooks had been pastor of Tenth Avenue Church in Vancouver for less than two years and was reluctant to leave his charge.[48]

More significant, the mention of Vancouver in the context of western Canadian affairs reopened the issue of district boundaries. Since Roffe's unsuccessful 1924 attempt to bring all of British Columbia into the Western Canadian District, the hope had remained in western minds (page 127). Shortly after Brooks became a Vancouver pastor under the Pacific Northwest District, he urged the Home Department to include Vancouver in the Western Canadian District.[50] To study the issue, the Home Department appointed an ad hoc committee, consisting of Rev. Gordon Wishart, a pastor in Pittsburgh (chairman), Rev. Cecil R. Thomas, superintendent of the Western District, and Rev. Linton D. Hill, a pastor in Dover, New Jersey.[51] The committee could not present a united recommendation, and the department ruled against any immediate change in district jurisdiction.[52]

---

* In 1953 Gordon Skitch relocated to the Eastern and Central Canadian District, where, still labouring under considerable handicap, he served as pastor, first in Brantford and then in Kitchener. In 1963, he returned to Calgary with the title of "evangelist," and retired two years later, thus closing a ministry spanning 41 years. He passed to his rest on May 30, 1974, still praising the Lord. In an *Alliance Weekly* obituary, he was correctly described as "a cheerful, buoyant, faith-filled man, known for his optimism, his humour, his generosity, and his evangelistic zeal."[49]

Forging a Consensus / 303

7.5

7.5 The Fifty-third General Council of 1950 convened in Cooke's Presbyterian Church, Toronto. Here, District Superintendent Nathan Bailey poses with one of the elaborate missionary displays.

7.6 The stained glass window depicting Al Lewis and "The Gospel Messenger," which was installed at Alliance headquarters in Wassenaar (The Hague), Netherlands.

7.6

304 / *Forging a Consensus*

7.7

7.8

7.9

7.10

7.7 Originally the Avenue Road Presbyterian Church, this fine old limestone building served as church home of the Avenue Road Church from 1941 to 1975. Here Dr. Tozer preached for four years.

7.8 Commencing in 1952, Clarence Jaycox and his wife, Ruth, began career ministries among the Indians of western Canada.

7.9 The popular pastor/evangelist, Rev. J. D. Carlson served Alliance churches in Edmonton, Vancouver, Toronto and Calgary, during the period 1939 to 1960.

7.10 Rev. and Mrs. David Caskey, long term missionaries to the Inuit at Eskimo Point.

In March 1949, on the recommendation of the Home Department, the district executive committee asked Rev. Harry L. Turner to fill the unexpired term of district superintendent, ending in December 1950. Turner consented, but the board of managers disapproved, on the basis that Turner's absence from St. Paul Bible Institute would "impair the progress" of that school.[53] The Home Department then suggested Rev. George Blackett, but the committee believed he should remain as president-dean of the school in Regina.[54]

Attention now returned to Willis Brooks, and during the conference of June 1949, he reluctantly agreed to become district superintendent, part-time, while remaining pastor of the Tenth Avenue Church, answerable to the superintendent of the Pacific Northwest District. All present, including Home Secretary Nelson, saw the absurdity of the arrangement, and on Nelson's recommendation,[55] the board approved a boundary change in December, and the following May, Council gave its approval. At last all of Canada had returned to the jurisdiction of Canadian-based districts.[56]

However, the part-time superintendence of a district from one extremity of its 1,500-mile breadth was not practical. Yet Willis Brooks steadfastly refused to relinquish his Vancouver ministry. Each year he resisted re-election, but with no other candidates, he took on again the impossible task. After the first year, he was assisted part-time by George Blackett for Saskatchewan, Manitoba and western Ontario, and by George Magnus or John Cunningham for Alberta.[57]

Notwithstanding, the Brooks years were characterized by enormous increases in missions giving—in those four years, annual contributions rose from $49,000 to $124,000. (Allowing for four percent inflation, this amounts to an annual increase of 22 percent, probably an all-time high for any four-year period.) However, growth in missionary giving was not matched by a similar home extension program. The tremendous extension momentum which had carried through even the years of Gordon Skitch's illness was not maintained during the Brooks era. The number of churches grew only from 63 to 66 (an annual growth of 1.4 percent).

This condition was not accidental. In his annual report to conference in September 1952, District Superintendent Brooks stated, "It has been the feeling of the superintendent that some consolidation should be done before many new centres are opened." Nevertheless, a successful pioneer effort was launched during the following April, when Roy Batchelor was dispatched to the Okanagan Valley to open a work in Vernon, based on a group of eighteen children. Soon a weekly radio broadcast was beamed from this centre. Late in 1955 an old church building was purchased and dedicated. Early in 1961, Pastor John Klassen of the Vernon church commenced holding Sunday services in Kelowna, and in October, Jack Schroeder was appointed pastor. Three years later, a church was started in Penticton under George Ross. Thus a new and important area was entered and consolidated.

In the area of specialized ministries there was an important first for the Brooks era. In June 1952, after graduating from Nyack, Clarence Jaycox was appointed a missionary to the Indians by the Western Canadian District. Jaycox, his wife Ruth, a registered nurse, and Mr. and Mrs. Phil Wilson first located in Fort Nelson, B.C. (500 miles northwest of Edmonton), where a work among the Slavie Indians commenced.

Over the next fifteen years, with the help of several other workers, six mission centres were opened among the Cree Indians of Alberta, about 100 miles north of Lesser Slave Lake. Spiritual work was combined with school teaching and nursing. Outstanding among all who had a part in these hard and discouraging tasks were Clarence and Ruth Jaycox who laboured for 38 years, until retirement. Today, at Loon Lake, Alberta, a school is named in his honour.

Rev. Willis Brooks recognized that in terms of home extension, the situation must not be allowed to continue, and he resigned his part-time superintendency, effective December 1953.[58] In his final report to conference, he thanked all concerned for their support and then added:

> We trust you will not think too unkindly of us for our inability to devote our full time to this ministry. As God has given strength and wisdom we have been willing to carry this dual responsibility.... However ... a continuance of this adjusted relationship would not be in the will of God, nor in the best interests of the work.[59]

Conference of September 1953 elected Rev. Cyril H. Steinman, an Alliance pastor in Portland, Oregon, superintendent of the Western Canadian District. However, one month later, before he took office, he "declined" to come.[60] In November, Brooks advised the Home Department that his district executive committee was unable to propose another candidate, but that a sub-committee had been charged to do so.[61]

The need for a new district superintendent coincided with the resignation, effective December 31, 1953, of President-Dean Blackett from the Bible college in Regina. With the approval of the district executive committee, the Home Department immediately appointed him district superintendent.[62]

Rev. George Blackett was a quiet-spoken, articulate, immaculate and deeply spiritual man—perhaps not the prototype of a popular western superintendent of the period. Nevertheless he was held in deep respect by those who knew him. During his six-year term of office, the district experienced moderate and sustained growth. The number of churches grew at an average annual rate of three per cent, and missionary offerings at four percent (in constant dollars). In 1958, western Canadian missionary contributions surpassed the east at $194,000. Never again would the west take second place to the east in this respect.

Blackett was a true churchman at heart. It was his conviction that there would be far fewer ailing church members if more care was taken to prepare prospective members for their responsibilities. In response to this need he prepared an excellent manual, "Preparation for Membership." Thousands of copies have been used by Alliance candidates and teachers throughout Canada and the United States—a lasting spiritual and practical legacy to his posterity. In his farewell address to the 1959 conference, Blackett said:

> In my last official word to you I should like to emphasize a matter that is vital in life and ministry. The living heart of the glorious message that our Lord has entrusted to us is love—Calvary love. It does more to solve problems than anything could do. . . . Closely associated with love are such beautiful graces as humility, meekness, lowliness, kindness and sympathy. . . . Let us "covet earnestly the best gifts", and strive to excel in the things that are nearest to the heart of God.[63]*

---

* George Blackett retired in April 1960, following the conclusion of his superintendency at the end of 1959. He died at the age of 70 on Thanksgiving Day morning, October 9, 1960, rejoicing in a recent vision he had had of the Saviour and the life beyond.[64]

308 / *Forging a Consensus*

In eastern Canada, District Superintendent Nathan Bailey persisted in his efforts for better relationships with the west, and in George Blackett he found a kindred spirit. Old issues were put to rest, including the location of a single educational centre. In 1956, the Western Canadian Bible Institute became the national Alliance school, changing its name to Canadian Bible College.[65]

A MISSIONS TRAGEDY

In the mid-1950s the worldwide Alliance community was drawn together through a traumatic series of events. In June 1938, a scientific expedition had discovered the land-locked "Grand Valley of the Baliem River" in Dutch New Guinea, and had reported that the valley, 40 miles long and 10 miles wide, had a native population of about 60,000. With the onslaught of World War II, the world soon forgot the intriguing valley with its stone age occupants.

Then, in May 1945, an American Air Force C-47 crashed in the mountains not far from the Baliem Valley. Survivors brought back tales of a strange aboriginal culture in the valley, which newsmen dubbed "Shangri-La," to add glamour and mystery. The Baliem Valley was back in the newspapers and also in the minds of the people in the Foreign Department of the Alliance.

Meanwhile, Alliance post-war missionary activity resumed in Indonesia. In view of the great distances involved in the archipelago, it was decided in 1948 to purchase a plane, and Foreign Secretary Dr. A. C. Snead began to look for a pilot to head up the project. In the divine juxtaposition of events and people, it happened that William (Bill) Newell, a Nyack student from Hamilton, was with Home Secretary H. E. Nelson when the need was mentioned. Newell suggested Albert (Al) Lewis, an elder in his home church of Delta Tabernacle. A war-time flying instructor with the Royal Canadian Air Force, Lewis was by that time a successful building contractor. Soon, he and his wife, Mary, were interviewed in New York, and he agreed to become a missionary pilot for Indonesia. Writing some time later about his decision, Lewis stated, "It is going to cost, I know, but I am willing to pay the price."

A reconditioned Beechcraft D17S, built in 1945, was purchased for $8,900. Floats from Oshawa and struts from Winnipeg were fitted to the plane in New Jersey, and it was shipped to Borneo. Early the following year, when flying from Borneo to Java, Lewis stopped for fuel and tied the Beechcraft to a pier. By the time he returned, insurgents had cut the aircraft adrift, to founder and break up against a shoal.

On Lewis's return to New York, he found that the Foreign Department had shifted its interest to the Baliem Valley of New Guinea. However, there would be no easy way to fly in to the valley. It was surrounded by 10-12,000-foot mountain peaks, except for a hopelessly narrow gorge to the southeast and a somewhat wider pass to the northeast. The only feasible way was to approach through the pass, drop down rapidly, turn sharply up-river and land on the longest straight stretch of the river, at an elevation of 1,500 feet. Flying out of the valley was even more hazardous, involving a sharp turn and a high climb rate immediately following lift-off. The Dutch government gave their consent for the venture on the condition that a twin-engined aircraft would be used. It was Lewis's task to find a suitable plane.

By July 1949, Lewis recommended a Sealand Twin-engined Amphibian, manufactured by Short Brothers in Belfast, Northern Ireland.[66] After several visits to Belfast, many flight tests, and a few minor design changes, Lewis was satisfied and the plane was ordered in April 1950 at a cost of $69,800.[67]

However, many months passed before the plane was ready, and by then, the price had risen to $100,000. At an impressive dedication ceremony on November 13, 1953, at Belfast, it was christened "The Gospel Messenger." Lewis and his co-pilot Edward W. Ulrich, an ex-United States Navy flier, flew it to London, where additional radio equipment was installed, then across Europe and Asia to Sentani Airport base, on the north coast of New Guinea.

Flying time from the base at Sentani to the Baliem Valley was about an hour and a half. Recalling his first flight over the valley, Lewis wrote, "When I realized that down below me in those villages were thousands of people who had never heard the gospel . . . my heart cried out for an opportunity to reach them." After many trial flights and mock landings, all was ready for the historic entry on April 20, 1954. The initial missionary force consisted of Einar Mickelson (in charge) and Lloyd Van Stone. A native pastor from the Wissel Lakes area accompanied them, along with his wife and two-year-old daughter, who were included in the hope that their entry would be seen as peaceful. Describing the landing, Lewis wrote:

> It was quite an experience flying down into that narrow valley and trying to put the Sealand Amphibian plane

down on the narrow, winding Baliem River. I had to approach it on a curve and trust I would not clip a tree with the wings or hit a floating log. The Lord was good and we made it.

Within fifteen minutes of touchdown, all passengers and supplies had been unloaded. The plane then returned to Sentani.[68] The following day it returned with Myron Bromley, a linguistic specialist, and a Kapauku tribesman from the Wissel Lakes. These eight souls comprised the entire beachhead party. Later, after friendly contacts had been made with the inhabitants, the wives and children of the missionaries were added. Thus was the Baliem Valley first entered with the gospel.[69]

For one whole year Al Lewis and "The Gospel Messenger" served the infant mission station. Then came the sad day of April 28, 1955. While ferrying supplies to the valley, unaccompanied, Lewis encountered dense cloud and rain squalls. However, since clear skies over the valley had been reported, he pressed on through the pass. He never arrived at his destination. Extensive searches by planes of the Royal Dutch Navy and the Missionary Aviation Fellowship failed to locate "The Gospel Messenger." Not until a month later was the wreckage spotted on a rocky slope at an elevation of nearly 11,000 feet.

The loss of pilot and plane sent a lasting shock ripple throughout the Alliance community. In a crowded Delta Tabernacle in Hamilton, an awesome memorial service was held on November 6, featuring Lewis's almost prophetic words, "It is going to cost, I know, but I am willing to pay the price."

In December 1959, more than four and a half years after the tragedy, an overland party reached the crash site. The body of Lewis was found in the convoluted cockpit, his chest crushed but his head unmarred. The orientation of the wreckage suggested that he might have been turning back. Missionary Harold Catto of Owen Sound conducted a committal service, and the body was lowered into a nearby rock crevice. Then a Dutch official unfurled a flag and officially named the peak "Lewis Top."[70]

The name of Al Lewis became almost a legend. At Alliance headquarters in Wassenaar (The Hague), Netherlands, a stained glass memorial window was installed, depicting Lewis and "The Gospel Messenger." Alan and Marguerita Howarth, of Rexdale Alliance Church, donated money to establish the Al Lewis Memorial Scholarship at Canadian Bible College in Regina. At Glen Rocks Bible

Conference grounds, a circle of flowers around the flag pole at the main crossroads was officially named Lewis Circle. "In a very real sense," Russell Hitt wrote in his book, *Cannibal Valley*, "Pilot Lewis had become Martyr Lewis, a faithful witness, who laid down his life in bringing the gospel to the tribespeople of Dutch New Guinea."[71]

The saga of Al Lewis was not yet ended. Early in 1990, tribesmen removed his skeletal remains from the crevice on Lewis Top. Missionaries managed to recover them, and on March 10 re-interred them at Wamena, in the heart of the Baliem Valley. A memorial service was attended by "several hundred of the Wamena community, including government officials." It was fitting that Dr. Myron Bromley, who 36 years previously had been in the original party flown into the valley by Lewis, spoke at the service. It is also fitting that the remains of Al Lewis should rest with the people of the valley, for whom his heart had cried out. Surely, he had proven his love for them—"Greater love hath no man than this, that he lay down his life for his friends."

A Decade of Change

In 1955, the east followed the lead of the west in appointing its first full-time Youth and Sunday School secretary, Ruth Bailey. She served from October 1954 until September 1959. Largely due to her efforts, the district achieved "an enviable position" among the districts with respect to these ministries.[72]

In Unionville, Ontario, a church destined to become of note joined Alliance ranks. A small group had commenced holding independent services in May 1949 as the Unionville Gospel Centre, in the old Unionville Congregational Church building on Main Street at Fred Varley Drive. Four years later, led by the Rev. Percy R. Barley, a former minister of the United Missionary Church, land was purchased and a church building erected further north on Main Street. In September 1956, the centre and Barley were accepted into the Alliance fellowship, and the centre reorganized with 45 charter members as the Unionville Gospel Centre Church. A few years later the name was changed to Unionville Alliance Church. Under Rev. David G. Petrescue, the congregation purchased a ten-acre property on 16th Avenue and on February 28, 1988, dedicated a new sanctuary accommodating 1,200 persons.[73]

On April 29, 1956, under the leadership of Pastor Richard W. Bailey, the congregation of the Alliance Community Church on Pie IX Boulevard in the north end of Montreal (formerly the Alliance Gospel

Hall), dedicated its new church building. Dr. H. M. Shuman personally donated the handsome oak pulpit and offered the dedicatory prayer. The comfortable sanctuary, seating barely 150, could hardly be called important in terms of its size or architectural grandeur, but it was historically unique because it was the first church building erected by the Alliance in Quebec. Unfortunately, the subsequent migration of the English-speaking population from the area to the west island communities or out of the province altogether, necessitated closure of the church on May 26, 1974, after 48 years of ministry. However, the historic little building was not lost to the Alliance. It now serves L'Eglise de L'Alliance Chrétienne et Missionnaire (Haitian) congregation.[74]

In May 1958, General Council convened for the first time in western Canada. Meeting chiefly in the Knox United Church in Winnipeg, the Saturday evening and Sunday services were held in the Civic Auditorium. The featured speaker was the well-known Dr. J. Sidlow Baxter, of Edinburgh, Scotland.[75]

In December 1959, after serving the large Southside Alliance Church in Chicago for 31 years, Dr. A. W. Tozer became "preaching pastor" of the Avenue Road Church of Toronto. The famous preacher had also become known as the "spicy-penned author" both from his books and his editorials in the *Alliance Witness*. During his three and a half years of ministry in Toronto, huge crowds were drawn to "Dr. Tozer's church." Stricken before leaving for church on Sunday morning, May 12, 1963, Dr. Tozer was taken to Scarborough General Hospital, where he died early the following morning in his sleep from a coronary thrombosis. He had served as an Alliance pastor for 44 years, as editor of the *Alliance Witness* for 13 years, as a member of the board of managers for 22 years and as vice-president of the Alliance for 4 years. His greatest fame would come after his death. Today, his published writings and sermons are acclaimed the world over by evangelicals of almost every stamp.

The 1950s brought sweeping change in both the composition of the Alliance hierarchy and, as a result, in policies. It all started in 1952, when Treasurer Rev. David Mason retired, and Council elected Rev. Bernard S. King as his replacement. Strong-willed and influential, his opinions would carry much weight with the board of managers for the next 24 years. He is credited with establishing the Church Extension Loan Fund, which greatly assisted churches to finance their building programs. Four years later, President Dr. Harry M. Shuman stepped

Forging a Consensus / 313

7.11 Dr. Harry Turner was the fifth president of the Christian and Missionary Alliance, from 1954 to 1960. Through his influence, the Alliance gained a foothold in Winnipeg and Saskatoon.

7.11

7.12 Rev. John Cunningham is representative of the many long-term pastors whose service commenced during the late 1930s.

7.12

7.13

7.14

7.13 Pastor A. H. Orthner prepares to address his radio audience in Moose Jaw during the 1950s.

7.14 "Spicy-penned author" Dr. A. W. Tozer was preaching pastor at Avenue Road Church (Toronto) from December 1959 until May 1963.

314 / *Forging a Consensus*

7.15

7.16

7.15 Dr. Nathan Bailey was superintendent of the Eastern and Central Canadian District from 1946 to 1960. He also served as the sixth president of the Christian and Missionary Alliance, from 1960 to 1978.

7.16 Ruby Johnston, known as "the mother of Chinese Alliance Churches in Canada," ministered for more than half a century.

7.17

7.18

7.17 Rev. Augustus Chao became the first pastor of the first Canadian Chinese congregation in Regina, in June 1960.

7.18 Rev. William J. Newell was superintendent of the Eastern and Central Canadian District from 1960 to 1973. He provided vital leadership during the early years of the movement to Canadian autonomy.

down at the age of 76, and Council elected Rev. Harry L. Turner to the top Alliance job. Shuman had held the position for 29 years—a record exceeded only by the founder. He had guided the Alliance through the harrowing years of world depression and world war, effecting changes which, for good or bad, forever changed the Alliance image.

In 1956, Foreign Secretary Dr. Alfred C. Snead retired after 34 years. He was replaced by Rev. Louis L. King, a former missionary and area secretary for India and the Far East, where he had "earned his spurs" by implementing tough new indigenous policies. Just three years later, while King was renovating the Foreign Department, Council replaced Home Secretary Rev. H. E. Nelson with Rev. Leslie W. Pippert. Under his command, the Home Department was ordered to advance on the twin fronts of evangelism and extension.

After serving for six years as president, Dr. Turner declined to allow his name to stand for re-election in May 1960. In his final report to Council, he had the courage to say what some still did not want to hear:

> Rightly or wrongly, the days are past when we were only a fellowship. Today we are a church. We must tell the world what we believe and why we believe it.[76]

Then, warming to his theme for a better educational program, he told the delegates:

> We need to re-think, re-emphasize, consolidate and expand our educational obligations. Too little, too late can rob us of desirable candidates and make us followers, rather than leaders.[77]

Council elected Rev. Nathan Bailey,* then serving as superintendent of the Eastern and Central Canadian District, as their new president. They also took to heart Turner's warning and elected Dr. Gilbert Johnson as the first full-time Education Secretary. In time this would have great significance for the Alliance in Canada.

In 1960, both Canadian districts acquired new superintendents. In the west, Rev. George Blackett had retired the previous December, and Rev. Roy McIntyre became district superintendent as of January 1, 1960.[78] (He it was who had been sent to open up the Peace River

---

* One month later, President Bailey was awarded an honourary Doctor of Laws degree by Asbury College.

area—see pages 267, 268.) Born in northern Ontario in 1913, McIntyre was raised on a northern Saskatchewan homestead. He was converted when seventeen through the ministry of an itinerant team from Prairie Bible Institute. Upon graduation from that school in 1935, he became an Alliance worker, and over the next 25 years proved himself an energetic and capable pastor. At that time pastor of the University Drive Tabernacle in Saskatoon, McIntyre was elected unanimously to the superintendency by the conference of September 1959.[79] His predecessor, George Blackett, commented, "He needs the wisdom of Solomon, the strength of Samson, the perception of Daniel, the legal talents of Moses and the faith of Abraham."[80] McIntyre appears to have possessed a good measure of all these.

In the east, Dr. Bailey continued as district superintendent in addition to his new duties as president until the conference of September 1960. He had provided sound leadership at a critical time. During his superintendency of fourteen years, the number of churches had grown from 24 to 44—an average annual growth rate of nearly four per cent. This was the highest ever achieved in the east over a fourteen-year period (see Figure 2). From May through September, with Bailey in New York much of the time, District Treasurer Rev. L. Latimer Brooker, of the Alliance Tabernacle on Yonge Street, took a leading role in district business. It was not surprising therefore, that the delegates of conference nominated him for superintendent, although the nominating committee had put forward the name of Rev. William J. Newell, associate pastor of the Avenue Road Church. On the second ballot Newell received the required number of votes and was declared the new district superintendent. [81]

Born in Belfast, Northern Ireland, in 1922, William (Bill) Newell grew up in Hamilton, where he made Delta Tabernacle his home church. After serving with the Royal Canadian Navy during World War II, he attended the Missionary Training Institute, and in 1949 graduated and became pastor of the Alliance Tabernacle in Chatham, Ontario. Ordained in 1953, he pioneered the Key City project work in Oshawa a year later, where he served until called to the Avenue Road Church late in 1959.

Both new Canadian superintendents welcomed headquarters' home evangelism and home extension emphasis. However, the Western Canadian District had been heavily engaged in these fields for several decades. In fact, by 1960, the district was adding new churches at the astonishingly high average annual rate of seven percent. Moreover, in the area of home missions, the district supported five missionary couples plus helpers in six locations among the Slavie and Cree Indians.[82] The following year McIntyre reported that the district was operating nine missions works, supported by offerings amounting to $44,000.[83] So it was that McIntyre had reason to believe that he knew how to proceed with these policies. As a result, the programs issuing from the Home Department sometimes were given short shrift in western Canada, much to the annoyance of Home Secretary Pippert.

CHINESE AND INUIT MINISTRIES

McIntyre's interest in special ministries extended beyond a witness to the Indians. The year 1962 saw the organization of the first Chinese Alliance church in North America in Regina. The church had its beginnings in 1932, when Ruby Johnston of the Alliance Gospel Hall first realized that no gospel work was being done among the Chinese of her city. Assisted by other young friends from the Hall, Miss Johnston purchased and distributed Chinese tracts. Within three years, home meetings were started, including one for children in Miss Johnston's home, in which future WEC missionary Beth Allinger and future pastor "Alf" Orthner were of special help.

By 1945, meetings were being conducted on Sunday afternoons, at which future missionaries Garth Hunt and Dave Douglas, and future pastor Paul Edwardson and his wife-to-be, June Sanborn, all of the Western Canadian Bible Institute, gave valuable assistance. In 1955 the work was named the Regina Chinese Christian Fellowship. A full-time Chinese pastor was needed, but money was scarce. Hearing of the need, the Davao Chinese Church of the Philippines, together with several local friends, undertook to support a Chinese pastor in Regina. In June 1960, the Rev. Augustus Chao arrived from Hong Kong and was appointed pastor.[84]

On January 29 of the following year, a church was organized as the Regina Chinese Alliance Church.[85] In 1967, the congregation purchased the old tabernacle on 13th Avenue and Osler Street, which remained its home for the next 21 years.

Rev. Augustus Chao came to Regina with a vision for fifty Chinese Alliance churches in North America. Within fifteen years there were seventeen in Canada and nine in the United States. The continuing presence of Ruby Johnston throughout this long and developing ministry caused her to become affectionately known as "the mother of Chinese Alliance churches in Canada," which she faithfully served in various capacities for more than a half century until called to higher service in July 1983.

The Western Canadian District's several ministries to Indians were not its only attempts to evangelize Canada's aboriginal peoples. A thousand miles north of Winnipeg, and two hundred miles north of Churchill lies the settlement of Eskimo Point, on the shores of Hudson Bay. It is populated by the Inuit, descendants of a brave, nomadic people who for centuries followed the caribou herds on which they depended for food. When the caribou supply failed in the 1950s, the government of Canada brought the starving Inuit into settlements, mostly along the coast where supplies and services could be made available.[86]

In February 1962, the district took over the work of the Eskimo Gospel Crusade, founded in 1946 by the Rev. Gleason H. Ledyard at Maguse River some twelve miles inland from Eskimo Point. The two resident missionary couples, the Ron Castles and David Dyes, came into the Alliance fellowship.[87] Because the Inuit were being moved to coastal settlements, it was decided to relocate the mission to Eskimo Point. On June 5, Ron Castle, a 36-year-old experienced pilot, flew his Stinson aircraft towards Churchill to pick up helpers for the move. Flying into a "white-out," he crashed and was instantly killed.[88] A week later, he was buried at Star City, Saskatchewan, Rev. Alf H. Orthner conducting the service.[89]

Living and working in the Northwest Territories can be particularly difficult for those who come from more temperate latitudes. The hardships are physical, spiritual and psychological. As a result, short-term ministries have been usual. Unique among Alliance workers to have served at Eskimo Point are David and Marian Caskey. They persevered for fifteen years, from 1965 to 1980, until relocated to Churchill.

Other more recent attempts to evangelize the Inuit people have come and gone but the work at Eskimo Point has persisted. In April 1970, new facilities were dedicated and enlarged five years later. In November 1981, the work was organized with a charter membership of 22 (plus 24 adherents), as the Arviat Alliance Church.

Advances West and East

Among several well-known churches in western Canada that had their start during this period was the work at Surrey, some twenty miles from Vancouver. In 1960, prayer meetings began in the home of

Arnold Neufeld, and in April 1961, Sunday services were commenced in the Dell Hotel under the leadership of Rev. Gordon Fowler, assistant pastor of the Alliance Tabernacle in Vancouver. Property on 96th Avenue was purchased, and on September 17 President Nathan Bailey turned the first sod to initiate a building program.[90] At the end of 1961, Fowler resigned in Vancouver to become pastor in Surrey. Three months later, on March 11, the new 350-seat sanctuary was dedicated, and on April 17, the Surrey Alliance Church was organized.[91]

Fowler left Surrey in 1966 to become a missionary in Hawaii,[92] and Rev. Melvin Shareski was installed as pastor.[93] Plans were made for a larger sanctuary, and on February 18, 1968, a 650-seat sanctuary was dedicated.[94] During Shareski's eight-year ministry at Surrey, Sunday morning attendance grew from 200 to 500. In 1974, the congregation daughtered a new church at White Rock and again in 1978 at Coquitlam. Notwithstanding a plateauing of attendance between 550 and 600, this zealous congregation dedicated a third new sanctuary, seating 1,400 persons, on April 4, 1982.

The seeming boundless confidence of this remarkable congregation was typical of the west, as compared with a cautious and measured approach that was typical of the east.

By 1960, it was obvious that the Western Canadian District was getting too large for one man to look after. Each year, McIntyre asked the Home Department, unsuccessfully, for an assistant. In March 1963, with 98 churches under the district's care, the Home Department and the board of managers decided to divide the district. The new district would comprise Saskatchewan, Manitoba and that part of Ontario and the Northwest Territories lying between the 88th and 110th meridians, and would initially include 39 churches.[95]

Western leaders wanted to name the new district "Central Canadian District." But since this would have necessitated a name change for the east, and McIntyre was determined to avoid another strain in east-west relationships, he put the matter before his eastern counterpart, Superintendent Newell.

On August 21, the district executive committee in the east adopted the following resolution:

> Whereas Ontario is usually considered to be geographically Central Canada, and
>
> Whereas a further division of the Eastern and Central Canadian District could form an Eastern Canadian District in

320 / Forging a Consensus

our Maritime Provinces and create a problem in naming Ontario and Quebec, and

Whereas Manitoba is usually considered to be the commencement of Western Canada,

We recommend that the new district for Manitoba and Saskatchewan be called "The Mid-Western Canadian District". . . . [96]*

So it was that the new prairie district obtained its name, which was slightly altered to the Canadian Midwest District. At the September 1963 conference of the Western Canadian District, delegates unanimously selected Rev. Alf H. Orthner as the founding superintendent of the Canadian Midwest District.

The new district commenced functioning on January 1, 1964.[97] For several months it was headquartered in the Canadian Bible College. Then, a house on Parliament Street was acquired and suitably equipped, and served as district parsonage and office for the next eleven years. The first district conference was held at Morden, Manitoba, in September 1964, attended by Home Secretary Rev. Leslie W. Pippert. Among district officers elected were Rev. Melvin P. Sylvester as secretary and Clare Heagy as treasurer.[98]

The vigorous western programs for extension and home missions during the first half of the 1960s were not matched in the east. Between 1960 and 1966, the number of churches in the east decreased from 44 to 41. However, there were a few significant gains. Perhaps the brightest star was that of Rexdale, on the northwest fringe of Metropolitan Toronto.

In July 1959, the West End Alliance Church**, on St. Clarens Avenue, sold its property and a down payment was made on a property in Rexdale on Islington Avenue, near the Humber River crossing. Services started in rented premises, but the congregation was fraught with problems, and was disbanded in October 1960.[99]

---

* The district executive committee might have added that historically the Eastern and Central Canadian District was meant to be a temporary combination of two districts until such a time as a separate district for the maritimes could be justified (see page 140).

** The West End Alliance Church had its origin in 1912, when an independent work became the Emmerson Avenue Tabernacle of the C&MA, the first church in Canada to adopt the Alliance constitution. In 1914, the Emmerson Avenue Tabernacle linked up with another independent work and became Lappin Avenue Alliance Tabernacle. Relocating again in 1949, to St. Clarens Avenue, it became the West End Alliance Church.

In August 1961, at the request of District Superintendent Newell, Rev. Ross Ingram of Cobourg accepted the challenge to start a new work in Rexdale.[100] A generous gift enabled the purchase of a parsonage and a month later door-to-door visitation commenced.

The first services were held on October 1 in Elms Public School, on Golfdown Drive. Sunday school was attended by one Christian friend and the members of Pastor Ingram's family. Three others from the community attended the worship service. The pastor's text was Luke 4:18: "The Spirit of the Lord is on me, because he has anointed me to preach good news. . . ."

One year later, Sunday School attendance was 77, and Sunday morning and evening attendance was between 50 and 60.[101]

Using the property purchased by the former West End Church, a church home was erected, and on January 20, 1963, more than 250 people crowded into facilities designed to seat 164 for the dedication service. Over the years, adjacent property was acquired and the sanctuary extended twice, despite the fact that the congregation sent off several of its members to daughter two churches. On February 4, 1979, a beautiful new 750-seat sanctuary was dedicated with Alliance president Dr. L. L. King preaching the sermon.

In April 1963, the Missionary Rest Home in Mimico, founded in 1913 by A. W. Roffe and dedicated by A. B. Simpson, was closed. In return for providing an annuity for its last resident, the Eastern and Central Canadian District fell heir to the proceeds of sale of the property.[102] The development sparked interest in a district missionary home, and a 24-acre property in Unionville was considered.[103] However, interest in this property began to wane after Rev. William Moreland, pastor of the Alliance church in Waterdown, met with Myrtle Osborne, Cecil Ambridge and William Henderson one month later. Together with a Mrs. Gertrude Baker, the four were the last survivors of the Church of God Sojourning in Aldershot, five miles away. According to tradition, in 1913 a few friends began to meet for Bible study in the attic home of Emily Carr in downtown Toronto. While sweeping the floor after a meeting, a Mr. Schulkins came across a scrap of crumpled paper. It turned out to be a pamphlet written by a Dr. Ivan Panin, of Grafton, Massachusetts. The message of the pamphlet appealed to the members of the group who invited Panin to address them.

Forced to leave Russia in 1872, Panin completed his education in the United States, and became a writer and teacher of some note. After an introductory visit to Toronto, Panin became the leader of the group. By 1926 they numbered fourteen or fifteen adults plus children. Having developed communal aspirations, Panin and his followers purchased a farm near Aldershot, where they built houses and established themselves as the Church of God Sojourning in Aldershot, of which Panin was high priest or at least prime minister.

By the time of Panin's death in 1942, the children had grown up and left the parental commune. In his will, Panin had made certain that the little company of aging adults would be financially secure. By 1960, only four members remained. Realizing that there was no one to look after them in their final years, they began to visit neighbourhood churches and concluded that the Alliance most nearly reflected their beliefs. During the meeting with Moreland, the triumvirate offered their beautiful 40-acre farm to the Alliance in return for care during their old age.[104] Besides this one legal obligation on the part of the district, there was a mutual understanding that the district intended to use the land in order of priority for a "Missionary Rest Home—Furlough Centre, Senior Citizens Complex, district Parsonage and Administration Building."[105]

The deal was soon completed,[106] and great plans laid in accordance with the original intentions.[107] However, "greenbelt" regulations invalidated almost every attempt at progress. Nevertheless, in the presence of Rev. William F. Smalley, general secretary of the Alliance, the property was dedicated January 29, 1966, "to the glory of God and in accordance with the authorized designation—viz. Missionary Rest Home—Furlough Centre, Senior Citizens Complex, district Parsonage and Administrative Building."[108] District Superintendent William Newell added:

> It is hoped that more active participation by the Society will be enjoyed by recognizing this development as the retiral centre for Canadian missionary personnel. When detailed studies have been made . . . and approval to proceed from proper municipal authorities, it will be our express wish to receive . . . endorsement from the Board of Managers and/or the Foreign Department to have the program recognized officially.[109]

In April 1970, the former Ambridge House opened as the Cama Woodlands Nursing Home.* Among its initial twelve residents was

---

* Late in 1990, a new 60-bed nursing home was opened and the old Ambridge House converted into a district headquarters. It seems doubtful that the original trust priority of a Missionary Rest Home—Furlough Centre will ever be realized.

Cecil Ambridge. That year a district parsonage and office was erected. Five years later, Henderson House became a seniors' residence.

Missed Opportunity

Early in 1960, overtures were made by representatives of the Alliance in New York and the Missionary Church Association of Fort Wayne, Indiana, regarding a possible merger. Founded in 1898, of Mennonite background, the Missionary Church Association had enjoyed for many years a close association with the Alliance. Indeed, it had first learned of the Fourfold Gospel from Rev. Albert E. Funk, Simpson's associate in German ministries. There had also been a close tie between the missionary work of both societies. In fact, over the years, many missionaries of the Missionary Church Association served under the Alliance banner.

In April, fraternal committees of both organizations met in Pittsburgh to iron out adjustments necessary for merger.[110] The Alliance Council of 1962 approved the merger by a majority of 82 percent. However, the polity of the Missionary Church Association required approval at the local church level, and the proposal for merger was defeated by less than one per cent of the votes cast.[111]

Throughout the procedures, Alliance churches in Canada registered only limited interest, because the Missionary Church Association had no churches in Canada. However, two years later, the United Missionary Church, a Canadian body founded in 1883 as the Mennonite Brethren in Christ Church, became interested in union with the Alliance in Canada. The founders of the United Missionary Church, concentrated in the German settlements around Kitchener (formerly Berlin), Ontario, had enjoyed close relationships with the Missionary Church Association in Indiana, but fundamental differences in the area of church government had stymied their attempts at union. The United Missionary Church also had close relationships with Rev. Albert E. Funk of the Alliance in New York and with Rev. John Salmon and Dr. Reuben J. Zimmerman of the Alliance in Ontario. Indeed, the relationship with Salmon had produced a "gentleman's agreement" not to encroach on each other's territory.

In 1965, the United Missionary Church appointed a commission to explore merger with "other organizations," including The Christian and Missionary Alliance and the Missionary Church Association.[112] Exploratory talks were opened between District Superintendent Newell and Rev. Kenneth E. Geiger, general secretary of the United Missionary Church. Hopes mounted. Newell was invited to attend the annual Ontario conference of the United Missionary Church in June 1966, in Gormley. He was seated with great courtesy as a special "advisory delegate" by Rev. Ward Shantz, the district superintendent. The leaders and delegates were clearly enthusiastic about a merger with the Alliance in Canada, which they made clear was their first preference. The United Missionary Church was largely a rural and small town church in Ontario, whereas the Alliance in that province, since Roffe's day, had concentrated on the cities and larger towns. The strength of the United Missionary Church was in the east, whereas, by that time, the strength of the Alliance was in the west. Furthermore, the United Missionary Church was already operating a successful Bible college in Kitchener and was anxious to increase its student body. The Alliance in the east was smarting under the recent loss of several of its young men to other denominations after attendance at "neutral" schools in the east, so the possibility of an "official" school in the east held appeal. All things considered, it appeared the two bodies would complement rather than compete with each other.

Apparently, it was a great disappointment to the delegates of the United Missionary Church when Newell pointed out that he represented only his own district, and could not speak for the Home Department or the board of managers. However, he promised to take the matter up with his superiors, and he wrote a lengthy and well expressed report, clearly indicating the advantages of merger to the Alliance in Canada. He then directed copies to both President Bailey and Home Secretary Pippert. No encouragement emerged from New York. Neither the president nor the Home Secretary had any interest in merger with the small Canadian denomination, regardless of the benefits to be gained, unless it could be part of eventual union with the Missionary Church Association of Fort Wayne.[113]

For another year the Eastern and Central Canadian District and the United Missionary Church continued to exchange fraternal conference delegates, discuss merger details and enjoy inter-fellowship socialities that "we may pursue every necessary step towards the encouragement of ultimate merger."[114] However, because of the lack of support from New York, the fraternization ceased. What a pity that such an opportunity was thrown away.*

---

* In 1969, two years after negotiations with the Alliance collapsed, the United Missionary Church merged with the Missionary Church Association, to form the Missionary Church, headquartered in Fort Wayne. Ten years later, the Missionary Church (Fort Wayne) attempted to reopen merger negotiations but the Alliance (Nyack), absorbed in its centenary church doubling program, had lost interest in merger. In 1987, the Canadian section of the Missionary Church again became autonomous, and today is known as the Missionary Church of Canada, with headquarters in Willowdale, Ontario.

However, as Canada's centennial approached, a national spirit of self-determination began to grip Canadians. Had the movement towards merger with the United Missionary Church come a few years later, or had the movement towards Canadian self-determination come a few years earlier, The Christian and Missionary Alliance in Canada and the Missionary Church of Canada might today be sharing a common purpose with a resulting greater impact.

REFERENCES

1. John Webster Grant, *The Church in the Canadian Era* (Burlington: Welch Publishing Co. Inc., 1988), p. 160.
2. A. C. Forrest, *Religion in Canada* (Toronto: McClelland and Stewart, 1968), p. 64.
3. Annual Report, May 1942, p. 96.
4. Eastern and Central Canadian District Conference Records, 4 Sep 1946; Home Department Minutes, 3 Sep 1946.
5. Lindsay Reynolds, *Footprints* (Toronto: The Christian and Missionary Alliance in Canada, 1982), p. 125.
6. *Alliance Weekly*, 17 Dec 1949, p. 813.
7. Eastern, Conference, 12 Sep 1951.
8. Eastern, Conference, Superintendent's Report, Sep 1941.
9. Alliance Tabernacle, Executive Board Minutes, 3 Feb, 7 Apr, 26 May 1941; ibid., Congregational Meeting, 4 Jun 1941; *Footprints*, pp. 421, 422.
10. Alliance Tabernacle, Executive Board, Minutes, 27 Sep 1945.
11. Eastern and Central Canadian District, Minutes, 12 Jan 1946.
12. *Alliance Weekly*, 24 Jul 1948, p. 472; 23 Oct 1948, p. 684.
13. Annual Report, May 1944, p. 62.
14. Report of Home Department to Board of Managers, 7 Sep 1944, p. 5.
15. Board of Managers, Minutes, 7, 8 Sep 1944, pp. 74, 76, 93.
16. Eastern, Conference, Superintendent's Report, 1947, p. 8.
17. Board of Managers, Report of President's Council, 10 Mar 1948, p. 6.
18. Eastern, Minutes, 28 Sep 1948.
19. Board of Managers, 8, 9 Dec 1948.
20. *Alliance Weekly*, 1 Apr, p. 194; 20 May, p. 308; 27 May, p. 325, 1950.
21. Charles B. Templeton, *Charles Templeton—An Anecdotal Memoir* (Toronto: McClelland and Stewart, 1983), pp. 33, 34.
22. *Toronto Star*, 27 Sep 1941, p. 17; 4 Oct 1941, p. 11.
23. Eastern, Minutes, 20 May 1949.
24. Avenue Road Church Board Minutes, 30 Mar 1950.
25. Ibid., 19 Apr 1950.
26. Ibid., 6 Jun 1950; Eastern, Minutes, 18 May 1950.
27. Avenue Road Church Board Minutes, 6 Jun 1950; Eastern, Minutes, 5 Oct 1950.

326 / Forging a Consensus

28. *Alliance Weekly*, 21 May 1952.
29. Eastern, Conference, Superintendent's Report, 1955, p. 11.
30. *Western Workers' Bulletin*, Apr-May-Jun 1946, p. 2.
31. Home Department, Minutes, 22 Jan 1947; *Western Workers' Bulletin*, Jan-Feb 1947, p. 4.
32. Home Department, Minutes, 13 May 1947.
33. Board of Managers, Minutes, 13 May 1947.
34. Home Department, Minutes, 19 Jun 1947.
35. Western, Conference, May 1947, p. 1.
36. *Western Workers' Bulletin*, Mar-Apr 1947.
37. Ibid., Jan-Feb 1948; Western Conference, 1948, 1950, 1951, Superintendent's Report.
38. *Western Workers' Bulletin*, Jan-Feb 1952; Western Conference, 1952. District Superintendent's Report.
39. Home Department, Minutes, 2 Sep 1947; Board of Managers, Minutes, 4 Sep 1947.
40. Home Department, Minutes, 8 Oct 1947; *Western Workers' Bulletin*, Fall 1947, p. 2.
41. *Western Workers' Bulletin*, Jan-Feb 1948, p. 3.
42. Home Department, Minutes 14 Jun 1948; Board of Managers, Minutes, 6 Sep 1948.
43. Western, Conference, Superintendent's Report, June 1948.
44. Ibid.
45. *Western Workers' Bulletin*, Oct-Nov 1956.
46. *Western Workers' Bulletin*, Sep-Oct 1948, p. 4.
47. Home Department, Report to Board of Managers, 14 Jun 1948.
48. Western, Conference, Home Secretary's Report, Jun 1949.
49. *Alliance Weekly*, 28 Aug 1974, p. 29.
50. Home Department, Minutes, 7 Mar 1947, p. 98.
51. Ibid., 11 Mar 1947.
52. Ibid., 8 Dec 1947.
53. Home Department, Minutes, 6 Sep 1949; Western, Conference, Report of Home Secretary, Jun 1949; Board of Managers, Minutes, 7 Apr 1949.
54. Western, Conference, Report of Home Secretary, Jun 1949.
55. Home Department, Minutes, 6 Sep 1949.
56. Western, Conference, Report of Home Secretary, Jun 1949; Home Department, Minutes, 6 Sep 1949.
57. Board of Managers, Minutes, 7, 8 Dec 1949; Annual Report, May 1950; Board of Managers, Minutes, 5, 6 Sep 1950; Annual Report, May 1951; Home Department, Minutes, 7 Dec 1951; *Alliance Weekly*, 9 Apr 1952, p. 237; Annual Report, May 1952.
58. Western, Conference, Sep 1953, District Superintendent's Report; Annual Report, May 1954.
59. Western, Conference, District Superintendent's Report, Sep 1953.
60. Home Department, Minutes, 27 Oct 1953.

Forging a Consensus / 327

61. Ibid., 10 Nov 1953.
62. Ibid., 9 Dec 1953.
63. *Western Worker*, Nov-Dec 1959.
64. Letter written to "Art and Vi" by Mrs. Lucy Blackett, 5 Feb 1969.
65. Eastern, Minutes, 18 Aug 1955.
66. Board of Managers, Minutes, 9 Jul 1949.
67. Ibid., 13 Apr 1950.
68. Russell T. Hitt, *Cannibal Valley* (Harrisburg: Christian Publications, Inc., 1962), pp. 16, 17.
69. Ibid., pp. 18, 19.
70. *Alliance Witness*, 24 Feb 1960, p. 4.
71. *Cannibal Valley*, p. 108.
72. Eastern, Minutes, 4 Oct 1954, 16 May 1959; Eastern, Conference, Superintendent's Report, 1959, p. 18.
73. Eastern, Minutes, 17 Sep 1956; Eastern, Conference, Superintendent's Report, 1956, p. 12.
74. *Alliance Weekly*, 27 Jun 1956, p. 12.
75. *Alliance Witness*, 9 Apr 1958, p. 4; 23 Apr, p. 8; 7 May, pp. 5, 6.
76. Annual Report, May 1960.
77. Ibid.
78. *Western Worker*, Jan-Feb 1960, p. 2.
79. Ibid., Sep-Oct 1959, pp. 6, 7.
80. Ibid.
81. Eastern Conference, 1960, p. 10; *Alliance Witness*, 2 Nov 1960, p. 15.
82. *Western Worker*, Jan-Feb; Mar-Apr; May-Jun 1958; ibid., Mar-Apr; May-Jun; Jul-Aug; Sep-Oct 1959; Western, Conference, Superintendent's Report, Sep 1958.
83. Western, Conference, Superintendent's Report, Sep 1961.
84. *Alliance Witness*, 27 Jul 1960, p. 16; Western Conference, District Superintendent's Report, p. 6, Sep 1960.
85. *Alliance Witness*, 14 Jan 1961, pp. 16, 19; *Western Worker*, Apr-Jun 1961, p. 7; Western, Conference, Superintendent's Report, p. 5, Sep 1961.
86. *Alliance Witness*, 17 Sep 1969, pp. 15-17.
87. *Western Worker*, Oct-Dec 1961, p. 6; Apr-Jun 1962, p. 4.
88. *Western Worker*, Apr-Jun 1962, p. 10; Western, Conference, Superintendent's Report, pp. 5, 6, Sep 1962.
89. *Western Worker*, Jul-Sep 1962, 1962, p. 4.
90. Ibid., Apr-Jun 1961, p. 5; Jul-Sep 1961, p. 5; Oct-Dec 1961, p. 8.
91. Ibid., Apr-Jun 1962, p. 10; Western, Conference, Superintendent's Report, p. 2, Sep 1962.
92. *Western Worker*, Jul-Sep 1966, p. 6.
93. Ibid., Oct-Dec 1966, p. 10.

94. *Alliance Witness*, 8 May 1968, p. 19.
95. *Western Worker*, Jul-Sep 1963, p. 3; Oct-Dec 1963, p. 4.
96. Eastern, Conference, Sep 1963, p. 62; Eastern, Minutes, 21 Aug 1963, p. 3.
97. Annual Report, May 1965, p. 175; *Alliance Witness*, 8 Jan 1964, p. 16; *Western Worker*, Jan-Mar 1964, p. 4.
98. Canadian Midwest District, Conference, Sep 1964.
99. Eastern, Minutes, 17 Oct 1960.
100. Ibid., 17 Apr 1961.
101. "Outlook," Oct 1962; Eastern, Conference, District Superintendent's Report, Sep 1961.
102. Eastern, Minutes, 22 Apr 1963, p. 4.
103. Eastern, Minutes, 22 Apr 1963, p. 5.
104. Ibid., 6 Jun 1963, p. 1; 17 Jun 1963, p. 2.
105. Eastern, Conference, Superintendent's Report, p. 19, Sep 1966.
106. Eastern, Minutes, 16 Sep 1963, p. 1.
107. Eastern, Conference, Superintendent's Report, pp. 15, 16, Sep 1965; Eastern, Minutes, 10 Jan 1966, p. 1.
108. Eastern, Conference, Superintendent's Report, p. 19, Sep 1966.
109. Ibid.
110. *Alliance Witness*, 5 Oct 1960, p. 19; 2 May 1962, pp. 10, 11.
111. "Outlook," Feb 1963, p. 3.
112. Eastern, Conference, Sep 1966, Report of District Superintendent to the District Executive Committee, 20 Jun 1966.
113. Ibid., Sep 1966, pp. 15, 16, 67-69.
114. Eastern, Minutes, 21 Sep 1966, p. 5; 17 Oct 1966; 6 Mar 1967; Eastern, Conference, Sep 1966.

CHAPTER EIGHT

The Education Struggle

Poet John Milton wrote, "It is a fond error to think that the university makes a minister of the Gospel." A product of Cambridge himself, Milton was nevertheless convinced that however important a university education was to the leadership of the church, such knowledge, by itself, fell short of equipping the Christian ministry with the basic tools of the job.

Christianity is a religion of the heart. Its truths are meant to be spiritually experienced even more than intellectually understood. Its message has often been communicated better by the simple than the profound.

No sooner had the last of the apostles died, around A.D. 100, than error began to take hold of many segments of the church. The early church writings which evangelical Protestants today regard as Spirit-inspired, were as yet uncanonized, and had to compete with other writings, sometimes of a spurious or contradictory nature. Thus, church tradition which claimed precedence over writings in determining matters of faith and practice was developed. The institutions of the clergy, the episcopacy and eventually the papacy were devised, at least in part, as a system to maintain truth in tradition.

However, tradition seldom remains static. Modified by pressure from without and moral laxity within, many traditions and the institutions that were to have been their watchdogs, became corrupt.

By A.D. 200, the four Gospels, the Acts and the Pauline epistles had become generally accepted as authoritative. With the widening gulf between the teachings of these scriptures and the traditions of the church, the need for study became apparent. The church's first catechetical school was founded in Alexandria in A.D. 185 by Pantaenus of Egypt, and it was attended by both men and women. One of its early graduates who succeeded to the principalship was Origen, the great Greek theologian. Under his tutelage, the school reached the zenith of its influence. Later, Origen established a second school at Caesarea, in Roman Palestine.

Over the next two or three centuries, many private theological schools were established. During the fifth century, monasteries became the chief centres of learning. When, in the ninth century, these were forced to restrict their teaching to monks, episcopal schools became prominent. With the rise of the universities in the eleventh and twelfth centuries, these became the great seats of both theological and secular education.

By the fourteenth century, Christendom was in a state of decadence in faith and practice. In England, around 1370, John Wycliffe, an eminent scholar and teacher in Oxford, began to criticize the false beliefs and practices of the church, and to teach a Bible-based Christianity. He completed the first translation of the entire Bible into the English language. Although very few clergy were sympathetic to his cause, a growing body of the laity believed in his presentation of the gospel. Wycliffe realized that if his message were to take root in England, it would be with the help of the laity. Gathering a few friendly clergy helpers, he set up a school—the first English Bible school—at Oxford and later at Lutterworth to train laymen and send them out as preachers (called "Lollards") to all parts of England with the gospel message. Wycliffe and his followers were denounced as heretics. Some lost their lives and the movement was finally silenced. But Englishmen would never forget the experiment of training and sending out lay preachers with the message of the gospel.

About the middle of the fifteenth century, a series of events began which transformed Europe. The capture of Constantinople by the Turks in 1453 caused the flight of learned Greeks to the west. They carried with them priceless manuscripts of Greek literature, long forgotten by the darkened west. Soon, Greek professors were teaching the ancient literature, including that of the early church, in western universities. The restoration and re-examination of the Greek texts of the New Testament laid the foundations for the most powerful change in European life, and gave birth to the Protestant Reformation.

Throughout Europe, work began toward reform in faith and practice and a return to Biblical principles. At Zwingli's Bible exegesis classes in Zurich, ministers, missionaries, preachers and teachers received a thorough grounding in the Scriptures. A century later in England, privately supported free-lance clergy trained lay leaders through the institution of the Puritan "lectureships."

The tide of reformation and revival came in gigantic waves. With each successive wave, laymen were trained to do their part. During the great evangelical revival of the eighteenth century, John Wesley spent much of his time preparing study materials for his lay preachers. The Countess of Huntington, an associate of George Whitfield, built Trevecka College in Wales for the training of lay leaders in the Calvinistic branch of Methodism.

The Origins of Bible Schools

The great revivals in Europe of the nineteenth century gave rise to the birth of the modern foreign missions movement. Dozens of missionary societies were formed, but the seminaries could not train the great number of missionaries needed. As many were volunteering who had less than an adequate education, the prerequisite of a university education began to be seriously questioned. In quick succession Bible schools were opened on the continent and in Britain. In 1872, the East London Institute for Home and Foreign Missions was established by Rev. H. Grattan Guiness, "to increase the number of missionaries; to provide education and training for zealous young people who desire to engage in missionary work but are thwarted by lack of education and means." During its first sixteen years, this institute graduated 500 who became Christian workers at home or abroad.

News of this English Bible school spread across the Atlantic, where several Christian leaders began to consider a similar venture in the United States. The first to take action was Dr. Charles Cullis of Boston, who in October 1875 opened Faith Training College on Beacon Street "to train for Christian work such consecrated men and women that are desirous of fitting themselves in the widening fields of lay activity, such as Bible exposition, exhortation, preaching, evangelism, home and foreign missionary labour." Using as its motto, "Jesus Only," the college emphasized evangelical faith, sanctification through full consecration, divine healing and the pre-millennial return of Christ. Thus was founded the first Bible college in North America.*

In 1883, Rev. A. B. Simpson organized and opened the Missionary Training College for Home and Foreign Missionaries and Evangelists in a rented house on Eighth Avenue in New York. Patterned after Guiness's school in London, Simpson wrote, "The aim will be to qualify consecrated men and women who have not received, and do not wish to receive, a regular scholastic education." The curriculum, he said, would consist of "a thorough Scriptural training and a specific and most careful preparation for practical work."[1]

After several relocations and name changes, the school settled at Nyack in 1897 and was known for the next 59 years as the Missionary Training Institute, the only Alliance school in the United States until 1916.

Canadian Beginnings

Around the year 1867, Lucy Drake of Boston experienced a remarkable healing from tuberculosis and a malignant tumour through the ministry of Dr. Cullis. After serving as a deaconess in one of the Cullis churches for six years, she was sent to India as a missionary. After two terms, she returned to the United States as Mrs. William Osborne. Renting a large house on the Methodist Conference grounds at Niagara Falls, Ontario, she opened the Mission Training School in

---

* In 1862, Dr. Cullis, an evangelical Episcopalian, accepted the doctrine of sanctification as taught by his close friend, Dr. William E. Boardman. That same year, feeling a call to spiritual as well as physical ministries, he founded an enterprise in Boston which within the next ten years included three hospitals, two orphanages, a nurses' home and school, a seamen's home, rescue mission, tract repository, publishing house and two churches which sent out several missionaries to India. In addition, he established home missions for the freed slaves of Virginia and the Chinese of California. In 1873, after firming up his belief in divine healing, Cullis commenced a ministry of healing, and opened the Faith Cure Home in Boston. Largely through the results of this ministry, Boardman was convinced of the truth of divine healing. After settling in London, Boardman opened a work which featured sanctification and divine healing.

In 1874, after reading an "old musty" copy of Boardman's book, *The Higher Christian Life*, Simpson embraced Boardman's basic teaching on sanctification. Seven years later he experienced healing through Cullis's ministry. While attending some of Boardman's meetings in London in 1882, Salmon embraced his teachings of sanctification and divine healing. Three years later, Salmon experienced healing through the ministry of Simpson.

Thus were these four men linked together in matters of faith, experience and ministry.

March 1885. Patterned largely after the Faith Training College of Dr. Cullis in Boston, this was Canada's first Bible school.

In 1887, William Gooderham and Mayor William H. Howland erected a building on Richmond Street in Toronto and founded the Christian Institute, committed to the "study of the Word of God, the fostering of a missionary spirit and the promotion of Christian work." Alfred Sandham served as principal of this, Toronto's first Bible school, for six years. By that time, both Gooderham and Howland had died, and the institute, becoming insolvent, was forced to close down.[2]

For some years, Salmon had wanted to set up a Canadian version of Simpson's school in New York. Clearly, there was room for only one Bible school in Toronto, and out of deference to Howland and Sandham, Salmon made no move to compete. With the demise of the Christian Institute and with the encouragement of Sandham, Salmon opened the Toronto Missionary Training School "to train young people, male and female, for missionary and evangelistic work." Classes commenced on October 16, 1893, in Bethany Chapel on University Avenue. Instruction was provided by Salmon and several others, in which the Alliance distinctives of sanctification, divine healing and the pre-millennial return of Christ were featured. Although the tiny Alliance community supplied only a fraction of the student body, this was the first Bible school venture in Canada under the banner of the Alliance.[3]

However, there were those in Toronto who were not prepared to support the Alliance with its special teachings. In May 1894, ten influential evangelicals formed the Toronto Bible School (which became Ontario Bible College and Seminary), under the tutelage and principalship of the Rev. Elmore Harris, minister of Walmer Road Baptist Church. In 1894, to improve general acceptance and to provide lodgings for out-of-town students, Salmon removed his school from Bethany Chapel to a rented house on Elm Street and renamed it the Toronto Missionary Training Institute. But it was all to no avail. The Alliance community was unable to compete for students with the larger appeal under Baptist support. Two years later, Salmon's dream of a Canadian Bible school in full sympathy with the Alliance cause came to an end. The experiment would not be repeated for another quarter of a century.[4]

Meanwhile the Alliance concept of a Bible school was changing. Training Christian workers at a sub-university or even sub-high school level was no longer seen to be fundamental. Attempts to raise the level of education were slowly gaining ground. By 1912, William C. Stevens, dean of the Missionary Training Institute, and Dr. J. Hudson Ballard, principal of Wilson Academy (an Alliance private high school at Nyack), were advocating a junior college, liberal arts college and seminary—indeed a "Nyack Missionary university . . . which would give us a hold upon the best minds in the country."[5] However, changes came slowly and sometimes painfully, and the idea would not be fully achieved for another half century. In October 1916, Rev. J. D. Williams founded the second Alliance Bible school in the United States, at St. Paul, Minnesota. First named the Alliance Training Home, it later became known as St. Paul Bible College, and in 1991 was renamed Crown College. In 1920, Council approved a recommendation to establish a network of "regional or sectional schools."

In October 1920, the District of Canada Committee was formed (pages 58, 59), "to consult with and advise the superintendent in the work." On that occasion, Home Secretary Rev. E. J. Richards "laid before the gathering the great opportunities and needs of the Alliance, for the presentation of the great Scriptural truths for which it stands, and above all the pressing call from missionaries . . . for reinforcements."[6]

A few weeks later, District Superintendent Roffe pointed out to his committee the new Alliance policy to open regional schools. What better way, asked Roffe, was there for Canadians to teach Alliance truth and to provide qualified Alliance missionaries than to launch an Alliance training school in Canada? As Roffe conceived the project, it would be a "national school" for all Canada which "would offer the spiritual provisions of Nyack." Regarding location, Toronto was the centre of Protestant faith in Canada and also the hub of the Alliance community. No other location could be expected to supply the leadership, financial support and student response required.

The first half of 1921 was largely taken up with the first Canadian Bosworth campaign in Toronto. However, by September other matters were receiving more attention. With enthusiasm at an all-time high, it was decided to proceed with plans for a Bible school.[7]

One month later, President Rader visited Toronto and addressed the committee. The minutes read:

> Mr. Rader mentioned that he understood something was being said regarding opening a school in Toronto. He

wished to state that so far as the Board was concerned, they had no thought of any such thing; that Toronto had a good Bible school now and the Alliance would never consider competition with such a school.[8]

The reference was to the Toronto Bible School. Rader's statement seems to have shocked both the superintendent and the committee into a seven-month silence on the subject of an Alliance school for Canada. Then almost unexpectedly, Council of May 1922 approved the Canadian venture, and within a week, Dr. Walter M. Turnbull, dean of the Missionary Training Institute at Nyack, addressed the committee. A member of the leading founding family of Bethany Church, Peterborough, and a graduate of McMaster University in Toronto, he personally looked forward to a Canadian equivalent of the Missionary Training Institute. However, said Turnbull, only a regional school for Canada was presently authorized. The standard of education at Nyack was to be raised immediately, so that a regional school might attain the current standards at Nyack. In the meantime, in deference to the strong views of President Rader, he urged that a meeting be held with Principal McNicol of Toronto Bible School to solicit the blessing of that institution on an Alliance venture.[9]

Early in June, Rev. Oswald J. Smith and Lionel Watson, assistant to Roffe, visited McNicol. The meeting was cordial, and Smith and Watson were encouraged to open an Alliance school. It was, said McNicol, "a very wise and timely move."[10]

Thus reassured, a sub-committee was appointed "to organize and manage the Alliance Bible Institute, Toronto," and a "first class" circular was prepared, announcing details of the courses to be taught, starting in September.[11] The first task of the sub-committee was recognized as being "to secure a principal."[12] At least six prospects were interviewed. Two offers were made and both were rejected. By August, the sub-committee concluded that "a strong Alliance man" was indeed needed, but could not be found in Canada.[13] And so the "opening day" came and passed without the school being opened.

Delays and False Hopes

Events in the west now began to affect plans in the east. Back in 1914, Edward and Hattie Kirk had graduated from Nyack and returned to their farm home near Cornwall, Ontario. Six years later, the Kirk family relocated to Three Hills, Alberta, where they found themselves without a church. Using Hattie's Nyack notes, they started teaching their neighbours' children the gospel. Meanwhile, William C. ("Daddy") Stevens, dean and principal at Nyack, becoming impatient with the Alliance aversion to change in education, resigned his position in 1915. Three years later, he founded the independent Midland Bible Institute in Kansas City where Leslie E. Maxwell came as a student. Early in 1922, during Maxwell's last year, Stevens received a letter from the Kirk family in Three Hills, asking if he could send someone to give Bible instruction to the local teenagers. Maxwell agreed to go and started classes in a farmhouse in September. And so Prairie Bible Institute, western Canada's first Bible college, was founded. Soon the story of the "prairie miracle" reached John Woodward in Edmonton and A. W. Roffe in Toronto.

It was a disturbed district superintendent who addressed the subject of Bible schools before his committee in April 1923. He told them that Prairie Bible Institute was just finishing the first "very successful winter with eighteen students." In his view, "this school had been begun because we had not been progressive enough to undertake one, and it would appear that we had missed our opportunity." He now questioned his former vision for a single national Canadian school. Perhaps there should be "one near Toronto and one in the West." He believed the Toronto school should have boarding accommodation and be located outside the city.[14]

In August, Turnbull was again in Toronto to review progress. The committee, having once wavered on the original concept, were now faced with several alternative proposals. John Woodward was urging that a western school take precedence over an eastern location, claiming that the critical need was for permanent workers for the west, which could not be obtained from the United States schools. Now that the west had a school, his prospective workers from western Canada would not travel to Toronto for their training. If they trained at Three Hills, they would be lost to other organizations on graduation. Rev. Edgar Capel (page 72) of Knowlton, Quebec, could see Woodward's point. However, he viewed it from the opposite direction. He believed that students from the maritime provinces would not travel as far west as Toronto. He urged that there be two schools, one in the west and one in the Eastern Townships of Quebec, where eastern and central Canada could be served from a more geographically central point. To help with the realization of this proposal, he offered to donate land on his Knowlton conference ground and to pay half the cost of erecting a building.[15]

In response to Roffe's preference for a location outside the city, the committee had carefully examined four suburban sites and evaluated the pros and cons of each. To top off all the uncertainties, one member of the committee had resigned, because the inability to secure a principal had led him to believe that they did not know the mind of the Lord in the matter.[16]

It was Walter Turnbull who brought order out of chaos. He reminded the committee that the only approval they had received was to open a national school in or around Toronto. It was not the policy of the board or Council to approve more than one school in a district. He urged that party spirit be put aside, and Canada as a whole be kept in mind. The committee, he said, needed to make practical decisions, and to this end he held out the carrot of financial assistance from New York.

For the next two months, nothing more was said about alternate views—at least as recorded in official records. However, neither Roffe nor Woodward had lost their convictions for the need of some form of Alliance-controlled instruction in the west.

In October 1923, Roffe and Woodward visited Maxwell in Three Hills. To the visitors, Maxwell appeared to welcome the possibility of some connection with the Alliance. Indeed, on his return, the superintendent reported that "it was the unanimous desire of the school (at Three Hills) to affiliate with the Canadian District."[17]

It would seem that fancy had taken over from fact. In March 1924, an article appeared in the *Alliance Weekly* about Maxwell's school, which stated:

> The school, feeling its development to be of God, asked Mr. Roffe, Canadian Superintendent, to take over the school. While arrangements have not yet been completed for the transfer, students from the Canadian West are being sent there in preparation for Nyack.[18]

Maxwell had no such intentions. He was prepared to have Woodward assist with the teaching, to have Roffe address the student body, to take up an annual collection for Alliance missions, and, in the event that the Alliance opened a school in Edmonton, to recommend it to his students living in Edmonton. However, he was not prepared

338 / *The Education Struggle*

to turn over his school to them. For the sake of his school, it was just as well that Maxwell remained obdurate.[19]

Two Schools Begin

During the Toronto conference of May 1924, a decision was made to purchase land adjacent to the Christie Street Tabernacle for a Bible school, to draw up plans for a building and to prepare to open the national school in September.[20] At the same conference, Woodward revealed that he was ready to start "study classes" in Beulah Tabernacle, and he pled for permission to proceed. At first fearing that the plan would impair attendance in the east, the delegates agreed in the end that "in view of the progress already made in Edmonton," district permission would be given to go ahead under the name of "Alliance Bible Classes" which "should not involve the District financially." Woodward assured conference that this arrangement "satisfies the friends in Edmonton."[21]

Developments in both locations now moved forward in rapid succession. In Toronto, on May 31, a board of governors was formed which included Dr. W. M. Turnbull, chairman; E. T. Young, secretary; and W. C. Willis, treasurer. One week later, the governors offered the principalship to Rev. John R. Turnbull (brother of the chairman), who had just arrived home on furlough from India. He agreed to accept the offer for the first academic year.[22]*

New York headquarters made a grant of $8,000 and a loan of another $5,000. Members of the tabernacle contributed $2,500 and a mortgage of $25,000 was secured for the balance.[23] The Canadian Bible Institute building was constructed of brick, two storeys high, with ground measurements of 50 x 50 feet. It consisted of classrooms, offices and a "prayer auditorium."** The school and tabernacle shared common heating and sanitary facilities.[24]

It was decided to adopt the Nyack syllabus. The teaching week would consist of 32 periods of 45 minutes each, with one extra hour for music. The initial full-time teaching staff consisted of Rev. J. R.

---

* Starting with the second academic year, Dr. Ralph E. Hooper, formerly dean of the Boston Bible School, became principal of C.B.I.

** One of the specifications passed on to the building architects from the governors, was the requirement of separate stairs for men and women students. Apparently, the governors believed that common stairs would be a temptation to linger.

Turnbull, Rev. S. P. Hamilton and Rev. and Mrs. R. A. Grupe. Part-time teachers were Rev. O. J. Smith, Rev. J. G. Inkster, Rev. H. S. Hallman and Rev. Dr. Campbell.[25] On July 7, the constitution of the Canadian Bible Institute was adopted.[26]

It then became clear that the new building would not be completed until late in the year. Accordingly, the tabernacle offered its facilities for temporary use. On Monday, September 15, 29 students from "various parts of Canada" were registered. On the following Sunday, the institute was officially opened,[27] and on December 12, the new building was dedicated by Home Secretary Rev. E. J. Richards.[28] About the occasion, Principal Turnbull wrote:

> Many of our young men and women have caught the vision, have heard the call and should be sent to the whitened harvest fields of the world and our great Canadian west. But first, they must be trained.... The Canadian Bible Institute is no longer a dream or project. It is a glorious reality. An additional and recent factor which makes a Canadian school necessary is the new immigration policy of the United States, which practically debars our young people from attending our Nyack school.[29]

After district conference in Toronto in May 1924, John Woodward immediately commenced "study classes" in Beulah Tabernacle, Edmonton. However, within a few weeks he concluded that such classes would never satisfy himself or his associates, who yearned for nothing less than an Alliance Bible School for western Canada. "God over-ruled," explained Woodward, as he began to plan and organize in that direction.[30]

In July, a large, dilapidated house on 120th Street was rented. For several weeks, members and friends of Beulah Tabernacle prayed, repaired, renovated and re-decorated, augmented by professional workmen who offered their services without remuneration. Gifts of money, dishes, silverware, bedding, furnishings and groceries poured in.[31]

Finally, on October 2, ten (later eighteen) students enrolled, and the Great West Bible Institute came into existence—without the approval (or opposition) of Council, the board of managers, the Home Department or the District of Canada. Woodward wrote of that occasion:

> I did not expect, in the beginning to have anything of this character develop so soon in our Canadian West. "What hath God wrought." Without one cent of money to commence the undertaking, we find ourselves today the possessors of a twenty-one room building. . . . Answers to prayer have come in thick and fast. Opponents have become ardent friends of the project, and while we have received very little cash, our expenses have been taken care of. The whole building has been renovated, even to electric fixtures and beautiful wall paper.
>
> We have had our first chapel service, and the presence of the Lord was marked by tears from some of the faculty and student body. . . . This morning we received two answers to prayer. Yesterday, we were on our knees asking for coal; the building was cold and the students were arriving. This morning two tons of coal were delivered. We also asked the Lord for a piano, and just following chapel service a beautiful player piano was delivered.[32]

Among the officers of the Great West Bible Institute were Rev. J. H. Woodward, president; A. Whitelaw, vice-president and treasurer; and H. W. Ambrose, secretary. The original all part-time teaching staff consisted of Woodward, dean; Miss M. Connor, superintendent of women; Miss A. M. MacDonald, registrar; Miss A. B. Rose, matron; and Rev. Arthur Murray, J. E. Cross, Henry McCleary and Miss C. MacLeod.

For a few months after the first academic year, the institute relocated to the former nurses' residence of the old Isolation Hospital on 92nd Street. Then, during the autumn of 1925, a school building was purchased as the home of the institute.

An Uncertain Future

In May 1926, district superintendent Woodward, prodded by the board of managers to do something about sagging missionary contributions (see page 220), resigned from Beulah Tabernacle to devote more time to district business. His increasing absences from Edmonton necessitated that he find a replacement for himself as dean and chief instructor of the Great West Bible Institute. This he tried to do, albeit unsuccessfully.

The Education Struggle / 341

8.1 Toronto Missionary Training Institute opened in October 1893, the first attempt to establish an Alliance Bible school in Canada.

8.2 As dean of the Missionary Training Institute in Nyack, Dr. Walter M. Turnbull supplied the vital leadership necessary to push through the idea of a national Canadian Alliance Bible school to be situated in Toronto.

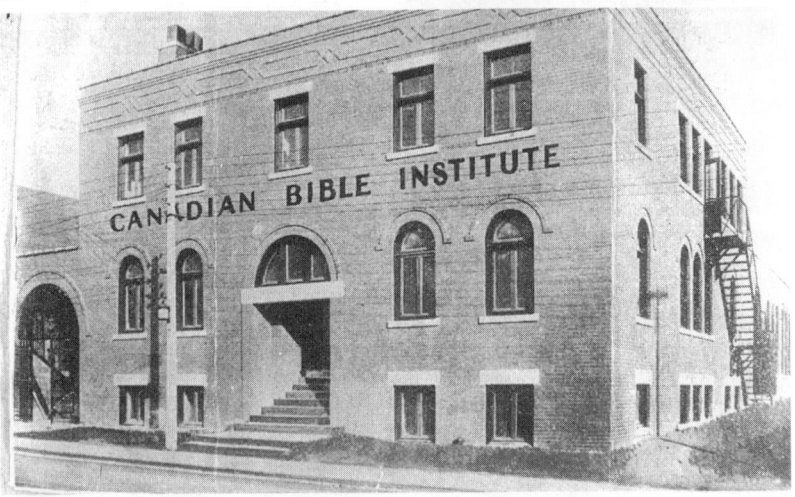

8.3 The Canadian Bible Institute building was erected and officially opened in Toronto on December 12, 1924. After the closure of the school in 1929, the building served as the district headquarters and adjunct of the tabernacle. The property was sold in 1947 and the building demolished two years later.

342 / *The Education Struggle*

8.4

8.5

8.4 Faculty and students of C.B.I. for the first year, 1924-1925. In the back row, third from the left, is future missionary F. W. Elroy Roffe. In the centre of the row is Principal John R. Turnbull, Rev. H. S. Hallman and Rev. Oswald J. Smith.

8.5 Faculty and students of C.B.I. for 1925-1926. In the back row, third and fourth from the left, are Bob Lennox and Gordon Wishart. In the centre of the front row are Rev. Oswald J. Smith, Principal E. Ralph Hooper and Assistant Superintendent Lionel Watson.

8.6 Dr. E. Ralph Hooper was principal from 1925 until 1929.

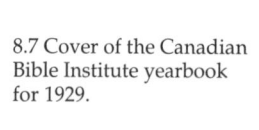

8.7 Cover of the Canadian Bible Institute yearbook for 1929.

8.6

8.7

Still facing declining missionary incomes two years later, Council instructed the board of managers to take steps to reduce Bible school costs. Accordingly, the board dispatched a letter to the Western Canadian District Conference, which read, in part:

> Inasmuch as there seems to be great difficulty in securing qualified leaders for our District Bible schools and
>
> Inasmuch as we do not wish to confine our superintendents to work in the schools, and
>
> Inasmuch as we have good Bible schools already established in Toronto and St. Paul, to which students from Western Canada could be sent,
>
> Therefore, the Board of Managers begs to advise the Conference of the Western Canadian District that in our opinion, it would be best for all concerned if the Great West Bible Institute would be discontinued.[33]

The Western Canadian District Conference was not prepared to accept the Board's recommendation, nor its veiled portent. "Since the development of the Alliance work in this District centres around the Institute," the conference decided, "the young men and women of the prairies . . . must be trained there. Therefore the school at Edmonton must continue."[34]

Coincidentally, the delegates to that conference considered an offer from Principal Rev. P. Cundy to turn over the Winnipeg Bible Institute to Alliance auspices. In view of the Alliance policy to reduce Bible school encumbrances, the offer was regretfully rejected.

Within a year, the board's designs for school closures extended to locations far beyond the Canadian prairies. In May 1929, President Shuman told delegates to the Toronto conference of the board's conviction that all "the smaller schools should be closed." Rev. George Blackett of Owen Sound expressed the view that at least Canada's national school should be kept open. Rev. W. E. Powers of Ottawa believed that "Canada occupied a unique position" within the Alliance, and there was a "special need" to maintain a national school. President Shuman suggested that if the school were to continue at all, it should become a place "where already trained men coming into the Alliance might come for a short time to get acquainted with the principles and practices of the Alliance." In this way, the Canadian school would not duplicate the work of Nyack.[35]

The cloud of uncertainty persisted until July, when the board closed both Canadian schools, together with Simpson Bible Institute in Seattle and the Boston Bible Institute. Canadians from coast to coast viewed this action with shock. For westerners, the continued operation of the Great West Bible Institute was believed to be necessary for the supply of workers for the west. To emphasize the finality of the decision, the Edmonton school property was ordered to be sold and the district executive committee instructed to "wait for clear leading from God for the future."[36]

For many westerners, however, the clear leading from God, already apparent, was to reopen the school. For this they planned and schemed for two years (see page 237), until the board took stern action to terminate all such attempts until "firm approval of the Board be granted."[37]

In the east, disappointment was no less acute than in the west, but easterners were more inclined to accept the board's decision as final, until circumstances changed. Speaking of the episode many years later, Rev. Edgar Lorimer commented, "I guess it never occurred to us to oppose constituted authority." Meanwhile, the school building was to be retained, pending a reopening.

If by closure of the Canadian Bible Institute the board hoped to channel into missionary offerings what had previously been categorized as school operating expenses they were mistaken. The institute building, a contiguous part of the tabernacle complex, shared common heating, light, water and sanitary facilities, which had to be maintained. Although the district office would occupy one room of the institute building, the district rarely had enough money to meet mortgage and tax payments on the institute property, the burden of which was borne by the tabernacle. It was a heavy burden, made tolerable only by the expectation of better days ahead, when the institute would be reopened.

When Simpson Bible Institute reopened in 1934, the question of the Toronto school came to the fore. The board explained that it had felt it essential to reopen a school on the west coast. With three American schools (west, central and east) located reasonably close to the Canadian border, the board saw no urgency for a Canadian school. Again eastern Canadians acquiesced. Three years later, the "Canadian matter" surfaced again.[38] The Great Depression was over, the economy was booming and missionary offerings from Canada were far higher than they had ever been. Unfortunately, a world war appeared to be approaching. What was more, District Superintendent David Mason, himself a member of the board of managers, did not support a national school for Canada. The board reasoned that it would be unwise to attempt to launch and staff another school under these uncertain conditions, and the decision of the board was accepted by eastern Canadians.

A New School is Born

In October 1934, Rev. George Blackett ended ten years of service with the Eastern and Central Canadian District by becoming pastor of the Winnipeg Gospel Tabernacle. A few months later, he also became a part-time teacher of pastoral theology at the Winnipeg Bible Institute. A year later he was appointed principal, while retaining his pastorate at the tabernacle. Under pressure from the board of the institute, Blackett resigned his pastorate in 1939 to devote his full time to the institute.

Early in April 1941, the board of the institute acted to restrict the prerogatives of the principal. Tensions mounted, and on April 7, Blackett tendered his resignation.[39] A few days later, Blackett wrote to Pastor Willis Brooks of Regina, telling him that he believed the time had come to open an Alliance Bible school in western Canada. "Knowing his ministry in Winnipeg had come to a close," Mrs. Lucy Blackett recalled of the occasion, "... there came a great desire to my husband's heart to launch out anew, without a promised support."[40]

Probably the same day, Brooks penned a letter to Blackett in which he told of his burden for an Alliance Bible school in western Canada. He asked Blackett if the Lord was speaking to him along these lines, and if so, he offered the use of the tabernacle basement for such a venture.[41]

These historic letters crossed in the mails. It was no wonder that the two writers concluded they had discerned the will of the Lord to proceed. As Mrs. Blackett later commented, "In a remarkable way God showed us His will."[42]

Blackett arrived in Regina and Board Representative Gordon Skitch arrived from Calgary and the triumvirate agreed that Blackett should present a plan for a school to conference, due to meet the following month. Blackett told conference that he felt led to return to an Alliance ministry and that God had laid upon him a burden for an Alliance Bible school in western Canada.[43] Conference gave approval for the immediate formation of a Bible school in Regina under the name of Canadian Bible Institute, and the appointment of Rev. George Blackett as principal and dean.[44] In the first issue of the institute's official organ, the *Messenger*, Principal Blackett wrote:

> We have acted in obedience to God's command. Now it is His to give the necessary wisdom, to supply the physical, mental, and spiritual strength, and to meet all the needs.[45]

Friends from the tabernacle congregation undertook basement renovations. Walls were finished, partitions and doors set in place and a "beautiful red linoleum" laid. According to the *Messenger*, the cornerstone of the college library was "well and truly laid" through the gift of a *Young's Analytical Concordance* and an English dictionary. The *Messenger* also claimed that a rug was donated for the principal's office so that students might be "properly called on the carpet."[46]

The training initially offered was described as being:

> Carefully planned to enable those taking it to become efficient witnesses of the Lord Jesus Christ. Its purpose is to train for service rather than scholarship. It seeks to train the heart as well as the mind. It is practical rather than theoretical, and spiritual more than academic.[47]

Among the original eight-member full- and part-time faculty, Blackett taught Bible, homiletics, pastoral theology and prophecy; Rev. Murray Downey, theology, Bible and evangelism; Miss Nora Bassingthwaighte, church history; Rev. Willis Brooks, Bible and public speaking.

On October 1, classes commenced for a student body of 50. For the staff at least, those were days of testing and trusting. Murray Downey wrote:

> My wife and I had been asked to assist in the launching of the program. So we set out from Peace River Bible Institute in Sexsmith, Alberta, with a Model A Ford pulling a trailer containing all our earthly possessions, and two babies. Nothing for travel expenses was forthcoming and nothing was said about living expenses or housing accommodations when we reached Regina late in August. The first

cheque, our monthly allowance, was for $120. Mr. Blackett was almost in tears when at prayer meeting in his home he told us at the end of the next month that there was no money for allowances. We assured him that we had come trusting in the Lord and not in him, and that he was not to take the matter personally.... I don't think there was a full allowance in the school months that followed to the end of April, sometimes 50 percent, or 60 percent but not more. We got nothing in the summer months when school was out.—We lacked nothing.—The Lord in marvelous ways provided.... Brother Blackett and his dear wife taught all of us in those days that God does really answer prayer, that He often purposefully leads us to the Red Sea that He might acquaint us with the wonder of His power and presence. We had days of prayer, weeks of prayer, and once we had ten days without classes when we went about on tip-toe, so conscious that God was present.[48]

Response in Toronto and New York to the opening of a Bible school in Regina has already been described (pages 274-276). Disregard for constituted authority in New York and for eastern Canadian concerns carried its own penalty. Although the school was reluctantly allowed to continue, it had to alter its name to Western Canadian Bible Institute, and to agree to "confine the appeal of the Institute to the Western Canadian District."[49] Furthermore, official recognition was withheld for four years.[50] What was more serious for the well-being of the Canadian fellowship was that the incident severed workable relationships between the two districts and impeded the development of a Canadian consensus for seven or eight years until both superintendents had been superseded.

EASTERN EDUCATIONAL CONCERNS

In the east, it was feared that sheer economics would forever rule out the viability of two Canadian schools, and thus frustrate the reopening of the national school in Toronto. However, the eastern superintendent shared no longings for a Canadian school anywhere. "I have opposed the official recognition of the school in Regina," Rev. David Mason said, "for if that was to become an official Alliance school, we would be barred from sending anyone to Nyack."[51]

In any event, the thinly populated prairies, already blessed with twenty Bible schools, gained yet another, while the relatively heavily populated east was thwarted from reopening an existing and much needed facility. What should have been a cause for thanksgiving and cooperation within the whole Canadian Alliance community became an instrument of national division, as nothing else had.

Back in 1928, as part of the cost saving plan, Council closed down the Education Department in New York. In 1941, "with the rapid expansion of the work at home and abroad," the department was reinstated, "having jurisdiction over all educational institutions in the United States and Canada."[52]

In December 1942, after reviewing another request from the Western Canadian Bible Institute for recognition,[53] the board of managers decided that "further consideration of recognition by the Society of a Bible school in Canada will be postponed for the duration of the war."[54]

At the Eastern and Central Canadian District Conference of September 1943, Superintendent Mason noted with alarm that:

> Many of our promising Canadian young men who attended the Nyack Missionary Training Institute have remained in the United States instead of returning for service in their own land. In order to overcome this handicap it may be essential to either subsidize students who attend Nyack, with an agreement that they return to work in their own district, or else if that is not feasible, some form of training in the district may have to be devised.[55]

This brought the reopening of Canadian Bible Institute into open discussion. Charged with making a recommendation, the district executive committee disagreed with the principle of subsidizing Canadian students to attend American Bible colleges. Furthermore, the problem was not just the lure of American opportunity, but also of increasing border and monetary restrictions, which were making it impossible for many Canadians to obtain their training in the United States. Since the Canadian Bible Institute could not be reopened immediately, the committee recommended "that the District superintendent commence negotiations with the Western Canadian District, through the Home Department, for the setting up of a Bible Training Centre for students of both Canadian districts."[56]

In January 1944, Mason reported to the district executive committee, and later to conference:

> In accordance with the resolution of last Conference, as regards a union effort on the part of the Western and Eastern and Central Canadian Districts for a Bible Training Centre, I conferred with Home Secretary Nelson, and a brief conference was arranged with Mr. Skitch, Mr. Nelson and myself. It was evident as a result of this conference that our western brethren would not look kindly upon any union effort, unless we should decide to cooperate with them in the West, in their present venture in Regina.[57]

This seemed to close the door to a reconciliation between the two districts. The best time to have negotiated in the interests of the whole Alliance community in Canada would have been before the western school acquired property and became permanently located in Regina. However, the opportunity was lost.

THE YOUNG SCHOOL MATURES

Meanwhile, the Western Canadian Bible Institute in Regina pursued its own course, seemingly oblivious to the unfolding drama in the east. In his first commencement address, President Blackett told his first three graduates, "You are the vanguard of the army that is to follow."[58] His words proved true. The original student body of 50 had swollen to 106 by the fourth year, causing housing problems and overcrowded classrooms. Clearly, what was needed was much larger permanent quarters, including residential facilities.

In April 1945, the three-storey Clayton Hotel on Broad Street, near the railroad station, was offered for sale. Blackett determined that it could be purchased for $65,000. Excitedly, he called on Pastor Brooks, at the tabernacle, and together they mused over the possibility of acquiring it. Brooks recalled:

> I went home that day at noon, just after he [Blackett] had spoken to me. While having lunch, the Lord put a thought in my mind, "Go and see Stuart Champ." So, I got up from the table and went down town to see the owner of the Champ Hotel. He was a Brethren and a good friend of the

Alliance. I asked him what the Clayton Hotel building was worth and he replied that he believed he could buy it for $50,000, cash. I said, "Stuart, you may be able to, but we don't have any money." To my astonishment he replied, "Why don't I buy it for cash and sell it to you."[59]

Champ purchased the building and friends contributed $20,000 in gifts. On August 15, the transaction between him and the school was completed, and the old hotel building became the new home of the Western Canadian Bible Institute. After extensive and speedy renovation and redecoration (described as "transformation from wine to worship, from beer to Bible and from blasphemy to blessing"),[60] the school moved into the premises, which included rooms for 170 students, an auditorium seating 200 and a dining room for 225.[61]

In December 1944, the board of managers approved a recommendation of the Education Department:

That the Western Canadian Bible Institute be granted recognition as one of the regional schools of The Christian and Missionary Alliance (1) when standards of the school meet the requirements of the Education Department, (2) if students in eastern Canada are not jeopardized in their desire to go to Nyack by such recognition, (3) and that such recognition become effective at the close of the war.[62]

The war in Europe ended in May 1945 and in Asia three months later. However, the board seemed to be in no hurry to implement their plan to recognize the Western Canadian Bible Institute. In December, Rev. E. F. Mapstone of Beulah Tabernacle in Edmonton urged the board of managers to immediately recognize the Regina school, and requested a loan of $10,000 to help pay off the mortgage on the school property. At first it was agreed to grant "modified" recognition as a regional school with a grant of $5,000, pending achievement of "required standards."[63] However, by March 1946, the board agreed to propose full recognition to Council.[64]

In May 1946, Council recognized Western Canadian Bible Institute as a regional college of The Christian and Missionary Alliance. "It means," the *Messenger* stated, "that graduates of the Institute may now be accepted as candidates for the mission field or for home work without the necessity of taking further studies at Nyack."[65]

To make this possible, the standard of entrance was raised to grade eleven (junior matriculation). By then, the many Bible schools

Great West Bible Institute
EDMONTON, ALTA.

The students' rooms in the Institute are furnished as follows:

    Bed and Mattress.
    Pillows.
    Table.
    Chair.
    Mirror.
    Washstand.

Students will be required to bring sufficient bedding, towels, etc., for their own use.

The cost of Board and Room in the Institute will not exceed $5.50 per week, payable in advance.

A Registration Fee of $10.00 per term for day students and $5.00 per term for evening students is charged on entrance.

Text Books will be supplied students at cost.

Further information and Application Forms obtainable from

        Rev. J. H. WOODWARD,
        10643 - 98th Street,
        Edmonton.

8.8 Brochure for the opening year of the Great West Bible Institute, 1924-1925.

8.9 The institute's second location in this former nurses' residence on 92nd Street.

8.10 The third and final location of the Great West Bible Institute was this former school building, which was occupied by the institute late in 1925. Here the first studio of station CHMA was located.

8.11 The first class of the Great West Bible Institute at the first location on 120th Street. Behind them stands A. W. Roffe (in the centre of the doorway), with John Woodward to the left, and, to the right, missionary to Palestine Mary Butterfield and Margaret Connor. The photograph was taken during the Edmonton Missionary Conference of November 9 to 16, 1924.

352 / *The Education Struggle*

8.12 **8.13** **8.14**

8.12 In September 1941, Rev. George Blackett, with the help of Rev. Willis Brooks and the approval of Gordon Skitch, launched the Canadian Bible Institute in the basement of the Alliance Tabernacle in Regina. He was president for thirteen years.

8.13 Rev. William McArthur was the second president of the Western Canadian Bible Institute, for the period 1955-1958. During his tenure, the institute officially became the all-Canada Alliance Bible school, changed its name to Canadian Bible College, relocated to the present campus site, and commenced a massive building program.

8.14 Rev. Alvin Martin was president of Canadian Bible College from 1958 until 1972. During his term of office, the college became a full member of the Accrediting Association of Bible Colleges, conferring its first degree in 1959.

8.15 In October 1945, the renamed Western Canadian Bible Institute relocated into the downtown Clayton Hotel building.

8.15

8.16 Students fill the chapel of the old hotel building in Regina.

8.16

of the prairies were experiencing phenomenal growth, to some extent due to the influx of ex-servicemen and women. In Alberta alone, enrollments increased from 800 in 1940 to 2,100 in 1947.[66] W.C.B.I. shared fully in this development as its initial enrollment in 1941 of 50 increased in 1947 to 192, bringing special commendation from headquarters. President Shuman stated that the school had come into being and had developed as a result of "divine pressure."[67] In 1949, by an Act of the Legislative Assembly of Saskatchewan, W.C.B.I. was incorporated as a non-profit educational institution.

Eastern Uncertainty

Back in May 1944, the board of managers had approved the division of the homeland into five "school regions"—four in the United States and one in Canada, with the rider that "within these regions there shall not be more than one school."[68] This was just what the district executive committee of the Eastern and Central Canadian District feared would happen, and they issued a strong protest to the board of managers. As a result, in September 1944, the board made an amendment to its policy "that owing to the immensity of the area, the diversity of the need, challenge and opportunity, the demand seems to require that we establish two school regions instead of one for the Dominion of Canada."[69]

The news was passed on by both President Shuman and District Superintendent Mason to the Eastern and Central District Conference, which met in Toronto three weeks later.[70] The Committee on Matters Referred exclaimed:

> We welcome with joy our President's report. We are glad that action has been taken [regarding] our Bible schools, and we look forward to the day when a school shall be opened in this part of the Dominion.[71]

The Committee on Home Work stated that "we can not but be aware of the need of a Bible school for our Eastern and Central Canadian District," and introduced a successful motion that "Conference favours the establishment of a Bible school in the Eastern and Central Canadian District."[72] A committee consisting of Revs. Nathan Bailey, William McArthur, Ernest J. Bailey and William H. Lewellan was appointed to develop plans and report to the district executive committee in January 1945.

The report was duly delivered. It expressed alarm at the increasing number of district young men being lost from Alliance ministries through attendance at non-Alliance schools in eastern Canada. Adverse currency exchange rates had made attendance at Nyack impractical, and the lure of local schools was proving to be irresistible to many. The committee deplored the continuing delays and restrictions imposed upon its work. It had been hoped that Rev. Harry L. Turner of Hamilton might serve on the faculty, but he had left the district to teach at St. Paul Bible Institute. The report concluded that plans must be finalized quickly to reopen the Canadian Bible Institute in September 1945.[73]

In July 1945, signs of impatience in Toronto brought President Shuman to address the district executive committee on the subject of Bible colleges. He stated that post-war operating costs for colleges were expected to rise enormously. Furthermore, neither he nor District Superintendent Mason was convinced that the existing institute building was suitable, as it lacked living quarters. Post-war construction costs were already skyrocketing and indications were that this might not be an appropriate time to rebuild and relocate elsewhere. The president and district superintendent suggested that the district subsidize its students at Nyack with the money it had earmarked for the Toronto school. The suggestion apparently fell on deaf ears for the committee passed a motion "that a Bible school be established in this District."[74]

By the time of the district conference in September 1945, the district superintendent reported that Rev. William McArthur of Owen Sound, whom it had been expected would serve on the faculty of the Bible institute, had left the district to join the faculty in Regina. The continuing inability to locate a suitable head for the Toronto school had made it impossible to proceed further with the venture. However, a survey of district churches indicated that a majority favoured a Bible school within the district. If this could not be achieved, they favoured their young people being encouraged to attend the Nyack or St. Paul schools.[75]

During the next several months, District Superintendent Mason and his executive committee were largely occupied with the disastrous Crone crisis (pages 189-194). As a consequence, the school project received little attention. The Council of May 1946 elected David Mason as treasurer of The Christian and Missionary Alliance, and within a few weeks he had relocated in New York. It was all that acting superintendent Nathan Bailey could do that summer to maintain the ministry at the Gospel Tabernacle in Ottawa and to give leadership in the crisis affairs of the district, without trying to secure a faculty for a defunct Bible school. The annual conference in September elected Bailey as their new district superintendent. At that same conference, the Home Work Committee, with the strong backing of the newly elected superintendent, proposed the purchase of the Glen Rocks estate for a district camp and conference ground,[76] and Home Secretary H. E. Nelson, who was present, gave his "candid opinion" that the "District should own and operate a summer camp or conference ground."[77] Conference approved the proposal.

However, the district had only one source of assets large enough to acquire the estate. Within four months, an offer to purchase the debt-free institute building was accepted, and in due course, the Glen Rocks Bible Conference was purchased (see pages 291-292). Henceforth, all serious talk about reopening the Canadian Bible Institute in Toronto ceased. In point of fact, the east was surrendering to the west its historic claim to leadership in a national education facility and program. More importantly, the tenor of eastern Alliance thought would undergo change. The growing predominance of western pastors, together with western-trained eastern pastors, would bring eastward a willingness to pioneer new trails in the ministry. Over the next quarter of a century, eastern conservatism, with its historic concern for the preservation of its confessional faith, would give way to western innovation, more attuned to the social or relational aspects of the gospel.

A NATIONAL SCHOOL EMERGES

In any event, if District Superintendent Bailey appeared to be more interested in camp than college, it was certainly not because of disinterest in the training of Alliance young people in Canada. He was a realist. He saw the Western Canadian Bible Institute as an established fact and he believed that economics would preclude more than one Alliance Bible school in Canada. What was more, he was not prepared to perpetuate the strained relationship that separated the two Canadian districts, which was certainly not of his making.

The year-long interval between the superintendencies of Gordon Skitch and Willis Brooks in the west (September 1948 to September 1949) gave Nathan Bailey an opportunity to have a talk with George Blackett. He found the soft-spoken, gentlemanly president-dean eager to work towards a new era of cooperation. As if to cement the new accord, three graduates of the Western Canadian Bible Institute were appointed to eastern churches that year.* However, full integration of educational aspirations would only come a step at a time over the next seven years.

In the spring of 1950, newly elected Superintendent Willis Brooks launched a campaign to liquidate all remaining debt on the institute property. His eastern counterpart, Superintendent Nathan Bailey, sent him a letter of encouragement:

> We here in eastern Canada have an interest in W.C.B.I., as we feel that it is our school too! Canada needs this vital ministry. Here is not just another Bible school, but a place of preparation for Christian service dedicated to the highest standards of spiritual and scholastic achievement. Let us join in prayer, faith and action that the burden of debt may be removed, thus assuring an even greater ministry for the school. An investment now will bring dividends throughout eternity.[78]

The old hotel building had been considered a godsend in 1945, but by 1952, many were thinking again of relocation. The noisy downtown location was not conducive to study and reflection. The building had been designed as a hotel, and some of its unalterable features were far from ideal. There were no campus or recreational facilities. In addition, a tax-exempt status could not be obtained because it was in a commercial zone of the city. The conference of 1952 was persuaded to approve relocation in principle, and Administrator Rev. William McArthur was appointed Director of Extension, to head up a committee responsible for the locating and securing of a suitable new property.

In March 1953, the committee urged the immediate purchase of the present property on Fourth Avenue. The school board was persuaded, and with no available cash, borrowed $11,000 to secure the purchase of the thirteen-acre plot. District Superintendent Willis Brooks told the conference in September:

> We should look forward to the day when Western Canadian Bible Institute is not only a Western Canadian school, but is recognized as the "all Canada" school of our society.[79]

---

* During the previous eight years of the Regina school's existence, only two of its graduates received eastern charges.

Reinforcing this forward look was another matter brought to the attention of the delegates. After the presentation of an educational survey report, Council that year had recommended:

> That as a minimum requirement, all of our schools seek for and maintain accreditation with the Accrediting Association of Bible Institutes and Bible Colleges in its Collegiate division.[80]

Fired with this additional challenge, conference charged the school board with the responsibility of appointing a committee "which would take initial steps toward the bringing of our school to a place of accreditation," and at its meeting of November 11, the board appointed a Committee on Accreditation composed of the school president and Revs. M. Downey, R. M. Kincheloe and R. F. Merrill.[81]

As if not to be outdone by the movement towards academic excellence, McArthur and his committee set a high priority on the achievement of physical plant excellence. Eager that the benefits and attractions of relocation, modernization and enlargement should be offered to students as soon as possible, and urged forward by others of the faculty, the Relocation Committee presented on November 11, 1953, a proposal for a large debt-financed rebuilding program for the new site. A majority of the school board approved of the plan. However, President-Dean Blackett had always been opposed to large church debts, and his convictions applied equally to Bible schools. Of particular concern to Blackett was the fact that the viability of the financial plan hinged on selling price estimates for the old hotel building ranging as high as $200,000. In addition, enrollment had been dropping from a high of 192 in 1947 to 125 in 1952, and indications were that it might drop even further.* Under such conditions he did not see the wisdom of incurring large debts. As a matter of conscience, he could not agree to be part of such a venture. Moreover, Blackett had noted an increasing number of occasions when his views did not coincide with the majority views of the board.** As a result, Blackett tendered his resignation, effective at the end of the year, and he was replaced immediately by William McArthur.

---

* Enrollment would continue to drop to a 1957 nadir of 92 and would not again reach the 1947 level until 1961.

** Blackett's experience with the board of W.C.B.I. in 1953 is reminiscent of his experience with the board of Winnipeg Bible Institute in 1941 (see page 345).

During the summer of 1954, a giant step toward achieving the dream of a national school for Canada was taken. Superintendent Blackett invited Superintendent Bailey to appoint two members to the school board. In response, the eastern executive committee elected Revs. David Anderson and Nathan Bailey as the first eastern members.[82] The goodwill western gesture was reciprocated by the August 1955 resolution of the eastern executive committee "that the Western Canadian Bible Institute be recognized as the all-Canada school." Cautiously, a rider added:

> This action, it was understood, would not exclude other Alliance schools in their approach to the churches of the Eastern and Central Canadian District, and would not exclude our young people from entering them.

After some further discussion, it was agreed "that there would be no objection to dropping the word 'Western' from the name of the school."[83] The eastern conference of one month later ratified the executive action with some wording modification,* and requested the Home Department to pursue the matter to implementation.[84]

The Western Canadian District executive and the school board were more than pleased and immediately enlarged the board from eight to twelve members to include four from the east. That same year, 1955, the school amended its constitution to conform with those used by other Alliance schools.

In May 1956, General Council made Canada a single school zone, and W.C.B.I. was declared to be the official school.[85] A great barrier to Canadian Alliance unity had been breached. The centre of deepest cleavage became the instrument of inter-district reconciliation and the focal point for the further development of a national consensus. For the first time, the president of Western Canadian Bible Institute reported to an eastern conference in 1956, and also for the first time, eastern churches were urged to send their young people to the western school and to help support its financial needs.[86]

Strangely enough, the school board did not drop the word "Western" in the school name until thirteen months later. At that time it received permission from the board of managers to not only make that change but also to replace the word "Institute" with "College."[87]

---

* The motion adopted by conference granted Canadian Bible Institute "the privilege of dropping the word 'Western' . . . if they so desire."

By Act of the Saskatchewan Legislature, on April 10, 1957, Western Canadian Bible Institute legally became Canadian Bible College.

Meanwhile, the campus building plans were pushed forward with skill and vigour.[88] The first phase of construction involved the men's and women's dormitories and the administration building. On August 7, 1955, ground was broken, and just fourteen months later, by delaying the start of the school year by two weeks, the move from downtown was effected. Undoubtedly, President-Dean McArthur deserves much credit for his administrative prowess. He reported:

> The new buildings, though not completely finished are proving all that has been desired for comfort and smooth working operations. So different is life on the new campus from that of the old Broad Street location, that living spiritually, physically, socially, and scholastically has taken on new meaning and blessing.[89]

Notwithstanding the joy of the occasion, deep concern accompanied the move. The project had been approved in 1953 at an estimated cost of $200,000 which, it was hoped, would be largely covered by the sale of the old hotel. Costs amounted to $332,000, and Blackett's fears proved well-founded when the 1956 sale of the old building netted only $50,000.[90] Increasing the burden, student enrollment decreased to a 1957 low of 92. Because, as McArthur explained, "Student fees in Western Canada must of necessity be kept as low as possible because of the very highly competitive element of scores of surrounding Bible schools," the enrollment trend resulted in a serious loss of operating income.[91]

The financial crisis sparked a wave of goodwill and generosity throughout the Canadian Alliance community. In 1957, the Western Canadian District established a policy of donating 30 percent of its annual home missions fund to the college (about $10,000 a year). That same year, both Canadian districts began collecting special annual donations towards debt reduction at the college which by 1958 amounted to nearly $10,000.[92] In 1960, the western and eastern districts agreed on a 75 percent and 25 percent split, respectively, in their financial support of the college, roughly proportional to district attendance.[93] However, the greatest help came from New York headquarters which, in 1956, advanced a loan of $170,000, repayable over a fourteen-year term.[94] It fell to District Superintendent Blackett to express official thanks:

The generous assistance and sympathetic understanding of the Education Department and Board of Managers have meant more to the school than words can tell. We desire to express our heartfelt gratitude to God for the very wonderful help that has come from our own Society making the expansion program possible.[95]

The prevailing shortage of capital dragged out the completion of the relocation project over the next five years. Gradually classrooms were finished, dining hall and bathrooms tiled, sidewalks laid, roads paved and lawns extended. The provision of five staff houses and the furnishing and decoration of the chapel were major items. On May 12, 1961, the completed new campus, valued at $400,000, was dedicated with appropriate ceremony, and attended by many of the great within and without the Alliance fellowship. Congratulations were expressed by Regina Mayor H. H. P. Baker and Saskatchewan Premier the Hon. T. C. Douglas.[96]

COMING OF AGE

Back in November 1953, a committee had been appointed "which would take initial steps towards the bringing of our school to a place of accreditation." A year later the school's charter was amended by Provincial Act to permit the granting of the B.Th. degree in the theological and missions courses. At the same time the school year was extended from seven to nine months and other changes to the curriculum effected. An application for affiliation with the University of Saskatchewan, Regina College, was turned down because of the minimum educational requirements for full-time staff teachers. Nevertheless, an arrangement was made with Regina College to provide courses leading to senior matriculation and first-year liberal arts standings. Entering Canadian Bible College with these qualifications, a graduate of the three-year theological or missions courses would qualify for the Bachelor of Theology degree.

However, progress towards accreditation lagged during the peak years of the construction program. After four and a half years as president, McArthur resigned in May 1958 to accept a church ministry in Seattle, and he was replaced by Rev. Alvin Martin.* That same

---

* From Nobles County, Minnesota, and a graduate of St. Paul Bible Institute, Martin was an Alliance missionary in Palestine, Israel, from 1947-1954. In 1956, at 37, he joined the faculty of W.C.B.I. as an instructor in Bible, homiletics, Hebrew, theology and missions.

month, the Education Department urged all schools to "secure accreditation on the highest academic level."[97] In response, the school board, under the new leadership of Martin, set a goal to reach the accreditation requirements of the Accrediting Association of Bible Colleges by 1960.[98]

There then ensued a fifteen-month period during which numerous changes were made in conjunction with a team of representatives from the accrediting association. On October 26, 1960, the college was granted associate status, pending final conformities, and on October 25, 1961, became a fully accredited member.[99] Canadian Bible College was the third of 54 Bible colleges in Canada to achieve this level of qualification.[100]

That same year, the college again revised its constitution and changed the name of its governing body from school board to board of managers.[101] The degrees of Bachelor of Theology and Bachelor of Religious Education were first conferred in 1959[102] and 1961,[103] respectively.*

During the Council of 1955, the Education Department had reported:

> The youngest of our Bible schools, located ... on the great prairies of western Canada, has not yet been able to attain to the same level scholastically as its American sisters.[104]

Certainly by 1961 this was not true. Moreover, by that time 61 percent of western, 31 percent of eastern, or just over half of all Canadian Alliance pulpits were filled by its graduates.[105] In a very real sense, Canadian Bible College had become the national training centre for new leaders and the national emblem of consensus for the Alliance in Canada.

REFERENCES

1. *Word, Work and World*, July 1883, p. 113.
2. Lindsay Reynolds, *Footprints* (Toronto: The Christian and Missionary Alliance in Canada, 1982), pp. 121, 122.
3. Ibid., p. 193.
4. Ibid., pp. 194, 195.
5. Robert L. Niklaus, *The School that Vision Built* (Nyack: Nyack College, 1982), p. 17.

---

* In 1959, Arnold Cook of Owen Sound became the first graduate of Canadian Bible College to receive a degree.

362 / The Education Struggle

6. Eastern, Minutes, 1 Oct 1920.
7. Ibid., 21 Sep 1921.
8. Ibid., 10 Oct 1921.
9. Ibid., 27 May 1922.
10. Ibid., 13 Jun 1922.
11. Ibid.; *Alliance Weekly*, 12 Aug 1922, p. 351.
12. Eastern, Minutes, 13 Jun 1922.
13. Ibid., 21 Jul 1922.
14. Ibid., 2 Feb 1923; 20 Apr 1923.
15. Ibid., 23 Aug 1923.
16. Ibid., 21 Jul 1922.
17. Ibid., 16 Oct 1923.
18. *Alliance Weekly*, 15 Mar 1924, p. 42.
19. Eastern, Conference, 29 May 1924, pp. 2, 3.
20. Ibid., pp. 1-15.
21. Ibid., 28 May 1924, p. 3; 29 May, p. 10.
22. C.B.I. Board of Governors, Minutes, 31 May, 19 Jun 1924.
23. Board of Managers, Minutes, 4 Nov 1924.
24. Ibid., 13 Aug; 12 Sep 1924; Board of Governors, Minutes, 30 Jun; 7 Jul 1924.
25. Ibid., 27 Jul 1924.
26. Ibid., 7 Jul 1924.
27. *Alliance Weekly*, 27 Sep 1924, p. 202; *Toronto Star*, 20 Sep 1924, p. 12.
28. "Himself," Toronto, 3 Jan 1925, p. 3.
29. Canadian Alliance, Toronto, Sep 1924, pp. 1, 2; Canadian Bible Institute, Opening and Dedication Bulletin, Nov 1924, pp. 1, 2.
30. Catalogue of the Great West Bible Institute, 1925-1926, p. 5.
31. *Alliance Weekly*, 17 Jan 1925, p. 47; 25 Jan 1925, p. 62.
32. Ibid., 15 Nov 1924, p. 239.
33. Board of Managers, Minutes, 2 Mar 1928.
34. *Alliance Weekly*, 2 Jun 1928, p. 349.
35. Eastern, Conference, May 1929.
36. Home Department, Minutes, 10 Dec 1929.
37. Ibid., 3 Jan 1920.
38. Eastern, Conference, 20 Sep 1940.
39. Edward Hildebrandt, "A History of the Winnipeg Bible Institute and College of Theology" (unpublished, 1965), pp. 66-84.
40. Mrs. Lucy Blackett's reminiscences, undated.
41. Willis Brooks, interview, 6 Oct 1983.
42. Mrs. Lucy Blackett's reminiscences, undated.

The Education Struggle / 363

43. Western, Conference, May 1941, pp. 6, 7.
44. *Alliance Witness*, 6 Sep 1941, p. 571.
45. *Messenger* (Regina: Canadian Bible Institute), Sep 1941.
46. Ibid., Jan 1944.
47. Canadian Bible Institute, Prospectus, 1942-1943, p. 4.
48. Letter, Downey to Reynolds, 6 Apr 1983.
49. Home Department, Report to Board of Managers, 16 Jun 1942.
50. Board of Managers, Minutes, 21 Mar 1946.
51. Eastern and Central Canadian District, Letters, Mason to Bailey, 30 Jun 1944.
52. Eastern, Conference, Sep 1941, Report of Education Dept.; ibid., Sep 1943, Letter of President Shuman; ibid., Superintendent's Report.
53. Home Department, Minutes, 16 Jun 1942.
54. Board of Managers, Minutes, 9 Dec 1942.
55. Eastern, Conference, Sep 1943, Superintendent's Report.
56. Eastern, Conference, Sep 1943, Home Work Report.
57. Eastern, Minutes, 27 Jan 1944; Eastern, Conference, Sep 1944, Superintendent's Report.
58. W.C.B.I. *Challenger*, 1942, p. 8.
59. Willis Brooks, interview, 6 Oct 1983.
60. W.C.B.I. *Challenger*, 1946, p. 15.
61. Special edition of W.C.B.I. *Messenger*, May 1945; W.C.B.I. *Messenger*, Dec 1947.
62. Board of Managers, Minutes, 14 Dec 1944.
63. Ibid., 5 Dec 1945.
64. Ibid., 21 Mar 1946.
65. W.C.B.I. *Challenger*, Jul 1946, p. 2.
66. Journal of Proceedings of the Fifteenth Session of the General Synod of the Church of England in Canada (Toronto, 1943), p. 264.
67. H. M. Shuman, "Bible Training Work in the Home Field—A Survey" (unpublished), 12 Dec 1947.
68. Board of Managers, Minutes, 31 May 1944.
69. Ibid., 7 Sep 1944.
70. Eastern, Conference, Sep 1944, Letter, Shuman to Eastern and Central Canadian District Conference; ibid., Superintendent's Report.
71. Ibid., Report of Committee on Matters Referred.
72. Ibid., Report of Committee on Home Work.
73. Eastern, Minutes, 23 Jan 1945.
74. Ibid., 3 Jul 1945.
75. Eastern, Conference, Sep 1945, Superintendent's Report.
76. Eastern, Minutes, Report of N. Bailey to District Executive Committee, 29 Jul—1 Aug 1946.

364 / *The Education Struggle*

77. Eastern, Conference, Letter, Nelson to Eastern and Central Canadian District Conference, 4 Sep 1946.
78. W.C.B.I. *Messenger*, Spring 1950, p. 1; *Alliance Weekly*, 15 Apr 1950, p. 230.
79. Western, Conference, Sep 1953, Superintendent's Report.
80. Annual Report, 1953, p. 256.
81. W.C.B.I. School Board Minutes, 11 Nov 1953, p. 3.
82. Eastern, Minutes, 23 Sep 1954.
83. Ibid., 18 Aug 1955.
84. Eastern, Conference, Sep 1955, pp. 7, 50.
85. Annual Report, 1956, p. 240.
86. Eastern, Conference, Sep 1956, pp. 40, 44.
87. W.C.B.I. School Board Minutes, 24 Oct 1956, p. 2.
88. W.C.B.I. *Challenger*, 1956, p. 4.
89. Annual Report, 1956, pp. 22, 23.
90. Ibid., 1961, p. 40.
91. Ibid., 1958, p. 22.
92. Ibid., 1959, p. 25.
93. Eastern, Minutes, 9 Mar, 17 Oct 1960.
94. Annual Report, 1957, p. 22; Canadian Bible College, Dedication Bulletin, May 1961, p. 2.
95. Western, Conference, 1956, p. 3.
96. *Western Worker*, Jul-Sep 1961, p. 6; Annual Report, 1962, pp. 39, 40.
97. Ibid., 1958, p. 214.
98. Canadian Bible Institute, *Messenger*, Oct 1958, p. 3.
99. *Alliance Witness*, 29 Nov 1961, p. 16.
100. Annual Report, 1962, pp. 39, 40.
101. Canadian Bible College, Annual Report, Sep 1961, p. 2.
102. *Western Worker*, May-Jun 1959, p. 10.
103. Annual Report, 1962, p. 40.
104. Ibid., 1955, p. 180.
105. Ibid., 1962, p. 40.

CHAPTER NINE

Canada's Other Sheep

French Canada, like English Canada, is a product of its history. There are reasons—good ones—why the two differ, and no amount of political rhetoric will change the facts of history. The two societies were, are and likely will remain distinct. An understanding of the history of French Canada is essential to understanding its religious ethos.

Contrary to general understanding, British victories at Québec in 1759 and at Montréal a year later, did not constitute unconditional surrender on the part of the French. At Québec the French offered to surrender if the British would agree to 11 conditions and at Montréal to 55 conditions. Most of these were accepted by the British, including articles relating to the prerogatives of the Roman Catholic Church and the pervasive authority of its bishops. In addition, the British undertook to collect "tithes and all other dues" on behalf of the church. This made the Roman Church the only church in Canada ever to be "as by law established," and gave its bishops an authority and privilege nowhere else recognized in the British Empire. In addition, the British agreed to govern French Canadians "according to the custom of Paris and the laws and usages established for this country."

The British had no intention of suppressing the French language in Québec. Protestantism and the English language would be for English immigrants, and Catholicism and the French language for the Québecois. They hoped to quickly populate the new territory with settlers from Britain and New England, and in this way to anglicize and Protestantize Québec by majority influence.

The Québec Act of 1774 reaffirmed and enhanced the prerogatives and privileges of the Roman Church and its bishops, thus making this vast area, in all but name, a French Catholic British colony. This was intended to settle the question whether French Canadians would be swallowed up by English-speaking co-settlers, or, retaining their language, religion, civil law and other customs, should maintain their distinction and develop side-by-side with them. The intent was that French Canadians would form a distinct society within the country, where their cherished rights and distinctives would be safeguarded by constitutional guarantees. The prospect of an ever-increasing English Protestant majority throughout North America was of particular concern to the French Roman Catholic hierarchy in Québec.

The Role of the Church

Throughout the vicissitudes of French Canadian history, the church hierarchy continued to dominate and to intrude into every aspect of French society "wherever he [the Bishop] shall see fit." The church-oriented educational system taught subjects suited to produce priests and lawyers, but failed to equip leaders for commerce and industry. Anglophones became the owners and managers of business, while Francophones became their employees. English became the language of business. In matters of religion, the French and English drifted into a tacit recognition of Catholicism as the religion of the French and Protestantism as that of the English.

As a result, there developed in Québec what Hugh MacLennan has so aptly described as "The Two Solitudes." English and French lived side by side in almost closed societies, interfacing only in matters of business and politics.

Attempts to evangelize the French were met with vigorous and even violent opposition from the Catholic clergy, and because of their dominant influence, by police, government officials and even by the courts. Not infrequently, French converts to Protestantism found themselves without employment, schools or cemeteries. For their own preservation, they usually became anglicized and absorbed into the English society, thus losing their French heritage.

English Protestant missionaries often felt the sting of the French Catholic clergy, but their mistreatment was not solely because of racial-religious antagonism. The hierarchy opposed any perceived threat to its authority or prestige.

A classic case against one of their own was l'affaire Guibord. L'Institut Canadien de Montréal was founded in 1844 to raise cultural standards in French Canada. Over the years it became a centre of political and religious liberalism. Bishop Bourget of Montréal became alarmed, condemned the institute and excommunicated all its members. In 1870, one of them, Joseph Guibord, died. The request of his family for burial in the consecrated ground of a Catholic cemetery was refused.

After making temporary arrangements for the body, the institute and the Guibord family took the case through the courts, and obtained a favourable decision from the Privy Council five years later. Guibord's long overdue remains were then taken to the Catholic cemetery under protection of English-speaking soldiers, and to preclude grave robbery, concrete was immediately poured around the coffin. It appeared that the bishop had lost the battle, but his ingenuity had been underrated. On that same day he declared the plot where Guibord lay encased to be forever unconsecrated ground.

Perhaps the first significant attempt to evangelize the French was the Feller Institute at Grande Ligne (south of Montreal), founded in 1836 by Madame Henriette Feller. Her successful work was supported by the English Protestant public at large, but it was really a Baptist venture. Another early evangelistic attempt was the French Canadian Missionary Society, organized in 1839. It was greatly opposed and maligned, but remained active for about forty years.

In 1876, the Presbyterian Board of French Evangelism, already engaged in a colportage program, opened a Mission House in Montréal. In one year there were enough converts to found L'Eglise du Sauveur, the first French-language Protestant church in Montréal. In that same year the Presbyterian board received into its membership the converted ex-priest, Father Charles Chiniquy. His preaching and writing featured exposure of Roman Catholic malpractices. Travelling widely, his ministry was accompanied by riots, tumults and opposition of every description, while his books were banned from sale in Québec.

Early Alliance Efforts in Québec

It was under such conditions that in September 1891 Rev. John Salmon, patriarch and vice-president of the Dominion Auxiliary of the Alliance, conducted the first Alliance convention in Montréal, which featured Rev. A. B. Simpson. At that convention, held in the Dominion Square Methodist Church, the first Alliance fraternal branch in Québec was formed, with engraver George Bishop as president.[1] That the language of the convention was entirely English and was directed solely to the English-speaking community is not surprising. In those days, the Alliance saw itself as a fraternity of evangelical Christians from many churches. As there were almost no French-speaking evangelical Christians, there was little need to consider French Canadians.

English-French disharmony, never very far beneath the surface, erupted in 1918 over the conscription issue. The insistence of many French Catholic Québecers on their historic right to remain neutral in the event of war, together with the rounding-up of defaulters, often at the hands of armed English Protestant officers, pitted the two races and two religions against each other. French Canadians would never forget the indignity of this episode.

By 1922, when District Superintendent Roffe reinstated the annual conference in Montréal (see pages 71-72), the Alliance was essentially a foreign missionary society, and the convention's attention was almost exclusively given to foreign missions. Reports of the Montréal conferences from 1922-1925 contain not a single mention of home evangelism or the spiritual plight of French Canadians. Even the prevailing ecclesiastical barrier in Québec is mentioned only once, and that only to blame an exceptionally low attendance at the 1924 convention on the fact that the city consisted mainly of Roman Catholics.[2] It is regrettable that the Alliance of those days, including its Canadian District, was more concerned about French-speaking souls living beyond the borders of North America.

The first sign of Alliance concern for the evangelization of French Canadians in their own language came from a Major Neate of the Canadian army, a member of the Gospel Tabernacle in Ottawa. During the summer of 1926, 24-year-old Jean Emile Funé, a graduate of the Nogent-sur-Marne Bible School in France who was at Nyack preparing to become an Alliance missionary to Vietnam, came to the capital at the request of Neate and the tabernacle committee. There he engaged in colportage work among the French of Ottawa and Hull for three months.

By the following summer, Major Neate had been transferred to Québec City, where his concern for his French-speaking neighbours became even more acute. He wrote to Foreign Secretary Rev. A. C. Snead, urging that Funé's home work assignment be spent in the provincial capital. Both Snead and Funé were agreeable but missionary appointees were expected to receive support from working with home churches, and the Alliance had no churches in Québec City.

With the assistance of Neate, arrangements were made with the Grande Ligne Mission to accept Funé on their payroll. He was appointed pastor of a small Baptist congregation—the only French-language Protestant church in the city. In order to conduct marriages, baptisms, and burials, Funé was ordained by the laying on of Baptist hands. One of Funé's Sunday school scholars was nine-year-old Robert Richardson who would become the first appointed Alliance missionary to the French Canadians.

Funé left for France and Vietnam in September 1928. Meanwhile, Fred Sparke and several of his congregation from the Alliance Gospel Hall in the north end of Montréal had started holding street meetings—no easy task. Street meetings required a police permit, which was impossible to obtain by Protestants, including even the benign Salvation Army. So Sparke's group placed lookouts to watch for policemen or robed members of the Catholic clergy. They were surprised to observe the number of French-speaking people who stopped to listen or even ask questions in French or broken English. It immediately became apparent that a knowledge of the French language was imperative if the gospel was to be effectively communicated to French Canadians. Sparke reported the limited success of the Montréal street meetings to newly-appointed District Superintendent J. D. Williams, adding, "this work is greatly handicapped through the need of a person capable of delivering a message in French."[3] That same year, Harold Meadows, secretary of Sparke's church, urged Williams to provide a French-speaking worker, and pointed out that an investment in a Québec witness would yield a rich harvest of French-speaking missionary candidates for Alliance mission fields in French colonial countries. It is not known if either Sparke or Meadows received a reply to their dispatches.[4]

Sparke resigned his Montréal pastorate in March 1929 and was replaced by Rev. T. J. Spier the following January. The new Chicago-born pastor soon became alarmed at the spiritual need and isolation of most of his neighbours. Within a few months, one or two people joined his congregation who could converse in French. With their help, the first bilingual Sunday school and children's meetings were conducted in the Alliance Gospel Hall in 1930. "Our work here is very peculiar," Spier reported to the district superintendent in his annual report that year, "principally because of 75% of the people speaking French. There would be numberless openings for the full Gospel in the French language if we had French-speaking missionaries."[5]

That same year, the Home Department logged the following minute:

> The matter of defining Pioneer Home Missionary areas to the Home Department was referred to the Superintendents' meeting held at Council 1930. It is the judgment of the Home Department that pioneer areas are illustrated by such Districts as the Western Canadian District and the Southwestern District.[6]

Apparently, District Superintendent Williams thus far had failed to impress the Home Department with the immensity and urgency of the need to establish a pioneer mission to the four million members of Canada's other founding race.

In September 1931, Williams, Spier, their wives,* and a young convert as an interpreter, made a thousand-mile survey of twenty cities and towns of Québec. The only evangelical witnesses in Québec City were a Baptist congregation of 25 and a Salvation Army group of three. While handing out tracts at the close of a service in Farnham, the group was mobbed by an angry crowd, but were able to leave without injury. Reporting the tour to both the conference of October 1931 and the *Alliance Weekly*, Williams stated:

> We were compelled to say that we found religious conditions simply appalling. The province is not only sadly neglected, but almost destitute insofar as faithful preaching of the full Gospel is concerned. We found cities of over ten thousand population with only one small Protestant witness. . . . Of course all the cities and towns are fully supplied with great imposing buildings of the Roman Catholic faith. Surely, our Protestant people everywhere in Canada and in the United States should be informed of the sad conditions existing in the province of Québec, and stirred to prayer and action that Gospel witnesses and missionaries be thrust forth into this most destitute of all the provinces of Canada.[7]

At the conference, Williams's report generated considerable talk. Williams called for "special prayer for labourers to be thrust forth into Québec." This was echoed in a call by the Committee on

---
* Mrs. Williams was an aunt of Mrs. Spier.

Evangelism and Extension Work for district workers to "do all in their power to encourage prayer and faith for the great unreached territories within our District, especially Québec." The board representative, Home Secretary Rev. G. Vernor Brown, was asked about the possibility of help from New York. He believed that the evangelization of Québec should be a district project. District treasurer Fred Sparke reported that no funds were available, but he recommended that "this Conference should consider most seriously the question of the disposal of the Bible Institute building and the use of the proceeds for challenges such as Québec and the Maritimes." His proposal did not meet with general approval, and the question of a Québec missionary was dropped.

Also in 1931, a French Canadian formerly with the Pentecostals, A. Ratelle, joined Spier's congregation. The little congregation subsidized Ratelle to visit French homes, and in the spring of 1932, this led to the first Alliance sponsored, French-language weekly church services, conducted "under the stimulus of tomatoes, stones, etc." from a few of the neighbours.[8]

Another French family that joined Spier's congregation was that of Rev. Joseph and Mde. Amélie Giguère. Ordained an Oblate priest in 1906, Giguère was converted through the witness of a former shoemaker and left the priesthood in 1917. He taught at the Feller Institute and then pastored a Baptist church at Marieville. Moving to Montréal in 1930, the family lived close to the Alliance Gospel Hall, and, attracted to its brave attempts to evangelize the French, made the little hall their church home. A few years later, Giguère founded a mission to French Canadians which met in a Communist hall in downtown Montréal.*

In October 1932, the Alliance Gospel Hall appointed Ratelle and Spier as their delegates to conference. Ratelle read the "Report from the branches, Montréal," in which he related details of the struggling, part-time, locally subsidized French ministry, emphasizing the urgent need for a full-time, fully supported ministry by French-speaking missionaries. In response to a question about how such a missionary might be supported since neither the Home Department nor the district was prepared to do so, Ratelle enquired if it would be possible to place Québec under the Foreign Department. The subject was dropped, and insofar as the written records indicate, it was not

---

* All four Giguère daughters married Christian workers. Marcelle, Elise and Clemence (Dawn) married Alliance pastors Ray Sawler, Robert Richardson and Robert Willoughby, respectively, while Marguerite became the wife of Brethren worker Raymond Taylor.

brought up at a district conference or district executive committee meeting for another sixteen years.

That conference was a turning point in Ratelle's relations with the Alliance. He returned to Montréal a disillusioned man. Two months later, Spier terminated his ministry in Montréal. By April 1933, Williams was superintendent of both Canadian districts, and was becoming increasingly involved with the great home missions work in western Canada. Convinced that the Alliance was not interested in evangelizing French Canadians, Ratelle severed his Alliance connection. As a result, the first Alliance-sponsored French-language church services and door-to-door ministry in Montréal came to an end.

A Woman Pioneer

About the year 1920, the Kenyons, a Baptist family descended from the Puritans of the Rhode Island settlement of Roger Williams, began attending the Alliance church in West Brownsville, Pennsylvania. Two of the boys, Paul and Donald, became Alliance pastors, and their sister, Dorothy, felt called to be a missionary. After graduation with honours from Taylor University and Houghton College, she believed Morocco would be her field of service. As the Alliance had no work in that country, she applied to another mission, and in the meantime became director of Child Evangelism Fellowship for Western Pennsylvania. In March 1940, Miss Kenyon was accepted for service in Morocco, but due to wartime conditions, her sailing was postponed.

Early in 1942, she had an opportunity to leave immediately by air for Morocco. While pondering the will of the Lord in the matter, she received a request from Child Evangelism to go to Montréal "to open up the French work there." After much prayer, she believed that God wanted her to go to Québec. "When I could say a wholehearted 'yes' to Him and give my willing consent to serve Him in Québec for as long as He chose to use me there," she recalled, "a great peace flooded my soul and immediately the Lord gave token after token that this thing was of Him."[9]

One of the tokens given involved Marie Freligh,* an Alliance

---

* Marie Freligh came from an Alliance family long connected with the Gospel Tabernacle in St. Paul, Minnesota. A brother, Rev. Paul Freligh, was also a long-term Alliance missionary to French West Africa. Another brother, Rev. H. M. Freligh, was for some time principal of St. Paul Bible Institute. During the summer recess of 1929, he occupied the pulpit of Owen Sound Alliance Church, during an extended absence of the pastor.

Canada's Other Sheep / 373

9.1 In 1948, Dorothy Kenyon founded l'Institut Biblique Bethel in Lennoxville, Québec.

9.2 Robert Richardson, spiritually influenced as a boy by Alliance missionary candidate Jean Funé, became, in 1951, the first appointed Alliance missionary to French Canadians.

9.3 Started in October 1951 by Pastor Robert Richardson, La Mission Chrétienne Evangélique Française, in Welland, was the first French-language Alliance church in Canada. Pictured here is the service of October 1, 1952, held in the Free Methodist Church building. On the extreme left is Marguerite Giguère, a volunteer assistant.

9.4 Three of the four Giguère sisters, left to right, Elise Richardson, Marguerite Taylor and Clemence (Dawn) Willoughby. Not in the picture was Marcelle Sawler.

374 / Canada's Other Sheep

9.5 Members of La Chapelle Evangélique Cornwall, stand outside their parsonage / chapel, in 1958.

9.6 Mabel Quinlan was converted from Roman Catholicism through the ministry of Rev. and Mrs. William McArthur, in Bethany Tabernacle, Peterborough. In 1946, she commenced a life-long ministry among French Canadians in Québec.

9.7 The team of Mabel Quinlan (Alliance) and Jean Heidman (Brethren) on colportage work in Québec City, during the early 1950s.

missionary to French West Africa home on furlough and unable to return because of the war. She volunteered to go to Montréal with Dorothy Kenyon until such time as she could return to Africa. Convinced that this development was of the Lord, Miss Kenyon wrote:

> Knowing the French language, she [Miss Freligh] can begin work immediately while I will be privileged to study the French language under her. Québec is not ordinarily thought of as a mission field. Going up there does not carry with it the glory and glamour of one who is crossing the ocean. Nevertheless, the field is a most needy one and certainly a hard one; a field that needs the earnest prayers and supplications of the Lord's intercessors.... There are some of those "other sheep" that the Shepherd MUST bring.[10]*

Shortly after her arrival in Montréal, Miss Freligh wrote a report to *Alliance Weekly* readers:

> Miss Kenyon and I are comfortably settled in rooms in the home of French Christians, saved three years ago. Miss Kenyon started a weekly Bible class in this home.... Two in the class have volunteered to undertake child evangelism. Others are showing a hunger for the Spirit-filled life. ... Now is the time to reap a harvest, for so many French people are becoming dissatisfied with Romanism. We are praying our way forward a step at a time, and we have seen tokens of the spiritual showers we believe are going to fall. With return to Africa closed for an indefinite period, I do rejoice that the Lord has let me come to work in a field as needy as this.[11]

After a little more than a year, Miss Freligh returned to Africa, By that time, a vision that the two women shared materialized in the purchase of a children's camp.[12]

---

* Dorothy Kenyon not only learned French from Marie Freligh, but also took a French language course at McGill University in which she distinguished herself by sharing with another student a Québec government prize for the second highest achievement in her section.

In time, Dorothy Kenyon had another, even greater vision for a French-language Bible school where converts could be prepared in their own language to become missionaries to their own people. Miss Kenyon spent ten days on her knees pleading for the needed funds, and God answered her prayer. Her undimmed vision became a reality in 1948, when, with the help of others from several denominations, Bethel Bible School (later renamed Institut Biblique Béthel) was established through the purchase of a 90-acre farm and buildings on the outskirts of Sherbrooke.* Classes began in January 1949 with just one student—Raymond Taylor. In time, he would commence French-language services in Montréal under the Alliance.

A few years later, the school was taken over by Baptist and Brethren interests, and all semblance of Alliance influence disappeared. Bethel Bible School continued to make a significant contribution to the training of workers of many creeds (including the Alliance), in the cause of French evangelism.

A Québec City Ministry

Contemporary with Dorothy Kenyon's later ministry in Québec, was that of Mabel Quinlan. Raised in Peterborough as a strict Roman Catholic, in 1939 at twenty years of age Mabel became a domestic in the home of a Christian woman who patiently brought to her attention the need for a spiritual rebirth. One day Mabel passed by old Bethany Tabernacle, where Rev. William McArthur was pastor. A large sign on the building read:

> By grace are ye saved through faith; and that not of yourselves; it is the gift of God; not of works, lest any man should boast.

To Mabel, this was disturbingly different from the teaching she had received. On the first of three services she attended at the tabernacle, the congregation sang:

> Once for all, O sinner, receive it:
> Once for all, O brother, believe it;
> Cling to the Cross, thy burden will fall,
> Christ hath redeemed us, once for all.

---

* Dorothy Kenyon succumbed to cancer in 1959, at the age of 48. Marie Freligh retired after 37 years of foreign missionary service, and passed on in 1984 at the age of 90.

"It thrilled me," Mabel recalled, "but I couldn't quite believe it was true." On her third visit she learned that Mrs. McArthur had been a Catholic. After the service Mabel went to the McArthur home, where a talk with Mrs. McArthur cleared up all questions, as she related:

> It was so simple! And so wonderful! In a few moments we knelt with the pastor, and I opened my heart to the Lord Jesus. At that moment on August 2nd, 1939, I knew I was born again, that Christ had come into my heart to live for ever.[13]

Mabel Quinlan attended Western Canadian Bible Institute and the Missionary Training Institute, graduating from the latter in 1946. Sensing a call to a ministry to French Catholics, she proceeded to Québec City on her own, since the Alliance appeared to have no interest in such a work. Having never studied French, she enrolled in a French language course at Laval University, and helped in colportage work with Child Evangelism. "I will never forget the results of the first Bible I sold in Québec City," she recounted. "The man who purchased it became a Christian, and his transformed life led his landlady to accept Christ also."[14]

When Dorothy Kenyon opened Bethel Bible School in 1948, Mabel Quinlan joined the staff as a cook and general housekeeper, and in addition took part in house-to-house visitation in the vicinity of Lennoxville and Sherbrooke. During the summer of that year, Mabel distributed Bibles and tracts to immigrants landing at Québec City, and did colportage work with the Canadian Bible Society.

In the 1930s, the Brethren Assemblies commenced a French ministry in Québec and became the dominant factor in French evangelism. During the following decade, the Pentecostal Assemblies and the Evangelical Baptists achieved much success. News of chinks appearing in the Catholic armour of Québec became a topic of discussion in Canadian evangelical circles. In September 1948, there was a general consensus among the delegates to district conference that the Alliance, which considered itself a "pioneer mission" should, without further delay, take steps to enter "the world's second largest (after India) unevangelized missions field, still open to the Gospel." A motion was adopted "to refer the matter of home missions in Québec to the District Executive Committee, with power to launch such a program."[15]

The district executive committee, which met ten days later, was not about to be carried along by the emotional decision of conference. Its official minute reads, "The possibility of mission work in Québec was discussed and tabled until suitable personnel is forthcoming."[16] So an Alliance ministry to French Canadians again fell by the wayside.

THE VISION SURVIVES AND EXPANDS

In the spring of 1950, Robert (Bob) Richardson, the former Sunday school pupil of Jean Funé, graduated from Western Canadian Bible Institute and made enquiry of District Superintendent Bailey of the Eastern and Central Canadian District regarding the possibility of starting a French-language Alliance work in Québec. He recalled being advised that the Alliance was not yet ready for this, so he accepted an assignment in Montréal with the Child Evangelism Fellowship. In November of 1950, he doubled as interim pastor of the Montréal Central (Notre Dame de Grace) Church, for four months.[17]

Meanwhile, Marguerite Giguère (Richardson's sister-in-law), also a graduate of Western Canadian Bible Institute, was sent by Youth for Christ to Welland, in the Niagara Peninsula, during the spring of 1950. She conducted home visitation and youth ministries in the "Frenchtown" section. Her contacts were largely with anglicized Francophones, most of whom felt as much at home with the English language as with the French.

During the summer of 1951, in response to a report from Marguerite Giguère, Richardson asked District Superintendent Bailey if he could be appointed as an Alliance home missionary to the French in Welland. On September 12, during conference, the district executive committee credentialed Richardson as the first "Home missionary to the French Canadians."

Richardson had accepted his appointment "with details of his support to be worked out."[18] One month later, Bailey appealed to the Home Department for a $100 a month subsidy towards the support of Richardson, with another $40 per month to come from the district.[19] He was not successful. As a result, most of the burden of support during the early months and even years of the project fell on the shoulders of relatives and friends. Ironically, it had been Richardson who, a year earlier, had put his finger on the reason for the historic shortage of district funds for home missions and extension that had long characterized the Eastern and Central Canadian District. In a letter to District Superintendent Bailey, Richardson had reported a situation in the Montréal Central (Notre Dame de Grace) Church, in which local expenses were not being met, let alone any giving to home missions, while at the same time foreign missions were generously supported. He had termed this "an unbalanced budgeting of foreign and home missions offerings."[20]

Two years later, Bailey drew attention to the continuing low home missions contributions and chided the delegates to conference by pointing out that western Canadians had given $20,000 to home missions while easterners had given only $6,500. He attributed the problem to a "loss of vision, love and zeal," adding, "If some of our churches . . . would lose themselves in an all-out effort to seek and to save the lost, most of our internal troubles would be over."[21]

However, consideration of the wider picture reveals something quite different. The 65 western churches had given $110,000 to foreign missions and $20,000 to home work, while the 32 eastern churches had contributed $130,000 to foreign missions and $6,500 to home work. Clearly, it was not a matter of "love and zeal" but of differences of priority.

The first home-based prayer and study sessions of La Mission Chrétienne Evangélique Française in Welland were attended by two or three believers and "a few others interested in hearing the gospel." Two months later, a Free Methodist church building was rented and the first regular public church services commenced. However, door-to-door visitation and tract distribution continued to be the most effective means of making contacts.[22]

In 1953, the congregation moved to Winstonville Community Hall, in a more heavily populated area, consisting of 65 percent French Catholic residents. Although the hall allowed for a much larger ministry, it "failed to be a drawing card," according to Richardson.[23]

Under the impact of several large "Frenchtown for Christ Crusades," many professed faith, but between campaigns attendance declined to the faithful few. For six months, a weekly fifteen-minute radio broadcast, "La Chapelle," beamed the gospel in French to the residents of the Peninsula.[24] In 1956, after a prolonged attempt to purchase a church building, an old Hungarian Presbyterian church building became the home of Chapelle Chrétienne Evangélique, in Welland.[25]

In November 1955, in response to the invitation of a small group of evangelical French Christians in Cornwall, Ontario, Richardson commenced a monthly week of services in that city in addition to his work in Welland. In September 1956, the Cornwall group made application to the district office to establish a mission work in Cornwall, with Richardson as the missionary.[26] During the conference of 1956, James McQuade, a new worker "acquainted with the French language," was approved for ministry in Welland under Richardson's general supervision, thus enabling Richardson to spend more time in Cornwall.[27]

A Broadening Support Base

McQuade's appointment released Richardson temporarily for another important task. By that time, the Home Department was beginning to think of an integrated home evangelism program. In Canada, this pointed to a better inter-district cooperation, in order to meet the larger Canadian need. In response to an invitation from some western churches (with the blessing of District Superintendent Blackett) to present the urgent need of French Canada, Richardson made a seven-week tour in October 1956 of 24 cities and towns from Fort William to Victoria. The round trip of some 9,000 miles consisted of 43 presentations to some 6,000 persons.[28]

From that time onward, an increasing number of contributions flowed from the west to help push back the frontier of spiritual darkness in the east. The east was now beckoning to the west for help. The historic tide had turned![29]

Coinciding with this development, the district executive committee appointed an ad hoc French Work Committee, consisting of Revs. R. G. Simpson of London, D. R. Shepson and L. L. Brooker of Toronto "to consider the whole question of the French work."[30] In January 1957, this committee issued a detailed report with recommendations that would become the basis for financial and administrative policies of the French work program for many years to come.[31]

At the end of January 1957, McQuade took over the Welland work fully, and Cornwall became the full-time responsibility of Richardson.[32] By September, Richardson was able to report that his original Cornwall congregation of "two soundly converted families" had grown to 24, from Huguenot, Lutheran, Baptist, Presbyterian, Brethren and Pentecostal backgrounds.[33] The congregation first met in a school auditorium, then in December 1957 a large old house was

9.8 Jean Heidman teaches a group of children in Québec City.

9.9 In May 1959, Jean Heidman persuaded District Superintendent Bailey and Pastor Robert Richardson of Cornwall of the urgency to commence the evangelization of French Canadians in Québec.

9.10 A group in front of the Chouinard Avenue chapel/parsonage in Québec City, during 1961.

382 / *Canada's Other Sheep*

9.11

9.11 Formerly the St. Andrews Presbyterian Church, this fine old building in Lévis became the permanent church home of La Mission Chrétienne Evangélique in 1961.

9.12 Rev. Raymond Deitz, pastor of the Alliance Community Church in Montréal provided a valuable link between the district superintendent in Toronto and the French workers in Québec.

9.13 The Lévis congregation meets for Bible study under the ministry of Jean Heidman and Mabel Quinlan.

9.12

9.13

rented, which provided for "an attractive chapel" on the ground floor and a parsonage on the upper floor.[34]

All appeared to be going well, when in the spring of 1958, Richardson's health began to falter. He rallied during the summer and in September was appointed "head of the French Work" of the district.[35] In November he was forced to take a complete rest for a month, but by the end of the year he seemed to be much improved. The improvement was short-lived; in February 1959, he suffered a serious nervous breakdown, requiring hospitalization. For several weeks his wife, Elise, kept the Sunday services going, but by April they had to be discontinued. It was not until July that Bob Richardson was able to resume work. By that time his erstwhile congregation had dispersed and settled in English-language churches.

Nor was that all the bad news. As early as February 1959, the district executive committee had to face up to the fact that the Welland church was in an alarming state of decline. As a result, a few months later it was placed on "final trial."[36] It appeared that the bright hopes for a French ministry in Ontario were coming to naught.

A Productive Partnership

At this very time of distress and discouragement, a remarkable series of "coincidences" occurred. Back in January 1952, while on colportage work with the Canadian Bible Society in Québec City, Mabel Quinlan met four young ladies who were conducting colportage work for a new Brethren Assembly. Among these was Jean Heidman, from Toronto. Mabel and Jean became fast friends. Five years later, Mabel left the employ of the Canadian Bible Society and commenced working in fellowship with Jean and other Brethren workers.

In the spring of 1959, the Brethren Assembly suffered a sad disintegration. During this crisis, Mabel and Jean entertained Alliance missionaries Rev. and Mrs. Alwyn Rees on their way to Africa. The two told their guests about their need for a church and pastor with whom they could work. The Reeses answered a few of Jean's questions about the Alliance and mentioned that the annual Alliance Council was due to convene in Buffalo from May 13-18. Jean decided to visit her home in Toronto, and from there attend some of the Council meetings and also try to arrange an interview with District Superintendent Bailey. Jean subsequently attended the Council services of Sunday, May 17. She returned to Toronto prepared to cast in her lot with the Alliance provided it was prepared to establish a French-language bridgehead in Québec City.

The historic interview with District Superintendent Bailey, which took place in the district office on May 21, was also attended by Rev. L. L. Brooker of the Yonge Street Tabernacle. From all accounts it was cordial but non-committal. Jean stated her case. She and Mabel wanted to become co-workers with an Alliance pastor in Québec City. The district superintendent suggested that she have a talk with Bob Richardson. However, Bailey's letter to Richardson, reporting the interview and impending visit, merely mentioned that Miss Heidman had called "about the possibility of becoming associated in some way with our French work."[37]

Jean Heidman visited the Richardsons in their Cornwall home four days later.[38] It is Jean's recollection that the visit came to life when she proposed a team of four, working to establish a French-language Alliance church in Québec City and disclosed the existence of several converted families without a church home, and an unused Brethren chapel.

In the interest of first establishing a working relationship, it was agreed that Jean and Mabel would spend the month of July with the Richardsons in a final colportage ministry in Cornwall.[39]

Early in August, after the women returned to Québec City, the Richardsons visited the city to see for themselves what had been told them. Convinced that a move to Québec was the thing to do, Richardson returned to Ontario, asked for and obtained the superintendent's approval to officially close the work in Cornwall, and move to Québec City, effective September 15.[40]

The Richardsons made the "surprise move" (to use his own words) at the beginning of September. Reporting the development to conference later that month, District Superintendent Bailey stated:

> It has been upon our hearts for a number of years that our testimony to the French Canadians should be in the Province of Québec. It now seems that the Lord is answering prayer. . . . When the work at Cornwall was without consistent leadership, the congregation returned to former congregations . . . and it was felt that God was pushing us out into the more direct responsibility of a ministry in French Canada. Because of this and other providential happenings, the Richardsons have moved to Québec City.[41]

Among "other providential happenings" was Jean Heidman's determined attempt to prod the Alliance leadership into taking action in Québec City. Without her initiative and drive, it is unlikely that the Alliance would have entered French Québec at what turned out to be the crucial time and location. Reporting to conference that same month, Bob Richardson closed his lengthy report from Québec City, with the ringing challenge:

> We are confident that you will fully realize this to be the greatest hour of opportunity that has come to us in our French work. Also, we are sure you will not hesitate to make a definite commitment with your churches to pray and help us as never before in our enlarged ministry, its additional challenges, responsibilities and needs, and for continuing daily strength and health for all workers. "En avant, sous la bannière de la Croix."[42]

With the Richardsons' move to Québec City, Mabel Quinlan and Jean Heidman were recognized as "associate workers."[43] On December 21, they were examined and credentialed as "missionaries in the French work of the District."[44]

At first it was hoped to be able to rent the disused Brethren chapel on Belvedere Street, before commencing regular services. However, it became evident that the trustees had not yet abandoned the hope of reopening the chapel for Brethren use.[45] So weekly Bible studies and prayer sessions were commenced in the Richardson's apartment in September. Almost immediately Richardson found that "it is impractical and inadvisable to continue meetings much longer in our home ... as we have five other tenants in the apartment block, all Roman Catholics, and we have indulged almost to the limit of their tolerance."[46] An application to rent a room in the YMCA was turned down for fear of a resulting disturbance.[47] Finally, the hall of St. George's School (the only Protestant school in the city), was rented, and the first service held there on October 18, with 24 persons present.[48] So La Mission Chrétienne Evangélique Française was founded in Québec City.

Montréal Developments

Another Alliance French-language church in Québec had its start in October 1959. During the previous month, French-speaking attendees of the Alliance Community Church (formerly the Alliance Gospel Hall/Alliance Chapel) on Pie IX Boulevard in the north end of

Montréal, approached their pastor, Rev. Raymond Deitz, about the possibility of holding French-language services. Raymond Taylor, who had been the first student at Bethel Bible School and was now a French-speaking Brethren worker and husband of the former Marguerite Giguère, was willing to conduct services in French for the Alliance for a six-month period, but because of his commitment to the Brethren, could not devote time to home visitation.[49] Under the authority of Pastor Deitz, Taylor and his able wife started services in the lower hall of the Alliance Community Church on October 11 with 25 persons present.[50] Thus, two French-language Alliance churches had their start simultaneously, one in Montréal and one in Québec City. For the small English-language Alliance church in the north end of Montréal, it was the second time it had been involved in holding French-language church services (page 371).

Realizing that the arrangement with the Taylors was temporary, Pastor Deitz made vigorous requests of District Superintendent Bailey for a full-time qualified pastor for his French congregation. On December 1 he wrote:

> I am greatly concerned about our French congregation in respect to a pastor or worker.... Such a fine, ready made congregation must not be left shepherdless.... When you get 35 to 40 people with no visitation or regular pastoral work among French people, it is not something to let slide out of our hands.[51]

Bailey replied, "The work of the French people is indeed most encouraging.... It is too good to drop and we must plan to do something."[52] What that might be was not stated. Bailey's problem was two-fold: How could he find a French-speaking Alliance homeland worker, and if he did, how could he find the money for his support?

In December, Taylor was asked to become an Alliance worker, but declined. In March 1960, James McQuade resigned from the tottering work at Welland to assume duties with the Canadian Sunday School Mission. The Welland work was then closed and McQuade's support transferred to the French work in Montréal. Accordingly, Edouard Barbin,* a graduating student of Canadian

---

* Edouard Jean Baptiste Barbin, a native of Québec, was converted from Catholicism while on active service with the Royal Canadian Navy.

Bible College, was examined, approved and appointed pastor of Mission Chrétienne Evangélique Française, Montréal, effective in September 1960.[53]

The apparent burst of opportunity for the Alliance in French Québec was no illusion. The founding of the two churches in Québec City and Montréal coincided with the beginning of what is generally known as the "quiet revolution" in Québec. Following the demise that year of Québec's ultra-conservative premier, Maurice Duplessis, and the changes in the Roman Catholic Church brought on by the Second Vatican Council, Québécois entered a period of self-examination and self-assertion. They discovered a new freedom from church control and began to make far-reaching changes in the life of their province. A new openness to the evangelical gospel appeared.

The unprecedented change caught most evangelicals by surprise, including the Alliance. Following the unplanned opening of the two new French churches in Montréal and Québec, the district became alive to the opportunities in French Québec, but the Home Department apparently remained unmoved. The district conference of 1960 spent much time discussing the Québec situation and the delegates concluded that the district was unable to obtain French-speaking workers or to financially support them if they were available. It seemed to the delegates that Québec must be placed under the jurisdiction of the Foreign Department, and a motion was entered, as follows:

> In view of the sentiments expressed by conference, we move that this conference communicate with the Foreign Secretary that consideration be given by the Foreign Department to the end that the work in French Canada be operated on the basis of a foreign mission field.[54]

After further discussion, during which the more politically-minded delegates urged caution, the following substitute motion was carried:

> In view of the sentiments expressed by Conference, we move that this conference communicate with the Home Secretary that unusual consideration be given by the Home Department to the end that the work in French Canada be operated with greater interest and support of the Home Department.[55]

However, the Home Department would take no significant action in this regard for many more years to come.

BEGINNINGS IN LÉVIS

Early that same month, the district purchased a large house on Chouinard Street in Québec City to serve as chapel and living quarters for the Richardsons, Jean Heidman, and Mabel Quinlan.[56] The new facility, which would serve the congregation for nine years, was dedicated on October 9.[57]

The winter of 1960-61 was a "time of testing" for the Richardsons. The strain of being "head of the French Work" and pastor of the new work in Québec City proved to be too much for him. Coupled with the traumatic loss of an infant daughter, he suffered another severe breakdown in health which affected working relationships. In the spring of 1961, he was relieved of all responsibility outside of Québec City, but carried on as pastor of the Québec church without the assistance of Mabel Quinlan and Jean Heidman.[58]

At the same time, the district extension committee urged the formation of a "French Work Committee," with Rev. Raymond Deitz as "chairman and co-ordinator," to "give guidance to the ministry to French speaking Canadians."[59] The district executive committee approved this plan,[60] and during conference that year appointed Raymond Deitz, William Newell, Gordon Wishart, Paul Valentine, Lindsay Reynolds and Sidney Grierson as the founding members of the French Work Committee.[61] This committee would supply a general coordinating function for the French work program for the next ten years.

The decision to detach Jean Heidman and Mabel Quinlan from the work in Québec City presented no problem in reassignment. During the summer of 1960, the two had distributed tracts in Lévis and Lauzon, across the river from Québec City. Towards the end of the year, they followed up resulting contacts and, just before Christmas, two women in Lévis professed faith in Christ. Armed with this encouragement, Jean and Mabel continued their follow-up work. In January, a man and his wife knelt to receive Christ as Saviour. There seemed to be good reason to believe that the area, totally devoid of any other evangelical witness, would be a responsive mission field.

While in Lévis, the women discovered the unused building of the defunct St. Andrews Presbyterian Church, which contained a chapel and apartment. In February 1961, Jean Heidman reported their experiences and findings in Lévis to District Superintendent Newell, adding:

> Mabel and I have been wondering if the Alliance would give us permission to move to Lévis and start a new work there.[62]

The district superintendent readily (and perhaps even eagerly) gave his consent.[63] The trustees of the old church building allowed the Alliance to occupy the premises for two years free of charge, as of May 1, provided they carried out a few rather minor repairs.[64] The women moved to Lévis at the beginning of May, and by June 1 the repairs, renovations, cleaning and redecorating were essentially complete at a total cost of $854. About two weeks later, the first service of La Mission Chrétienne Evangélique, Lévis, was held, with two French Canadians and two English-speaking visitors present.[65] Within fifteen months the missionaries were able to report attendances of as high as fourteen. Thirty-eight Roman Catholics had attended at least one service and there had been eight professions of faith.[66]

A FOUNDATION IS LAID

The Montréal venture was not as encouraging. The early good attendance under Raymond Taylor was not maintained under Edouard Barbin. By August 1963 only three or four were present for the Sunday morning service. Several of the early lay leaders had drifted over to Raymond Taylor's services, under Brethren auspices. The French Work Committee expressed "grave concern," and the district executive committee decided to terminate Barbin's ministry in Montréal. As no replacement could be found, the services were "temporarily suspended" as of September 29.[67] The suspension would remain in effect for six years.

The Home Department provided summaries of six "home missions" projects to the Council of May 1965. Among them was "The French Canadians," which it stated was "regarded by many people to be a great unreached mission field."[68] Four months later, with some exasperation, Rev. Richard G. Simpson, by that time pastor of the Alliance Community Church in Montréal, and chairman of the French Work Committee, submitted to the district conference a challenging report on behalf of the committee, in which he stated:

The Spirit which made the Apostle Paul a pioneer missionary in the first century has been the motivation for Alliance missionary advances into territories never before exploited for Christ.

While this is true of our foreign missionary program, we have been traditionally led to believe that a distinction must be made when we seek to evangelize people living within the scope of our own country; so we call this "Home Missions." But what does the Bible call it? Under the divine compulsion we are instructed to "Go into all the world beginning at Jerusalem." Would it then be correct to call our ten provinces in the Dominion of Canada our "Jerusalem?" Thus, Québec is an immediate obligation under the name of Foreign Missions. . . .

We must be alert to the opportunities that are expanding in this revolutionary day. A positive approach is imperative. Will God give to us a new day in French Canada? And if He does, what will we do to redeem the wasted years? Must we be prepared to employ any new methods available and pray for a rebirth of the old if we are to be found worthy of God's merciful goodness. . . .

It is our candid opinion that the time is before us for advance into new areas of operation heretofore neglected. We must appeal to the Home and Foreign Departments in New York for the kind of assistance that will mean men and money at our disposal. . . . We ask of this Conference a dedication to the task, calling for prayer—fervent prayer—prevailing prayer; yea, fasting and prayer. God wants to work; and without Him all of our efforts shall be in vain. God grant us the joy of bringing new life, and light and deliverance to our "foreign French neighbours" in Canada.[69]

Three months later, T. A. (Phil) Reeve, a lay leader in the Avenue Road Church, Toronto, dispatched a pleading letter to the President's Council in New York, with copies to the President, Foreign Secretary, Home Secretary, and District Superintendent Newell. In that letter Reeve wrote:

For some time, many of us have been aware of the tremendous opportunity and challenge to get the gospel into our

French Province of Québec . . . with a population of approximately 5 million.

However, Roman Catholicism does hold complete sway here so that very few things are done without the prior approval of the priest. It has the most dense Roman Catholic population in the world next to the Vatican.

We in the Alliance send missionaries to Colombia, Viet Nam, etc., and rightly so. However, a province completely Roman Catholic and French speaking has hardly had a dent made by the evangelical church.

Brethren, should we not be making a major thrust into this large area ripe for the Gospel? Does it not seem incredible that in North America, this Christian land, that we have neglected our own "Jerusalem?"

May I, as a layman, encourage you to launch into an immediate full scale effort to reach these 5 million people of Canada. Whether you call it Home Missions, Foreign or what, the fact remains that this situation is unique and I believe there is nothing in the U.S.A. of a similar nature.[70]

During the district conference of September 1966, District Superintendent Newell announced:

Our ministry to French speaking Canadians has been included in the program of the Home Department to nationalize all home missions projects within the Society. The details of this program will reach us presently as it receives the continuing attention of New York Boards. We believe it will greatly benefit our thrust in the Province of Québec.

However, help came slowly. It would be another six years before tangible help in the form of "special grants from the Home Department" would assist in the expansion of the French work in Québec.[71]

Despite the continuing cry for "men and money," an Alliance ministry to French Canadians had been successfully established by 1966. The churches in Québec City and Lévis would prove to be the centre of operations. Since 1927, many had made their contributions to the spread of the gospel in Québec, and new reinforcements were, in fact, now on the way for a new forward thrust. However, the real heroes who laid the lasting foundations were missionaries Bob and Elise Richardson, Jean Heidman and Mabel Quinlan.* But for their faith and intrepidity during those seven formative years, there would be no beachhead story to tell.

REFERENCES

1. Lindsay Reynolds, *Footprints* (Toronto: The Christian and Missionary Alliance in Canada, 1982), pp. 277, 279, 280.
2. *The Prophet* (Toronto), Apr 1924, p. 17.
3. Eastern and Central Canadian District, Annual Report of the Branches, 1928, Montreal.
4. Ibid.; Letter, Meadows to Williams, 16 Oct 1928.
5. Ibid.; Annual Report of the Branches, 1930, Montreal.
6. Home Department, Minutes, 9 Jun 1930.
7. *Alliance Weekly*, 17 Oct 1931, p. 685.
8. Ibid., 29 Oct 1931, p. 252; ibid., 28 Nov 1931, p. 784; Eastern and Central Canadian District, Report of the Branches, Montreal, 1932.
9. Child Evangelism, May 1942, p. 21.
10. Ibid.
11. *Alliance Weekly*, 20 Mar 1943, p. 192.
12. Child Evangelism, Oct 1944, p. 6.
13. Scripture Press, *Power*, 6 Dec 1959, p. 7.
14. Ibid.
15. Eastern, Conference, Sep 1948, pp. 6, 7, 21.
16. Eastern, Minutes, 27 Sep 1948, p. 1.
17. Eastern and Central Canadian District, Letter, Bailey to Richardson, 25 Oct 1950; ibid., Webster to Bailey, 9 Nov 1950; ibid., Richardson to Bailey, 13 Nov 1950; ibid., Webster to Bailey, 29 Jan 1951.
18. Eastern, Minutes, 12 Sep 1951.
19. Ibid., 17 Oct 1951; Home Department, Minutes, 28 Nov 1951.
20. Eastern, Letter, Richardson to Bailey, 13 Nov 1950.
21. Eastern, Annual, Sep 1953, Superintendent's Report, pp. 14, 15, 16.
22. *Alliance Weekly*, 13 May 1953, p. 6.
23. Eastern, Annual, Sep 1954, Report of Home Missions to French Canadians, p. 33.
24. Ibid., p. 31.
25. Ibid., Sep 1956, Report of French Canadian Work, p. 37.

---

*Jean Heidman and Mabel Quinlan would continue to give valuable service in the cause of French evangelism under the Alliance banner for 21 years.

Canada's Other Sheep / 393

26. Eastern, Annual, Sep 1956, Superintendent's Report, p. 16.
27. Eastern, Minutes, 20 Sep 1956.
28. Eastern, Annual, Sep 1957, Report of French Canadian Work, p. 46.
29. Ibid., p. 58.
30. Eastern, Minutes, 17 Dec 1940.
31. Eastern, Annual, Sep 1957, p. 46.
32. Ibid.; *Welland Evening Tribune*, 29 Jan 1957, p. 6.
33. Eastern, Annual, Sep 1957, p. 48.
34. "Outlook," Dec 1957, p. 6; Eastern, Annual, Sep 1958, French Work, p. 39.
35. Eastern, Minutes, 17 Sep 1958.
36. Eastern, Churches, Cornwall, Letter, Bailey to Richardson, 11 Feb 1959; ibid., Richardson to Bailey, 14 Feb 1959; ibid., Welland, Letter, Bailey to McQuade, 6 Jan 1960.
37. Ibid., Cornwall, Letter, Bailey to Richardson, 22 May 1959.
38. Ibid., Richardson to Bailey, 1 Jun 1959.
39. Ibid.
40. Ibid., Richardson to Bailey, 7 Aug 1959.
41. Eastern, Annual, Sep 1959, Superintendent's Report, pp 15, 16.
42. Ibid., Report of French Work, p. 43.
43. Eastern, Minutes, 23 Sep 1959, p. 4; "Outlook," Fall 1959, p. 5.
44. Eastern, Minutes (sub-committee), 21 Dec 1959; *Alliance Witness*, 13 Jan 1960, p. 15.
45. Eastern, Churches, Quebec, Letter, Richardson to Bailey, 3 Sep 1959.
46. Ibid., 1 Oct 1959.
47. Ibid., 21 Oct 1959.
48. Ibid.; ibid., 31 Oct 1959; French Work Newsletter, Christmas 1959.
49. Eastern, Churches, Montreal, Letter, Deitz to Bailey, 1 Dec 1959.
50. Ibid., 19 Oct 1959; ibid., Quebec, Letter, Richardson to Bailey, 21 Oct 1959; Eastern, Minutes, 21 Dec 1959.
51. Eastern, Churches, Montreal, Letter, Deitz to Bailey, 1 Dec 1959.
52. Ibid., Bailey to Deitz, 4 Dec 1959.
53. Eastern, Minutes, 9 Aug 1960, p. 2; "Outlook," Oct 1960, p. 2.
54. Eastern, Annual, 1960, p. 10.
55. Ibid., p. 11.
56. Eastern, Minutes, 23 Sep 1960.
57. "Outlook," Oct 1960, p. 4.
58. Eastern, Minutes, Extension Committee, 17 Mar 1961, p. 4; Eastern, Annual, French Work, 1961, p. 46.
59. Eastern, Annual, French Work, 1961, p. 46c.
60. Eastern, Minutes, 7 Jul 1961.

394 / *Canada's Other Sheep*

61. Eastern, Minutes, 18 Sep 1961.
62. Eastern, Churches, Quebec, Letter, Heidman to Newell, 3 Feb 1961; ibid., 27 Feb 1961.
63. Ibid., Newell to Heidman, 1 Mar 1961
64. Ibid., Royal Trust Co. to C&MA, 6 Apr 1961.
65. Ibid., Lévis, Letter, Heidman to Newell, 7 Jun 1961.
66. Eastern, Annual, French Work Committee, 1962, p. 43.
67. Eastern, Minutes, 21 Aug 1963, pp. 2, 3, 5; Eastern, Annual, Sep 1963, p. 57.
68. Annual Report, May 1965, p. 177.
69. Eastern, Annual, Sep 1965, French Work Committee, pp. 41, 43.
70. Eastern, Churches, Avenue Road, Letter, Reeve to President's Council, 3 Dec 1965.
71. Annual Report, May 1972, p. 202.

CHAPTER TEN

Canadian Identity Again

In the mid-1960s, Canadian churches in general were still basking in the sunshine of a post-war popularity. Some of the older and larger denominations had passed their peaks of influence, but several of the newer and smaller groups were still experiencing remarkable growth. Outstanding among the latter were the Pentecostals and, to a lesser extent, the Alliance (see figure 3). From 1966 to 1980, the Alliance in Canada grew from 157 to 229 local churches—an average annual growth rate of 2.4 percent. At the same time, the total of members and adherents grew at the rate of 5.3 percent annually. Thus, the ministry was both spreading and growing.

In 1966, General Council convened in the Queen Elizabeth Theatre in Vancouver, from May 11-16. The featured speaker was Dr. Stephen F. Olford, of Calvary Baptist Church in New York. On the Sunday afternoon, the missionary rally was held in the Agrodome, on the Pacific National Exposition Grounds.[1]

Eleven years later, the same district was again host to General Council, which, on that occasion, convened in the Convention Centre of the Four Seasons Hotel in Calgary, from May 10-15, 1977. Public services were held in the Southern Alberta Jubilee Auditorium, and the featured speaker was Dr. J. Glyn Owen, of Knox Presbyterian Church, Toronto. On that occasion, Rev. Edwin T. Holt (see pages 83, 84) was honoured for his "fifty-one years of pastoral work" in Canada.[2] As events would turn out, this would be the last General Council of the Alliance, headquartered in the United States, to be held in Canada. Over a period of 53 years, three had been held in Toronto and one each in Ottawa, Winnipeg, Vancouver and Calgary.

Between 1966 and 1978, the Western Canadian District, under Rev. Roy McIntyre, surpassed the other two Canadian districts with an average annual increase in number of churches of 3.5 percent for the twelve-year period. With 92 churches under its care, the district was sub-divided on January 1, 1979, releasing its 57 churches in British Columbia to form a new Canadian Pacific District, under the superintendency of Rev. Gordon Fowler.

On December 31, 1980, McIntyre retired from the superintendency. When he had first taken on the job in January 1960, the Western Canadian District included the 78 churches in the territory west of the eighty-eighth meridian (just east of Thunder Bay) to the Pacific Ocean. When he retired 21 years later, his territory consisted only of Alberta and northward with 66 churches. However, by then there were 168 churches within the scope of his former large territory. Of this increase of 90 churches, 68 were attributable to his superintendence. Thus ended a remarkable pastoral and superintendent career of close to 46 years.*

The first superintendent of the new Canadian Pacific District, Rev. Gordon Fowler, was no stranger to either British Columbia or Alberta. Born in Calgary of Christian parents (see pages 221 and 270) who had been long active in gospel work and the development of First Alliance Church in Calgary, he recalled coming into the kingdom through the influence of his brother:

> It was as a nine year old boy that my two year older brother, Gerry, talked to me in the darkness of the night in our bedroom. His conversation was quite impassioned as he expressed to me his concern for me, and my need to invite the Lord Jesus into my heart. In the quietness and darkness of the night I slipped out of my bed and knelt beside it, and at his instruction prayed the "penitent prayer." I have often shared this with people by saying that the greatest event in my life happened in the greatest place in my life, amongst the greatest people in my life.

---

* Among his many accomplishments, McIntyre was instrumental in establishing a Christian Publications outlet in Calgary. Since he took office in 1960, the district office handled all Sunday school supplies coming from Christian Publications in the United States for all western Canada. In 1976, McIntyre persuaded Christian Publications to open its own bookstore in Calgary. In September of that year, the district purchased a building on 17th Avenue S.W. The district office located on the upper floor, and Christian Publications occupied the ground floor.

After graduation from Canadian Bible College in 1957, Gordon Fowler married Eleanor McArthur, daughter of the president of the college. He served as assistant pastor of the Tenth Avenue Church in Vancouver for four years, and as founding pastor of the Surrey church for another four years. The Fowlers then became Alliance missionaries in Hawaii for five years (see page 319). Returning to Canada in 1970, he was pastor of the Foothills Alliance Church, Calgary, until appointed to the superintendency eight years later.

The Canadian Pacific District held its first annual conference in Penticton, from September 18-21, 1979. District Superintendent Fowler welcomed Rev. Melvin Sylvester, superintendent of the Eastern and Central Canadian District, as the official deputation of the board of managers. This was the only occasion that a Canadian resident appeared at a Canadian district conference in that capacity. Because of his involvement in the movement towards Canadian autonomy, Sylvester had come at the special request of President Louis L. King.

At Roy McIntyre's retirement, Rev. Harvey A. Town became superintendent of the Western Canadian District. Born into a Christian home in Portal, North Dakota, Harvey Town was converted when seventeen years of age. In 1955, he graduated from Canadian Bible College and married Joyce Lewis. The couple served as Alliance missionaries in Japan for twelve years. After returning home, and a six-year Alliance pastorate in Great Falls, Montana, Town became pastor of Beulah Church in Edmonton for four years before his appointment to the superintendency. Under his leadership, the district continued its well-above-average growth rate.

Western Revival

In September 1971, a revival broke out in western Canada which drew the attention of the Alliance fellowship throughout North America. It started in Prince George, British Columbia, when God broke upon that community through the ministry of visiting evangelists Lou and Ralph Sutera of First Alliance Church in Mansfield, Ohio. Moving on to Saskatoon for an October campaign, meetings were held in the Ebenezer Baptist Church. Along with revival preaching, the twins were backed by testimonies of beneficiaries of earlier Sutera campaigns. According to contemporary reports, it was the "unbelievable power of the testimonies" that brought on a massive wave of repentance.

398 / *Canadian Identity Again*

The first service in Saskatoon was attended by about 200 persons. Four days later, the church could not accommodate the crowds, so the meetings were relocated to a larger Anglican church. When that became inadequate, the University Drive Alliance Church offered its 800-seat sanctuary. When that also proved too small, the campaign secured the 1,800-seat Third Avenue United Church sanctuary.

Rev. H. Robert Cowles, editor of the *Alliance Witness*, came to Saskatoon to observe, and reported:

> On the night that I was there, two thousand people jammed every available square foot... [while] four hundred were across town in an overflow meeting in the Alliance church.... In rhythm with the waves of sound from the great pipe organ, the united voices of the Holy Spirit moved out over that pillared sanctuary, bathing us in the exhilaration of His presence.... The service lasted until well past ten o'clock, yet there was no restlessness or inattention.
>
> A ladies trio—a "transformed trio," Ralph Sutera called them—preceded their number with glowing testimonies.
>
> At the invitation to "share," several made their way at once to the platform.... A tall fellow... bared his coldness of heart and testified to Christ's complete infilling. A well-dressed middle-aged lady told of being cleansed from selfishness. A youth, a bit nervously, confessed to restitution he had made....
>
> The unhurried sharing lasted a couple of hours. Then Ralph... invited those with spiritual needs to go to a downstairs prayer room.... It was ten-thirty when the audience was finally dismissed, but the night was far from over. Probably two hundred made their way to the Alliance church to the announced "afterglow" session.
>
> In the informality of that after session, the sharing time continued.... The conviction of hearts was quiet but compelling.... Church elders confessed to sin in their lives.[3]

"I thought I had the best church in the district and maybe in the Alliance," said Pastor Walter Boldt of the Alliance church to Cowles, "but after the revelations of these weeks I wonder how we ever managed to hold things together."[4]

Revivals of similar character broke out in Moose Jaw, Regina and Winnipeg.

Pastor Wilbert McLeod of the Ebenezer Baptist Church in Saskatoon visited the Central Baptist Seminary in Toronto, and it was reported that the Holy Spirit fell "as he shared the revival blessings with students and faculty." Between the emotional sessions, student Edward Angrove telephoned his pastor, Rev. Raymond Deitz of the Alliance Tabernacle, urging him to come right away to witness the astonishing spectacle. It was reported that the dean remarked, "God accomplished more in a day and a half than in the last fifteen years."[5]

In the Eastern and Central Canadian District, Superintendent William Newell organized a small itinerant revival team, which featured the public confessions of the team members. However, generally, the attempt in the east was unsuccessful, where the large-scale public confessions of wrongdoing were not appreciated. The lesson to be learned was that the Holy Spirit has His own times, places and methods.

The revival continued in the west for four or five months, and left those provinces spiritually enriched and invigorated. As District Superintendent Roy McIntyre expressed it, "A spiritual awareness has come to Western Canada."[6] District Superintendent Alf Orthner was more specific. "During 1972," he said, "God gave us an increase of over one hundred percent in conversions, and a good increase in baptisms. This, of course, can be partly attributed to the Holy Spirit revival that so graciously swept through our churches."[7]

The effect on the University Drive Alliance Church in Saskatoon was dramatic. After the Sutera revival, the congregation decided it needed a larger building. A debt of $173,000 on the old 800-seat structure was liquidated in just nine months, while giving to foreign missions and local needs increased. "We began to realize our challenges were not great enough," commented Pastor Walter Boldt. "Small plans do not inflame great minds."[8]

A 30-acre piece of land on Circle Drive on the fringe of the city was purchased, and in November 1979, a magnificent 70,000-square-foot complex, costing $3.2 million, was dedicated in the presence of Alliance President Dr. L. L. King. Reporting a later visit to "the world's largest Christian and Missionary Alliance church," in terms of its 2,100-seat capacity, *Alliance Witness* editor Rev. Robert Cowles wrote:

> To those who might feel not all of this is absolute necessity, Mr. Boldt has an answer. "We do not save the Lord's money, we invest it."[9]

The building of large Canadian Alliance church complexes did not begin in Saskatoon. In 1968, First Alliance Church of Calgary, under Rev. Lowell Young, sold its 700-seat church building on 17th Avenue and built an 1,100-seat (later expanded to 1,700) sanctuary on a 4.5-acre site on Glenmore Trail. When dedicated in December 1969, it was the largest new sanctuary for the Alliance in Canada since the completion of the Ottawa Gospel Tabernacle in 1924.

Thus began a trend among visionary congregations towards "super churches."* However, the concept of an expensive complex with various social and physical amenities, although more common in the United States, was still generally viewed in Canada with both admiration and uncertainty. History leaves us with many warnings about very large and costly church structures. Frequently they come into existence through the appeal of a charismatic ministry or local enthusiasm. Whatever the reason, the appeal eventually disappears, and the congregation size and financial support dwindles. It is seldom possible to restore the early fortunes, and the building becomes a burden and embarrassment. Both the Toronto and Ottawa tabernacles were classic examples. The philosophy of daughtering other churches has generally yielded longer-term benefits.

In September 1975, the board of managers appointed Rev. Alf Orthner as General Director of Canadian Ministries, to take effect "as soon as possible." One month later, the Canadian Midwest District elected its assistant to the superintendent, Robert (Bob) J. Gould, as its new superintendent in Orthner's place.** Under Orthner, the Canadian Midwest District had experienced twelve years of moderate growth, increasing the number of its churches from 41 to 56—an

---

* Large complexes have been erected at Bayview Glen (Toronto), Sherwood Park (Edmonton), Cranbrook, B.C., Sevenoaks (Abbotsford, B.C.) and Beulah (Edmonton).

**Robert Gould, a native of Moose Jaw, was converted when thirteen years of age. Shortly thereafter, during the challenge of a missionary convention, he consecrated his life to the full-time service of God. After completing high school he entered Canadian Bible College, graduating in 1960. After pastorates in Invermere, B.C., Assiniboia, Saskatchewan, and Morden, Manitoba, he became assistant to the superintendent for special ministries in the Canadian Midwest District.

average growth rate of 2.7 percent.[10] Under Rev. Robert Gould, the growth continued.

EDUCATIONAL INITIATIVES

A growing concern for the loss of its young people to non-Alliance institutions of learning was chiefly responsible for the appointment in 1960 of the first full-time education secretary, Dr. Gilbert Johnson. That same year, Jaffray School of Missions was opened on the Nyack campus. However, the new institution's one-year course in theology, missiology and sociology beyond the baccalaureate level had limited appeal to students desiring post-graduate degrees.*

The General Council of 1963 then designated Wheaton Graduate School of Theology as the "officially recognized" seminary of The Christian and Missionary Alliance, until an Alliance seminary could be established. Johnson and Dr. Merrill C. Tenney, dean of the seminary, agreed that Alliance students, in addition to following the Wheaton curriculum, would follow a special "Alliance course," featuring Alliance polity, doctrinal emphasis and missionary methods, taught by a teacher "of our own choosing." Graduates of Nyack Missionary College (which a year previously was accredited by the Middle States Association of Colleges and was becoming a liberal arts college), would not be required to take entrance tests, but those of all other Alliance colleges would have to do so or make their own "special arrangements" with Wheaton.[11] The plan was not received in Canada with much enthusiasm.

The question of a post-graduate Alliance theological education in Canada was then taken up by President Dr. Alvin Martin and Academic Dean Dr. Samuel Stoesz, shortly after the latter's arrival in Regina in 1965. In response to their urging and the approval of the Education Department, the General Council of 1967 authorized Canadian Bible College to develop its own graduate school, consistent with Canadian needs and possibilities. In the fall of 1970, a graduate school was opened on the campus of Canadian Bible College (CBC), with an enrollment of twenty students.[12]

---

* The Jaffray School of Missions became the Alliance School of Theology and Missions in 1974, with a two-year course leading to the Master of Professional Studies, and in 1979, with a full three-year seminary program leading to the Master of Divinity, became the Alliance Theological Seminary.

On March 29, 1973, the Saskatchewan legislature granted Canadian Theological College (CTC) a provincial charter, and on June 2 of the same year, the graduate school was approved as an affiliate of the University of Saskatchewan.[13] Under this arrangement, the granting of master's degrees in divinity, missions and religious education became recognized. Although sharing the campus and general facilities with CBC, CTC moved into its own classroom and office building and appointed its own dean in 1979.[14]

In June 1982, by means of a private bill in the Saskatchewan Legislature, the name of Canadian Theological College was changed to Canadian Theological Seminary. The same month, the seminary was granted associate standing with the Association of Theological Schools in the United States and Canada.*[15]

Dr. Alvin Martin resigned from the presidency of CBC/CTC in 1972, to pursue further studies,[16] and was replaced by Dr. David Rambo, a professor at CBC and former Alliance missionary to the Philippines, with earned doctorates from New York University and Southern Baptist Theological Seminary.[17] His eight-year presidency was characterized by a 50 percent growth in student enrollment and major campus additions. He resigned in 1979 to become president of the Nyack educational institutions, and was replaced in Regina by Rexford A. Boda, the academic dean.[18] In 1982, the present beautiful 1,000-seat chapel was completed and the Centre for Evangelism established.

Eastern Developments

In 1970, for the third and last time, General Council convened in Toronto,** where it had all begun, insofar as the propagation of the Fourfold Gospel in Canada is concerned. "Toronto the good," as it was known in the time of Mayor William H. Howland, first president of the Alliance in Canada, had by 1970 undergone much change. Rev. G. B. Smith, assistant to President Nathan Bailey stated:

> The City . . . has been "switched on" in recent years, with an explosion of modern energy and creativity that even the residents are amazed at the blithe manner in which the capital of the Province of Ontario is shedding its conserva-

---

* Full accreditation by the Association of Theological Schools was granted in 1989.

** The Sixth Biennial General Assembly of The Christian and Missionary Alliance in Canada is scheduled to convene in Toronto in June 1994.

Canadian Identity Again / 403

10.1 Rev. Gordon Fowler became superintendent of the newly-formed Canadian Pacific District in January 1979.

10.2 Rev. Harvey Town became superintendent of the Western Canadian District in January 1981.

10.3 Ralph and Lou Sutera, of Mansfield, Ohio, conducted a remarkable revival campaign in western Canada during the fall of 1971 which revitalized the prairie churches.

Courtesy Saskatchewan Archives

10.4 Rev. Walter Boldt in the balcony of Circle Drive Alliance Church in November 1979.

10.5 The impressive tower of the Circle Drive complex can be seen from several miles' distance.

404 / *Canadian Identity Again*

10.6

10.6 Pastor William Goetz conducts a service in the massive Sevenoaks Alliance Church in Abbotsford, B.C.

10.7

10.7 Dr. David Rambo, president of CBC/CTS from 1972 until 1979. During his presidency the campus experienced a 50 percent growth in enrollment and major building additions.

10.8 In 1979, Rexford Boda became president of CBC/CTS. Three years later a 1,000-seat chapel was completed and a Centre for Evangelism established.

10.9 An aerial view of the CBC/CTS campus, looking northwest from the intersection of Fourth Avenue and Lewvan Drive. The chapel and its tower dominate the scene. The gymnasium is immediately behind the chapel.

10.8

10.9

Courtesy Bruce Draper

tive past. Once a tightly knit English centre, Toronto is undergoing both a transition and a renaissance as it faces the twenty-first century.... The population is now at least forty percent non-English, and the variety gives the City a flavour of being all things to all men.[19]

Already the metropolis of Canada, Toronto was becoming the chief centre of immigration and the greatest national challenge for evangelism among peoples of every race, culture, tongue and religion.

Council opened on May 18 in the historic King Edward Hotel, then moved to the O'Keefe Centre and concluded in Varsity Arena. Guest speakers were Dr. Myron S. Augsburger, president of the Eastern Mennonite College, and Dr. Philip Teng, president of the Alliance Church Union in Hong Kong. Among other decisions, Council 1970 ordered the appointment of a committee to study the "restructuring of the Society." This resulted in the first important constitutional change since 1912.[20]

Rev. William Newell's superintendency continued until September 1973, when he resigned to become executive director of World Vision International of Canada.[21] The last few years of his superintendency had been marred by what appeared to him to be a lack of cooperation in district programs on the part of some of the churches. In his final report he stated:

> The continuing failure of some [churches] to make any effort towards District objectives is more than perplexing ... to neglect a corporate program may suggest an attitude less than loyal.[22]

Newell concluded on a more conciliatory note: "While some remained aloof, others involved themselves totally and joyfully."[23]

The thirteen-year superintendency of Rev. William Newell was roughly bounded by the losses of two historic churches of the district. In October 1960, the West End Alliance Church of Toronto, which had joined the Alliance family in 1912, closed down. It had been the first church in Canada to adopt the new Alliance constitution of that year, which would outline the modus operandi of the Alliance for the next sixty years.[24] Late in 1973, the Gospel Tabernacle of Brantford, which in 1911 had been the final triumph of the patriarch, Rev. John Salmon,[25] ended its days. This left Bethany Church of Hopeville as the last survivor of the Salmon era. However, during Newell's leadership, the district experienced an overall modest growth. The number of churches increased from 44 to 52, an average annual rate of 1.5 percent. During the 1973 conference, the Eastern and Central Canadian District elected Rev. Melvin P. Sylvester as its new superintendent. Born in Grande Prairie, Alberta, of a Salvationist mother and Lutheran father, Melvin Peter Sylvester was converted at five years of age through the preaching of Board Representative Gordon Skitch. Five years later, the family moved to Beaverlodge, where Melvin completed his schooling and became active in the life of the new Alliance Church, under Pastor Norman Galbraith. While attending Canadian Bible College, he married fellow student Marion Samoila in 1955. After graduating a year later, he pastored churches in Glenside/ Outlook, Estevan and Swift Current, Saskatchewan; Brandon, Manitoba; and Delta Tabernacle in Hamilton, Ontario, before his election to the superintendency of the Eastern and Central Canadian District.

The 1974 General Council approved the recommendations of the committee appointed the previous year to study the "restructuring of our society." These clearly gave the Alliance the official status of a denomination. "After 87 years as a para-denominational organization dedicated to missionary activity," *Eternity* magazine commented, "The Christian and Missionary Alliance has officially recognized what many people have known for years: the Alliance is a denomination."[26] Four years later, General Council set itself the goal of doubling in size within ten years.

In April 1975, First Alliance Church of Metropolitan Toronto closed the doors of its Yonge Street Tabernacle for the last time and relocated to the Agincourt section of Scarborough. One or two Sundays later, veteran retired missionary Mrs. Marie Irwin, on her way to the new location, passed by the old tabernacle and saw a group of people attempting to enter the tabernacle. When she stopped to inform the group of the new location, she was delighted to recognize them as former members of her church in Vietnam. This was the first known Alliance contact with the new flow of Southeast Asian refugees arriving in Canada. With the help of another veteran retired missionary from Vietnam, Rev. D. Ivory Jeffrey, this group met every Sunday as a section of the First Alliance Church congregation, with the two missionaries acting as interpreters and intermediaries. In October of that same year, Vietnamese churches were formed in Vancouver, under Rev. Nguyen quang Thuan, and in Montreal under the guidance of Rev. and Mrs. John A. Fitzstevens of Fairview

Alliance Church, who were former Alliance missionaries in Vietnam.[27] The church in Montreal then called Nguyentan tan Canh as its pastor. A year later, the Vietnamese section of First Alliance Church, still under the general guidance of Rev. Jeffrey and Mrs. Irwin, formed their own church in Toronto, calling Rev. Nguyen van Van as their pastor.

The new district superintendent supplied much of the leadership in the movement toward Canadian autonomy. As a result, much of his time during his seven-year superintendency was taken up with matters not solely the concern of his district. Nevertheless, the number of churches grew from 52 to 69—an average annual growth rate of 3.7 percent, and inclusive membership grew at an average annual rate of 7.1 percent. This record was exceeded only during the superintendency of Rev. Nathan Bailey. Having been elected president of the autonomous Christian and Missionary Alliance in Canada in June 1980 (effective January 1, 1981), District Superintendent Melvin Sylvester tendered his resignation, effective at the turn of the year.

Also in June 1980, Rev. Ross Ingram of Rexdale Alliance Church accepted a special one-year assignment in England, to become effective at the end of September. At the request of the district nominating committee, he agreed to allow his name to stand for district superintendent, with the understanding that he would not be able to assume duties until September 1981. The committee also asked District Superintendent Robert Gould of the Canadian Midwest District if he would agree to become superintendent if requested. He agreed provided there was no contest. In its report to conference in September, the committee submitted its nomination of Rev. Robert Gould,[28] whereupon the name of Rev. Ross Ingram was nominated from the floor.[29] When advised by telephone of this development, Gould withdrew his name. Nevertheless, conference proceeded with the election. Although Ingram received a majority of the votes cast, because one-third of the voters returned their ballots unmarked, he failed to receive the required "two thirds majority of all ballots cast." The appointment of a superintendent was therefore referred to the board of directors of The Christian and Missionary Alliance in Canada, which duly appointed Rev. Robert Gould.[30] He assumed his duties on March 1, 1981.[31]

At the same time, Rev. Arnold Downey, senior pastor of Westgate Alliance Church in Saskatoon, was appointed superintendent of the Canadian Midwest District, effective in March.

Consolidation in Quebec

The bridgehead in Quebec French ministries established by 1966 grew slowly. In July of that year, the district entered negotiations with the Presbyterian Church in Canada for the purchase of the old church building in Lévis. The Alliance was fortunate in that the Presbyterian negotiator was its old worker and friend, Dr. Robert Lennox.[32] Some difficulties about the title deed were encountered, but in the end, the fine old property became the permanent home of Eglise Chrétienne Evangélique, Lévis, for $25,000.[33]

Eugene McNutt, a native of Truro, Nova Scotia, and a senior student at Canadian Bible College, spent most of the summer of 1964 in Quebec City, studying French and helping out with the work under Pastor Bob Richardson.[34] The following May he returned to Quebec City as a part-time worker and part-time French-language student.[35] After Eugene McNutt married Shirley Miller, they were appointed French work missionaries in March 1967. Eleven months later they were assigned to Lévis, to assist Jean Heidman and Mabel Quinlan in door-to-door work.[36]

In November 1968, the McNutts became burdened for the lower St. Lawrence and Gaspé Peninsula areas of the province. After two investigative visits to the areas, the missionary couple was reassigned in January 1970 to Rimouski, a town of 30,000 generally regarded as the hub of the Gaspé Peninsula.[37] Within a year, a little group of believers and inquirers were meeting in houses, but no public services had yet begun.

In February 1971, a white clapboard church building, formerly used by the Anglicans, and seating barely 50 persons, was purchased for the amazing sum of $6,000, and the first public services began. Seven years later, the Rimouski congregation was organized as an Alliance church with 30 charter members, and construction began on a fine 260-seat building on an adjoining lot. The new structure, dedicated on October 21, 1979, in the presence of federal, provincial and municipal officials, was the first evangelical church to be built in Rimouski.[38]

That city was not the sole interest of McNutt during his ten-year residency. Among the surrounding towns explored, informal extension works were started in Matane* and Mont Joli. In August 1980 the

---

* The work in Matane was organized in December 1982 under pastor Marc-Andre Roy, and is known as L'Alliance Chrétienne et Missionnaire.

McNutts relocated to Montreal, where they worked for another eight years.[39] In all, they served the cause of French Canadian evangelism for 21 years, in a ministry characterized by Eugene's contagious enthusiasm.

In June 1968, Pastor Robert Richardson of Quebec City was granted leave of absence (which became permanent) to work for the Canadian Bible Society. Six months later, Lois Stewart, a graduate of Toronto Bible College and a French course at Bethel Bible Institute was credentialed by the district as a deaconess and assigned to the Quebec City church. For the next five years, although there were several short-term pastorates or pulpit ministries, the church had no regular pastor. During the pastoral gaps, the congregation was held together largely by the good work of Lois Stewart.*[40] In November of 1969, the house and chapel on Chouinard Street in Quebec City was sold and the former Brethren chapel on Belvedere Street was purchased. The church is now known as L'Eglise Evangélique Belvédère.[41]

In June 1969, Anna Rempel, a two-term Alliance missionary in Zaire, became an official home worker in Montreal. Her task was to revive the former French-language work that had been closed down in September 1963. Renting an apartment close to the English-language Alliance Community Church, she was soon successful in gathering together a small group, which met informally in her home.[42]

Four months later, Edgar Guerette, a graduate of Bethel Bible Institute, became an Alliance worker and was assigned to the new Montreal project as pastor. In January 1970, Guerette and Anna Rempel began holding French services in the Alliance Community Church as L'Alliance Chrétienne et Missionnaire, with an initial attendance of seven.[43]

The Montreal work grew steadily but slowly. Within three years Guerette reported attendances as high as 47. Then Haitian immigrants settled in the vicinity of the church, and evangelicals among them began to attend Guerette's services. As long as the proportion of Haitians remained small, the congregation welcomed them. "The Lord has opened a door of service to us," Guerette reported to conference, "among the thousands of Haitians in the city."[44]

However, the congregation soon was predominantly Haitian, and the character of the services became more and more in keeping

---

* In 1973, Lois Stewart obtained leave of absence from the district (which became permanent) to pursue social studies.

with their cultural preferences and less to the liking of the French Canadians. Their attendance at the services decreased to the vanishing point.

In May 1974, the English-language Alliance Community Church became extinct (see pages 311, 312). Immediately, the French language congregation acquired the church building from the district, and was organized as a church on August 18 with 37 charter members.[45] Two years later, Guerette resigned his charge and the Haitian congregation called one of its own members, Rev. Joseph Omicile, of previous Baptist connection, to its ministry. The church prospered, daughtering two other Haitian congregations.

Several other attempts were made to establish a permanent work among French Canadians in Montreal, notably in the Outremont and Rosemont areas under Pastor McNutt. None of these met with long-term success. However, in 1978, Rev. Daniel Wolfe commenced visitation work in Dollard des Ormeaux—a West Island community on the fringe of the metropolitan area. In August 1979, public services were commenced, using the premises of the English-language Fairview Alliance Church.[46] In February 1982, Eglise Alliance Chrétienne et Missionnaire de Dollard des Ormeaux was formed, under the pastorate of Wolfe.[47] Today, the church remains the sole Alliance church for French Canadians within the greater Montreal area, where nearly half the population of Quebec resides.

Since its formation in 1961, the French Work Committee had attempted to abide by its mandate "to give guidance to the ministry to French speaking Canadians" (see page 388). Centred as it was in Montreal, and usually chaired by the pastor of the English-language Alliance Community Church, it proved to be somewhat lacking in its effectiveness to the chief centre of operations around Quebec City. By 1970, it had become obvious that the committee had to be more in tune with details of the operation. Thus was conceived the position of "coordinator" of French work—the district's man-on-the-spot, to be "regarded as senior pastor and overseer of the personnel and work in the Province of Quebec."[48]

In November 1970, the 68-year-old Alliance missionary to Cambodia, Rev. Jean Funé, who had first ministered to French Canadians in 1927, retired after 42 years of service (see pages 368-369). News of his return to North America reached District Superintendent Newell, and he asked Funé to become the Quebec coordinator.[49] Funé agreed,[50] and assumed his duties on June 24, 1971. The Funés made

Canadian Identity Again / 411

10.10 **10.11** **10.12**

10.10 Rev. Mel Sylvester was superintendent of the Eastern and Central Canadian District from September 1973 until December 1980. During his tenure, he supplied much of the leadership towards Canadian Alliance autonomy.

10.11 Rev. Robert Gould was superintendent of the Canadian Midwest District from October 1975 until March 1981. He was appointed superintendent of the Eastern and Central Canadian District, commencing in March 1981.

10.12 Rev. Arnold Downey assumed the duties of superintendent of the Canadian Midwest District in March 1981.

10.13

10.13 In 1968, the Eastern and Central Canadian District acquired the Salle Evangelique Belvedere in Quebec City from the Brethren Assemblies. Thereafter it became the church home of l'Eglise Chrétienne Evangelique.

10.14 Rev. Eugene McNutt, a native of Truro, Nova Scotia, ministered to French Canadians in Quebec for 24 years. In 1970, he founded a church in Rimouski, and initiated another in Matane.

10.14

412 / *Canadian Identity Again*

10.15 Eugene McNutt baptizes an early convert at Rimouski.

10.16 The tiny former Anglican building which became the first permanent home of the Rimouski church in 1971. To the left is the new and larger church building erected eight years later.

10.17 In 1976 the building of the former English-language Alliance Community Church became the church home of an Alliance Haitian congregation.

10.18 In January 1970, Edgar Guerette was appointed pastor of the small group gathered by Anna Rempel. French-language services were then started in Alliance Community Church on Pie IX Boulevard. Here Guerette leads the singing, accompanied by Anna Rempel.

10.15

10.16

10.17

10.18

their home and headquarters in part of the Lévis parsonage. The district superintendent then advised all French workers:

> Mr. Funé will be resident in Lévis, but it is clearly understood that his ministry will be more far-reaching than one fellowship. He is regarded as senior pastor and overseer of the personnel and work in the Province of Quebec. He will be working closely with the District Executive Committee ... and in relationship with the French Work Committee.[51]

Funé had not come to be a figurehead or father confessor. He intended to give unambiguous direction. In October 1972, he was the prime mover in a Quebec City interdenominational campaign, "Operation Espérance" (Hope), which united Baptists, Brethren and the Alliance in a way never before experienced. Rev. Alain Choiquier of Paris, France, was the featured evangelist.

The spirit of the campaign spilled over into the following year, and formed part of the continent-wide "Key 73" emphasis on evangelism.[52] A campaign was held in March, featuring Dr. Arthur Johnston. Choiquier returned in October 1973, when additional campaigns were held in Quebec City, Montreal, Sherbrooke and Rimouski, assisted by Brethren evangelist Fernand St. Louis.[53] All in all, it was a wonderful time of witness, and a new spirit of interdenominational cooperation prevailed.

In January 1975, the faculty and students of Bethel Bible Institute were shocked at the tragic highway death of Principal Dr. Sheldon Bard. "This is an awful loss for the French work, but God is in control," reported Jean Funé to District Superintendent Melvin Sylvester. The sad event had a good side, drawing into closer fellowship French workers from several denominations. Pending the appointment and arrival of a new principal/teacher at the institute, Funé lectured on doctrine and missions for several weeks.

Jean Funé carried out his responsibility as coordinator with the vigour normally expected of a much younger man. Used to working independently in the past, some of his workers resented his intrusions on occasion, but on the whole the arrangement was helpful and necessary. By his own assessment, he had been "hindered" by having to fill the pulpit of the Belvedere church for all but seven months of his tenure. At long last, on November 5, 1974, Rev. Richard G. Nester, on loan from Global Outreach (U.S.A.) became pastor.[54] The Belvedere church owes much to the ministry of Rev. Jean Funé during those critical years.

On June 1, 1975, Funé retired from his responsibility as "Coordinator of the French Work." During the almost four years, his only income had been his missionary pension. To demonstrate its "love and appreciation," the district underwrote the cost of a "final visit" to his native France.

A District is Born

The district did not replace Funé. Addressing the conference of September 1976, District Superintendent Sylvester referred to "the great need and present potential" of the province, and expressed the belief that "the day will come when the French speaking churches of Quebec will form a new district of The Christian and Missionary Alliance in Canada."[55] To the conference of the following September, it was clear that a full-time, French-speaking, resident director for Quebec was required.[56] But a suitable prospect was not to be easily located.

Early in 1980, the position was offered to Rev. Jesse D. Jespersen, who had served for fifteen years as an Alliance missionary in the Ivory Coast. A native of Spruce Grove, Alberta, the 43-year-old missionary held a Bachelor of Arts degree from the University of Saskatchewan and a Bachelor of Theology degree from Canadian Bible College. He accepted the offer and commenced his new duties on September 1, 1980, locating in Ste. Foy.[57]

Seven months later, in March 1981, the board of directors of the newly autonomous Christian and Missionary Alliance in Canada, created a special study commission to investigate the needs of Quebec. At their meeting in Montreal on June 19, the commission members unanimously endorsed the idea of a separate Quebec district, subject to the views of the French Work Committee and the district executive committee. Both committees agreed and the recommendation was then approved by the board of directors in October of that year, to be implemented in January 1983. However, to allow more time for the normal flow of events, the date was reset to coincide with the next district conference in May 1983.

On May 25, the eighteen clergy and nineteen lay delegates from seventeen Quebec churches held their own elections, and the new St. Lawrence District came into being, headquartered in Ste. Foy.[58] The founding elected officials were:

District Superintendent
　　　Rev. Jesse D. Jespersen
District Executive Committee
　　　Rev. Jesse D. Jespersen
　　　Claude Dubé—Rimouski
　　　Tim Nhon—Dollard des Ormeaux
　　　Rev. Daniel Wolfe—Dollard des Ormeaux
　　　Fernand Cancelier—Quebec City
　　　Michael Gagnon—Farnham
　　　Alain Moreau—Ste. Claire
Alliance Women President
　　　Mme Marika Cancelier—Quebec City
Alliance Men President
　　　Jean Boisseau—Lévis

During the 1920s, 1930s and 1940s, much was heard of the need to train western workers in the west. During the 1960s and 1970s, the need to train Quebec workers in Quebec was heard with increasing frequency. In April 1979, Rev. Harold Catto, Director of Church Growth for the district, proposed Theological Education by Extension (TEE) courses for potential Quebec leaders, and some students did follow such courses from Institut Biblique Béthel. In February 1982, Director Jespersen, with the cooperation of Academic Dean Dr. Robert Rose of Canadian Bible College, devised an Alliance "Training Program for Church Leadership in Quebec, under the Academic umbrella of CBC." The program recognized:

a) The instruction must be in French
b) The course work must be accredited in Bible College circles
c) It must be developed within the context of Quebec
d) It must be geared to serve an initial small group
e) Start-up costs must be minimal

The proposal, adopted with some modifications, provided for a course director to be a faculty member of the college, paid for by the college, assigned to live in Quebec. Jean Martin, of the Belvedere church, graduated from Canadian Theological Seminary in 1983 with a Master of Divinity degree. He accepted the invitation to direct the

ETAQ (Enseignement Théologique de l'Alliance au Québec) program. The annual courses, conducted in Lévis, Montreal and Rimouski, commenced in the fall of 1983, with a total enrollment of 42. Diplomas were granted under the authority of CBC.[59]

THE ROOTS OF AUTONOMY

The movement back towards a self-governing Canadian Alliance probably consumed more time, dominated more thought and altered more relationships than any other domestic dispute faced by the homeland constituency of the Alliance in forty years. When the movement became an issue in the 1960s and 1970s, many of the distraught within the American Alliance blamed it on "Canadian nationalism," while some Canadians blamed it on "opportunism." While there was some truth in these allegations, the root cause was the frustration of a minority that cannot achieve its aspirations simply because it is always in the minority. That was why the American colonists rebelled against the majority rule of the British Parliament, why the United Empire Loyalists left the United States for Canada, and why the Southern Confederacy fought a civil war against the majority rule of the United States. It was the reason French Canada never wholeheartedly embraced Canadian confederation, and why Canadian Indian political issues are so awkward at the present time.

Traditionally, Americans have been charmed with their own accomplishments, and have tended to believe that what is good for the United States must be good for the rest of the world, and particularly for Canada. Americans within the Alliance have not been shielded from these tendencies. They have found it difficult to remember that every nation is the product of its own history, geography, politics and institutions.

The Fourfold Gospel movement in the United States received its founding impulse from a Scottish Canadian with a much modified Presbyterian outlook. The sister movement in Canada was initiated by another Scottish Canadian of Methodistic stamp, with strong Adventist, Baptistic and Congregational overtones. From their inception, therefore, the two sister movements were bound to have different perspectives. Moreover, Simpson's movement was born in a post-Civil War victorious north, steeped in a conviction of American destiny, and marked by a profusion of emerging religious movements. In contrast, Salmon's movement was forged in an over-churched, ultra-conservative Loyalist Ontario, which valued its time-honoured British institutions and resisted any form of American intrusion.

The joining of Salmon's and Simpson's movements in 1889 was based on the mutual acceptance of two concepts:

1. An interdenominational fraternity of faith and experience in the Fourfold Gospel, which would not interfere in the prerogatives of the churches.*

2. A Canadian ("Dominion") Auxiliary of The Christian Alliance, directed by its own freely elected president and executive body.

There is no evidence that Dr. Simpson or his team in New York ever interfered in the affairs of the Canadian auxiliary during the eight years of its existence. However, when the Alliance scrapped the Canadian auxiliary in 1897, making Canada just one of many Alliance districts, and, based on American conditions, shifted its interest from fraternal branches to church branches, Canadians reacted with shock and demoralization. In fact, they began to lose interest in the Alliance.

When, in 1910, again in response to American conditions, the Alliance took steps to acquire or control the properties of affiliated churches, Canadians refused to comply. The first Alliance constitution for local churches was approved by General Council in 1912, but no existing Canadian churches would adopt it because the "reversion clause" was considered to be contrary to Canadian convictions. Again during the 1920s, when eastern and central Canada experienced its greatest opportunity to establish new churches of the holiness tradition but the Alliance showed little interest in churches except as supply bases for the foreign missionary program, many Canadians lost interest in the Alliance as a viable alternative to church union or modernism.

In the 1930s, the Alliance showed little tangible concern for the evangelization of the Canadian prairies, and western Canadians veered towards their natural bent of self-determination. Apparent Alliance insensitivity to the need for even one Bible school in Canada was an important reason why western Canadians rebelled against the clear directive from New York and opened their own school in Regina in 1941.

---

* District Superintendent Roffe highlighted the differences between Alliance work in Canada and the United States to the Councils of 1921 and 1922 (see pages 54, 55).

418 / Canadian Identity Again

During the 1960s and 1970s, the inability of Canadians to persuade Councils and boards to help in Canadian home missions projects was the final straw. Almost in desperation, Canadians began to look towards nationalization of the several ethnic and native ministries in the west and the ministry to French Canadians in the east. By then, the achievement of a Canadian consensus by Canadians had become a goal of Canadians. The wonder is not that Canadian autonomy came in 1981, but that it did not come much sooner.

Several signs along the way pointed to the inevitability of a return to Canadian identity in some form. In 1923, a self-appointed cabinet of the Toronto members of the district executive committee had taken it upon themselves to conduct the district's business. District Superintendent Roffe attributed this to a tendency to think of "a Canadian Alliance." Indeed, the self-styled "official organ" of the district in those days was named the *Canadian Alliance*. In response, the board of managers had taken precipitous action to stamp out such wild fire by placing the district office under the direct oversight of the financial secretary (see page 88).

In 1944, General Council had recommended the establishment of a "representative agency" for Canada. Although supported by the Home Department, the board of managers shelved the project (see pages 292, 295). In 1947, District Superintendent Nathan Bailey had tried to obtain a Canadian consensus to establish a "Canadian Office," as a tool for repairing and maintaining inter-district relationships in Canada. The plan failed, largely because of western indifference (see page 295). Later that year Bailey made a last attempt to achieve a "Canadian Agency" by persuading the Eastern and Central Canadian District Conference to "make a formal request to the Board of Managers, reminding them of the action of the Council of 1944." The strategy failed to produce any results.[60]

A Spark of Nationalism

The movement towards Canadian Alliance autonomy was aided and abetted by external influences. After the conclusion of the Second World War, Canada took steps to develop her image as an independent nation. In 1867, the principal impulse for confederation had been to provide a united defense against possible new American territorial demands. After 1945, it was obviously impossible to provide a military defense, so Canada concentrated on defending itself from political, economic and cultural intrusion from the south.

John G. Diefenbaker was prime minister of Canada during the early 1960s when John F. Kennedy was president of the United States. It was well known that the two men were not enamoured, and Diefenbaker's views and sentiments were widely discussed throughout Canada. Former Alliance President Dr. L. L. King recalled an Alliance conference in Saskatoon at which he heard much talk about Diefenbaker—and some talk about American Alliance leadership that was not very flattering. On his return to New York he advised President Bailey that he foresaw trouble ahead. Apparently, the president dismissed the warning with his own opinion that Canadians just liked to talk. However, Canadians were in fact questioning some aspects of Alliance government as it pertained to Canada.

As the Canadian centennial year of 1967 approached, all levels of governments and other institutions began to devise centennial projects to mark the national event. The three Alliance districts did not escape the contagion of celebration. Spontaneous ideas emerged from several quarters, but it was not until the September 1966 conference of the Eastern and Central Canadian District that a project for all three districts was urged. In his annual report, District Superintendent Newell stated:

> Our centennial year celebrations afford us unique opportunity as the Eastern and Central Canadian District or as a Tri-District family (Canada-wide) to make a valid contribution to our Dominion. We can not legislate for the Alliance family throughout Canada, but perhaps some action here might well encourage the Midwestern and Western Canadian Districts to join us in a vital ministry. A common objective to catch the imagination of our Canadian Alliance family should be considered. . . . The Committee to which this report is referred may further reflect on the potential of a Tri-District Centennial Plan.[61]

The delegates were enthused with the proposal and passed a resolution that:

> The chairman appoint a Committee to study and implement a Centennial Project in conjunction (if possible) with the other Canadian Districts, with priority to be given to evangelistic endeavour on a Canada-wide basis, sponsored by The Christian and Missionary Alliance in Canada.[62]

It would appear that District Superintendent Newell appointed himself as a committee of one. A short time later, he met with District Superintendents Roy McIntyre and Alf Orthner, together with President Alvin Martin on the Canadian Bible College campus. All four men were in full agreement with the idea of a Tri-District Conference.

The next step was to obtain the approval of Home Secretary Rev. Leslie W. Pippert. Later that fall, the three Canadian superintendents attended a superintendents' meeting in New York, at which time they presented their proposal to Pippert. He could not have been altogether surprised (he was in the chair when Newell read his report to conference a few weeks previously), but he was not pleased. President Bailey and Treasurer Bernard King then joined the discussion. All three New York leaders were apprehensive. After all, no regional group of American districts had ever attempted to meet apart from General Council. President Bailey's oft-quoted remark, that if you build a railroad track, someday someone will run a train on it, is attributed to this uneasy meeting. Rev. William Newell recalled that permission was reluctantly granted only after the president was told that as all three Canadian districts wanted to hold the conference, an explanation from the president would be required if permission were denied.

A Conference, a Corporation, and a Charter

The historic Tri-District Conference convened in Hillsdale Alliance Church, Regina, from September 7-11, 1967, under the theme "Guidelines for Tomorrow." Both President Bailey and Home Secretary Pippert were in attendance. In a lengthy "Centennial Declaration," it was stated that the "First National Conclave of Alliance Churches in Canada" was more than a celebration of past achievements, or an enlarged fellowship convened for the sake of strengthening national unity. It was to be a convocation for self-examination and study in the present methods of evangelism.[63] Among the visiting speakers were evangelist Richard Bennett of England and the Honourable E. C. Manning of Alberta. More than 1,500 persons met in the Regina Exhibition Auditorium on the Sunday evening.[64]

During the conference, District Superintendent Newell struck a portentous note:

> Though the Spirit of Nationalism and independence has gripped us as many other nations, we express gratitude to

Canadian Identity Again / 421

10.19   **10.20**

10.19 Rev. and Mrs. Jean Funé. In 1926 and 1927, Funé was the first Alliance worker to carry the gospel to French Canadians in their own language. After 42 years of missionary service in Vietnam and Cambodia he returned to Quebec in 1971 as coordinator of French work.

10.20 In 1980, Rev. Jesse Jespersen, above, a fifteen-year missionary in the Ivory Coast, was appointed director of French work. On May 25, 1983, the new St. Lawrence District came into being, with Rev. Jesse Jespersen as its superintendent.

10.21

10.21 In 1972 and 1973, Funé was the prime mover in the interdenominational campaigns, "Operation Esperance." Pictured in March 1973 are, left to right, Jean-Paul Berney, Brethren; Dr. Arthur Johnston, St. Paul's Bible College; Rev. George Roger, Baptist; Rev. Jean Funé.

422 / *Canadian Identity Again*

10.22

10.22 The first District Executive Committee of the St. Lawrence District. From left to right: Claude Dube, Rimouski; Fernand Cancelier, Quebec City; Michael Gagnon, Farnham; Rev. Jesse Jespersen; Alain Moreau, Ste. Claire; Daniel Wolfe, Dollard; Tim Nhon, Dollard.

10.23 In 1983, Jean Martin was appointed director of the ETAQ program. Courses were conducted annually in Lévis, Montreal and Rimouski, with diplomas granted under the authority of Canadian Bible College.

10.23

10.24

10.24 Hillsdale Alliance Church, host to the first Tri-District Conference in 1967, with the assembled delegates.

10.25 Rev. A. H. Orthner, a long-service pastor in Western Canada. The Canadian Corporation elected him secretary in 1972, president in 1974 and general director in 1975.

10.25

God for the continuing tie with our Parent Body. Doubtless, changes will come with governmental demands peculiar to Canada, but the international flavour of the Society must be maintained.[65]

The Canadian delegates returned to their homes rejoicing, while the two senior officials from New York returned home uneasily. Just as President Bailey had feared, the conference had been more than a conference. It had whetted Canadian appetites for more freedom of expression and action.

President Bailey's opposition to anything that smacked of Canadian independence did not mean that he had forgotten his attempts in 1947 to form a "Canadian Office." To use his own words, he had a "growing conviction that the Society should have a national identity" in Canada.[66] Since 1925, the Alliance in Canada had been operating under provincial charters, the districts acting independently of each other. There was no legislative structure for unified action, no common voice to government or to the Canadian constituency as a whole. With the growing emphasis on Canadian culture and national identity during the 1960s, the time had come for a country-wide organization.

Dr. Bailey called a special meeting for August 25, 1969, in Regina. Treasurer Dr. Bernard S. King, Home Secretary Rev. Leslie W. Pippert, and eleven representatives from the three Canadian districts voted unanimously that a proposal to incorporate the Alliance in Canada be referred to the Canadian districts for adoption. The proposal was endorsed at the three district conferences in September. In November, an "application for incorporation" was submitted, but it was not until May 29, 1972, that the Deputy Registrar-General officially recorded the petition granted by the Minister for Consumer and Corporate Affairs for a federal charter.

The new corporation, known officially as "The Christian and Missionary Alliance in Canada (1972)" but usually referred to as "The Canadian Corporation," comprised twelve members: three, including the district superintendent, from each district, plus the president, secretary and treasurer of the C&MA in New York.* Its first officers, elected in October 1972, were: president, Rev. William Newell; vice-president, Rev. A. H. Orthner; secretary, Rev. Roy McIntyre; treasurer, Dr. Bernard S. King.[67]

---

* Two years later, the Vice-President of North American Ministries was added to the members of the corporation.

Dr. Bailey described the Canadian Corporation as "a vehicle and a channel through which the churches and districts in Canada can consult and act in cooperative efforts without disturbing the historic and fraternal relationships which have bound the Society together."[68] Perhaps its function was better described by an *Alliance Witness* reporter: "The board of the Canadian Corporation now serves as a liaison for Canadian affairs with the Division of North American Ministries."[69] The Canadian Corporation was, in reality, a wedge between the three Canadian district superintendents and the vice-president of the Division of North American Ministries. Therein lay the problem.

In 1973, the Canadian Corporation elected to become a member of the Evangelical Fellowship of Canada. It also decided to hold a second Tri-District Conference in the fall of 1974. In September 1973, Rev. William Newell resigned from the positions of district superintendent and president of the Canadian Corporation. As the new district superintendent, Rev. Mel Sylvester automatically became a member of the corporation's board of directors. In June 1974, the board elected the following slate of officers: president, Rev. A. H. Orthner; vice president, Rev. Roy McIntyre; secretary, Rev. Mel Sylvester; treasurer, Rev. Bernard S. King.

The second Tri-District Conference was held in Hillsdale Alliance Church, Regina, September 5-9, with the stated purpose to strengthen the bond of fellowship within the Alliance in Canada and to establish goals for church growth in Canada. The conference theme was "Growing with Canada." At the first business session, Rev. Ernest J. Bailey, of Bramalea, Ontario, read a lengthy paper entitled, "Restructuring The Christian and Missionary Alliance in Canada for Church Growth." Of course, the Tri-District Conferences had no power to legislate, only to suggest. Ernest Bailey made many suggestions for the greater impact of the Canadian operation, and the conference approved and passed on to the board of directors the following recommendations:

> RECOMMENDATION #1
> "that the Canadian Corporation, as presently constituted, be given a mandate to perform specific tasks in the interests of growth and unity of the C.&M.A. in Canada as directed by the District Conferences in concert."
>
> RECOMMENDATION #2
> "that our Home Missions ministries be nationalized and

that the control of the funds, and the oversight of the Home Missions operations be committed to the Canadian Corporation."

RECOMMENDATION #3
"that the Canadian Corporation study and develop a revolving loan fund for the purpose of creating and strengthening church works in Canada."

RECOMMENDATION #4
"that the Canadian Corporation give consideration to and implement a Canadian publication that would include the Districts and College in a united voice across Canada."*

RECOMMENDATION #5
"that the next Tri-District Conference convene not later than the Fall of 1977, and that the Canadian Corporation work toward the implementing of this."

RECOMMENDATION #6
"that the Canadian Corporation be requested to further study other proposals and report back their recommendations to the constituency through the District Conferences or the next Tri-District Conference."

Perhaps the most important contribution of Ernest Bailey's report was that it clearly identified many of the grievances inherent in the existing system of American control. Bailey had stated in public and in the presence of top Alliance officials what many Canadians believed in their hearts but expressed only in private conversation. The Canadian Charter clearly implied self-government of the Alliance in Canada, but the Alliance Constitution made it subordinate to the Division of North American Ministries, the board of managers, and General Council.

THE MOVEMENT ACCELERATES

The 1974 Tri-District Conference was the turning point in the movement towards Canadian autonomy. No longer could there be any serious doubt among informed Canadians—nothing short of full

---
* Recommendation #4 had its origin in a proposal of District Superintendent Roy McIntyre.

domestic autonomy would enable the Alliance in Canada to develop according to its own genius.

During the Tri-District Conference of 1974, Dr. Keith Bailey, Vice-President of the Division of North American Ministries, presented a paper on "Canadian Church Affairs" which closed with the following:

> We believe the social phenomenon of nationalism so manifest in contemporary Canada can be a blessing to The Christian and Missionary Alliance churches in the Dominion. This strong force can be harnessed to produce an unprecedented level of church growth and development in your country. We believe the only healthy way to do this job is to open the door for Canadian leadership to creatively develop, nurture and carry out its own programs for advancement. The Division stands ready to help you in this great purpose.

In keeping with this new policy, together with the Tri-District Conference recommendation to nationalize Canadian home missions, the directors of the Canadian Corporation in October 1974 requested Keith Bailey to approve the concept of a full-time executive director for Canada. Two months later he gave his approval, and at the same time the board of managers took the following action:

> WHEREAS, the three districts of Canada in response to the strong feelings of nationalism have sought for a degree of self-determination in their program, the Division of North American Ministries has been willing for the Canadian Corporation on the behalf of Canadian churches to devise programs of extension, home missions, evangelism and church loan fund that would be particularly fitted to the Canadian scene; and
>
> WHEREAS, at a recent meeting of the Canadian Corporation action was taken to request that the Canadian portion of the 10 percent of the budget allocated to the Division of North American Ministries be budgeted by the Canadian Corporation in consultation with the Vice-President of North American Ministries; and

WHEREAS, this presents a considerable departure from the procedure practiced throughout the history of The Christian and Missionary Alliance, it is therefore

RECOMMENDED, That the Canadian portion of the Budget allocated to the Division of North American Ministries be used for the Canadian operation. . . .⁷⁰

In June 1975, the corporation nominated its own president, Rev. A. H. Orthner, to be the new General Director of Canadian Ministries, and he was duly appointed by the board of managers in Nyack, effective October 1. For the next twenty months he travelled extensively across the country, promoting extension, evangelism and special ministries.* His was an increasingly difficult task, attempting to serve two masters who were becoming ever more possessive and polarized in their views. The district superintendents began to feel distant in their relations with the Vice-President of North American Ministries. After the appointment of Orthner as general director, Roy McIntyre was elected president, and Rev. Walter Boldt vice-president of the Canadian Corporation.

Back in May 1975, delegates to the General Council read the following paragraph in the annual report of the society:

> The growth of The Christian and Missionary Alliance churches in Canada has reached a level where more self-determination is needed for the programming of their work. The Board of Managers has approved the Canadian Corporation acting as a liaison committee to the Division of North American Ministries for the purpose of designing plans for evangelism, extension, home missions and Christian education that will be tailored to the Canadian scene.⁷¹

The report had not been worded with Canadian sensitivities in mind. The Canadian members of the corporation could not rationalize "self-determination" with "acting as a liaison committee." In their

---

* The recommendation of the 1974 Tri-District conference to have an all-Canadian Alliance periodical came to fruition in January 1977 when Director Orthner first issued the *Canadian Alliance News*. Originally published biannually, it was intended to be a supplement to the district serials. In 1980, it replaced them and was issued three times a year.

June meeting, the corporation noted that "the Canadian district superintendents feel in some degree a conflict of loyalties and priorities between the Canadian Corporation and the Department of North American Ministries" and concluded that "Canadian autonomy would seem to be in the best interests of expansion of Alliance ministries in Canada and ultimately in the worldwide work of the Society."[72]

As a consequence, the corporation authorized the appointment of a "Study Commission on Canadian Autonomy, to develop purposes, plans, programs and effective dates of implementation."[73] Initially serving on that important commission were:

Western Canadian District	Rev. Roy McIntyre
	Rev. Gordon Fowler
Canadian Midwest District	Rev. Robert Gould
	Rev. Walter Boldt
Eastern & Central Canadian District	
	Rev. Melvin Sylvester
	Rev. Ernest Bailey*
The Canadian Corporation	Rev. A. H. Orthner

The commission explored the implications of several degrees of autonomy. This required much more time than was at first thought necessary. Early in the process, the opinions of lawyers and accountants were obtained to determine the legal requirements of the Canadian Charter. Among the reports and recommendations was the "Western Report," which suggested that Canadian ministries relate to the American Alliance through a Canadian vice-president, on the same level as all other Alliance vice-presidents. The legal studies led to two major conclusions:

1. The Canadian Charter clearly called for the self government of the Alliance in Canada.

2. In at least one aspect, American accounting practice for Canadian contributions was not in compliance with Canadian law.

---

* After the sudden death of Rev. E. J. Bailey in June 1976, Rev. Ross Ingram served on the commission.

Canadian Identity Again / 429

10.26
10.26 The huge crowd in the Regina Exhibition Centre for the Sunday evening service of the first Tri-District Conference.

10.27
10.27 Dr. Louis L. King became president of The Christian and Missionary Alliance in May 1978. Alone among the senior Alliance officials of the 1970s he spoke favourably of the idea of a self-governing Alliance in Canada.

10.28
10.28 Cover of the *Alliance Witness*, depicting Dr. L. L. King presenting the new Canadian president, Rev. M. P. Sylvester, with a framed text of the official minutes authorizing Canadian autonomy.

430 / *Canadian Identity Again*

10.29

10.29 Dr. L. L. King delivers a charge to Rev. M. P. Sylvester during the commissioning service of the founding General Assembly. Standing behind them are the members of the founding board of directors, left to right, Rev. Jack Schroeder, Rev. Arnold Reimer, Mr. Lloyd Matheson, Rev. Gordon Fowler, Mr. Yvan Fournier, Dr. Raymur Downey, Rev. Walter Boldt, Rev. David Anderson, Dr. Phillip Ng. Not pictured are Messrs. Robert Conroy, Q.C., and Jack Klemke.

10.30 The newly elected President and Mrs. Melvin P. Sylvester, at the founding General Assembly.

10.30

10.31   **10.32**   **10.33**

10.31 Among the founding officers, Gerald L. Fowler was executive vice-president.

10.32 G. Lloyd Matheson was appointed treasurer of The Christian and Missionary Alliance in Canada.

10.33 Arnold L. Cook became director of personnel and missions.

RESISTANCE EMERGES

During a meeting of the directors of the corporation in Burlington in May 1976, these infringements of Canadian law were brought to the attention of the Nyack representatives, Drs. Nathan Bailey, Robert Battles (secretary of the Alliance), Keith Bailey and Bernard King. Up to this point in time, the American officials had maintained a stoney detachment from all hints of independent Canadian action. Now to have Canadian law cited as an irresistible argument for autonomy was more than the president and his lieutenants were prepared to take. The discussion became tense, and the suggestion of "insubordination" was made.[74] Canadians were warned that they neither possessed the necessary leadership or financial resources required to "go it alone."* To top it off, the president is reported by several witnesses to have treated the Canadian Charter disparagingly by words and action.

This regrettable incident needs to be seen against the backdrop of the whole Nathan Bailey. Although he had earned the reputation of a strong parliamentarian, he was a very sensitive and kindly man. Easily moved to passion and compassion, he was known to have openly cried during a service in Westminster Abbey, overcome by a compelling sense of history and beauty. He was passionately loyal to the historical Alliance and its founder, Dr. Simpson. Believing erroneously that Dr. Simpson had personally established the Alliance in Canada, at Peterborough (see page 290, footnote), anything that might weaken the historic Alliance ties between the United States and Canada he thought should be opposed with all his might. In any event, the hardening line taken by the American officials at the meeting in May 1976 severely damaged relationships between the two main segments of the Alliance homeland for many months. At this same meeting, Roy McIntyre declined to allow his name to stand for re-election as president of the Canadian Corporation, and he was replaced by Mel Sylvester.

The Study Commission, meeting in August 1976, recorded in its minutes:

> It was the general consensus that the members were disappointed in the attitude and actions expressed by

---

* A warning often sounded but seldom heard throughout the history of struggles between freedom and authority.

Headquarters' personnel.... We feel they do not have a grasp of the climate in Canada and they have pre-judged the entire situation.... The Charter places certain responsibilities on the Canadian leadership. We have an obligation on behalf of the C.&M.A. in Canada and the Canadian Government. We can not just consider the Charter as an "article of convenience."[75]

Sylvester and Boldt were dispatched to Nyack to meet with the president on September 18, 1976, in the hope of bringing about "a better understanding and a more wholesome atmosphere."[76] Unfortunately, we have only Canadian minutes of that historic occasion. It would appear that all participants were frank but well-behaved. The president thought that Canadian district superintendents were not being loyal. He reminded his visitors that superintendents were paid from the General (Missionary) Fund of the Alliance and were answerable to the Division of North American Ministries—not the Canadian Corporation. In his opinion, there were perhaps as many as twenty Canadians who wanted to lead their constituency into complete autonomy. The rest of the Canadian membership would be against the move.

The Canadian view was that the president still did not take the Canadian Charter seriously. He felt it could be interpreted to serve the Canadians' own purposes, and he accused Canadian leadership of doing just that. The president appeared to be hurt that Canadians, who he said had been given everything they had asked for, were now out for independence. He admitted such independence could come about in five years' time, but certainly not as long as he was president. The Canadian visitors hoped to alleviate some presidential suspicions about the motives of the Study Commission, and that some initiative would be taken by the Nyack officers to resolve differences.[77]

In May 1977, the Study Commission submitted its long-awaited report to the directors of the Canadian Corporation in Calgary. The commission made specific recommendations only to bring accounting procedures into conformity with Canadian tax laws. After discussing the implications of various degrees of self determination, the commission summarized its thoughts under five scenarios:

A. Full Autonomy
B. Canadian Autonomy—cooperative ministry overseas
C. Canadian Vice-President for Canadian affairs

D. Dissolution of Canadian Corporation
E. Maintain the status quo

The directors adopted the report and decided that the time had come to solicit positive leadership from the board of managers. The board was asked to:

1. Give its permission to use appropriate means to determine the sentiment of the Canadian constituency towards the concept of autonomy.

2. Appoint a "Fraternal Committee," composed of four members each of the Canadian Corporation and the Board of Managers to study the question of Canadian autonomy and present the terms, provisions and steps required to achieve these goals, and report back to the Board and Corporation, annually or as may be required.[78]

The directors had in mind the next Tri-District Conference as the vehicle through which the "sentiment of the Canadian constituency" would be determined. However, the previously planned date of September 1977 had been postponed by one year to allow more time for committee work to progress, and because the General Council of 1977 was to convene in Calgary.

During the fall of 1977, the board of managers appointed a Fraternal Committee composed of:

Board of Managers	K. M. Bailey
	R. W. Battles
	M. C. Feather
	W. Sandell
The Canadian Corporation	M. P. Sylvester
	R. McIntyre
	R. J. Gould
	J. E. Clemenger

A CHANGE OF LEADERSHIP

The year 1978 would be an important one in the life of the Alliance. After eighteen years as president, Dr. Nathan Bailey's tenure was at an end, and a new president would be elected at General Council in May. Because of the imminent change in top leadership, and in a spirit of avoiding further damage to relationships, the Canadian members of the Fraternal Committee refrained from exerting pressure for the resolution of the sensitive issue until a new president was elected. During Council, Dr. Louis L. King, the existing vice-president of overseas ministries, was elected president. He who had vigorously implemented the policy of indigenous overseas churches, alone among the senior Alliance officials, spoke favourably of a self-governing Alliance in Canada.

Following Council, on June 5 and 6, the Fraternal Committee met in Winnipeg with the retiring president and the president-elect in attendance. The alternatives and their implications were reviewed. The committee decided to issue its report in favour of a plan to establish a "Vice-president of Canadian Ministries."[79]

In July, Drs. Louis King, Robert Battles and Keith Bailey prepared critiques of the Fraternal Committee's report and proposal. King concluded that to attempt to meet the requirements of both the Alliance constitution and Canadian law was impossible and impractical. Battles doubted that the proposal would "enhance the work of The Christian and Missionary Alliance in Canada" and concluded that "if Canadian autonomy is to go the way that is indicated here, it has to mean a separate general council for Canada." Keith Bailey believed that for Canadians to make "full use of their charter they must forfeit their franchise in General Council." He had reached the opinion that Canadians should be given their autonomy and that the president of the Alliance in Canada should be given fraternal membership in the President's Cabinet and on the board of managers "as long as they continue to operate their mission program through the Division of Overseas Ministries."[80]

The third and last Tri-District Conference convened from September 7-11, 1978, at Canadian Bible College, under the theme "His Dominion: From Sea to Sea." The topic of Canadian autonomy dominated all three morning sessions. During the first session, the chair called on Dr. King to present the report of the Fraternal Committee, which recommended the establishment of a vice-president of Canadian ministries. However, Dr. King chose to provide a short verbal summary of the committee's work and then presented the response of the board of managers to the report and recommendation of the Fraternal Committee.[81] The board, said Dr. King, wished to obtain an expression of the "concerns of the Canadian constituency" in the matter of "Canadian autonomy," and to that end he authorized the Tri-District Conference to conduct a poll by ballot vote of the official delegates of district conferences "who are representatives of the Canadian constituency."[82]

A CONVINCING RESULT

After three days to think, talk and pray it over, the delegates reassembled on Monday morning, September 11, for the historic vote. After a "lengthy discussion," the majority of the delegates were ready to express what they knew deep down in their hearts they wanted. As John Robinson had expressed to King James I in 1616, the constituency wanted "the right of spiritual administration and government in itself and over itself by the common free consent of the people," and they wanted it "without tarrying any." In modern parlance, they wanted self-determination—now!

The ballots provided for three choices:

1. Continue as now
2. Move to autonomy
3. Possible alternative

There were 536 delegates present. Of the 379 ballots cast, 87.6 percent voted to move to autonomy. The people had spoken.[83]

The Fraternal Committee's tasks were now completely changed. Meeting in Winnipeg at the end of October 1978, the committee prepared "The Enabling Legislation Leading to Autonomy for The Christian and Missionary Alliance in Canada." On December 7, the legislation wording was unanimously accepted by the board of managers for presentation to General Council in May 1979. Among other actions, the legislation recommended that Council:

1. Authorize The Christian and Missionary Alliance in Canada to establish an autonomous church body for the "total governance" of the Alliance in Canada.

2. That the Canadian members of the Canadian Corporation be empowered to arrange for and call a Canadian Council no later than June 1980 to determine an organizational and administrative structure, to draft and adopt a constitution and bylaws, and to elect officers.

3. That the transition follow a schedule authorized by the board of managers for a gradual Canadian takeover of

operations now handled through the international headquarters, to be completed by January 1981.

Meanwhile, in the interest of saving time, and in anticipation of a favourable decision from General Council, the Fraternal Committee, in conjunction with the directors of the Canadian Corporation, appointed sub-committees to begin preliminary work on a proposed constitution and bylaws, the location of headquarters, the selection of personnel, the division of assets, the preparation of a budget and a working agreement between the Division of Overseas Ministries and The Christian and Missionary Alliance in Canada.[84]

The General Council of 1979 convened in Lincoln, Nebraska, from May 15-20. Among the first items of business, the enabling legislation and recommendations of the Fraternal Committee through the board of managers was presented to Council, which referred it to the Committee on the Division of North American Ministries. After a "lengthy discussion," the legislation and recommendations were returned to Council floor with the committee's endorsement and recommendation that it be adopted. After more than two hours of additional question and debate, including two delaying motions, the legislation and recommendations were adopted by well over the required two-thirds majority.[85]

It was a very emotional occasion. According to an *Alliance Witness* reporter:

> One delegate skeptically likened the separation to a no fault divorce. Another saw it as the coming of age of a child—a strangely condescending observation, as another debater remarked, for a church whose founder was a Canadian.[86]

Oddly enough, no one seemed to realize that the Canadian Alliance was simply returning to something like its self-governing days as the "Dominion Auxiliary of the Christian Alliance" (1889-1897), or was aware that the Dominion Auxiliary had had its origin as a native Canadian movement in the Fourfold Gospel.

The adopted legislation called for a "Canadian Council" to convene not later than June 1980, to adopt a constitution and bylaws and to elect officers. In the meantime there would begin a gradual transfer of the administration of Canadian affairs to a Canadian headquarters, with the transition to be completed by January 1981.

THE FIRST ASSEMBLY

The historic "Canadian Council," later to be dubbed the "First Biennial General Assembly of The Christian and Missionary Alliance in Canada," convened from June 3-8, 1980, in the University Centre of the University of Manitoba, in Winnipeg. Evangelist Dr. Ravi Zacharias was the featured speaker at the public services. Other speaking ministries were provided by Dr. Louis King, Dr. David Rambo, Dr. Robert Henry, Dr. Arnold Cook and Rev. Wendell Grout. A total of 530 official and 170 corresponding delegates were present at the founding Assembly. According to Rev. Robert Cowles, editor of the *Alliance Witness*, Assembly moderator Gerald Fowler guided the business sessions through to completion and "remained unruffled and in possession of his disarming sense of humour throughout."[87]

The delegates adopted a constitution and bylaws, establishing an autonomous Canadian church body as of January 1, 1981. The constitution contained a statement of faith identical with that of the Alliance in the United States. Canadian missionaries would continue to serve while overseas under the Division of Overseas Ministries, which would be reimbursed for expenses. The Alliance in Canada would handle recruitment and appointment of Canadian missionary candidates, and the deployment of Canadian missionaries while on furlough. The *Alliance Witness* would remain the official mouthpiece of the Alliance throughout North America.[88]

Bylaws called for a biennial General Assembly, which would elect the president and members of the board of directors. In turn, the board would elect its own chairman, vice-chairman, secretary and treasurer, and make appointments to positions on the president's team. Elected at the founding assembly were:

President: Rev. Melvin P. Sylvester
Board of Directors:
    Canadian Pacific District   Rev. Gordon Fowler
                                           Rev. David Anderson
    Western Canadian District   Mr. Jack Klemke
                                           Rev. Jack Schroeder
    Canadian Midwest District   Mr. Lloyd Matheson
                                           Rev. Walter Boldt
    Eastern and Central Canadian District
                                           Rev. Arnold Reimer
                                           Mr. Yvan Fournier

At Large   Rev. Raymur Downey
             Dr. Philip Ng
             Mr. Robert Conroy

Highlights of the Assembly were the charge to the new president, and the presentation of a framed copy of the congratulatory resolution by the 1980 Council, both by Dr. King. After the last business session, the delegates met for a time of celebration. Robert Cowles described the occasion:

> The first General Assembly of the C. & M.A. in Canada, in addition to being a business meeting, a spiritual feast and a study convocation, was a celebration. And celebrate the participants did—at a sit-down banquet for 700 delegates and guests.
>
> A special audio-visual presentation entitled "Canada" prepared by the Bowker brothers preceded the message by Wendell Grout, "New Horizons".... The solemnity of the message continued as Dr. King introduced the newly elected Board of Directors and set them apart by prayer. They in turn laid hands on the first president, Rev. Melvin P. Sylvester, currently superintendent of the Eastern and Central Canadian District, as he was commissioned for his new responsibilities.
>
> The long, joyous evening ended with the singing of "O Canada."[89]

Of course, technically, Canadian autonomy was still more than half a year away. The board of directors would have to appoint other officers and tend to many other details between the conclusion of General Assembly and January 1, 1981. Meeting on August 5, the board appointed five of their members to various functions:

Gordon Fowler	Chairman
Robert Conroy, Q.C.	Vice-Chairman
Arnold Reimer	Secretary
Lloyd Matheson	Treasurer

On the same occasion, they appointed Gerald Fowler as executive vice-president, Dr. Arnold Cook as director of personnel and missions and Mrs. Beverly Howell as national president of the Womens' Missionary Prayer Fellowship. Having decided to locate the head office in the Toronto area, office space was rented at 235 Yorkland Boulevard, near the intersection of the Don Valley Parkway and highway 401, in the city of North York, for November 1 occupancy.

In September 1980, Dr. King deputized for the board of managers for the last time at both the Canadian Pacific and the Western Canadian district conferences. In Victoria, District Superintendent Gordon Fowler said:

> Not only are we honoured to have the president of The Christian and Missionary Alliance with us on this final occasion of having an official representative from the Board of Managers with us, but, in Dr. King we welcome one of the finest preachers of the Word that we know.[90]

In Calgary, retiring District Superintendent Roy McIntyre said:

> For about ten years I have been ... vitally involved in the move to Canadian autonomy. It has been long and at times tedious, but that day will arrive on January 1st, 1981. ... We appreciate the part Dr. King has had in bringing this to fruition.[91]

A REGAINED INDEPENDENCE

On Monday, November 3, 1980, President Mel Sylvester unlocked the door to the new head office so that the movers could bring in two desks and chairs, a small table, an orange crate and several boxes of records. Together with his secretary, Esther Reimer, Director of Finance Menno Dirks and File Clerk Mrs. Verna Dirks, they began the task of setting up operations. Over the next few months, they were joined by Executive Vice-president Gerald Fowler, Director of Personnel and Missions Dr. Arnold Cook and other staff members.

On December 19, 1980, President Louis L. King dispatched his last message to all Canadian workers and missionaries on furlough:

Dear Canadian Friends:

How can I express the deep feelings which well up in my heart today! When the New Year dawns across the North

American continent, you will set out on your own to realize the great vision God has given The Christian and Missionary Alliance in Canada—a vision of God's dominion from sea to sea. I strongly share with Rev. Melvin Sylvester, your first president, the desire to see the glory of Jesus Christ cover the earth and to see men and women brought out of darkness into His marvelous light.

Several years ago my son stood before me moments before his departure for the mission field.... My words to him at that parting hour I now also leave with you: "Make it your consuming desire to be *All for Jesus*."[92]

Eleven days later, as the clocks chimed the arrival of the new year, a new Canadian denomination was born.

On February 1, 1887, Rev. John Salmon had stepped out on an independent ministry. Amid tearful farewells, he had told his congregation that he did not know where he was going but would trust the Lord to open up another "sphere of usefulness" to him. His friend, Rev. John Burton, had expressed the hope that Salmon would find a "suitable field."[93] Both Salmon's trust and Burton's hope were fulfilled in the Canadian movement in the Fourfold Gospel. By January 1, 1981, the "sphere of usefulness" had undergone several metamorphoses and was now appearing as a Canadian denomination, with 239 churches and in full support of its 111 overseas missionaries.

The story of the achievement of Canadian autonomy is more than an exposition of Canadian quirks and American dominance. Our American brethren, with few exceptions, were not able to view the unfolding drama as anything other than the result of the rise of Canadian nationalism. While nationalism certainly was the spark to ignite the flame, the episode should be viewed as a classic illustration of the age-old tension between authority imposed from without and vitality expressed from within. In addition, since 1897, within the Alliance there had been a cleavage between the American philosophy of the melting-pot society, with the Canadian counterpart of the multi-cultural or multi-regional society. The two divergent ideas are not compatible, and it may be questioned why Canadians acquiesced for almost 84 years. However, in the light of current Canadian trends, the achievement of Canadian autonomy begs the question of Canadians themselves. The Canadian Alliance may one day be asked to

Canadian Identity Again / 441

submit to fragmentation along cultural or regional lines. If and when that occurs, will the Canadian majority prove to be more understanding of minority aspirations than the American majority was in the all-Canada struggle for self government in the 1960s and 1970s?

REFERENCES

1. *Alliance Witness*, 27 Apr 1966, pp. 6, 7; 11 May 1966, pp. 6, 18.
2. Ibid., 15 Jun 1977, pp. 8-10.
3. Ibid., 19 Jan 1972, pp. 6-9.
4. Ibid., p. 9.
5. Ibid., p. 8.
6. Western Annual Conference Records, District Superintendent's Report, Sep 1972, p. 1.
7. Mid-Western Annual Conference Records, District Superintendent's Report, Sep 1973, p. 2.
8. *Alliance Witness*, 9 Jan 1980, p. 6.
9. Ibid., p. 8.
10. Mid-Western Annual Conference Records, District Superintendent's Report, Oct 1975, pp. 1, 11.
11. *Alliance Witness*, 26 Jun 1963, p. 8; 11 Dec 1963, p. 8.
12. Ibid., 9 Apr 1975, pp. 6, 7; Annual Report of the President of CBC/CTS, 1971, p. 1.
13. *Alliance Witness*, 6 Nov 1974, pp. 8, 9; 18 Mar 1981, p. 10.
14. Ibid., 18 Mar 1981, pp. 10, 11; Annual Report of the President of CBC/CTS, 1980, p. 2.
15. *Alliance Witness*, 15 Sep 1982, p. 29.
16. Ibid., 5 Jan 1972, p. 21.
17. Ibid., 24 Aug 1987, p. 14.
18. Ibid., 7 Mar 1979, p. 11.
19. Ibid., 29 Apr 1970, p. 18.
20. Ibid., 13 May 1970, p. 8; 24 Jun 1970, pp. 8, 10.
21. Eastern and Central, Minutes, 11 Jun 1978.
22. Eastern and Central, Annual, Sep 1973, District Superintendent's Report, pp. 47, 48.
23. Ibid., Proceedings, p. 16.
24. Lindsay Reynolds, *Footprints* (Toronto: The Christian and Missionary Alliance in Canada, 1982), pp. 356, 357.
25. Ibid., pp. 293, 356.
26. *Eternity*, Aug 1974, p. 8.
27. *Alliance Witness*, 5 Nov 1975, pp. 2, 18, 19.

28. Eastern, Annual, Sep 1980, p. 111.
29. Ibid., p. 4.
30. Ibid., p. 7.
31. *Alliance Witness*, 18 Jan 1981, p. 28.
32. Eastern, Minutes, 16 Jul, 22 Oct, 25 Nov 1966.
33. Eastern, Annual, 1967, p. 61.
34. Ibid., 1964, p. 29.
35. *Alliance Witness*, 10 Nov 1965, p. 16.
36. Eastern, Minutes, 6 Mar 1967.
37. *Alliance Witness*, 13 May 1970, p. 17.
38. Ibid., 6 Feb 1980, p. 28.
39. Ibid., 26 Nov 1980, p. 29.
40. Eastern, Annual, 1969, p. II-J-2.
41. Ibid., 1970, p. II-J-1.
42. Ibid., 1969, p. II-J-1; Quebec Newsletter, Nov 1969.
43. *Alliance Weekly*, 13 May 1970, p. 16; Quebec Newsletter, Feb 1971; Eastern, Annual, 1970, p. II-J-1.
44. Eastern, Annual, 1973, p. 85.
45. Ibid., 1975, p. 88.
46. Ibid., 1979, p. 77.
47. Ibid., 1983, p. 37; *Alliance Witness*, 12 May 1982, p. 29.
48. District memo to French workers, 2 Jun 1971.
49. Letter, Frost to Orthner, 27 Nov 1970.
50. Eastern, Minutes, 29 Apr 1971.
51. District memo to French workers, 2 Jun 1971.
52. *Alliance Witness*, 3 Jan 1973, p. 15.
53. Ibid., 30 Jan 1974, p. 30; Eastern, Annual, Sep 1973, pp. 83, 84.
54. Letter, Funé (Christmas), Nov 1974; Letter, Funé to French Work Committee, 5 Nov 1974; Eastern, Annual, Sep 1976, p. 89.
55. Eastern, Annual, Sep 1976, p. 54.
56. Ibid., Sep 1977, p. 145.
57. Letter, Sylvester to French Workers, 8 Sep 1980; *Alliance Witness*, 2 Apr 1980, p. 27.
58. *Alliance Witness*, 22 Jun 1983, p. 29; *Canadian Alliance News*, Sep 1983, p. 1.
59. *Canadian Alliance News*, Sep 1983, p. 7; Feb 1984, p. 5.
60. Board of Managers, Minutes, 4, 5 Sep 1947, p. 160.
61. Eastern, Annual, Sep 1966, p. 18.
62. Ibid., Sep 1966, p. 6.
63. Ibid., Sep 1967, p. 5.
64. *Alliance Witness*, 22 Nov 1967, pp. 14, 15, 16, 23.

65. Eastern, Annual, Sep 1967, p. 18.
66. Statement by Dr. Nathan Bailey to Tri-District Conference (1974) re. The C&MA in Canada (1972), p. 3.
67. *Alliance Witness*, 6 Jun 1973, p. 5.
68. Statement by Dr. Nathan Bailey to Tri-District Conference (1974) re, The C&MA in Canada (1972).
69. *Alliance Witness*, 6 Nov 1974, p. 10.
70. Board of Managers, Minutes, 5 Dec.
71. Annual Report, May 1975, p. 22.
72. Canadian Corporation, Minutes, 11-12 Jun 1975.
73. Ibid.
74. Meeting with Dr. N. Bailey, Rev. M. Sylvester, Rev. W. Boldt in New York, Minutes, 18 May 1976.
75. Study Commission, Minutes, Aug 30-31, 1976.
76. Ibid.
77. Nyack meeting of Dr. N. Bailey, Rev. M. Sylvester, W. Boldt, Minutes, 8 Sep 1976.
78. Canadian Corporation, Minutes, 16-17 May 1977.
79. Fraternal Committee, Minutes, 5-6 Jun 1978.
80. Letter and attachments of King to members of Fraternal Committee on Canadian Autonomy, 15 Aug 1978.
81. Tri-District Conference, Minutes, 8 Sep 1978, p. 3.
82. Ibid., p. 13.
83. Ibid., pp. 8, 9.
84. Fraternal Committee, Minutes, 26 Feb, Mar 1979.
85. *Alliance Witness*, 27 Jun 1979, pp. 9, 10; *Canadian Alliance News*, Jun 1979, p. 1.
86. *Alliance Witness*, 27 Jun 1979, pp. 9, 10.
87. Ibid., 23 Jul 1980, p. 6.
88. Annual Report, May 1981, p. 3.
89. *Alliance Witness*, 23 Jul 1980, p. 9.
90. Midwest Annual, Sep 1980, District Superintendent's Report, p. 3.
91. Pacific Annual, Sep 1980, District Superintendent's Report, pp. 111-6.
92. Annual Report, May 1981, p. 3.
93. *Footprints*, pp. 88, 89.

EPILOGUE

Until He Comes

Some thirty years ago, the writer was vacationing in Cape Cod, and as there was an excellent Baptist church close by, he joined with them for Sunday worship. It so happened that there was a well-known guest preacher present that day, not of either Baptist or Alliance connection. His sermon was on divine healing, which he concluded with the words, "That is what The Christian and Missionary Alliance used to teach. Unfortunately, they no longer believe it."

The writer was shocked—even angered. However, with the passage of time he has come around to think that perhaps there was more truth in the preacher's statement than he had been prepared to admit at the time. Moreover, the allegation might well have been applied to other distinctives of Alliance heritage.

Every movement, whether religious or secular, starts out on the basis of an impelling conviction. As the movement grows, an administrative organization develops. Eventually, the administrators become motivated by considerations of institutional (and even personal) aggrandizement, while the founding convictions cease to be determinative in the affairs of the movement.

More to the point, church history teaches us that movements of the Spirit, almost without exception, finally lose their way and fail to fulfil their destiny. This may be abetted through alien forces growing up from within, or infiltrating from without, but is seldom due to calculated policy, accidental misfortune or even failure to adjust to the times. Generally, it is caused simply by failure to abide by the convictions and principles with which they started out.

John Dillenberger and Claude Welsh, in their work on the development of Protestant Christianity, have been very specific in their observations of the experience of movements and denominations like the Alliance. They write:

> Groups which came into existence to revitalize the life of churches and to share in the work of evangelization, quickly become self-conscious and concerned for institutional self-preservation. Each society becomes concerned with extending its own membership and promoting its own particular methods of evangelization and religious education.[1]

These denominations, they go on to tell us, have most commonly first appeared among depressed and disinherited social levels of society. As they grow older, there is a tendency to become identified with the upper middle class.[2] National and economic matters assume increasing importance. The old distinctive beliefs no longer touch the heart or the head. They become mere dogma, to which assent is presumed, rather than expressions of living faith and experience.[3] Vitality wanes while a shell of orthodoxy lingers on.[4]

No accusations are being made. I merely state a fact which we dare not ignore. There are striking similarities between these general historical observations, the condition of Canadian Methodism at its first century mark one hundred years ago, and the condition of the Alliance at its first century mark today. We need to be warned. I do not suggest that we should "bind ourselves to a changeless yesterday," nor yet that we must have unity devoid of variety. Indeed, the history of Christian organization is one of successive adjustment of form to meet the demands of changing environment. However, we must not confuse form with faith. Our first business is to understand and believe our faith.

No denomination can continue to exist without a vital, distinctive faith that sets it apart. The mere pursuit of a program, however commendable, will not be sufficient to withstand the growing pressures of economy which call for mergence and loss of identity.

The right of the Alliance to independent existence rests upon its proclamation, faith and experience in the Fourfold Gospel truths. These are its articles of faith by which it began, and by which it will either stand or fall. They are pivotal among all it teaches and practises.

The Alliance drive to double its constituency within a ten-year period, ending with the centenary, met with much success, largely because of a growing acceptance and even popularity. The Alliance has been hailed as a highly respectable, middle-of-the-road denomination. Perhaps we need to listen to Professor T. A. Kantouen, who says that increasing popularity and prestige for a denomination is seldom the result "of deepened conviction, but of growing indifference to beliefs, which for the fathers were matters of vital importance. Attention," he claims, "tends to shift to externals so that while a form of godliness is maintained, its soul changing power is lost."[5]

In spite of its success in the realm of church growth, and perhaps in a sense because of it, Alliance churchmanship is no longer a seamless robe, but a coat of many colours. Notwithstanding an official statement of faith, within the Alliance today, one finds a broad spectrum of belief or disbelief in its distinctive doctrines; so broad in fact, that those near one extreme may be embarrassed by those near the other. Our once unifying beliefs appear to have lost their relevancy, and we hear little about them from our pulpits. Perhaps we need to ask ourselves a few questions. Have our distinctive doctrines become religious catch phrases, lacking the ring of truth? Have we made a museum piece of the Fourfold Gospel, which is dusted off for special occasions and then put back on the shelf? Have we become content with a program to follow, rather than a faith to be experienced? Have we gained a spurious respectability at the cost of a muted message?

As the Alliance proceeds into its second century, the time has come for its doctrinal house to be put in order, or pay the price. Failure to reverse the drift away from its founding faith will undoubtedly result in it following the usual downward path of aging denominations. The denomination that thinks it can keep its distinctives in the shadows deceives itself. They will either be important or soon they will not be at all.

It will be necessary to first admit that the Fourfold Gospel is not in robust health within the fellowship. Reginald W. Bibby says that "recognition of religion's poverty can lead to the discovery of its potential."[6] Our founding distinctives must again become more than sentimental platitudes. They must be restored to their original causative role. We have been guilty of putting the proverbial cart before the horse. Belief and experience in the Spirit-filled and Spirit-motivated life must once more become the "first objective," the foundation on which the "ultimate objective," or superstructure of world evangelism, is built.

In the meantime, the Alliance can rejoice in a century of worldwide missionary progress, and in a numerically growing home constituency. Many have been and continue to be brought to know Jesus Christ as Saviour through the agency of the Alliance. While our leaders must wrestle with the place of our distinctive doctrines within the Alliance economy, there must be no slackening in the area of God-given opportunity in the work of the Great Commission. In these critical last years of the twentieth century, this is the way that clearly beckons us on. Let us head down the road of our second century, guided by our founder's enjoiner:

> Let us never forget the special calling of our Alliance work. It is first to hold up Jesus in His fulness. Next, to lead God's hungry children to know their full inheritance of privilege and blessing for spirit, soul and body. Next to witness to the imminent coming of the Lord Jesus Christ as our millennial king. And finally, to encourage and incite the people of God to do the neglected work of our age and time among the unchurched classes at home and the perishing heathen abroad. God will bless us as we are true to this trust.

REFERENCES

1. John Dillenberger and Claude Welsh, *Protestant Christianity* (New York: Charles Scribner's Sons, 1954), p. 290.
2. Ibid., p. 286.
3. Ibid., p. 137.
4. Ibid., p. 136.
5. T. A. Kantouen, *Resurgence of the Gospel* (Philadelphia: The Muhlenberg Press, 1948), p. 204.
6. Reginald W. Bibby, *Fragmented Gods* (Toronto: Irving Publishing Co., 1987), p. 271.

Tables and Figures

Table 1
CANADIAN ALLIANCE OVERSEAS WORKERS—1924

Retired
Rev. Sidney Hamilton
Miss J. C. Fraser
Rev. David McKee
Mrs. David McKee
Rev. Louis Turnbull
Miss Christina
  MacDougall

Detained at Home
Mrs. A. E. Thompson
Mrs. H. D. Stoddard
Rev. Walter Turnbull
Rev. C. Eicher
Mrs. C. Eicher
Mrs. A. W. Field
Miss Anna Little
Rev. H. V. Andrews

Africa
Rev. Earnest Howard
Miss Ethel Roffe
Miss Agness Killer
Rev. A. E. Loose
Miss Nora
  Bassingthwaighte

India
Miss H. C. Bushfield
Mrs. K. D. Garrison

Rev. E. G. Glenn
Rev. John R. Turnbull

China
Miss E. E. Moull
Mr. J. A. McMillan
Mrs. J. A. McMillan
Mr. Walter Oldfield
Mrs. Walter Oldfield
Mr. E. Fred Page
Miss M. J. Quinn
Rev. W. A. Shantz
Mrs. W. A. Shantz
Mr. James Smith
Mrs. James Smith
Mrs. W. G. Davis
Miss Marion Grobb
Rev. W. B. Williston
Mrs. W. B. Williston
Miss Lida White
Miss A. N. Young
Mrs. I. L. Hess
Rev. R. A. Jaffray
Mr. A. M. Lopston
Mrs. Charles E. Lumpp
Rev. M. B. Birrell

Japan
Rev. C. P. Green
Mrs. C. P. Green

Rev. W. A. Barber
Mrs. W. A. Barber

French Indo China
Mrs. D. W. Ellison
Rev. E. F. Irwin
Rev. D. J. Jeffrey
Mrs. D. J. Jeffrey
Rev. W. C. Cadman
Mr. Wm. Robinson
Rev. H. C. Smith
Mrs. R. M. Jackson
Mrs. H. C. Smith

Palestine
Mrs. R. A. Clark
Rev. E. O. Jago
Mrs. E. O. Jago
Miss Laura Beecroft

South America
Rev. W. H. Johnston
Mrs. H. W. Feldges
Rev. S. T. Burman
Mrs. S. T. Burman
Miss Grace Morrison
Rev. E. A. Prentice
Rev. Paul Young
Mr. George Moffatt
Miss Muriel Owen

/ 449

Table 2
Canadian Alliance Overseas Workers—1981

Retired
Mrs. Muriel A. Edmonds
Rev. Jean E. Funé
Mrs. Myrtle Funé
Miss Pearl Fustey
Mrs. Marie M. Irwin
Rev. D. Ivory Jeffrey
Mrs. Gladys M. Little
Miss Ethel K. Marsh
Mrs. Muriel E. Moffat
Miss Grace Morrison
Miss Blanche Palmer
Rev. Robert Patterson
Mrs. Esther G. Patterson
Rev. F. W. E. Roffe
Dr. G. Edward Roffe
Mrs. H. Curwen Smith

On Special North American Assignments
Rev. Ted Cline
Mrs. Marjorie Cline
Rev. Garth Hunt
Mrs. Betty Hunt
Rev. F. James Pratt
Mrs. Doris J. Pratt

Argentina
Mrs. Mora Bundy
Rev. Jack M. Shannon
Mrs. Jean Shannon

Chile
Miss Joan A. Meger

Colombia
Rev. C. Stuart Lightbody
(on leave of absence)
Mrs. Jo Anne Lightbody
(on leave of absence)
Rev. David Peters
Mrs. Arlene Peters

Ecuador
Dr. John W. Hall
Mrs. Penelope Hall
Rev. Bruce A. Jackson

Miss Evelyn Jensen
(on leave of absence)
Rev. Jacob P. Klassen
Mrs. Mavis B. Klassen
Rev. David Miller
Rev. Henry C. Miller
Mrs. Vera C. Miller
Rev. Richard P. Reichert
Mrs. Hope Reichert
Rev. Theodore A. Sauvé
Rev. Cecil M. Smith
Mrs. Eunice Smith
Miss Marjorie D. Sproxton

Peru
Rev. Eugene Kelly
Mrs. Muriel G. Kelly
Rev. Ernest E. Klassen
Mrs. Marilyn Klassen
(both temporarily in Costa Rica)
Rev. James K. McKerihan
Rev. Donald J. Scarrow
Miss Betty Sproxton
Mrs. Lois Thiessen

Surinam
Rev. Vincent Lone Cheung
Mrs. Sylvia Cheung

Great Britain
Rev. Ross F. Ingram

France
Rev. Donald I. Dirks
Rev. Norman Ens
Mrs. Marie Ens
Rev. George Irwin
Mrs. Harriette Irwin
Miss Ruth F. Patterson

Netherlands
Rev. Clement R. Dreger
Mrs. Madalene G. Dreger

Mali
Miss Joan Foster
Miss Sandra H. Scott
Miss Kay M. Thompson

Upper Volta
Mrs. Myrna Ballard
Rev. A. Eric Persson
Mrs. Gwen Persson

Guinea
Rev. James H. Elliott
Mrs. Carol Elliott
(both temporarily in France)

Ivory Coast
Rev. Jesse Jespersen
Mrs. Ann Jespersen
(both on leave of absence)

Gabon
Miss Julie R. Fehr
Mrs. Maurine Holcomb
Miss Esther I. Lutzer
Rev. J. Laurie McLean
Mrs. Nancy McLean

Zaire
Rev. Ronald W. Brown
Mrs. Myra Brown
Miss Marion Dicke
Rev. Raymur Downey
Mrs. Viola A. Downey
Miss Leona Embury
Rev. James R. Sawatsky
Mrs. Dawn E. Sawatsky
Miss F. L. Ruth Stanley
Miss Anne Stephens
Miss Cheryle A. Wilson

India
Rev. Elmer J. Entz
Mrs. Muriel M. Entz
Miss Ferne A. Gerrie
Rev. Fred Roth
Mrs. Cora E. Roth

Table 2 (continued)

Thailand
Miss Irene G. Hearn
Miss Dorothy Hubert
Rev. Richard H. Johnston
Rev. Reg Reimer (refugee work)

Malaysia (Dalat School)
Mr. Edward J. Wiens
Mrs. Helen Wiens

Indonesia
Rev. Gordon V. Chapman
Mrs. Adina Chapman
Rev. Floyd J. Grunau
Mrs. Joyce Grunau
Rev. Harold Klassen
Mrs. Maureen T. Klassen
Miss Margaret Lee
Miss Lorna Munroe
Rev. Frank A. Peters
Mr. Alex Valley
Mrs. Irene Fleming (refugee work)

China—Hong Kong
Rev. Elisha L. Cheung
Mrs. Shiu Mai Cheung
Miss Ruth Sanders
Rev. Douglas F. Wiebe
Mrs. Hilda Wiebe

China—Taiwan
Rev. James M. Chuang
Mrs. Esther Chuang
Miss Laura J. Roszell (on leave of absence)

Japan
Miss Susan Dyck

Philippines
Mrs. Helen Douglas
Rev. D. Franklin Irwin
Rev. Ronald P. MacKinnon
Mrs. June MacKinnon
Mrs. Marilyn Maves
Miss Ethel J. Moorehouse

Miss Margaret A. Schick
Miss P. Lynn Walsh (on leave of absence)

Irian Jaya, Indonesia
Miss Marcia H. Thomas (awaiting visa)
Miss Lois R. Belsey
Rev. Harold W. Catto
Miss Elfrieda S. Toews
Miss Elsie Toews
Rev. Pat A. Worsley
Mrs. Ardyce Worsley

Australia
Rev. Harold M. Collins
Mrs. June Collins

New Zealand
Rev. John Bergen

452 / Tables and Figures

Figure 1

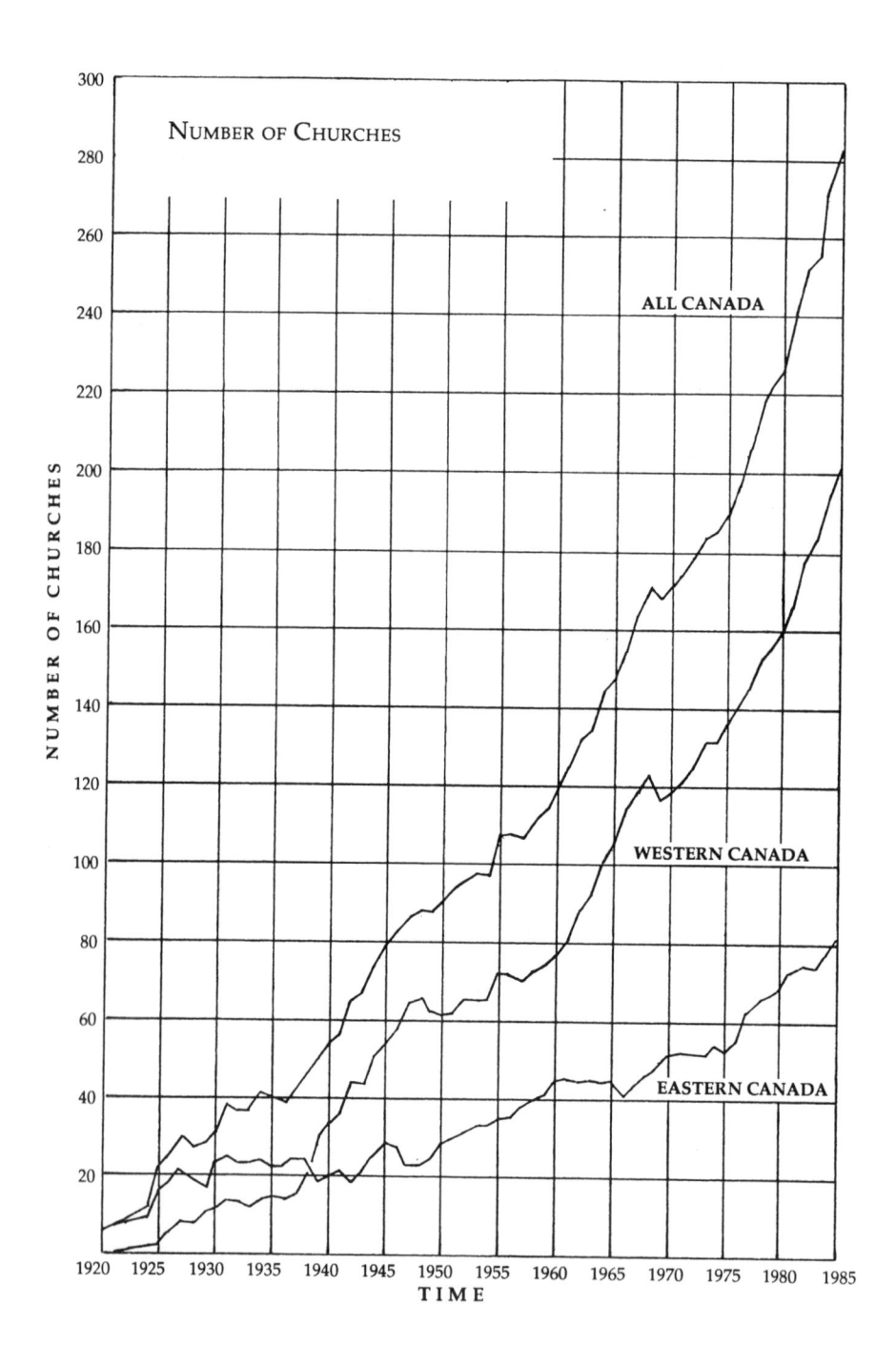

NUMBER OF CHURCHES

(y-axis: NUMBER OF CHURCHES; x-axis: TIME, 1920–1985)

ALL CANADA
WESTERN CANADA
EASTERN CANADA

Tables and Figures / 453

Figure 2

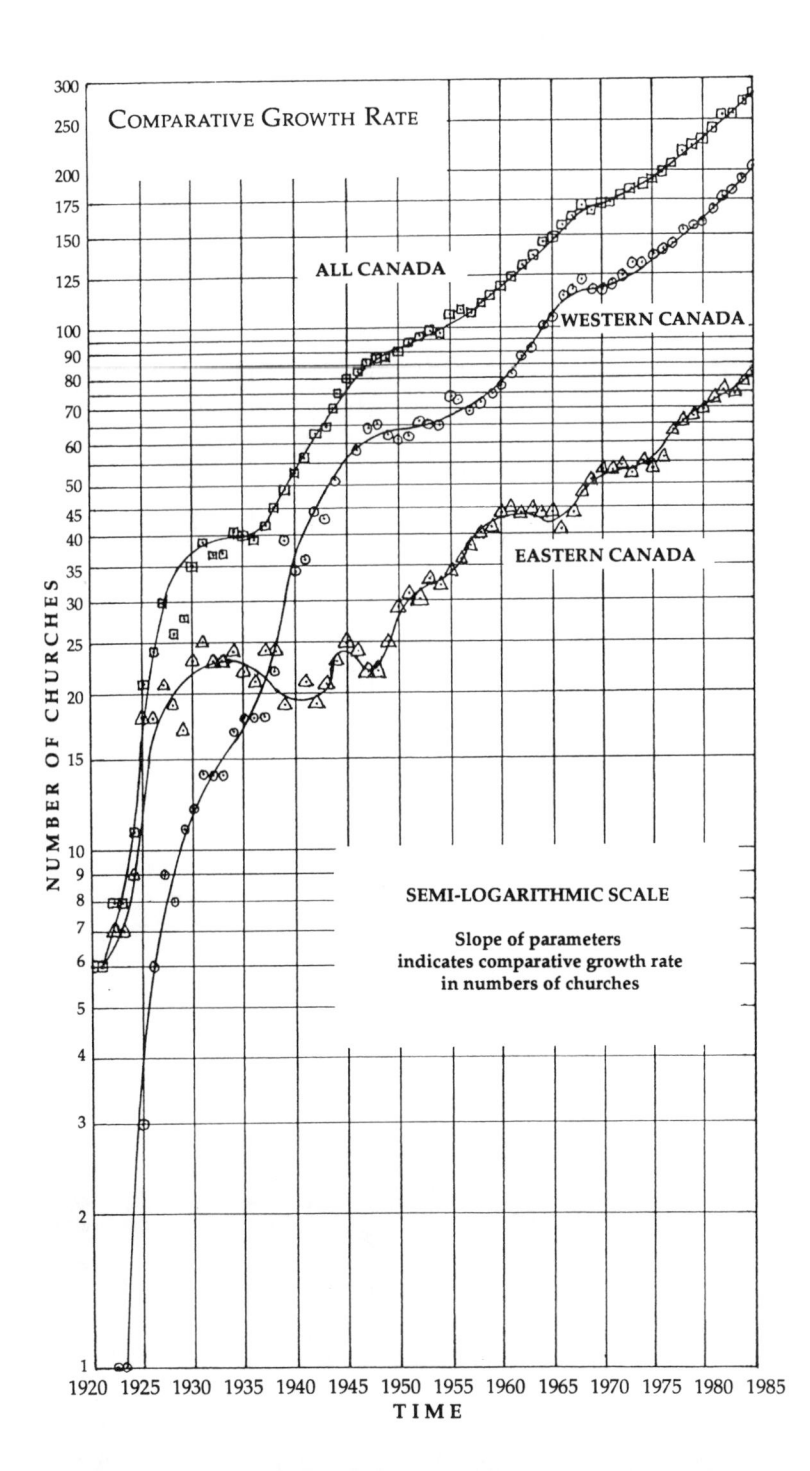

COMPARATIVE GROWTH RATE

ALL CANADA
WESTERN CANADA
EASTERN CANADA

SEMI-LOGARITHMIC SCALE

Slope of parameters
indicates comparative growth rate
in numbers of churches

NUMBER OF CHURCHES

TIME

454 / Tables and Figures

Figure 3

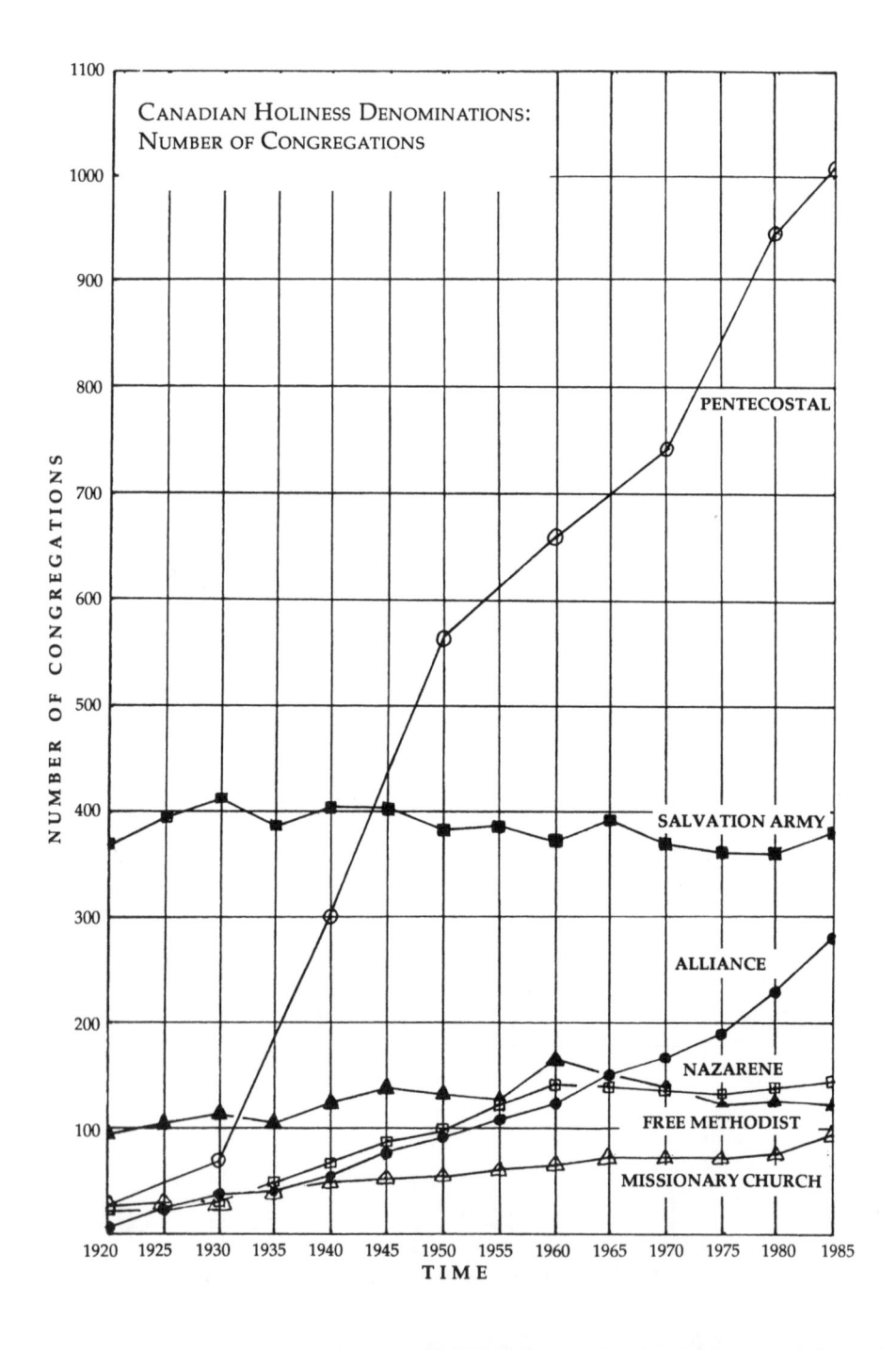

Index

A

Abbotsford, B.C., Alliance work 301.
  See also Sevenoaks Alliance
Abee, Alberta 126
Aberhart, William 221
Accrediting Association of Bible Colleges 352, 357, 361
Adamson, W. H. 58
African missions 288
Albert College, Belleville 76, 206
Alberta Bible Academy 224
All for Jesus 183
Allenbach, Sask. 119
Alliance Bible Institute, Toronto 335
Alliance cavalry 118, 126
Alliance Chrétienne et Missionnaire, Dollard des Ormeaux 410
Alliance Church Union, Hong Kong 405
Alliance Community Church, Montreal 72, 311, 385, 386, 409, 410
Alliance Gospel Hall, Montreal 148, 369, 371
  depression hardships 172
  extension work 165
  losses to Pentecostals 160
  Sparke as pastor 161–162
Alliance Gospel Hall, Regina 255, 271, 271–272
Alliance Gospel Tabernacle, St. John, N.B.
  decline of 178–182
  reaffiliation with the Alliance 182
Alliance Men 289
Alliance Publications 185

Alliance School of Theology and Missions 401
Alliance Tabernacle Willowvale Park Corp. 68, 151. *See also* Christie Street Tabernacle
Alliance Theological Seminary 401
Alliance Training Home 334
Alliance World 88
Allinger, Beth 248, 317-318
Allinger, Henry 255
Ambridge, Cecil 321, 323
Ambridge House 322
Ambrose, H. W. 340
American Conference of Undenominational Churches 217
Anderson, David T. 278, 430, 437
Anderson, Mavis 274, 293, 299
Anderson, Selma 209
Anderson, Sydney F. 259
Angrove, Edward 399
Ansley, Chester 277
Apostolic Church, Saskatoon 243
Archibald, J. R. 236
Arminianism 7
Arminius, Jacobus 7
Arviat Alliance Church 318
Ash, Mr. 219
Assiniboia, Sask. 400
Associated Gospel Churches of Canada.
  See Christian Workers Churches
Association for the Promotion of Holiness 33
Association of Theological Schools 402
Augsburger, Myron S. 405
autonomy, Canadian 407, 416–418
  ballot results 435

/ 455

456 / Index

Council deliberation   436
enabling legislation   435
fraternal committee   433, 434, 435, 436
opposition to   416, 431–432
study commission   428, 431
recommendations of   432
Avenue Road Alliance Church, Toronto   304, 312, 316
origins   296–298
Avenue Road Church of the Nazarene   297
Avenue Road Presbyterian Church   297
Avenue Road United Church   297

B

baby boomers   287
Bailey, Keith   431, 431–432, 433, 434
Bailey, Mabel   239
Bailey, Ernest J.   182, 187, 353, 424–425, 425, 428
Bailey, Nathan   192, 194, 293, 303, 314, 353
  presidency of   315, 319, 324, 433
    Canadian autonomy   420, 423, 424, 431-32
  role in French work   378, 383, 384, 386
  superintendency of   289, 291, 295, 298, 316, 354
  work for district cooperation   295, 355, 418, 423
Bailey, Richard W.   311
Bailey, Ruth   311
Baker, Charles   145
Baker, Gertrude   321
Baker, H. H. P.   360
Baliem Valley, New Guinea   308–311
Ballard, J. Hudson   334
Bangor, Maine   223
baptism
  of infants   65
  Simpson's belief   3, 11
Baragar, H. W.   76
Barbin, Edouard   386–387, 389
Bard, Selwyn   413
Barley, Percy R.   311
Barr, Mrs. Norman   168
Barton, Ben   126
Barton Street Methodist Church   76
Bassingthwaighte, Nora   264, 268, 346
Batchelor, Roy   305
Battles, Robert   431, 433, 434
Baxter, J. Sidlow   312
Bayview Glen Alliance   400
Beach, George and Ruth   144–146

Beal, Elton   86
Beattie, J. T.   84
Beaverlodge, Alta., Alliance work   277, 406
Bell, George   105, 108, 111, 112, 115, 117
Bell, Mr. and Mrs. George   64, 187
Belleville, Ontario   75. *See also* Quinte Alliance Church, Belleville
Bennett, Merle   239
Bennett, Richard   420
Berachah Mission, Truro   186–187
Berney, Paul   421
Berry, Mrs. W. H.   65
Bethany Chapel   36, 333
Bethany Church, Hopeville   34, 405
Bethany Church, Peterborough   34, 251, 289, 290, 335, 431
Bethany Church, Toronto   34
  Bethany Gospel Wagon   34
  Bethany Home for Healing   34
  Bethany Mission   34
  Bethany Orphanage   34
  Bethany Working Men's Home   34
Bethany Constitution   34, 38, 188–189, 190
Bethany Tabernacle, Peterborough   188–189, 191
  Crone as pastor   190
  independence of   192–193
Bethel Bible Institute   409, 413. *See also* Institut Biblique Béthel
Bethel Church, Kingston   138
Bethel College and Seminary   278
Beulah Alliance   130, 204, 206, 213, 220, 222, 265, 339, 397, 400
  Carmichael as pastor   170
  conventions at   109, 115-116, 128
  early hardship   101
Beulah Mission   98–99
Beuler, Miss   148
Bibby, Reginald W.   447
Bible Institute for Women   186
Bible schools, origins   331–332
  in Canada   332–333
Big Bay, Alta.   126
Bingham, Rowland V.   53
  view of Bosworths   64
Birrel, Matthew   36
Bishop, George   367
Black Thursday   239
Blackett, G. M.   80–81, 138, 258, 343, 352, 356
  as board representative   262
  Bible school leadership   274, 305, 345-346, 349-350, 355
  resignation   357

Owen Sound pastorate   81
western superintendency   307–308, 359
Blackett, Mrs. Lucy   345
Blythe Cottage   35
Boardman, William E.   32, 332
Boda, Rexford A.   402, 404
Boisseau, Jean   415
Boldt, Walter   398, 400, 403, 427, 428, 430, 432, 437
Boston Bible School   338
Bosworth, B. B.   60
Bosworth Brothers   60–64
   Alliance leadership view of   69–70
   1921 Toronto campaign   60–64, 76, 334
   after effects of   69, 149
   effect on west   99–100
   opposition to   64
   1924 Ottawa campaign   78, 82–85, 170, 210
Bosworth, F. F.   61, 226–227
Bourget, Bishop   367
Bowker brothers   438
Bowker, Martin   270, 277
Bowman, Mr. and Mrs.   260
Boyd, Mrs.   187
Boydton Institute   73
Brabazon, James F.   172–173, 180
Bradley, Myrtle   233–234. *See also* Wishart, Rev. and Mrs. Gordon
branch meetings, early role   18
Brandon, Man., Alliance work   269, 277, 406
Brentwood Park Alliance Church   252
Brethren Assemblies
   Quebec ministries   377
Brimley Road Alliance Church   87
British Columbia
   district jurisdiction of   127, 267
Broad, H.   87
Bromley, Myron   310, 311
Brooker, L. Latimer   316, 380, 384
Brooks, Mr. and Mrs. Herman   87
Brooks, Mr. and Mrs. W. H.   248, 264
Brooks, W. H.   224
   Alliston ministry   156
   conversion of   154–155
   Faith Mission ministry   156–159
   Saskatoon ministry   256-258, 270
   Vancouver ministry   299, 301, 302
   Wallaceburg ministry   155–156
   WCBI leadership   274, 275, 345, 346, 349
   western superintendency   305–306, 355, 356

Broughton, Clifford   243, 254, 257
Brown, R. R.   294, 296
Brown, E. G.   76
Brown, G. Vernor   52, 142, 172, 174, 246, 371
Brown, O. P.   167
Brownlee, Mr. and Mrs. W. J.   87
Brussels Street Church, St. John   58, 61, 167–168, 182
Bryant, Sir Arthur   45
Burton, John   440
Butcher, Louis J.   108, 110, 116, 121, 122
Butterfield, Mary   73, 127, 128, 351

C

Cactus Lake, Sask.   235
Calgary, Alta., Alliance work   102, 225, 256. *See also* First Alliance Church; Foothills Alliance Church
   missionary convention of 1923   115
   origins   110, 120, 269–270
Calgary Gospel Mission   128
Calgary Prophetic Bible Institute   221
Calvary Temple, Winnipeg   207
Calvinism   7
Cama Woodlands Nursing Home   322
Campbell, Alexander B.   11
Campbell, Dr.   339
Campbell, Duncan   132, 233, 255
Canada-U.S. relationships, Alliance   416–418, 419, 425, 440
Canadian Alliance   418
Canadian Alliance News   425, 427
Canadian Bible College   169, 308, 310, 320, 401–402, 406
   accreditation   360–361
   degree programs   360, 361
   Fourth Ave. campus   359, 360, 404
   naming of   359
   Quebec extension   415
Canadian Bible Institute, Regina   275, 346. *See also* Western Canadian Bible Institute
Canadian Bible Institute, Toronto   155, 156, 170, 210, 211, 274, 341, 342
   closure of   172, 344
   origins   338–339
   reopening considerations   348, 353–355
   sale of property   291
Canadian Bible Society   377, 383, 409
Canadian centennial   419
Canadian charter, Alliance   423, 425, 428, 431, 432

458 / Index

Canadian Corporation, Alliance 295, 427, 432, 436
   origins 423–424
Canadian District, incorporation of 89
Canadian Midwest District
   Downey superintendency 407
   origins 319–320
Canadian Mission to India 185
Canadian Pacific District
   conference, 1979 397
   formation of 396, 397
Canadian Pioneer Evangelism 191
Canadian representative agency 292–295, 418, 423
Canadian Sunday School Mission 207, 386
Canadian Theological College 401–402
   name change 402
Canadian Theological Seminary 402, 404, 415
   accreditation 402
Cancelier, Fernand 415, 422
Cancelier, Marika 415
Canh, Nguyentan tan 407
Cannibal Valley 311
Capel, Edgar T. 72, 73–74, 336
Capital Hill Union Church 247, 251
Capitol Hill Alliance Church 252
Carey, William 273
Carlson, J. D. 273, 297–298, 304
Carmichael, A. M. 170, 221
Carseland, Alta. 256
Carstead, Della 156
Carter, R. Kelso 22
Carter, W. P. 185
Caskey, Rev. and Mrs. David 304, 318
Castle, Ron 318
Castleton, Ont. 165, 170
Catholicism, Quebec 365–366, 366–367
Catto, Harold 310, 415
Cedarvale Gospel Tabernacle 61, 65–66, 85, 88
Centennial Declaration 420
Central Alliance Church, Detroit 168, 169
Central Baptist Seminary 399
Central Canadian District 90, 140
Central China Conference 36
Central Church of Christ, Regina 131
Central City Mission, Vancouver 227
Centre for Evangelism, CBC/CTS 402
CFRN radio 223, 224, 273
chair shower 66
Champ, Stuart 349
Chao, Augustus 314, 317–318
Chapelle Chrétienne Evangelique, Welland 379, 383, 386

Chapman, Roger 103
Chatham, Maude 260
Chatham, Ont., Alliance work 316. *See also* Gregory Drive Alliance Church
Child Evangelism Fellowship 372, 377, 378
Chilliwack, B.C., Alliance work 277
China Inland Mission 251
Chinese Alliance Church, Regina 248, 317–318
Chinese Christian Institute 185
Chiniquy, Charles 367
CHMA radio 351
Choiquier, Alain 413
Chouinard Avenue chapel, Quebec City 381
Chown, S. D. 138
Chown United Church, Vancouver 260
Christian Alliance
   amalgamation with Evangelical Missionary Alliance 37
   effect in Canada 37
   early objectives 17
   founding of 16–18
Christian and Missionary Alliance in Canada (1972) 423
Christian Institute 333
Christian Publications, Calgary 396
Christian Worker 49
Christian Workers Bathurst Street Tabernacle 49, 116
Christian Workers Churches 49
Christie, William 265
Christie Street Tabernacle 62, 86, 88, 149, 209, 217, 290, 291
   depression hardships 171
   Hollinrake at 176
   incorporation of 151
   Lewellan at 176
   Mason at 173
   origins of 66–69
   response to Dunkerque 184
church debt, warning against 205
Church Extension Loan Fund 312
Church of England 30
Church of God Sojourning in Aldershot 321–322
Church of the Redeemer (Independent) 193
church tradition, origins 329
Church union, 1925 201. *See also* Unionism
   effect in west 201–202
Circle Drive Alliance Church 255, 403
   formation of 399–400
City Mission, St. John 167

Clark, A. W.   84
Clark, S. D.   137
Clayton Hotel   349–350, 352
Clemenger, J. E.   433
Clemmer, Raymond   232, 239, 244
Cleveland Coloured Quintette   73, 76, 77, 81, 82, 87, 110, 116
Clifford, N. Keith   138
Colbourne, Sir John   30
Colley, T. E.   277
Collins, B. F.   204, 205, 225
Committee of Evangelism   164, 176
Committee of Home Work   176, 192
Compass   299
confederation, Canadian   97
Congregationalists   32
   response to church union   138
Connor, Margaret   116, 118, 119, 299, 340, 351
   Beulah ministry   204, 220, 230
   district executive   236
   Saskatchewan ministries   235, 258
Conroy, Robert   430, 438
consecration meetings   5
Constantinople, capture of   330
constitution, Alliance.   *See also* Bethany Constitution; Restructuring
   1912 constitution   24, 417
conventions, origins   37
Cook, Arnold   361, 430, 437, 438, 439
Cook, Reid   290
Cooke's Presbyterian Church   295
Cooper, D.   169
Cooperative Commonwealth Federation   170
Coquitlam, B.C., Alliance work   319
Cornwall, Ont., French ministry   374, 380–383, 385
Countess of Huntington   331
Courtney, John   169
Cowles, H. Robert   398, 400, 437, 438
Cox, Winnie   248, 255, 271
Cranbrook, B.C., Alliance work   400
Cree Indian ministry   306, 317
Crockford, Oliver   65, 85–86, 88
Crone, H. W.   190, 193
Crone, Walter S.   189–194
Cross, J. E.   340
Crosby, Edson   229
Cross, Mrs. Edward   209, 216, 219
Cross, Edward   111, 112-113, 118, 129, 130, 204, 209, 215, 216
   death of   218
   Great West Mission work   114, 117
   Gwynne ministry   124-125, 126, 128
   ordination of   206

Crown College   334
Cullis, Charles   32, 331, 332
Cults
   in western Canada   98, 122, 202
   post-union rise of   137
   post-war rise of   46
Cundy, P.   343
Cunningham, John   126, 268, 270, 274, 305, 313
Cutler, Mrs. L. J.   71, 73, 75, 116

D

Danforth Avenue Methodist Church   209
Darby, L. L.   82
Darby, John N.   10, 46
Dartmouth, N.S.   74
Dauphin, Man.   235
Davao Chinese Church   317
Davey, James E.   167, 181
David, Ira E.   150-152, 162, 277
Davis, E. W.   115, 120, 121
deeper life   9, 16.   *See also* Sanctification; Fourfold Gospel
   as motivation for service   16, 71
   decline of emphasis on   23
Deitz, Raymond   382, 386, 388, 399
Delorimier Street Methodist Church   147
Delta Tabernacle, Hamilton   79, 101, 170, 243, 310, 316, 406
   origins as Ebenezer Tabernacle   76
denominationalism
   O. J. Smith and   68–69
   the Alliance and   20, 24, 34, 53, 90, 176, 315, 406
Denzil, Sask.   119, 235, 238, 248, 255, 258–259
Denzil Union Church   258
depression.   *See* Great Depression
Dibden, Charles   233
Dickenson, R.   160
Diefenbaker, John G.   419
Dillenberger, John   445
Dimmick, John F.   226, 227, 228
Dimmick, Ruby   226, 227, 228
Dirks, Menno   439
Dirks, Verna   439
Disciples of Christ   202
dispensationalism   10, 46
District of Canada
   division into three districts   137
   District of Canada Committee   58, 334
district relationships, Canada   308, 347, 355–356, 358

divine healing. *See* healing
Dobie, P.   147, 148
Dollard des Ormeaux, Que.   410
Dominion Auxiliary   33–39, 417, 436
   decline of   37
Dominion conventions   73
   1907   38
   1917   37, 50
   1927   158
Dominion Square Methodist Church   144, 367
Dominion-Douglas United Church   144
Doner, Archibald G.   159
Dougall, Muriel   239
Douglas, Dave   317
Douglas Methodist Church   144, 145
Douglas, T. C.   360
Downey, Arnold   407, 411
Downey, Murray   346–347, 357
Downey, Raymur   430, 438
Drake, Lucy   332
Dreger, Clement   301
Drummer Centre, Ont.   165
Dubé, Claude   415, 422
Duckworth, William   147, 148, 157, 158, 172
Duff, Charles   76
Dunkerque   184
Duplessis, Maurice   387
Dye, David   318

E

East End Alliance branch   86
East London Institute for Home and Foreign Mission   331
Eastern and Central Canadian District   278-279, 289
Eastern and Central Canadian Districts   140, 166
Eastern Canadian District   90, 139–141
   demise of   153
Eastern Mennonite College   405
Eastminster United Church   209
Ebenezer Baptist Church, Saskatoon   397
Ebenezer Bible Institute   162, 185
Ebenezer Tabernacle   101. *See also* Delta Tabernacle
Edmonds, Wes   216
Edmonton, Alta.   102.   *See also* Beulah Alliance
education, Christian
   origins   329–331
education, Methodist   30
education, Alliance   315, 401–402

in Canada
   eastern Canadian concerns   353
   Missionary Training Institute, Toronto   34
   origins of   334
   Quebec   415
   regional schools policy   334
   reinstatement of education dept.   348
   school closures   172, 343–345
Edwards, Harold   189, 193
Edwards, Thomas   186
Edwardson, Paul   317
Eglise Chrétienne Evangelique, Lévis   408
Egremont, Alta.   206
Eildon, Man.   206
Elim Tabernacle, Windsor   168–169
Elk, Sask.   119
Elsher, Lou   216
Elvins, Charles   76
Emmerson Avenue Tabernacle   320
Epworth League   147
Erickson, J. A.   237
Eskimo Gospel Crusade   318
Eskimo Point, N.W.T.   304, 318
Estevan, Sask.   406
ETAQ (Enseignement Théologique de l'Alliance au Québec)   415
Eternity magazine   406
Evangel Temple   160
Evangelical Baptists
   Quebec ministries   377
Evangelical Fellowship of Canada   424
Evangelical Missionary Alliance   34.
   See also Christian Alliance
   founding of   16, 19–20
Evangelistic Centre, Niagara Falls   189, 193
evangelistic movement   3

F

Fairbairn, A. M.   31
Fairview Alliance Church, Montreal   410
Faith Cure Home, Boston   332
Faith Training College   331
Fant, D. J.   145–146, 152–153, 185–187, 209
Farnham, Que.   370
Feather, M. C.   434
Fee, John   247, 251
Feller, Henriette   367
Feller Institute   367, 371
Ferguson, Gordon   277

Fewster, Lyle 272
Finlay, Rev. and Mrs. William 109
First Alliance Church, Calgary 270, 396, 400
First Alliance Church of Metropolitan Toronto 406
First Western Canadian District Workers' Prayer Conference 131
First Western Workers Prayer Conference 131, 204
Fisher, George 39, 49
Fishers of Men Band 164
Fitch, Elmer B. 77, 79, 236
   Ottawa ministry 82, 143, 171
   Winnipeg ministry 218, 234, 242
Fitzstevens, John A. 406
Foley, Mr. 86
Foothills Alliance Church, Calgary 270, 397
foreign missions movement 3, 331
Forrest, A. C. 139
Forrest, R. A. 296
Fort Chipewyan 111, 121
Fort Erie, Ont., Alliance work 189, 193
Fort Nelson, B.C. 306
Fort St. John, B.C., Alliance work 267–268
Fort Wayne Bible Institute 162
Fourfold Gospel 11, 12–15, 417
   decline of 25, 53, 55, 57, 70, 141–143, 204–205, 260, 445-448
   Shuman's re-emphasis on 143, 174–175
   similarity to Methodist teaching 148
   toleration of variation from 56
   topic of convention 21
Fournier, Yvan 430, 437
Fowler, Gerald 221, 396, 430, 437, 438, 439
Fowler, Gordon 221, 319, 396–397, 437, 438,
   as executive vice-president 430
   superintendency 403, 428, 439
Fowler, Mr. and Mrs. L. B. 221, 270
Francisco, Raymond 126
Franco, Francisco 183
Fraser, John 72, 144, 147, 147–148
fraternal branch organization 34
   decline of 34, 40, 53, 159–160
   unpopularity in west 39
Frazier, William 84
free grace 3, 7. *See also* Arminianism
Freeman, Charles Victor 169, 180
Freligh, H. M. 372
Freligh, Marie 372–376
Freligh, Paul 273, 372

French Canadian Missionary Society 367
French Work Committee 380, 388, 389, 410, 414
Frenchtown for Christ Crusades 379
Friendly Home 72, 144
Full Gospel Church, Windsor 168
Full Gospel Tabernacle, Windsor 168
Funé, Jean Emile 368, 378
   Quebec coordinator 410–414
Funé, Rev. and Mrs. Jean Emile 421
Funk, A. E. 52, 323

G

Gagnon, Michael 415, 422
Gainforth, Mary 156
Galbraith, N. J. 277, 406
Gardiner, S. O. 236
Garfield, James 4
Gaspé Peninsula, Que. 408
Geiger, Edmund 160
Geiger, Kenneth E. 323
General Assembly, 1980 437
General Councils, Alliance
   1912 Council 24
   1924 Council, Toronto 78, 89
   1925 Council 201
   1930 Council, Ottawa 170, 179
   1944 Council, 418
   1950 Council, Toronto 295, 303
   1958 Council, Winnipeg 312
   1966 Council, Vancouver 395
   1977 Council, Calgary 395, 433
   1979 Council, Lincoln 436
   origins of legislative role 24
George, H. H. S. 204, 236
Gerow, S. M. 169
Gibson, James 235, 255
Giguère, Clemence 371
Giguère, Elise 371
Giguère, Joseph and Amélie 371
Giguère, Marcelle 371
Giguère, Marguerite 371, 373, 378, 386
Giguère sisters 373
Gillies, Rev. 251
Gillies, Robert 105, 108
Glad Tidings Assembly, Winnipeg 207
"Glad Tidings Half Hour," 257
Glen Rocks Bible Conference 290–292, 310, 355
Glengate Alliance Church 193
Glenside, Sask. 406
Global Outreach (U.S.A.) 413
Glover, R. H. 52, 99, 251.

Goetz, William 404
Goforth, Jonathan 126
Goldsboro, Alta. 126
Gooderham, William 333
Gordon, Mr. 110
gospel car ministry 118, 123–124, 129, 225, 232, 235, 244
Gospel in All Lands 4
Gospel Lifeline Home and Foreign Mission Society 273
"Gospel Messenger" 303, 309–311
Gospel Tabernacle, Brantford 160, 405
Gospel Tabernacle, New York 34
Gospel Tabernacle, Seattle 227
Gould, Robert J. 411, 428, 433
  eastern superintendency 407
  midwest superintendency 400
Grande Ligne Mission 369
Grande Prairie, Alta. 406
Grandon, Alta. 126
Grant, John Webster 205, 287
Gray, G. Robert 187
Great Depression 239–242, 244–245, 266
  effects on Alliance 171–172, 240–241, 244–245, 250
Great West Bible Institute 242, 246, 250, 351
  closure of 172, 225, 234, 236–237, 340–343, 344
  origins 338–339, 339–340
Great West Mission 110–115, 204, 209, 210, 219, 224, 238–239, 244, 250. *See also* Gospel car
  founding of 108–109
Green, Percy 269
Greenvale, Sask. 119
Greenwood Avenue Tabernacle 86, 217, 218
Gregg, George R. 58
Gregory Drive Alliance 73
Grierson, Sidney 388
Griffith, A. 87
Griffiths, W. T. 22
Grobb, Charles H. 58, 76
Grobb, Franklin 188
Grout, Wendell 437, 438
Grupe, Mr. and Mrs. R. A. 338
Guerette, Edgar 409, 412
Guibord, Joseph 367
Guiness, H. Grattan 331
Gwatkin, H. M. 46
Gwynne, Alberta 124–126, 128, 129, 130, 209, 231

H

Haitian ministries 409–410, 412
Halifax, N.S. 58, 74, 160
Hallman, H. S. 339, 342
Hamilton, S. P. 338
Hammond, Ross 216, 225
Hanna, Alta. 277
Harris, Elmore 333
Harris, H. C. 193
Harris, Randall 219
Harvey, Reuben 58
Haven of Hope choir 248, 271
Hawkins, Gipsy John 154–155
Hay, William 87, 120, 154, 217–218
Hazelton Avenue Congregational Church 32, 138
Heagy, Clare 320
healing 3, 4–6, 14, 16, 99, 228, 333, 445
  atonement and 9–10, 21, 57, 60
  decline of emphasis on 21, 56, 85
  healing faith in 9
  holiness and 15
  missions and 15, 21
  sanctification and 22
  Salmon's teaching of 32
  Simpson's later view of 22
  use of medicine 9, 85
Heidman, Jean 374, 381–385, 388–389, 392, 408
"Hell's Half-Acre" 186
Henderson House 323
Henderson, John 108
Henderson, William 321
Henry, Robert 437
Heppner, Herbert 274
Heritage Park Alliance 169
Hess, Raymond 255, 261–262, 271
Hess, Robert C. 235
Hewitt, Dudley 290
Hiebert, Henry 193
Hill, Linton D. 302
Hill, Prof. J. W. 182
Hill, W. J. 84
Hillsdale Alliance Church 248, 272, 422
"Himself" 9
Hinton, Albert 147
historicism 10
Hitler, Adolf 182–183
Hitt, Russell 311
Hobson, Ralph 290
Hodge, A. A. 7, 10
Hokanson, Paul H. 302

holiness movement   3
Hollinrake, F. W.   76, 79, 101
Holt, Edwin T.   83, 157, 395
homeland work, Alliance   288–289, 316
  Crone dispute   190–192
  giving for   379
  in Canada   37, 426
    eastern Canada   163–166
    Quebec   370–371, 377, 387, 389–391
  low priority of   141–143, 174, 418
  post-war growth rates   143
  renewal of interest in   174–175, 189–190, 193
  subordinated to missions   24, 236, 379
Hooey, Dorothy   290
Hooper, Ralph E.   338, 342
Houghton College   372
Howard, E. P.   177
Howarth, Alan and Marguerita   310
Howell, Beverly   439
Howell, H. W.   81
Howland, William H.   33, 35, 89, 333, 402
Hughes, Thomas   120, 122
Hull, Marion   248, 258–259, 277
Humber Summit Congregational Church   138
Hunt, Garth   317
Hythe, Alta.   264, 268, 277

I

Immanuel Alliance Church   290
incorporation, the Alliance in Canada   87–89
Ingram, Ross   321, 407, 428
Inkster, J. G.   71, 339
Innisfail, Alta.   102
Institut Biblique Béthel   373, 376, 415
  See also Bethel Bible Institute
institutional self-preservation   446
Inter-Varsity Christian Fellowship   153
Interdenominational Prayer and Evangelistic League   230
Interdenominational Prayer League   214
International Missionary Alliance   19, 34
Inuit ministries   318
Invermere, B.C   400
Irwin, Marie   406
Irwin, E. Frank   174, 177

J

Jaffray, Robert A.   36, 48, 71, 188
Jaffray School of Missions   401
Jaffray, William G.   50, 58
Jago, E. O.   140
Jasper Avenue Mission   219, 225, 238
Jaycox, Clarence   304
Jaycox, Clarence and Ruth   306
Jeffrey, D. Ivory   80, 177, 406
Jeffrey, Lucy   80
Jenkin, B. A.   255
Jennings, John   295
Jespersen, Jesse D.   414, 415, 421, 422
Jessop, S. J.   214, 257
Johns, Grace   156
Johnson, Elmer   187
Johnson, Gilbert   165, 315, 401
Johnston, Arthur   413, 421
Johnston, H. B.   103, 204, 235
Johnston, H. H.   255, 257
Johnston, Kae   248
Johnston, Ruby   255, 314, 317–318
Jones, Nellie   81
Jones, Walter   111, 117

K

Kamloops, B.C., Alliance work   277
Kantouen, T. A.   447
Kelowna, B.C., Alliance work   306
Kennedy, John F.   419
Kenyon, Donald   372
Kenyon, Dorothy   372–376, 373, 377
Kenyon, Paul   372
Kepple, Ont.   165
Keswick conference   46, 47
Key 73   413
Key City Project Fund   289, 316
Kincheloe, R. M.   357
Kindersley, Sask., Alliance work   268
King, Bernard S.   312, 420, 423, 424–425, 431
King, Louis L.   397, 399, 429, 437, 439
  Canadian autonomy and   419, 430, 434, 438
  foreign secretary   315, 321
  presidency   434, 439
King's Messengers   159, 165
Kingston, Ont.   71
Kirk, Edward and Hattie   335
Kirkland, P. L.   217
Klassen, John   306
Klemke, Jack   430, 437
Klopfenstein, Sadie   111, 118

464 / Index

Knowlton Conference Grounds 72, 72–73, 158, 290, 336
Knox College, Toronto 295

L

La Chappelle Evangelique Cornwall. *See* Cornwall French ministry
La Mission Chrétienne Evangelique Francaise, Quebec City 385
La Mission Chrétienne Evangelique, Lévis 382, 389
Lac LaBiche, Alta. 126
l'affaire Guibord 366–367
L'Alliance Chrétienne et Missionaire (Haitian) 312
L'Alliance Chrétienne et Missionnaire, Matane 408
L'Alliance Chrétienne et Missionnaire, Montreal 409
Lamb, William 82
Lappin Avenue Church (Toronto) 87, 157, 190, 193, 320
Latchford, O. 76
Laughlin, W. J. 86
Laval University 377
Law, William 8
Le Mission Chrétienne Evangelique Francaise, Welland 373, 379–380
Leadley, H. F. 236
Leavens, William 81
Ledyard, Gleason H. 318
l'Eglise Chrétienne Evangelique, Quebec City 411
L'Eglise du Sauveur 367
L'Eglise Evangelique Belvedere 409
Lemieux, Rudolphe 170
Lennox, Robert 210, 212-213, 216, 219, 224, 238, 342, 408
Lesser Slave Lake, Alta. 306
Lethbridge Alta. 274
Levis, Que., Alliance work 388–389, 391
Lewellan, William H. 177, 353
Lewis, Al 303, 308–311
Lewis, Joyce 397
Lewis Top 310
Lewis, Ulysses 50
Lindsay, John 76
Lindsay, Ont. 182
L'Institut Canadien de Montréal 366
Linton, John 72
Livingston, Henry Gilbert 100
Lollards 330
London, Ont., Alliance work 159–160
Long, Louis J. 40–41, 47, 67, 82, 127, 189

Loon Lake, Alta. 306
Loptson, A. M. 99
Lorimer, Edgar 75–76, 77, 289, 344
Losee, William 29
Loveless, Norman G. 154–155
Lucas, J. R. 121
Lucy, John 82

M

MacArthur, William T. (Daddy) 47
MacDonald, Agnes 204, 206
MacKenzie, Kenneth 22, 71
MacLennan, Hugh 366
MacLeod, C. 340
MacMillen, John A. 185, 245
MacRoberts, William 296
Magnus, George 207, 235, 247, 269, 305
  assistant superintendent 299, 301
Major, Sask. 119
Malcolm, Augustus G. 59
Malicky, Charles 108, 111, 121
manifest destiny 97
Mann, William E. 98, 202, 224, 225, 274
Manning, E. C. 420
Mantle, Gregory 48, 73
Mapstone, E. F. 350
maritime provinces, Alliance work in
  barriers to expansion 39, 185
  conventions in 57, 74, 160
  separate district for 90, 139-41
  St. John work 166-168, 178-182
  Truro work 185-187
Martin, Alvin 352, 360, 401, 402, 420
Martin, Jean 415, 422
Mason, Harold C. 296
Mason, David 180, 185, 275–276
  as New York treasurer 192, 296
  Canadian schools and 345, 347, 349, 354
  Christie Tabernacle ministry 173–174
  Crone controversy 188–194
  homeland work and 176, 178–181, 189–190, 193
  retirement of 312
  superintendency of 173–174, 265
Massey Hall, Toronto 294, 296
Matane, Que. 408
Matheson, Lloyd 430, 437, 438
Maxwell, Leslie E. 336, 337–338
McAllister, William 296
McArthur, Eleanor 397
McArthur, Mrs. William 377

Index / 465

McArthur, William   169, 352, 353, 354, 360, 376–377
McCalden, S. B.   155
McCleary, Henry   340
McConachie, Robert   232, 244
McCoy, Catherine   111, 118, 119, 258
McCrae, W. L. Linton   206, 219
McCrossan, Thomas J.   226, 227–228, 231
McCully, Elizabeth   186
McCully, Louise H.   186–187
McDonald, A. M.   340
McElheran, Archdeacon   123
McEwan, William   145, 162
McGarvey, S. W.   273
McGill University   375
McIntyre, Mr. and Mrs. Roy   263
McIntyre, Roy   259
  Canadian autonomy and   420, 423, 424, 425, 427, 428, 431, 433, 439
  Moose Jaw ministry   270, 277
  Peace River ministry   267
  superintendency   315–316, 317, 396, 399
McKay, Mr. and Mrs.   270
McLeod, Wilbert   399
McNaughton, Walter   268
McNutt, Eugene   408–409, 410, 411, 412
McPherson, Aimee Semple   235
McQuade, James   380, 386
McTavish, D.   50
Meadows, Harold   148, 369
Meadows, John   147
Medicine Hat, Alta., Alliance work   102, 277
Meikle, William   186
Melanchthon, Philip   7
Melindy, Charles   108
Menninger, W. F.   110
Merrill, R. F.   357
Messenger   346, 350
Methodism   8, 30, 31, 98, 446
  Bible Christian Church   31
  church union and   138, 144
  holiness teaching of   30
  in Ontario   29–31
  Methodist Church of Canada   31
  Methodist Episcopal Church in Canada   31
  modernism in   31, 147–148
  Primitive Methodist Church in Canada   31
  the Alliance and   18, 32, 33, 74, 148
Methodist Cavalry   30

Metropolitan Bible Church of the Associated Gospel   171
Michelfeller, H.   205
Mickelson, Einar   309
Middleton, Hugh   105, 108
Middleton, M. R.   144
Midland Bible Institute   336
Midland, Ont., Alliance work   87, 217
Miller, Shirley   408
Mills, R. K.   165, 289
Milne, J. S.   82
Milton, John   329
Mimico, Ont., Alliance work   217
Minute Men   289
Mission Chrétienne Evangelique Francaise, Montréal   387, 389
Mission Training School   332
Missionary Aviation Fellowship   310
Missionary Church Association   323
missionary giving   19, 37, 55
  depression decline in   241, 245
  eastern Canadian   253, 278
  missions pledge   19
  sanctification and   14
  Western Canadian District and   220, 225–226, 234, 236, 250, 255, 278, 301, 305
  western Canadian resistance to   40, 119–120, 131
Missionary Rest Home, Mimico   49, 321
Missionary Training College for Home and Foreign Missions   332
Missionary Training Institute   6, 84, 108, 207, 251, 332, 334, 335, 377
Missionary Union for the Evangelization of the World   6
missions, Alliance
  indigenization of   288
  primacy of   6, 23, 55, 71, 141–143, 142–143, 146, 166, 174, 417
modernism   40, 45, 80, 202, 227, 417
Moffat, George   67, 111, 112, 114, 126
Moncton, N.B.   57
Mont Joli, Que.   408
Montreal, Que., Alliance work   143–148
  Alliance beginnings in   71–73, 144
  convention of 1921   71
  French work   385–387
  Montreal Central work   146, 148, 160–161, 378, 379
  north end work   146–147
Moody Bible Institute   116, 299
Moose Hill, Alta.   126
Moose Jaw, Sask., Alliance work   270
Morden, Man.   320, 400

466 / Index

Moreau, Alain   415, 422
Moreland, William   321, 322
Morris, Charles S.   73, 110
Moseley, Thomas   116
Moynan, Robert   126
Muir, Harry G.   155
Murray, Arthur   340
Murray, James M.   254
Musselman's Lake   165

N

nationalism, Canadian   418–419, 426, 440
Nazarene, Church of the   202, 224, 230, 297
Neate, Major   368
Nedstrud, E. J.   258
Neidpath, Sask.   235, 244, 250, 255
Neill, Stephen   45
Nelson, A.   81
Nelson, H. E.   193, 194, 291, 292, 298, 299, 301, 305, 308, 349, 355
   homeland growth under   189, 288, 289
   retirement of   315
Nester, Richard G.   413
Neufeld, Arnold   319
New Testament Baptist Church   87
Newberry, W. W.   228, 259
Newell, William   308, 314
   Canadian autonomy and   420, 423, 424
   Quebec ministry and   388, 391
   superintendency   316, 319, 322, 323, 399, 405
Newman, Albert H.   10
Ng, Phillip   430, 438
Nhon, Tim   415, 422
Niagara Conference   46, 59
Niagara Creed   46
Nicholls, Craig   58
Niklaus, Robert L.   183
Nogent-sur-Marne Bible School   368
Non-conformists   30
North Side Tabernacle, Chicago   233
Northwest District, Canadian   127, 259, 267
Noseworthy, Douglas   108
Nyack College   182, 401

O

objectives, Alliance
   confusion of   55–57
   primacy of missions   141–143

Old Knox Apostolic Church   237-238, 242–243
Old Orchard, Maine   13, 16
Olford, Stephen F.   395
Oliver, E. H.   97, 203
Omicile, Joseph   410
Onoway, Alta.   212–213
Ontario Bible College and Seminary   333
Ontario, evanglization of   30
Onward Gospel Church   72
Onward Mission, Verdun   62, 72, 74, 144
Operation Espérance   413, 421
Origen   330
orphanages   6
Orthner, A. H.   268, 270, 277, 301, 313, 318, 422
   Canadian autonomy and   423, 424, 428
   Chinese work   317
   director of Canadian ministries   400, 427
   superintendency   320, 399, 420
Osborne, Mrs. William   332
Osborne, Myrtle   321
Osiander, Andrew   8
Ottawa convention, 1923   82
Ottawa Gospel Tabernacle   77, 79, 218, 355, 400
   1931 division of   170–171
   extension work   143, 159, 165
   origins of   81-82, 84, 210
Ottawa Valley campaign   143
Ottewell, Ont.   165
Outlook, Sask.   406
Overbrook Gospel Tabernacle   159
Owen, J. Glyn   395
Owen, Muriel   111–112, 113–114, 118
Owen, Arthur de B.   227
Owen Sound, Ont., Alliance work   81, 180

P

Pacific Northwest District   127, 226, 256, 259, 267
pacificism, pre-war   182–183
Palmer, F. Noel   152, 153
Panin, Ivan   321–322
Pantaenus   330
Paramount Drive Alliance Church   80
Pardington, George F.   47
Park Street Alliance Church   290
Parkdale Tabernacle Church   36, 39, 47, 59, 66
   closing of   66–67

creation of Wayside Mission 107
Patton, John 59, 82, 158
Peace River Bible Institute 268, 346
Peace River district 267–268
Pearson, Reuben 125, 221
Pentecostal Assemblies of Canada 207, 224
   Quebec ministries 377
Pentecostal Assembly of God, Winnipeg 207
Pentecostalism 250
   benefits of church union 143, 202
   effects on Alliance 145, 146, 160–161, 168, 207
   post-war growth 395
   tongues issue 24, 34, 38
Penticton, B.C., Alliance work 306
Peoples Church, Toronto
   origins of 152–153
   support of Alliance missions 177
People's Church, Winnipeg 217
perfect love 8
perfect trust 9
Persing, H. B. 277
Peterborough, Ont., Alliance work 289–290. *See also* Bethany Church, Peterborough
   extension work 165
   Key City Project 289
Petrescue, David G. 311
Philpott, P. W. 41, 49, 52, 56, 59, 101
Philpotts, A. G. 168, 181
Pierson, M. P. 224
Pigeon, George C. 137
Pine Grove Congregational Church 138
Pippert, Leslie W. 315, 317, 320, 324, 420, 423
Plymouth Brethren 32
Pointe St. Charles Baptist Church 72
Poling, W. S. 88
Pomeroy, Walter 267
post-millennialism 10
post-war church growth 287, 395
Pouce Coupe, B.C. 268
Powers, W. E. 343–345
Prairie Bible Institute 212, 254, 258–259, 268, 316
   affiliation talks, C&MA 337–338
   origins 335–336
Prairie Gospel Tabernacle 235, 258
Prayer Conference, 1934 180
pre-millennialism 3, 6, 10, 46, 333
   implications for missions 11–12
   tolerance of other views 17
pre-tribulationism 10

Preacher's Chorus 294, 296
"Preparation for Membership" 307
Presbyterian Board of French Evangelism 367
Presbyterianism 32, 138
   opposition to church union 138
Pressman, W. E. 177
Presswood, Ernest 188
Price, Charles 169
   Victoria campaign 226–227
   Winnipeg campaign 214
Primitive Methodist Church in Canada. *See* Methodism
Prince Edward Street Church, St. John 167
Prince George, B.C. 277, 397
Princeton Theological Seminary 7, 297
Prophetic Baptists 202
Providence Church, Winnipeg 217
Providence College 207
Providence Theological Seminary 207
Provost, Alta. 255
Pugh, Effie 211
Pugh, Sidney Tobias 211, 219, 225
Pullyblank, Herbert 290
Puritan lectureships 331
Pyne, Lawrence J. 182, 271

Q

Quakers 32
Quebec
   English-French relations 368
   quiet revolution 387
   Québec Act of 1774 365
   Quebec City Alliance work 384–385, 388, 391, 411
Quebec ministry 367
   Alliance incorporation 161–162
   Alliance work 367–372
   Catholic opposition to 366
   spiritual need 370
   western support 380
Quinlan, Mabel 374, 376–377, 382, 392
   Lévis ministry 388–389, 408
   Québec City ministry 383-385
Quinn, Margaret 186
Quinte Alliance Church 75–76

R

Rader, Luke 116, 119, 209
Rader, Paul 48, 52, 68
   presidency of 55, 57, 66, 334
   resignation of 82, 116

468 / Index

tour cancellation 115
uncertain priorities of 142
view of Bosworths 69
radio broadcasting 221–225, 250
  Edmonton 109, 273
  Moose Jaw 263, 313
  Quebec 379
  Regina 255, 271–272
  role of Reuben Pearson 125, 221
  Saskatoon 257
  Vernon 306
Railton, Mabel 124
Railton, Margeurite 248, 258-259, 264, 277
railway, opening of 40, 97
Rambo, David 402, 404, 437
rapture, the 10
Ratelle, A. 371, 371–372
Read, T. William 261
Red Deer, Alta., Alliance work 277
Rees, Paul 262
Rees, Rev. and Mrs. Alwyn 383
Reeve, T. A. (Phil) 390–391
Reformation, Protestant 330
Reformed theology 3
Regina, Sask., Alliance work 102, 127, 255, 271–272
  convention of 1924 131–133
  origins of Alliance work 132, 225
Reid, R. S. 82
Reimer, Arnold 430, 437, 438
Reimer, Esther 439
Rempel, Anna 409, 412
rescue missions 6
restructuring, Alliance 406
Revelstoke, B.C., Alliance work 277
reversion clause 24, 38, 189, 417
revival
  eastern response to 399
  in western Canada 397–399
Revolutionary War, American 29
Rexdale Alliance, Toronto 320–321
Reynolds, Lindsay 388
Ribstone, Alta. 255
Rice Lake Reserve 191
Richards, E. J. 52, 54, 58, 88, 90, 122, 204, 206, 223, 230, 334, 339
  convention ministry 48, 70, 71, 99, 131, 225
  titular superintendency of 91, 139–140, 153
Richards, E. W. 289
Richards, John (Jack) 147, 162
Richardson, Elise 373, 383
Richardson, Robert 369, 371, 373, 378, 383, 409
  Quebec City ministry 384-385, 408

  Ontario ministry 379-380
Richardson, Robert and Elise 388–389, 392
Rickard, Rev. 122
Rimouski, Que. 408
Ritchie, Elizabeth 111
Ritchie, T. H. 269
Robinson, Charles 167
Rockford, Ont. 165
Roderickville, Sask. 244
Rodger, R. C. 122
Roffe, Ethel 64, 82, 112, 147
Roffe, F. W. Elroy 342
Roffe, Paul R. 185–187
Roffe, A. W. 52, 186, 321 351
  convention ministry 57, 81
  poor health of 90, 122, 133
  superintendency of 48, 49, 54–55, 58, 59, 70–73, 87-88, 89, 91, 217
  western Canadian involvement 98, 102–104, 105, 117, 134
  "vision of need" 104, 106, 127
  writings of 64
Roger, George 421
Roosevelt, Franklin D. 183
Rose, A. B. 126, 340
Rose, Robert 415
Ross, George 306
Ross, J. R. 236
Roy, Marc-Andre 408
Ryerson, Egerton 30

S

Salmon, John 32, 33, 35, 36, 49, 89, 138, 159, 290, 323, 333, 367, 405, 416, 440
  healing of 332
  Peterborough work 188–189
  resignation as superintendent 189
  resignation from Alliance 38
Salvation Army 33, 123, 369, 370
  Methodist secessions to 32, 49
Samoila, Marion 406
Sanborn, June 317
sanctification 3, 6, 7–9, 333
  opposition to Simpson's views 7
  Presbyterian view of 8
  Wesleyan view of 8
Sandell, W. 433
Sandford, B. A. 76
Sandham, Alfred 333
Sanger, Clarence 111
Saskatoon, Sask., Alliance work 247
  origins 237–238, 242–244, 254, 256
Sauvé, Firm 156, 232, 244, 276, 289
Sauvé, Firmin J., Sr. 160

Sawler, Ray 371
Scheidt, A. 270
Schellenberg, Abram 269, 270, 277
Schroeder, Henry 248, 271
Schroeder, Jack 306, 430, 437
Schwedler, R. F. C. 261, 273
Scofield, C. I. 10
Scott, Ephraim 137
Scott, Maggie 32, 33, 35
Scottsburgh, Sask. 244
second coming of Christ 10, 14
Second Vatican Council 387
sects. *See also* Cults
  effects of church union 139
sects, evangelical
  in western Canada 202–203
  opposition to 235
secularization, post-war 45
Senft, F. H. 52, 84, 89, 142
Senlac, Sask 259
Sentani Airport 309, 310
separatist movement 46
Sevenoaks Alliance Church 301, 400, 404
Shantz, Ward 324
Shareski, Melvin 319
Shaunavon, Sask. 110
Shaver, A. M. 76
Shaw Memorial United Church 147
Shea, A. J. 83
Shepson, Don 298, 380
Sherbrooke, Que. 377
Sherwood Park, Alta., Alliance 400
Shields, T. T. 71
Shuman, H. M. 52, 157, 296
  Alliance education and 276, 343, 353, 354
  Alliance distinctives and 143, 166, 174–175
  Canadian Alliance and 172, 177, 277, 312
  election of 142
  missions policy 142
  retirement of 312
Shutz, Mr. 87
Silcox, C. E. 138, 139
Simmons, E. D. 164, 179
Simpson, A. B. 290, 295, 321, 332, 367, 416, 431
  death of 25, 49–53, 51
  experience of healing 4–5
  founding of Alliance 3
  personal qualities 53
  role in Canadian Alliance 37
  sanctification, view of 7–9
Simpson Bible Institute 228, 344
Simpson, R. G. 84, 380, 389–390

Simpson, Thomas 263, 272
Sinderson, George H. 126, 207
Sipprell, W. S. 227
Size, F. B. 169
Skitch, Gordon 118, 240–241, 246, 247, 271
  declining health of 279, 298–299, 300
  evangelistic work of 124-125, 129, 229-230, 270
  Midland ministry 154–155
  ordination of 154
  resignation 300–301
  role in WCBI 275-276, 345, 349
  superintendency of 278–279
  western leadership roles 235, 236, 265, 266-267, 272–273, 274, 276-277, 406
Skitch, Mabel 240–241, 276
Slavic Indian ministry 306, 317
Smalley, William F. 322
Smith, Fred A. 268
Smith, G. B. 402
Smith, Hannah 72, 144
Smith, Oswald J. 62, 81, 151, 162, 296, 335, 339, 342
  Alliance missions and 177
  Christie Street ministry 66-69, 209
  church polity 69, 149
  denominationalism and 68–69
  doctrinal viewpoints 59
  Parkdale ministry 59-60, 66–69
  resignation from Alliance 152–153
  superintendency 150
  Watson's view of 150
Smith, William G. 202
Snead, A. C. 52, 85, 173, 308, 315, 368
Snider, J. B. 160
social concerns 6, 332
  decline of emphasis on 23, 56
  in early Canadian Alliance 34
  in Saint John, N.B. 181
Social Credit Party 221
social gospel 23
South American missions 288
Southside Alliance Church 312
Spain, Frank 159
Sparke, Fred 145, 147–148, 157, 158, 160, 369, 371
specialized ministries 306, 317
Spier, T. J. 165, 172, 369, 370, 371–372
Spies, Mr. and Mrs. R. P. 126
Spratt, Joseph C. 132, 236
Sprattsville, Man. 206, 210
Spruce Grove, Alta. 414

St. John, N.B., Alliance work 58, 160, 182
  Gospel Tabernacle 168
  origins 166–168
St. Lawrence district
  district executive committee 422
  origins 414–415
St. Louis, Fernand 413
St. Paul Bible College 334, 343
St. Paul Bible Institute 162, 296, 305, 354, 372
Standard Sunday School 300
Star City, Sask. 257, 318
Ste. Foy, Que. 414
Steele, E. V. 268
Steinman, Cyril H. 306
Stephens, Harold 39, 127, 189
  resignation as superintendent 40
  role in Calgary work 110
Stephens, Rev. and Mrs. Harold 228
Stephens, Lloyd M. 256–257
Stephenson, Elva and Clysta 119, 131, 225, 231, 233, 237
Stevens, William C. 334, 336
Stewart, Lois 409
Still, F. M. 131, 204, 233, 236
Stoesz, Samuel 401
Stone Church of the Pentecostal Assemblies 297
Stony Plain, Alta., Alliance work 274
Street, Norman H. 190, 193
Sunday School Booster 299
Sunrise Gospel Hour 273
"super churches," Canadian 400–401
Surrey, B.C., Alliance work 318–319
Sutera, Lou 397
Sutera, Ralph 397, 398
Sutera Twins 397, 403
Sutherland, T. M. 217
Sweet, H. O. 169
Swift Current, Sask. 406
Sylvester, Melvin P. 320, 411
  Canadian autonomy and 428, 431, 432, 433
  eastern superintendency 397, 406, 407, 424–425
  presidency 429, 430, 437, 438, 439, 440
Sylvester, Rev. and Mrs. Melvin P. 430

T

Tarlton, Bella 62, 72
Taylor, J. Hudson 251
Taylor, Jeremy 8
Taylor, Marguerite 373
Taylor, Raymond 371, 376, 386, 389

Taylor University 372
Teawoods, Alberta 126
Templeton, Charles B. 296–297, 297–298
Teng, Philip 405
Tenney, Merrill C. 401
Tenth Avenue Alliance Church 261, 263, 273, 299, 302, 305, 397
Teulon, Man. 239
The Higher Christian Life 332
Theological Education by Extension 415
Thirteenth Street Presbyterian Church 3
Thomas, Cecil R. 302
Thomas, W. H. Griffith 47, 48, 51
Thomas, John
  Calgary campaign 230–233
  Edmonton campaign 229
  Regina campaign 233
  Winnipeg campaign 234
Thomas, Robert 268
Thompson, A. E. 5, 22, 48, 52
Thompson, John J. 59, 99
Thompson, John O. 104
Thompson, Mary E. 140
Thorhild, Alta. 126
Thuan, Nguyen quang 406
Tinkler, Mrs. B. 236
Tinkler, Wilbert 250
Toronto Baptist Seminary 169
Toronto Bible College 36, 37, 80, 169, 170, 409
Toronto Bible School 333, 335
Toronto Mission Union 116
Toronto Missionary Training Institute 34, 333, 341
Toronto Missionary Training School 333
Town, Harvey A. 397, 403
Tozer, A. W. 296, 312, 313
Trenton Faith Mission 156–159, 256
Trevecka College 331
Tri-District Centennial Plan 419
Tri-District Conference, 1967 420–423, 429
Tri-District Conference, 1974 424–425
Tri-District Conference, 1978 434–435
Troyer, W. Cyril 187
Truro, N.S., Alliance work 74, 160, 185-187, 256
Turnbull, John R. 338, 342
Turnbull, Walter 52, 115, 151
  as Nyack dean 112, 341
  role in Canadian Bible Institute 335, 336, 338, 339
Turner, Harry L. 206-208, 267, 296,

as St. Paul dean 296, 305, 354
  presidency of 313, 315
  Saskatoon ministry 237-238, 242-243
  Winnipeg ministry 206-208, 211
Turner, Minnie 251
two solitudes, Quebec 366

U

Ulrich, Edward W. 309
unionism, Canadian 40, 45–46, 131, 417. *See also* Church union
  as opportunity for Alliance 141
  controversy regarding 46, 80, 90, 137, 227
  effects of 144, 137–138
  western movement towards 98
Unionville, Ont., Alliance work 311
United Church of Canada 201, 202, 203, 227, 288
  origins 137
United Empire Loyalists 29, 33, 416
United Missionary Church
  merger talks with 323–325
University Drive Alliance, Saskatoon 316, 398, 399
University of Manitoba 227
University of Saskatchewan 402
University of Saskatchewan, Regina College 360
Upper Canada Academy 30

V

Vacation Bible School 208
Valentine, Paul 388
Van, Nguyen van 407
Van Stone, Lloyd 309
Van Plew, Thomas 111
Vancouver, B.C., Alliance work
  origins 251–252, 259–261
Vancouver City Mission 259
Vegreville, Alta. 126, 205, 207
Vermilion, Alta., Alliance work 278
Vernon, B.C., Alliance work 306
Victoria, B.C., Alliance work 226–229
Victoria College 76. *See also* Upper Canada Academy
Victoria Ministerial Association 226
Vietnamese ministries 406–407

W

Wade, George 206
Walker, Daniel 226, 227, 228
Wallace, C. J. 155

Wallace, C. B. 73
Walmer Road Baptist Church 333
Warfield, B. B. 7
Warren, Bishop 83
Wassenaar, Netherlands 310
Watson, Lionel 149, 151, 152, 157, 158, 160, 177
  as assistant superintendent 49, 59, 73, 75, 88-89, 91, 121, 139–141
  New York appointment 154, 162
  nomination as superintendent 91, 153-154
  role in Canadian Bible Institute 335, 342
  role in Montreal 145, 148
  role in Windsor 168–169
  view of O. J. Smith 150
Wayside Mission 107–108, 111, 121
Webb, Mr. and Mrs. R. 87
Webster, Marjorie 146
Weisbrodt, Jacob 255
Welcome Hall Mission 72, 144, 147
Welsh, Claude 445
Wesley, John 8, 331
West End Alliance Church, Toronto 320, 405
Westboro (Ottawa) Baptist Church 169
Westbourne Baptist Church 221
western Canada
  differences from east 120, 205, 225, 355
  frontier conditions 103–104
  need for workers 133, 202–203, 207, 208, 236–237, 242
  settlement of 40, 97–98, 105
  spiritual needs of 40, 97–98, 102, 122, 131, 202, 254, 417
Western Canadian district
  conferences in 204, 215, 230, 236
  division of 319–320, 396
  growth of 143, 396
  incorporation of 235, 242
  leadership uncertainties 245–246, 252–254, 265
  missions giving in 220, 245, 250, 255, 278–279, 301, 305
  origins of 39, 90–91, 201, 203
  revival in 397–399
  under Skitch 266, 272, 276–284
Western Canadian Bible Institute 349–350, 355–360, 377, 417. *See also* Canadian Bible College
  as national school 356, 358–359
  incorporation of 353
  name change 308, 359
  official recognition of 348, 350–353, 358

472 / Index

origins 274–276, 345–347
relocation of 356, 357
Western Workers Bulletin 272
Western Workers' Witness 278
Westgate Alliance Church 407
Wheaton Graduate School 401
Wheeler, Seth 76
White Rock, B.C., Alliance work 319
Whitelaw, A. 103, 340
Whitfield, George 331
Whitman, C. L. 86
Whitmore, Earl 156
Wicks, Fred 110
Wigglesworth, Reginald 160
Willett, John G. 167, 168, 181
Williams, Fred W. 206
Williams, J. 81
Williams, J. D. 22, 52, 152, 162–163, 179, 334
  eastern and central superintendency 143, 153, 154, 162-163, 369, 370
  homeland initiatives 163, 166-168, 169, 172, 185
  Pacific northwest superintendency 172
  western superintendency 253-254, 255, 256, 258–259, 260, 261, 262
Williams, Juanita 75
Williams, Rev. and Mrs. F. W. 232
Williams, F. W. 126, 230, 236
Willis, W. C. 209, 338–339
Willis, William 177
Willoughby, Clemence (Dawn) 373
Willoughby, Robert 371
Wilson Academy 334
Wilson, Mr. and Mrs. Phil 306
Wimborne, Alta. 235
Windsor, Ont., Alliance work 168, 293
Winnipeg Bible College and Theological Seminary 207
Winnipeg Bible Institute 278, 343, 345, 357
Winnipeg Bible Training School 207
Winnipeg, Man., Alliance work 102, 110, 115, 211
  Gospel Tabernacle 217, 242, 243, 253, 254, 258, 345
  origins of 206–208, 214–218
  revival 399
Wiseman, Peter 83
Wishart, Gordon 216, 220, 230, 231, 233, 236, 302, 342, 388
  conversion of 209-210

Great West Mission ministry 211-212, 225
Wishart, Rev. and Mrs. Gordon 232, 234, 259–260
Witmer, Safara 105, 108
Wolfe, Daniel 410, 415, 422
women's ministries 25, 230, 239
Wood, John L. 206, 210, 235
Woodbine Heights Baptist Church 65
Woodward, John 105, 117, 118, 168, 223, 231, 253, 337
  Beulah ministry 98, 100-103, 220
  conversion of 100
  Great West Bible Institute 234, 241-242, 340, 351
  Great West Mission 108, 129, 203-204, 213-214
  ordination of 116
  resignation of 249-250, 254
  superintendency of 90, 122, 201, 203-204, 208, 225-226, 229, 233, 235, 237, 240, 243, 246, 336
  Winnipeg ministries 206-208, 217, 218, 241-242
Word, Work and World 4
World Vision International 405
World War I 45, 187-188
World War II 184, 185, 287
  Alliance Witness view 183–184
  events leading to 182–184
  post-war church growth 287–288
  U.S./Canadian response 183–184
World's Christian Fundamental Association 46
Wright, Elmer 120
Wycliff, John 330
Wycliffe College 47

Y

Yonge Street Tabernacle 298, 384, 406
Young, E. T. 338
Young, R. 122
Young, Lowell 400
Youth for Christ 378

Z

Zacharias, Ravi 437
Zimmerman, George 59, 89, 127
Zimmerman, R. J. 156, 259, 323
Zwingli, Ulrich 331